The Tante Marie Book of
TRADITIONAL
FRENCH COOKERY

The Tante Marie Book of
TRADITIONAL FRENCH COOKERY

Wendy T. Majerowicz
and Patricia Bourne

with photographs by Herbert Lees
of the Tante Marie School of Cookery, Woking

WILLOW BOOKS
COLLINS
St James's Place, London
1982

Willow Books
William Collins Sons & Co Ltd
London · Glasgow · Sydney
Auckland · Toronto · Johannesburg

First published in Great Britain 1982

Bourne, Patricia
The Tante Marie book of traditional French cookery
1. Cookery, French
I. Title
641.5944
II. Majerowicz, Wendy
TX719

ISBN 0 00 218084 7

Filmset by Ace Filmsetting, Frome, Somerset
Printed in Great Britain by
William Collins Sons & Co Ltd Glasgow

Contents

Acknowledgements   6

Introduction   7

General Information   9
Sauces   26
Soups   34
Hors d'Oeuvre   41
Egg and Cheese Dishes   50
Seafood   64
Meat   90
Poultry and Game   133
Vegetables and Salads   160
The Cheeseboard   186
Sweets and Ices   187
Cakes and Pastries   206
Wines and Menus   231

Index   235

Acknowledgements

This book owes its beginning to two women of great character. Firstly, to Iris Syrett who had the imagination and courage to start Tante Marie in 1954 and who built up a large collection of recipes as the foundation of the school – some of which form the basis of this book. Iris had a vivid and strong personality and this is evident in the fact that, even today, we are still very much aware of her ideals and love of cooking which are the inspiration of Tante Marie. This, in some great measure, must be due to Wendy Majerowicz who, when Iris died in 1964, became principal and, together with Herbert Lees, Iris's widower and the photographer for this book, directed the school until her tragic death in 1981 at the age of 47.

Wendy also had a great love: not only of cooking, but of teaching others to appreciate and understand it. Her knowledge on all topics pertaining to food was unsurpassed and she was forever researching new ideas and material.

I worked with Wendy for 12 years before she died – the last four of them as her head teacher – and we worked very closely on school affairs and in writing recipes and books. We became great friends, sharing the same ideas and writing in the same style, and it is to Wendy that I must acknowledge my greatest gratitude for the pleasure and humour we enjoyed together in the long hours of writing this book. I miss her dearly.

After her death I was appointed principal of the School by Mr Lees and I have very much appreciated working with him. In January 1982 Mr and Mrs John Childs became the new proprietors of the Tante Marie School, with Mr Lees still retaining an active interest in the School's activities.

Both Wendy and I realised how much we owed to others, in particular to Mr Lees for his constant support and friendly criticism and for all the care he took in producing the beautiful photographs of our food. We owe thanks, also, to our husbands who tolerated our writing late into the night and who were continually on hand to give advice or sympathy whenever it was needed. I trust that eating the results of all our recipe testing was considered a suitable reward for their not inconsiderable patience.

I must also thank all the past and present staff at the Tante Marie School who have helped in developing recipes; Susie Pullen, Alison Dodd and our students who tested some of the recipes for us; and Val Glass and Jean Crowle who magically transformed our scribbled notes into beautiful typescript.

Thanks are also due to all of the following for their help in providing information and supplying food and 'props' for use in the photography:

P. F. Conisbee, butcher, of Ripley
R. Stonnard, greengrocers, Woking
J. Clarke, fishmonger, of Woking
Anne Dare of M.E.A.T.
Gill Service of the New Zealand Lamb Information Bureau
John Pesek, Senior Lecturer, Food and Beverage Operations, Middlesex Polytechnic
Heal's of Guildford for the china used in photographs on pages 84, 87 and 147
Woking Tile Warehouse for background tiles for photographs
Drawings of herbs, meat and kitchen equipment by Eric Rose (reproduced by kind permission of Forbes Publications Ltd)
Jacket photography by Gina Harris

Patricia Bourne

Patricia Bourne

Introduction

France is a country renowned for its cuisine which has been developed over the centuries. Country cooking is careful and modest and makes the best use of local produce. It has developed from ancient peasant dishes of the past, with each generation making improvements and additions so that today it is one of the best in the world. Dishes are regional – you will not find a Breton Cotriade in Burgundy nor a Burgundian Meurette in Brittany. For the traveller this characteristic adds great charm.

The more elaborate cooking of haute cuisine traces its origins to the sixteenth century, when Catherine de Medici came to France, bringing her Italian chefs with her. From this time on, the great chefs of France developed a standard of cuisine unparalleled in other countries. This grew, not only from the traditional cooking of France, but from the best food of other countries of Europe as well. As a somewhat unsubtle form of flattery, dishes were often named after the rich and famous people of the day. Names like Dubarry, Richelieu and Suchet recall different periods of history and today are often found in the names of the classic dishes which are, after all, the long-established favourites. Although many of these dishes demand time and skill in their preparation, they are within the scope of the cordon bleu cook who can derive satisfaction from reproducing these great dishes of the past.

At Tante Marie we have specialised for many years in teaching French cooking to English-speaking people from all over the world. Some come to us to prepare for a professional career in cookery, some to prepare for their own home life; others are house-wives who have a love of cooking and come to gain new expertise. For all our students, both regional and haute cuisine dishes have a place in the repertoire of cordon bleu cooking of meals for informal and formal occasions.

The excellence of a menu is achieved partly by selecting the best of the fruit and vegetables, meat and fish, as they are in season and at their prime. You have only to watch the French housewife shopping, or to hear the earnest discussions as to whether the garden peas are at their best, to realise how much thought is put into the choice of foods. With this in mind, we have given you information on the seasons and availability of foods, and suggestions for planning menus and choosing wines.

The choice of meat is always important to the success of your cooking, so we have given you information on this, together with diagrams to illustrate the way in which meat is cut in Britain and France. These diagrams will be useful to anyone, wherever they shop, as it can be difficult to buy the cuts you require if you are not familiar with them.

You may prefer to use metric or imperial weights and measures, or to measure by volume in American cups. Recipes have all three quantities so you can use whichever you like. Do remember that accurate measurement is especially important for sauces, pastries and cakes.

The cordon bleu cook must know about the equipment to use in the kitchen and the use of herbs, wines and flavourings. The techniques of preparing food are vital. You must know how to truss or joint poultry, line a flan or make feather-light pastry. You will find these skills and many others illustrated in easy-to-follow picture guides.

You will notice at the end of some recipes we have included a Tante Marie tip. We are often told, particularly by visitors attending short courses, that some of the most useful things they learn at Tante Marie are the extra little points they are given on how to make a success of each recipe or how to store, freeze or decorate. We thought you might like to know some of them as well.

The recipes are the ones that we have found to be favourites with our students and with our families and friends. We hope that you will enjoy them too.

Bonne chance – bon appétit!

General Information

Weights and Measures

Some people cook well using a handful of this and a drop of that, but this instinctive knowledge comes only after long experience of familiar recipes. If you want to be able to cook from any unfamiliar recipe it is wiser to measure ingredients in order that you can achieve reliable results every time.

Metric, imperial and American cup measures are given in this book, so you can use whichever you prefer. But use only one or the other – the amounts are not always interchangeable. Sometimes metric quantities have been rounded up or down to the nearest convenient figure for shopping – for instance 450 g (1 lb) of a vegetable may be written as 500 g (half a kilogramme) as this is the amount you will purchase.

Metric units

Kilogramme	kg	
Gramme	g	1,000 g = 1 kg
Litre	l	
Decilitre	dl	1/10th of a litre
Centilitre	cl	1/100th of a litre
Millilitre	ml	1/1,000th of a litre

Imperial units

Pound	lb	16 oz
Ounce	oz	16 oz = 1 lb
Quart	qt	2 pt
Pint	pt	20 fl oz
$\frac{1}{4}$ pt = 1 gill = 5 fl oz		
Fluid ounce	fl oz	20 fl oz = 1 pt

Cup and spoon measurements

The American cup = 8 fl oz = 227 ml (2 tablespoons less than the 250 ml metric cup)

| 1 tsp | 5 ml |
| 1 tbsp | 15 ml |

All spoon measurements in this book are level unless otherwise stated.

Equivalent weights

Ounces	Equivalent in grammes to the nearest digit	Practical weight used in recipes
1	28.35 g	25 or 30 g
2	57 g	50 or 60 g
3	85 g	75 g
4	113 g	100 g
5	141 g	150 g
6	170 g	175 g
7	198 g	200 g
8	227 g	225 g
9	255 g	250 g
10	283 g	275 g
11	312 g	300 g
12	340 g	350 g
13	369 g	375 g
14	397 g	400 g
15	425 g	425 g
1 lb	454 g	450 or 500 g
1 lb 1$\frac{1}{2}$ oz	500 g	500 g
2 lb	907 g	900 g or 1 kg
2 lb 3 oz	1 kg	1 kg
3 lb 4$\frac{1}{2}$ oz	1.5 kg	1.5 kg
4 lb 6 oz	2 kg	2 kg

Some small quantities may be difficult to weigh. When measuring odd amounts remember that 1 level tsp holds approximately 5 g.

All eggs in this book are size 3.

Oven temperatures

The temperatures of individual ovens may vary a little, but should be reasonably accurate. This table gives a comparison of gas marks, compared with dial markings in °C and °F.

Gas mark	°C	°F
$\frac{1}{4}$	110	225
$\frac{1}{2}$	120	250
1	140	275
2	150	300
3	160	325
4	180	350
5	190	375
6	200	400
7	220	425
8	230	450

Kitchen Equipment – Ancient and Modern

The words batterie de cuisine conjure up an image of old farmhouse kitchens, with shiny copper bowls and scrubbed wooden tables. Far removed, perhaps, from the modern kitchen and yet having much in common.

You will already have your kitchen with its cooker, refrigerator and other major pieces of equipment, but there are many small tools that will be needed if your cooking is going to be both efficient and pleasurable. The most modern pieces are not only the best; so often there is a beloved but ancient knife that is just right for peeling apples, or an elderly wooden spoon that is a favourite for sauce-making. But no one can cook without the basic essentials: pans and bowls, knives and spoons, and it is pleasant and helpful to have a good selection. Without them the culinary repertoire will be sadly limited, but it is surprising how many homes do not have enough of these essential tools.

We are not advocating that every kitchen should have a great deal of elaborate and expensive equipment, although some of this can be most enjoyable to use. On the contrary, those of you who have cooked at Tante Marie will know that we tend to keep to the simpler pieces, but believe strongly in good knives and boards, whisks and wooden spoons. However, there are many pieces of specialist equipment which help to do particular tasks quickly and efficiently. These range from electric mixers with their attachments to the simple but effective little tools such as a zester for preparing julienne strips of orange peel.

The absolute essentials

Pans

A basic set of good quality heavy saucepans in graduated sizes is necessary. Special purpose pans can be added as you need them. Aluminium is still the most common metal and is very satisfactory. Choose heavy pans with a ground base for gas, electric or solid fuel stoves; lighter, smooth-based ones are suitable only for gas cookers. Non-stick pans are popular and certainly helpful for foods that tend to stick, such as porridge or scrambled eggs.

Saucepans useful for particular needs include a double boiler for melting chocolate and keeping milk or sauce warm. A sauté pan about 8 cm (3 in) deep with a lid is excellent for cooking many dishes such as sauté chicken or poached fish. For large whole fish use a fish kettle. This is not essential but its lift-out drainer makes the task of poaching much easier.

A deep-fat pan is needed for deep frying. Choose one with a wire basket with a reasonably fine mesh, otherwise you will find that food – especially straw potatoes – falls through into the fat. You can use an electric thermostatically controlled deep-fat pan which is very safe and also has the advantage of reducing the smells of frying which are absorbed by its filter.

A frying-pan, of course, will be needed for shallow frying. A heavy one is best.

An omelette pan can double up for making pancakes as well. Unless it is non-stick it should not be washed. Wipe clean after use with kitchen salt on a piece of kitchen paper or a damp cloth.

Pot stands

Wooden stands will protect your kitchen surfaces from hot pans and baking-trays.

Knives

Stainless-steel knives are expensive but easy to clean and cause less loss of vitamins than ordinary steel knives when used to cut fruit and vegetables.

For a basic set choose a 17 cm (7 in) *cook's knife* (plus a 22 cm [9 in] one if you are cooking larger quantities) and a 7 cm (3 in) *vegetable knife*. Have a small *serrated knife* for slicing tomatoes and cutting fruit and a *palette knife* for spreading and lifting foods. If you fillet fish and cut suprêmes of chicken a *filleting knife* is needed and, for boning meat or

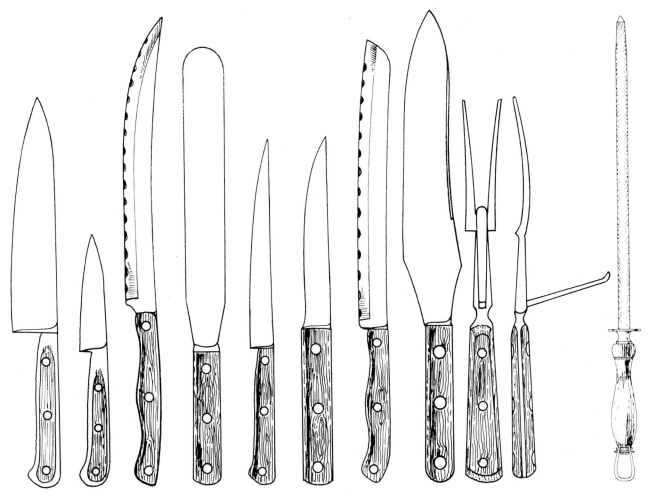

Knives, left to right: Cook's, vegetable, serrated, palette, filleting, boning, bread; carving knife and forks, steel for sharpening.

poultry, a *boning knife*. The household also needs a *bread knife* and *carving knife* and *fork*, and a *steel* for sharpening.

Boards
Knives cannot be used to good effect unless there is a suitable board to work on. A hardwood chopping-board is best for most purposes, but a kitchen can look attractive if there are one or two decorative boards as well. A pastry-board should be reasonably large and preferably made of a plastic laminate or a single piece of well-seasoned wood.

Rolling-pins
The old-fashioned wooden ones are satisfactory and difficult to improve on.

Bowls
Have a good selection of bowls in several sizes. They can be of glass, stainless steel, earthenware and plastic. A large mixing-bowl is good for making bread dough. A spherical copper bowl is ideal for whisking egg whites, but not essential.

Measuring
For measuring ingredients have a set of scales and a measuring jug, or cup measures. You will also need measuring spoons.

Gadgets
Gadgets can take many forms. Some that appeal to the eye or are well advertised sell well, but we must be able to see through the gimmicks to the realities. Kitchens, however large, have only limited storage space and it does not do to fill them with a multitude of gadgets that will be used once or twice and then discarded in a cupboard. Equipment must aid efficiency and help to do a job well and quickly. It must also be easy to keep clean and maintain in good

condition. Your individual choice of pieces depends on the type of cooking which you do and also on the manual skills you possess. It is all very well for a chef to say that a slicer is not needed but someone with no training in fast knifework may find one invaluable.

Tools for cutting

Besides the essential knives there are a number of tools useful for cutting particular foods.

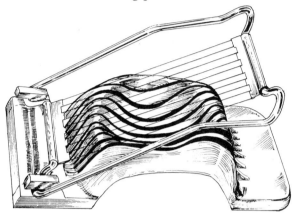

Egg slicers and wedgers
For cutting hard-boiled eggs quickly and easily.

Canelle knife or decorating knife
A knife with a small V-shaped blade for cutting strips out of cucumber, oranges, etc, to give slices a decorative edge.

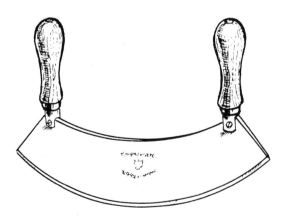

Hachoir or double-handed chopper
For chopping herbs, nuts and other ingredients quickly. Available in stainless steel, with from one to four blades.

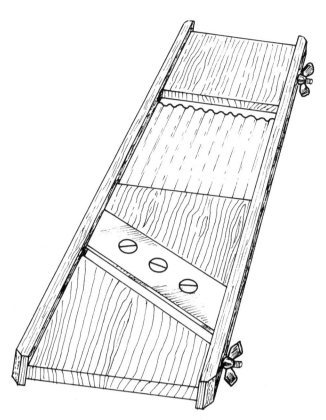

Mandoline or universal slicer
A wooden or metal frame with adjustable blades – one smooth for slicing potato, cucumber, etc, and one corrugated for cutting gaufrette potatoes and julienne strips of vegetables.

Mixer or food processor attachments
A number of machines have slicer and shredder attachments which are very fast and useful if you have a large amount of food to prepare. Bean and peel slicers help with the preparation of runner beans and marmalade.

Parisienne cutter or vegetable ball cutter
A sharp-edged scoop for cutting melon balls and vegetables. Various sizes available.

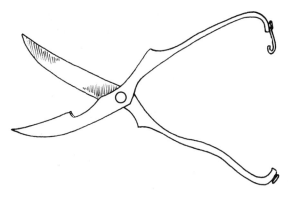

Poultry shears
An optional, but useful, tool for cutting poultry.

Scissors
Kitchen scissors are available with right or left hand cut.

Vegetable peeler
Choose one that you find speedy and which peels thinly. The Continental type with a swivel blade is excellent. Some models are adjustable for use with either hand.

Zester
A tool with a row of small sharp holes designed to grate rind from citrus fruit or to cut julienne strips without cutting into the pith.

Tools for making purées

Liquidiser and food processor
Fast and easy to use, this is one of the most time-saving pieces of electrical equipment. Use to make breadcrumbs as well as purées. When using dry ingredients always switch on first and then drop the food onto the moving blades through the hole in the lid. If you purée raspberries or tomatoes you can sieve the mixture afterwards to remove pips and seeds.

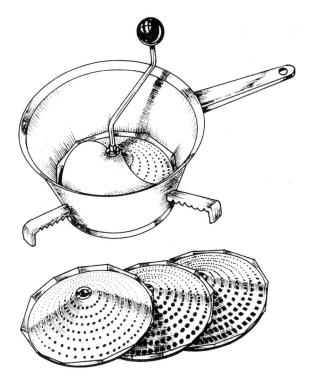

Vegetable mill
Easier than using a sieve when making fruit or vegetable purées, preparing soup, or sieving a pâté.

Pestle and mortar
Old-fashioned but effective and speedy for pounding praline, crushing large quantities of garlic, or crushing shrimps for a bisque.

Garlic press
Garlic can be crushed in a press or with a knife on a board.

Tools for beating

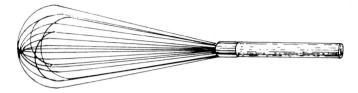

Balloon whisk
Used in a copper bowl, a balloon whisk will beat egg whites to a stiff froth of a consistency difficult to achieve in any other way. The bowl must be cleaned first with salt and either lemon or vinegar.

Sauce whisks
Essential for beating a sauce smooth or for making a light Hollandaise sauce. Stainless-steel beaters are easy to clean and a smooth handle is more comfortable than a ridged metal one.

Egg whisk
Choose a model (either a rotary beater or a wire whisk) that you find light and easy to use.

Electric mixer
Excellent for all kinds of beating and whisking. For small quantities the hand-mixers are suitable.

Moulds

A variety of moulds add interest to the appearance of many dishes. Select those suitable for your favourite types of food.

Jelly moulds for jellies, bavarois, and some savoury mixtures.

Charlotte tins for charlottes such as Charlotte Montreuil. They can also be used for meat or fish moulds and even for sponge cakes.

Spring-form tins for all those difficult-to-turn-out dishes, such as cheesecakes.

Moule à manqué – the indispensable French cake tin with sloping sides designed to make fondant icing easy. Use for gâteaux, bavarois and crème caramel.

Savarin or ring moulds, traditionally used for rum-soaked savarin. Also useful for gâteaux, rice rings and many other sweet and savoury dishes.

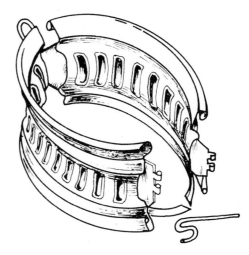

Game pies require the fluted tin with concave sides which can be unclipped at each end for removal.

Flan rings for flans of all kinds. Choose loose-based flan tins if you dislike lifting flans.

For piping

Forcing bags can be bought in several fabrics, nylon being perhaps the easiest to wash. Have a 22 cm (9 in) size bag for small quantities of cream and a 30 cm (12 in) size for piping meringues, choux paste or potatoes.

Pipes (in plastic or metal):
  3 mm ($\frac{1}{8}$ in) plain pipe for filling choux balls,
  12 mm ($\frac{1}{2}$ in) plain pipe for piping éclairs.

Small star pipes are used for piping cream, etc, and larger ones for potatoes and meringues. Especially fine tubes are required for cake icing, and are used with hand-made paper bags.

Brioche and **kugelhopf** demand their own special fluted tins.

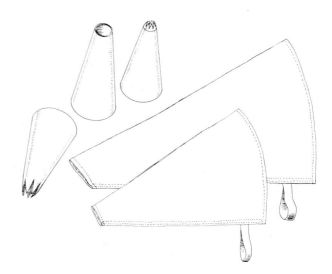

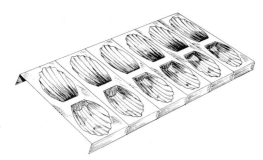

Madeleines require the traditional shell shaped tins.

Culinary Terms

French is the language of the kitchen. Many of the terms used to describe kitchen activities have passed into general use and most people are acquainted with terms such as bouquet garni, and indeed might wonder at the meaning of the old English term 'faggot'. However, there are some terms that may be less familiar.

à la: In the manner of.

à l'Anglaise: Literally, 'in the English style'. Used of fish coated in egg and breadcrumbs and deep fried, and of foods cooked in boiling water.

Aspic: A savoury jelly made from clarified stock. Used for coating cold savoury foods, and in the preparation of savoury moulds or mousses.

Bain-marie: A large pan, usually square or oblong but sometimes round, like a large saucepan, which contains about 4–5 inches of boiling water into which pans containing sauces, etc, can be placed to keep hot. When dishes are cooked in the oven in a bain-marie, a roasting-pan is normally used.

en Ballotine: Butchers' meat, e.g. shoulder of lamb boned, cut, stuffed and formed into a round ball shape for cooking. This term is also applied to boned poultry.

Bard: To cover the breast of game or poultry with pork fat or bacon while cooking.

Bark: The thin dry skin on the outside of a carcase of lamb or mutton which is removed from the chump, loin, best end and breast before cooking.

Baste: To spoon liquid over a food during cooking.

Beurre manié: A thickening for sauces. Butter and flour blended together with a fork in a bowl, using slightly more butter than flour by weight. Add this a little at a time and whisk into the boiling sauce to thicken it. Simmer for a few minutes.

Blanch: To plunge food into boiling water to remove skin, e.g. almonds and tomatoes. This term also means to plunge food into boiling water for a short time to partially cook, or to reduce an over-strong flavour, or to improve colour.

Bouillon: Stock or broth.

Bouchées: Small puff pastry cases.

Bouquet garni: A bunch of herbs, used for flavouring, which is removed from food before it is served. Usually a bayleaf, parsley or parsley stalks and thyme tied together with string. Other herbs sometimes added for special dishes include tarragon, fennel and chervil.

Braise: To cook a food such as meat or fish in stock or wine on a bed of root vegetables.

Casserole: A lidded baking-dish used for cooking stews and sauté dishes in the oven. The food is often served in the same dish.

Chaudfroid: Cold cooked food such as chicken or ham coated in a well-flavoured sauce set with aspic. This is decorated with designs cut in truffle, tomato or carrot, etc, then glazed with aspic.

Chiffonade: Leaves, such as those of lettuce or sorrel, which are rolled and cut into julienne strips.

Chine: To cut through the base of rib or loin bones close to the spinal column on cuts of meat in order to make boning or carving easier.

Concasser: To chop roughly.

Consommé: Soup made from well-flavoured stock which has been clarified. The name of the soup is given by the garnish, e.g. Consommé Julienne.

Court bouillon: A flavoured liquid used to cook fish. Basically water with either wine or vinegar added, with onion, carrot, celery and herbs cooked in it for about 20 minutes before the fish is put in to poach.

Croquettes: Minced meat, poultry, fish or egg, potatoes, etc, moulded into ball or cork shapes coated with seasoned flour, egg and breadcrumbs, then deep-fat fried.

Croûte: Either baked or toasted slices of French bread served with soup, *or* fried or baked slices of bread used as a base for poultry, steaks, etc.

en Croûte: Pâté, meat, poultry or fish enclosed in a pastry or brioche case.

Darne: A fairly thick slice of fish.

Déglacer: The addition of liquid (usually wine or stock) to a hot pan in which food has been fried or roasted. As the liquid is added the fat in the pan is emulsified and thickens the sauce.

Dégorger: To soak food in cold water to remove

impurities, or to sprinkle with salt to draw out strong flavours.

Dégraisser: To remove the fat from the surface of a liquid. Place a sheet of kitchen paper on the surface to absorb excess grease and repeat until the liquid is clear.

Diablotins: Slices of French bread, toasted on one side then coated with a thick cheese sauce and browned under the grill. These are handed with soup.

Duxelle: A savoury mixture of chopped mushrooms cooked with chopped onion or shallot and seasoning.

Escalope: A slice of meat or fish.

Farce: A savoury stuffing.

Fines herbes: A mixture of chopped herbs, e.g. parsley, chervil and tarragon. Can also be parsley only.

Flamber: To flame, as when brandy or other spirit is burnt over food to aromatise the flavour.

Fleuron: Crescent-shaped pieces of flaky or puff pastry used to garnish fish dishes.

Fold in: The sweeping movement used to incorporate ingredients into a light mixture with a minimum loss of volume, as shown in the picture on page 215.

Fond: Stocks of meat, poultry or fish.

Fondant: A soft shiny icing made from boiled sugar.

Fumet de poisson: Fish stock.

Glaze: To brush with melted jam, thickened fruit, syrup or aspic.

Gratiner: To brown the top of a dish in the top of a hot oven or under the grill.

Julienne: Any food cut into matchstick size pieces, e.g. vegetables used for garnish.

Kugelhopf: A rich yeast bread flavoured with raisins which is cooked in a fluted ring mould – a speciality of Alsace.

Larding: Strips of pork fat threaded through lean meat by means of a larding needle.

Liaison: A binding or thickening used for sauces, gravies, etc. Can be a roux, egg yolks, cream, beurre manié and so on.

Macerate: To soak fruit in liqueur or other flavouring.

Marinade: A flavoured liquid of wine or diluted vinegar, with herbs, vegetables and spices, used to soak meat or fish in order to flavour and tenderise it before cooking. The food is often cooked in it.

Médaillons: Either round or oval slices of meat or pâté, *or* chocolate rounds used as decoration on puddings and cakes.

Mirepoix: Diced vegetables used as a base for a braise.

Noisettes: Loin or best end of lamb boned, rolled, tied and cut into 2.5 cm (1 in) slices. See the picture of Noisettes d'Agneau Chasseur on page 109.

Pâte: A general name for pastries, doughs and batters.

Pâté: Literally, a pie, i.e. a savoury filling enclosed in a pastry case. Also used for smooth pastes, e.g. pâté de foie.

Paupiettes: Thin slices of meat or fillets of fish stuffed with a savoury filling and usually braised or poached.

Poach: To cook gently in liquid, e.g. eggs poached in water or fruit poached in sugar syrup.

Pot roast: To cook a joint of meat in a saucepan in fat and with a little liquid. Used to cook the less-tender joints or rather small ones.

Praline: Crisp almond toffee, which is pounded and used as a flavouring.

Purée: Food which has been sieved or mashed to a smooth mixture. May be meat, fish, vegetables or fruit.

Ragoût: Casseroles or stews of many kinds.

Reduce: To boil down a sauce so the flavour is intensified and the sauce thickened.

Réchauffé: Food which is re-heated and made into other dishes, e.g. croquettes.

Refresh: To pour cold water over vegetables after they are cooked or blanched in order to preserve the colour. They must be warmed through again if they are to be served hot.

Rissoles: Small pastry cases with a savoury filling. They are usually coated in egg and breadcrumbs and fried in deep fat.

Roux: A mixture of melted butter and flour cooked together as the thickening agent for a sauce. It may be white, blond or brown, depending on the sauce to be made.

Sabayon: Eggs and sugar beaten together with wine or a liqueur over hot water to a firm mousse and used as a sweet or a sweet sauce.

Sauter: Literally, to jump. Food cooked in fat over a good heat, with the pan shaken so that it jumps and does not stick to the pan.

Savarin: A light yeast cake baked in a ring mould, soaked in a flavoured syrup and decorated.

Slake: To mix flour or arrowroot with cold water to form a thin paste to add to soups, sauces, gravies, etc.

Tammy cloth: A piece of cloth – often double muslin – used for straining sauces when they need to be particularly smooth, e.g. for chaudfroid.

Vacherin: A sweet made with a meringue case filled with fruit and cream or ice-cream.

Vol-au-vent: A large puff pastry case filled with a savoury mixture.

Zest: The thin, coloured part of the skin of citrus fruits containing the flavour. The white pith underneath is bitter.

Bayleaves (*Laurier*): Bay trees, with their shiny dark evergreen leaves, can be grown from cuttings or purchased from nurseries. A well-established bay tree can be quite sizeable – Tante Marie used to have one 30 ft high but when the school moved to Woodham House our bay tree cuttings were carefully transplanted and in ten years they grew to a height of 12 ft despite constant cutting.

The bayleaf is an essential flavour of a bouquet garni and dried leaves can be perfectly satisfactory for this purpose. The flavour blends well with both meat and fish dishes.

Herbs

Every country makes use of its native herbs in its cookery, but few people do so with such skill as the French. One can learn much from them about the subtle use of herb flavours.

Dried herbs are not the same as fresh herbs although a few do dry well: notably bayleaves, thyme, rosemary and sage. Do not think that you can get a true herb flavour from a packet of mixed dried herbs – it is generally preferable to use some freshly chopped parsley. If you care to have some garden herbs to use for flavouring in the winter, they can be frozen very satisfactorily. A box of tarragon leaves, stripped of their stalks, will enable you to make a delicious Sauce Béarnaise to serve with a grilled steak in the winter. It is really necessary to grow your own herbs. A small area of garden or even a window-box or a few pots of herbs growing on a window-sill will give sufficient for family cooking.

Thyme (*Thym*): A hardy plant, the evergreen leaves of thyme can be used all the year round. It can be grown from seed or by division of plants. As it is low-growing and decorative it can make an attractive feature in a garden where the pale mauve flowers of a bank of thyme will attract bees all the summer long. It is a strongly flavoured herb and needs to be used with discretion. A sprig of fresh or dried thyme is included in a bouquet garni, and a little can be used in herb stuffings, but the flavour can all too easily predominate. One dish in which it really comes into its own is a Poulet Sauté à la Provençale, when sprigs of theyme are tied to each bacon-wrapped joint of chicken to give a unique flavour.

Parsley (*Persil*): Every gardener, if not every cook, knows that parsley is reputed to go to the devil seven times before it sprouts. Whatever the reason, it is inclined to germinate slowly, so wait patiently for the seeds to grow. Once established it will flourish, and can be grown either in the herb garden or used as a border in flower beds. Its uses are innumerable. A delicately flavoured herb, it can be used in many dishes and sprigs of parsley are, of course, invaluable as a garnish. Fried parsley makes an interesting crisp green garnish for fried fish.

Chervil (*Cerfeuil*): Grown from seed, it is always the first herb to appear in the year and it often starts to grow even when there is snow on the ground.

The leaves look rather like a flat form of parsley but the flavour is quite different. Use it mixed in equal quantities with chopped parsley for flavouring and decorating, or in a bouquet garni for flavouring Petits Pois à la Française. It is also pretty to use for decorating aspic work.

Chives (*Ciboulette*): These enjoy a sheltered spot with some shade. Too much sun makes them rather dry in summer. Clip the plants frequently to encourage fresh green growth, and remove the lilac-coloured flowers as they form. Chives appear as soon as winter turns to spring and the green tops can be cut to give a fresh mild onion flavour to soups, baked and boiled potatoes, salads and many other dishes.

Sage (*Sauge*): The silver-grey leaves of sage are seen in many gardens. It can be grown in a sunny position from seed or by propagation of root or stem cuttings. It is an evergreen herb which can be used both fresh and dried. As the flavour is pronounced, it must be used carefully. Some stuffings are flavoured with sage, particularly those for duck, goose or pork, and it is sometimes used for flavouring marinades.

easily from seed. It can be tall – about 5 ft when fully grown – when the golden flowers and feathery leaves make a good background to a herb border.

Fennel tastes faintly of aniseed and has a special affinity with fish dishes. A little blended with parsley gives a good flavour to a breadcrumb stuffing for fish, or it can be infused to flavour a sauce to serve with a white fish such as turbot. When you barbecue fish, place sprigs and dry stalks of fennel on the charcoal so they burn and enable the flavour to permeate the fish cooking above.

Savory (*Sarriette*): Winter savory is a perennial low-growing little bush which provides leaves for use in winter. Summer savory has to be grown each year from seed. Both have the same sharp aromatic flavour. The leaves are used to flavour beans (especially broad beans), winter vegetables and meat and fish dishes.

Tarragon (*Estragon*): A tall straggling plant which, once established, will grow well. French tarragon has a better flavour than the variety known as Russian. It comes into growth in late spring and continues until the first frosts. Its narrow dark green leaves can be chopped to add flavour to mixed herbs or a superb flavour can be given to Poulet à l'Estragon by roasting the dish in the French way with tarragon. It is also a useful herb with fish; use it for decorating and flavouring fish aspics, or in Truites à l'Estragon.

Marjoram (*Marjolaine*): Marjoram is a native of Britain and can be found growing wild in the summertime. The pinkish-mauve flowers are like thyme but the broader leaves have a different flavour and are very much milder. It is particularly good with tomato-flavoured dishes and in liver pâté.

Fennel (*Fenouil*): Another British herb, it grows

Rosemary (*Romarin*): Rosemary is a decorative

shrub which can be grown in a sunny spot in the garden, where the low-growing bush looks most attractive with its spiky lavender-green leaves and small blue flowers.

The leaves have a definite perfume which gives an aromatic flavour to food. Rosemary is used in France and Italy with roast lamb and kid, and a sprig can be put in the roasting-pan to give flavour to the sauce. Alternatively it can be finely chopped, mixed with garlic, and pressed into slits in the meat. A sprig is often added to the bouquet garni for a Coq au Vin.

Garlic (*Ail*): Another plant used more frequently in France than in England, garlic can be grown quite easily in this country although it is readily available in the shops. The whole bulb is known as the crown and each individual segment is called a clove of garlic.

No other plant gives such an emphasis to all the flavours of the dish and it is a vital ingredient of a good liver pâté. It is used, too, for flavouring casseroles of many kinds. The way in which garlic is used is important. Coarsely chopped, it can leave a bad taste in the mouth, and bad breath. Crush it finely with salt on a board or in a garlic press. Alternatively, leave it whole and remove it before the food is served. A few foods are highly flavoured with garlic, such as garlic toast and the unctuous, golden sauce, Aïoli.

In France more use is made of herbs than of spices, except for pepper which is used in almost every savoury dish.

Pepper (*Poivre*): Pepper can be bought ready-ground or as whole peppercorns. The flavour is best when you buy whole corns and grind them straight from a pepper-mill into the food you are cooking. Black peppercorns are the most aromatic and have the best taste. White pepper can be used ready-ground and is useful if you want to avoid suspicious-looking black specks in a mayonnaise or Hollandaise sauce. Bottled or tinned green peppercorns are often used in Steak au Poivre.

Flavourings

Vanilla (*Vanille*): Fresh vanilla is a predominant flavour in many cakes and puddings. The vanilla pod is the product of a climbing plant of the orchid family which comes from Mexico and is now grown in various tropical regions.

The pod can be used in several ways. For flavouring liquids, such as the milk to be used for a custard, the whole pod is placed in the warm liquid for a while to flavour it. The pod does not give up all its flavour in the process, so it is washed, the surface is dried by putting it in a warm place, and the pod is then placed in a stone jar or tube to be kept ready for use again. You can continue to use it for as long as it gives flavour. When this becomes weaker, slit the pod, and more flavour will be released.

Vanilla sugar: This is prepared in two different ways. A container – such as a plastic sugar-box – is filled with castor sugar and one or two pods of vanilla inserted into it. After a few days the sugar becomes impregnated with the flavour. When cooking, use a tablespoonful of this sugar as part of the weighed-out quantity required. Replace with fresh sugar in the container. Used in this way the pods last a very long time.

Concentrated vanilla sugar: If required, you can make a very much more concentrated vanilla sugar by blending 250 g (8 oz) sugar in a liquidiser with 2 vanilla pods cut into short lengths. Sift through a fine sieve to remove bits of pod that remain (these can be reground with a little more sugar). Store in an airtight container. Use a teaspoonful for flavouring.

Vanilla essence: Both artificial essence and true vanilla essence can be bought.

Wine in the Kitchen

Wine, beer, cider, spirits and liqueurs are all used to bring flavour and excitement to French food. Naturally, local produce is used in France: either wines of the region, or cider in Normandy, or beer in the north. If you are cooking in another country it is not always practical to use exactly the same wine as would be used in France. A recipe may specify a Vouvray or Chinon, which is fine when it is the local vin ordinaire but you might prefer to use a more readily available wine. In general, the wine used for cooking need not be of top quality. A comparatively inexpensive table wine can be very satisfactory indeed, but for the special occasion when you want to create a really memorable dish, a rather more expensive wine is indispensable. A dry cider can be used as a substitute for white wine on occasions. The flavour will be different, of course, but very palatable nevertheless.

Wine not only flavours the food cooked in it, but also makes meat, poultry and game more tender as the natural acidity of the wine softens the structure of the flesh. For this reason meat with a tendency to toughness, such as venison, is marinaded in wine before cooking.

The quantity used in a recipe depends on the way in which it is used. Sometimes only a few spoonfuls are needed and at other times the meat is cooked entirely in wine: for instance, to give the typically French flavour of a Coq au Vin.

Both red and white wine, as well as beer and cider, are used for cooking casseroles. They are added to the pan after the meat has been browned and allowed to bubble fiercely for a moment before the heat is reduced and the other ingredients added. This initial boiling concentrates the flavour and drives off the alcohol. When wine is used to finish sauces for small pieces of food such as escalopes of veal, steak or shellfish, it is added to the hot pan after the food has been cooked. It is then allowed to boil fiercely for a few moments, so the wine cooks and loses the raw taste of alcohol it will have if it were merely stirred in. Fortified wines such as sherry, Madeira or port are often used in this way.

Brandy gives a smooth flavour to pâtés and has the additional virtue of helping them to keep well. When it is added to a sauce it is sometimes only stirred in, but is more frequently flamed as it is put in so the alcohol is burnt off and a lovely aromatic flavouring remains. This is sometimes done in the kitchen – during the cooking of a Coq au Vin for instance – or it may be done in the dining-room, when a steak is flamed in brandy, or pancakes flamed in liqueur.

In either case, some care is needed. Place the measured spirit or liqueur in a jug and stand it in a pan of hot water for a few moments, in order that it has long enough to warm so it will light easily, but not so long that it loses its alcohol. Pour it over the food and put a light to it. As you do so, the blue flames will flicker across the dish until the alcohol is burnt off.

Safety points:

Do not pour the spirit straight out of the bottle: the flame can blow back. You will notice that, when a waiter flames your Crêpes Suzette, he always keeps his thumb over the opening;

Do not peer over to see if it is alight – there is sometimes a moment's delay;

Do not be over-generous. Too much may give a bigger display than you bargained for. If this happens, cover with a lid.

In puddings and cakes, liqueurs, sweet wines and some spirits are used as flavouring: a couple of tablespoonfuls usually give a good taste to a recipe to serve 4–6 portions. Add too much and a dish will lose all subtlety.

The fruit used in puddings is often macerated in a liqueur, or the liqueur can be added to the mixture for a hot soufflé or a soufflé omelette. Pancakes are flamed in a liqueur, too. Cakes can have liqueur added to the icing and filling for a much appreciated result.

These are some of the liqueurs and spirits most used in the kitchen.

Bénédictine: An aromatic, herb-flavoured liqueur used as a flavouring for soufflés, soufflé omelettes and sabayon.

Brandy: For flavouring pâtés and all kinds of fish, meat and poultry dishes, and chocolate puddings too.

Curaçao: A clear, sharp-flavoured liqueur made from bitter oranges, which is used in a similar way to Grand Marnier.

Grand Marnier: A sweet, soft-flavoured orange liqueur which is used wherever orange flavouring is to be introduced or emphasised. It is good with strawberries, too.

Kirsch: A clear liqueur made from bitter cherries. A less expensive cooking-quality kirsch is available for use in the kitchen. It brings out the flavour of many fruits such as cherries, strawberries and pineapple.

Maraschino: Slightly different in flavour but also made from cherries, maraschino can be used in the same way as kirsch.

Rum: Makes a superb blend with some flavours, notably chocolate, coffee, pineapple and banana.

Kitchen Lore

Some general knowledge of the kitchen.

Acidulated water: This is water with either a spoonful of malt vinegar or the squeezed-out skin of a citrus fruit added to it. It is used to prevent some vegetables and fruits from discolouring.

Almonds: Unless you are making praline you generally need to skin almonds or buy them ready prepared.

To skin almonds, place them in a bowl and cover with boiling water. Allow to stand for a moment or two, then slip the brown skin off each nut.

If you want to use browned almonds they can be coloured under a moderately hot grill or in the oven. Either way, they can burn fairly quickly, so watch them carefully and turn them over as they brown to keep the colour even. If they are to be chopped, use a sharp knife or a liquidiser, being careful not to pulverise them.

Apricot glaze: This is used for glazing fruits and sealing cakes and pastries. Sieve a jar of apricot jam and keep in the store cupboard ready to use. When required, heat the jam with a little water or lemon juice to make a smooth consistency and bring to the boil. Apply with a pastry brush.

Beurre Maître d'Hôtel (*Lemon and parsley butter*): Beat 50 g (2 oz/$\frac{1}{4}$ cup) butter in a bowl until it is soft and creamy. Beat in the juice of $\frac{1}{2}$–1 lemon. Finally mix in 1 tbsp chopped parsley and season to taste.

Place the mixture on a small piece of wet grease-proof paper and form into a roll approximately 2.5 cm (1 in) in diameter. Chill well before use. To serve, cut into slices and use as required.

This quantity is sufficient for 4–6 portions.

Beurre Manié (*Kneaded butter*): This mixture of butter and flour is used as a thickening for sauces, soups, etc. It is sometimes suggested in a recipe and it is also an invaluable help in correcting thin sauces.

Mix butter and flour together in a bowl, blending them with a fork. Equal quantities can be used, but it is easiest to mix if a little more butter is added. Bring the liquid to be thickened to the boil, then add the beurre manié gradually, and whisk it in using a sauce whisk. Add sufficient to achieve the desired consistency. Simmer for 4–5 minutes to cook the flour.

Breadcrumbs: Fresh white breadcrumbs are prepared from bread which is 1–2 days old. To make them speedily use a liquidiser or food processor. Switch on the motor and drop broken pieces of crustless bread onto the blades. When fine crumbs are needed, put them through a wire sieve.

Leftover bread can be dried in the oven until it is pale fawn and crisp. Crush with a rolling-pin or use a mincer. Put through a wire sieve and store in an airtight container.

Croûtons: These fried cubes of bread are served as

To make fresh breadcrumbs, switch on the liquidiser and drop the pieces of bread onto the moving blades.

a crisp accompaniment to soups, or larger ones cut into triangles or heart shapes are used to garnish savoury dishes.

Trim the crusts off some stale white bread, and cut into the shape required (see picture on pages 39 and 109). Heat 25–50 g (1–2 oz/2–4 tablespoons) of butter in a frying-pan with about 5–6 tablespoons of oil, to give about 1 cm ($\frac{1}{2}$ in) depth of fat. Heat until a piece of bread dropped into the fat will start to brown quickly. Remove this piece, then put in sufficient croûtons to give an even layer over the bottom of the pan. Turn the croûtons so they colour evenly. When they are golden brown, lift out and drain on kitchen paper. Allow to cool completely before use.

Grapes: To remove the pips from whole grapes, make yourself a useful tool for the job by pushing a clean hairpin into a cork. The rounded end of the hairpin is slid into the grape through the hole at the stalk end and the pips are scooped out.

Hazelnuts: The skinning and browning processes are done at the same time. Brown the nuts in the same way as almonds (see page 23). When they are coloured, place them in a tea-towel and rub briskly with the cloth. The skin will flake off and can be removed.

Larding: Unduly lean meat, such as venison or veal, can be made moister by the addition of pork or bacon fat. This is cut into small strips and threaded through the meat, using a larding needle.

To cut lemon for garnishing, use a canelle or decorating knife to cut strips from the lemon, then slice thinly.

Lemons: Slices are used for garnishing. Cut the skin with a decorating or canelle knife as shown in the photograph above. Slice thinly.

Liaisons: A cream-and-egg-yolk liaison gives a delicate thickening to some sauces and soups. Care is needed as it can curdle if it gets too hot. Always add the hot sauce to the cold egg-and-cream mixture – not vice versa. Reheat without boiling. Should it overheat and separate into a rough curdle, it can be corrected if you have a liquidiser. Place the sauce or soup in the liquidiser, turn onto high speed for a moment and it will become smooth again.

Olives: Olives can be stoned in one of two ways. An olive stoner is splendid if you have one. Place the olive in the cup-shaped holder, press the handles together and the stone should come out. However, olives come in a variety of sizes and some are too large or too small to fit. In this case, pare the flesh of the olive from the stone, holding the knife at a 45° angle, and work from top to bottom in a spiral. The olive will spring back into shape after the flesh is peeled off.

Oranges: To segment oranges or grapefruit use a sharp knife (a serrated blade is helpful) to cut the peel thickly from the orange so that all the pith is removed. Then cut out the segments of fruit by slicing on each side of the membranes.

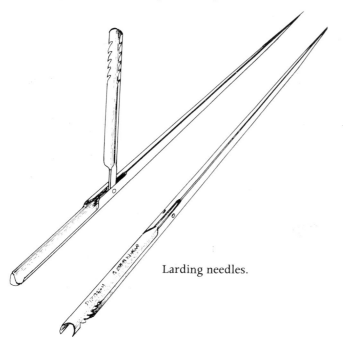

Larding needles.

'Turned' vegetables, which are used as a garnish. First cut them into blocks, then, using a small knife, trim into a neat barrel shape.

Tomatoes: To skin tomatoes, pour boiling water over them. As soon as the skins split, drop into iced water before peeling. Do not leave in very hot water for too long.

Peaches: Prepare as for tomatoes.

Seasoned flour: This is flour with salt and pepper added to it and mixed evenly.

When meat has to be tossed in seasoned flour, place 1 tablespoon flour per 500 g (1 lb) meat in a bowl with the seasoning. Add the cut-up meat, cover and toss together.

Food such as fillets of fish should not be coated until it is time to fry them. If the flour is put on too soon it makes a soft wet coating.

'Turned' vegetables: Root vegetables such as carrots, turnips and potatoes often have very uneven shapes. When they are to be used for a garnish they are 'turned', i.e. cut into neat barrel shapes.

To do this, cut the vegetable into blocks about 5 cm × 3 cm (2 in × $1\frac{1}{4}$ in) then hold them between the thumb and forefinger of one hand and, using a small sharp knife, pare off curved slices which are thicker at the top and bottom, to give a barrel shape.

Green vegetables: After boiling, drain in a colander and swish quickly under the running cold water tap to bring up the colour. Drain again and toss in a little butter to warm again before serving.

Sauces

Food and France conjure up visions or memories of country inns, back-street bistros or sumptuous hotels. Wherever you decide to eat, the food presented will have that special character of French cooking. But what is it that makes French food so special? In the smallest inn or greatest hotel, it is so often the sauce which accompanies a dish that is the foundation of its character – a sauce which adds to a well-cooked dish made from the best ingredients and does not attempt to disguise poor cooking or quality.

Master chefs throughout the history of cooking have invented sauces which are now the backbone of a cook's repertoire. To sauces such as Béchamel, Demi-glace and Mayonnaise, others have added variations so that a subtle balance of flavours is available to complement the food served. This surely is the essence of French food. It may not be a classic sauce; even a little wine or a dash of cream can transform a modest dish into something ambrosial. Imagine the delicate flavour of Sauce Suprême with eggs, the slight bite of Sauce au Vin Blanc with fish or the rich flavour of Sauce Madère with Tournedos Rossini. Each one contributes to the dish without overwhelming the palate so that, long after the meal is consumed, the memory still tries to recapture the flavour. This is the perfect sauce – this is the food of France.

Roux Sauces

These are basic sauces made from fat, flour and liquid. There are three types of roux:

White roux

This is used for making Sauce Béchamel. Butter is used as the fat, and milk as the liquid. The butter must be melted in a pan before the flour is added, and the mixture is then cooked slowly until it bubbles or feels slightly rough on the bottom of the pan. The roux must be cooked gently so that it does not colour. It is important that the roux is well cooked so that the starch cells burst, otherwise the taste of raw flour will remain.

Blond roux

This is used for velouté sauces. The fat used is generally butter, and the liquid is either a meat, chicken, vegetable or fish stock. The roux is cooked until it is a very light gold colour.

Brown roux

This is the basis of Sauce Demi-glace. Beef dripping is the fat normally used, and a good brown stock provides the liquid. The roux must be cooked very slowly until it is a deep golden brown. If it cooks too quickly it will burn and develop a bitter flavour which cannot be disguised.

Addition of liquids

When making all roux sauces, it is advisable to remove the pan from the heat once the roux is cooked and add the liquid a little at a time, beating well. If the sauce should go lumpy, replace over the heat and beat until smooth, then remove from the heat and add the liquid as before. Do not use a metal whisk in an aluminium pan for more than a moment when making a Sauce Béchamel or a velouté sauce, as the metals can react to each other and result in a grey sauce.

ALL ROUX SAUCES MUST BE BROUGHT TO THE BOIL AND COOKED AFTER ALL THE LIQUID HAS BEEN ADDED.

Sauce Béchamel

White sauce

In France this sauce is normally made simply with flour, butter, milk, seasoning and occasionally a pinch of nutmeg.

	Imperial	American
25 g butter	1 oz	2 tbsp
25 g plain flour	1 oz	3 tbsp
300 ml milk	½ pt	1¼ cups
salt and pepper		

Melt the butter in a pan, remove from the heat and add the flour. Mix well with a wooden spoon, return to the heat and cook the roux gently for 2–3 minutes, stirring well. Remove from the heat and add the milk gradually, beating all the time. Replace over the heat and bring to the boil, stirring all the time. Allow the sauce to simmer gently for 4–5 minutes before using. Taste and season.

Sauce à la Crème

Cream sauce

Use the same proportions of ingredients and make in the same way as Sauce Béchamel, but use half milk and half single cream.

Sauce Mornay

Cheese sauce

	Imperial	American
300 ml Sauce Béchamel	½ pt	1 cup
50 g cheese, grated	2 oz	½ cup

After the Sauce Béchamel is made, add the grated cheese and replace on the hob to heat through. The sauce must not be allowed to boil after the cheese has been added or it will become stringy, tough and indigestible.

Sauce Soubise

Onion sauce

	Imperial	American
450 g onions, finely sliced	1 lb	1 lb
50 g butter	2 oz	¼ cup
300 ml Sauce Béchamel	½ pt	1¼ cups
4 tbsp single cream (optional)	4 tbsp	4 tbsp
¼ tsp paprika pepper	¼ tsp	¼ tsp
a pinch of nutmeg		
salt and pepper		

Cook the onions in boiling salted water for 30 minutes. Drain thoroughly. Melt half the butter in a thick pan and finish cooking the onions in this. Add the Sauce Béchamel to the pan and mix well. Season with paprika, nutmeg, salt and pepper. Allow the sauce to warm through slowly and thoroughly. Pass it through a sieve or vegetable mill, or blend in an electric liquidiser. Stir in the cream. Add the rest of the butter gradually. Keep hot.

Velouté Sauces

Sauce Velouté

Velouté sauce

	Imperial	American
25 g butter	1 oz	2 tbsp
25 g plain flour	1 oz	3 tbsp
300 ml chicken, veal or fish stock	½ pt	1¼ cups

Melt the butter in a pan, add the flour and cook gently for a few minutes until the roux is blond. Remove from the heat and add the strained stock gradually, stirring it well. Bring to the boil and simmer for 5 minutes.

Sauce aux Crevettes

Prawn sauce

	Imperial	American
100 g whole prawns	4 oz	4 oz
40 g butter	1½ oz	3 tbsp
1 tbsp brandy	1 tbsp	1 tbsp
40 g plain flour	1½ oz	⅓ cup
300 ml fish stock	½ pt	1¼ cups
(see page 35)		
1 tsp tomato purée	1 tsp	1 tsp
150 ml double cream	¼ pt	⅔ cup
a pinch of cayenne pepper		
salt and pepper		

Shell the prawns, taking care to discard the eyes. Pound the shells well (this can be done in a pestle and mortar, with a wooden spoon or with the end of a rolling-pin in a bowl). Melt the butter in a pan and add the crushed shells. Cook gently for several minutes then warm the brandy, pour over and flame. Stir in the flour and cook the roux for 4–5 minutes. Remove from the heat and add the fish stock gradually, together with the tomato purée. Bring to the boil, stirring all the time, and cook for 4–5 minutes. Strain through a pointed chinois sieve. Add the cream and prawns, then reheat. Add the cayenne, taste and adjust the seasoning.

This sauce is an excellent accompaniment to poached fish.

Sauce Suprême

Creamy chicken sauce

	Imperial	American
40 g butter	1½ oz	4 tbsp
40 g plain flour	1½ oz	⅓ cup
450 ml chicken stock	¾ pt	2 cups
2 egg yolks		
150 ml double cream	¼ pt	⅔ cup
salt and pepper		

Melt the butter in a pan and stir in the flour. Cook over a low heat for 4–5 minutes or until pale gold. Remove from the heat and add the stock gradually, beating all the time. Bring to the boil, stirring all the time. Simmer gently for 5–10 minutes. Beat the egg yolks with the cream, then pour some of the hot sauce onto them. Return to the pan and mix together well. Taste and season. Reheat, whisking well, without bringing the sauce to the boil. The sauce should be of a good coating consistency and have a good gloss.

Sauce Aurore

Dawn sauce

	Imperial	American
25 g butter	1 oz	2 tbsp
25 g plain flour	1 oz	3 tbsp
300 ml chicken stock	½ pt	1¼ cups
2 tsp tomato purée	2 tsp	2 tsp
salt and pepper		
sugar, if necessary		

Melt the butter in a pan, add the flour and cook, stirring for 3–4 minutes until very pale gold. Remove from the heat and stir in the liquid gradually, then add the tomato purée and seasoning. Bring to the boil, stirring all the time, and simmer for about 5 minutes. Taste and adjust the seasoning, adding a small pinch of sugar if necessary.

Sauce au Vin Blanc

White wine sauce

	Imperial	American
25 g butter	1 oz	2 tbsp
25 g plain flour	1 oz	3 tbsp
150 ml fish stock	¼ pt	⅔ cup
(see page 35)		
150 ml white wine	¼ pt	⅔ cup
4 tbsp double cream	4 tbsp	4 tbsp
salt and pepper		

Melt the butter in a pan and stir in the flour. Cook gently, stirring for 4–5 minutes or until pale gold. Remove from the heat and stir in the fish stock and wine. Bring to the boil, stirring all the time. Cook for 5–8 minutes. Stir in the cream. Taste and season.

This sauce can be served with poached fish dishes.

Sauce au Fines Herbes

Herb sauce

Make this sauce as in the previous recipe and finally add 1 tablespoon finely chopped fennel or chervil.

This sauce goes particularly well with mackerel and other oily fish but the cream should be omitted.

Preparation of ingredients for Sauce Demi-glace.

Sauce Demi-glace being strained through a conical chinois sieve.

Brown Sauces

Sauce Demi-glace

Brown sauce

	Imperial	American
50 g bacon	2 oz	2 oz
50 g dripping	2 oz	$\frac{1}{4}$ cup
1 small onion, diced		
1 small carrot, diced		
3 tbsp plain flour	3 tbsp	3 tbsp
450 ml brown stock	$\frac{3}{4}$ pt	2 cups
100 g mushrooms *or* stalks and peelings	4 oz	4 oz
2 tsp tomato purée	2 tsp	2 tsp
75 ml sherry	$2\frac{1}{2}$ fl oz	$\frac{1}{3}$ cup
salt and pepper		

Cut the bacon into strips and fry in the dripping until golden brown. Take out the bacon and add the onion and carrot. Cook these slowly, until they are just beginning to turn a golden brown. This process cannot be hurried or the vegetables will be scorched. Sprinkle in the flour and cook over a low heat for 15 minutes or so until the roux browns, stirring occasionally. Add the stock, bacon and mushrooms. Bring to the boil, stirring all the time. Simmer, uncovered, for 30 minutes. Stir in the tomato purée and sherry. Cook for a further 15–20 minutes. Strain through a conical strainer, so that the liquid sauce is separated from the now overcooked vegetables. Taste and adjust the seasoning. The sauce should be of a medium coating consistency. Reheat before use.

Sauce Madère

Madeira sauce

Make as for Sauce Demi-glace but substitute 75 ml ($2\frac{1}{2}$ fl oz/$\frac{1}{3}$ cup) Madeira for the sherry.

Sauce Piquante

Spicy sauce

	Imperial	American
300 ml Sauce Demi-glace	$\frac{1}{2}$ pt	$1\frac{1}{4}$ cups
25 g butter	1 oz	2 tbsp
1 tbsp finely chopped shallots	1 tbsp	1 tbsp
150 ml wine vinegar	$\frac{1}{4}$ pt	$\frac{2}{3}$ cup
1 tbsp finely chopped gherkins	1 tbsp	1 tbsp
1 tbsp finely chopped parsley	1 tbsp	1 tbsp

Melt the butter in a small pan, add the shallots and cook until they are tender but do not allow them to colour. Pour in the vinegar and reduce by three-quarters. Add the Sauce Demi-glace and simmer for 15 minutes. Just before serving add the gherkins and parsley. Do not allow the sauce to cook once the gherkins have been added. Serve immediately.

This sauce is excellent with rechauffé and pork dishes.

Emulsion Sauces

Mayonnaise

This sauce is made by blending egg yolks and oil together to form an emulsion. It is important to remember that the oil must be at room temperature – if it is used straight from a cold larder it will not blend with the eggs and will separate or curdle. In cold weather, stand the jug of oil in warm water before starting to make the mayonnaise.

The type of oil used for making mayonnaise is a matter of personal preference. Olive oil is often suggested but this is expensive and, unless you have a first pressing and use it soon after it is opened, it can have a strong flavour. A first pressing is very light in colour; subsequent pressings get darker and stronger in flavour.

A good vegetable oil can be used instead. The French use arachide (groundnut) oil. This produces a bland sauce which needs careful seasoning. Corn oil can also be used but this has a more definite flavour. The quality of the vinegar is also important. A wine or cider vinegar gives a better flavour than malt vinegar, which is too harsh.

Sauce Mayonnaise

Mayonnaise

	Imperial	American
1–2 egg yolks		
$\frac{1}{2}$ tsp mustard	$\frac{1}{2}$ tsp	$\frac{1}{2}$ tsp
a pinch of sugar		
$\frac{1}{4}$ tsp salt	$\frac{1}{4}$ tsp	$\frac{1}{4}$ tsp
white pepper		
300 ml oil	$\frac{1}{2}$ pt	$1\frac{1}{4}$ cups
2–3 tbsp wine vinegar	2–3 tbsp	2–3 tbsp

Place the egg yolks, mustard, sugar, salt and a little white pepper in a bowl and beat them together, using either a whisk or a small electric mixer, until they thicken slightly. Stand the bowl on a damp cloth to prevent it moving and drip the oil in a little at a time, beating continuously. Dip the blade of a small knife into the oil and then drip into the eggs. Beat just enough to incorporate the oil before adding more. Once a good emulsion is formed, it is possible to add the oil a little more quickly, allowing it to drip off the tip of a small spoon. Do not let the sauce get too thick. When about a third of the oil has been

added, beat in half the vinegar, and then add the rest of the oil slowly, still beating all the time. When all the oil is added stir in the rest of the vinegar to taste.

To adjust the consistency of the sauce, add a little boiling water. This also helps to prevent the mayonnaise separating or oiling on the surface if it is to be kept. Store covered in a cool place, but not in a refrigerator.

Tante Marie tip:
If you are unlucky enough to curdle the mayonnaise, pour a tablespoon of boiling water into a clean bowl and *immediately* start to drip the curdled mixture into the water. An emulsion should form quite easily and the rest of the curdled mixture can then be added a drop at a time as previously described. This method is satisfactory only when beating by hand or using a hand electric whisk. It will not work with a large mixer although, if you are making a large quantity, the sauce can be transferred to one when about 300 ml ($\frac{1}{2}$ pt/$1\frac{1}{4}$ cups) of sauce has emulsified. If this method is not successful, try starting again with another egg yolk. Drip in a little fresh oil, making certain it is the correct temperature. When an emulsion has formed add the curdled mixture slowly.

MIXER METHODS

Liquidiser: Place the seasoning and one whole egg in the liquidiser. Just cover the blades with oil, cover with the lid and switch to fast speed until the sauce thickens. A change in the sound is usually a good signal. Then drip in the rest of the oil slowly, add half the vinegar when about a third of the oil has been used and continue as before.

Large mixers: Use a large mixer only when making a quantity such as 1–2 litres (2–4 pt/4–8 cups) of mayonnaise.

Food processor: This is the quickest and easiest way to make mayonnaise. Use the cutting blade. Place a whole egg and the seasonings in the bowl. Switch on, mix together for a second or two, then pour the oil in slowly. When all the oil has been incorporated, add the vinegar. Switch off, taste and check seasoning.

Aïoli

Garlic mayonnaise

	Imperial	American
2–4 cloves garlic, depending on size		
$\frac{1}{4}$ tsp salt	$\frac{1}{4}$ tsp	$\frac{1}{4}$ tsp
$\frac{1}{2}$ tsp mustard	$\frac{1}{2}$ tsp	$\frac{1}{2}$ tsp
white pepper		
1–2 egg yolks		
300 ml oil	$\frac{1}{2}$ pt	$1\frac{1}{4}$ cups
2–3 tbsp lemon juice	2–3 tbsp	2–3 tbsp

Peel the cloves of garlic and crush them to a pulp with the salt. Place in a bowl with the mustard, pepper and egg yolks. Add the oil slowly as for mayonnaise and flavour with lemon juice instead of vinegar.

Sauce Tartare

Tartare sauce

	Imperial	American
1 hard-boiled egg yolk		
1 raw egg yolk		
$\frac{1}{4}$ tsp mustard	$\frac{1}{4}$ tsp	$\frac{1}{4}$ tsp
white pepper		
300 ml oil	$\frac{1}{2}$ pt	$1\frac{1}{4}$ cups
1 tbsp wine vinegar	1 tbsp	1 tbsp
2 tsp chopped capers	2 tsp	2 tsp
2 tsp chopped gherkins	2 tsp	2 tsp
2 tsp chopped chives	2 tsp	2 tsp
2 tsp chopped tarragon	2 tsp	2 tsp
salt		

Sieve the hard-boiled egg yolk and place in a bowl with the raw egg yolk, mustard and white pepper. Add the oil and vinegar as for mayonnaise. When all the oil has been added, stir in the capers, gherkins, chives and tarragon. Season with salt to taste and adjust with boiling water to a thick pouring consistency.

Serve with fried fish.

Sauce Rémoulade

Rémoulade sauce

	Imperial	American
2 tbsp finely chopped capers	2 tbsp	2 tbsp
2 tbsp finely chopped gherkins	2 tbsp	2 tbsp
2 tbsp finely chopped tarragon	2 tbsp	2 tbsp
300 ml Sauce Mayonnaise	$\frac{1}{2}$ pt	$1\frac{1}{4}$ cups
1 tsp Dijon mustard	1 tsp	1 tsp
2 tsp anchovy essence	2 tsp	2 tsp
salt and pepper		

Mix the capers, gherkins and tarragon together. Stir them into the mayonnaise, together with the mustard and anchovy essence. Taste and season.

Sauce Verte

Green sauce

	Imperial	American
1 handful spinach		
1 handful parsley		
1 handful tarragon and chervil mixed in equal quantities		
300 ml Mayonnaise	$\frac{1}{2}$ pt	$1\frac{1}{4}$ cups

Strip the spinach leaves and herbs from the stalks and blanch in boiling, salted water for 1–2 minutes. Drain, refresh and drain well again, pressing out the surplus moisture. Place in a blender with a little of the oil for the mayonnaise and liquidise until smooth; or pass through a fine sieve or vegetable mill.

Make the mayonnaise with the remainder of the oil and add the purée a little at a time at the end. Taste and season. Use as required.

This sauce is an excellent accompaniment to cold poached fish.

Reduction Sauces

Sauces au Beurre

Butter sauces

Sauces such as Hollandaise, Béarnaise, etc, are made by boiling down a court bouillon, stock or vinegar and adding this reduction to egg yolks which are whisked over a pan of hot water until they thicken. Butter is then whisked in. The butter needs to be slightly soft but not runny. It must be whisked in a little at a time. If the sauce starts to curdle it is due to one of the following causes:

1. The butter was whisked in too quickly in large pieces. To remedy this, beat well until smooth before adding any more.

2. The butter was too cold. Stand over warm water and beat until smooth.

3. The sauce was allowed to get too warm. Remove from the heat and beat in a little more butter until the sauce is smooth again.

A reduction sauce is always served warm.

Sauce Hollandaise

Hollandaise sauce

	Imperial	American
2 egg yolks		
1 tbsp court bouillon *or* white stock	1 tbsp	1 tbsp
100 g butter	4 oz	$\frac{1}{2}$ cup
1 tbsp lemon juice	1 tbsp	1 tbsp
white pepper		

Place the egg yolks in a bowl and whisk lightly. Put the court bouillon or stock into a pan and reduce by half, pour onto the beaten egg yolks and mix well. Place the bowl over a pan of hot water, taking care that the water does not touch the bottom of the bowl. Whisk continuously until the eggs thicken. Beat in the butter gradually. Do not allow the sauce to get too warm. Remove it from the heat occasionally so that the sauce remains only warm; overheating will cause it to separate or curdle. When all the butter has been added, beat in the lemon juice and pepper to taste. Serve warm.

This sauce is used as an accompaniment to vegetables – see artichokes and asparagus (pages 45 and 46). It is also served with eggs and poached fish.

Sauce Béarnaise

Béarnaise sauce

	Imperial	American
2 egg yolks		
6 peppercorns		
1 shallot, finely chopped		
2 tbsp tarragon vinegar	2 tbsp	2 tbsp
1 tbsp white stock	1 tbsp	1 tbsp
100 g butter	4 oz	$\frac{1}{2}$ cup
1 tbsp finely chopped tarragon	1 tbsp	1 tbsp
salt and pepper, if required		

Beat the egg yolks lightly in a small bowl. Lightly crush the peppercorns and place them in a pan with the shallot and vinegar. Reduce by half, add the stock and strain onto the yolks. Continue as for Hollandaise sauce. Finally add the tarragon and season to taste.

This sauce is served with steaks, fish and eggs.

Sauce Choron

Choron sauce

This is Sauce Béarnaise flavoured with 1–2 tsp of tomato purée.

Sauce au Beurre Blanc

White butter sauce

	Imperial	American
6 shallots, finely chopped		
150 ml white wine	$\frac{1}{4}$ pt	$\frac{2}{3}$ cup
175 g butter	6 oz	$\frac{3}{4}$ cup
1 tbsp double cream	1 tbsp	1 tbsp
salt and pepper		

Make certain the shallots are very finely chopped and place them in a pan with the wine. Allow them to cook very slowly until soft. If the wine reduces too quickly before the shallots are cooked, add a little water and continue cooking. Reduce the wine to about 2 tablespoons. Beat in the softened butter a little at a time, taking care not to allow the sauce to become too warm. When all the butter has been added stir in the cream then taste and adjust the seasoning. Serve immediately.

This sauce is served with fish, particularly salmon.

Not all sauces can be described as specific types. The following sauces are examples: Sauce Raifort, a creamy horseradish sauce, is served with smoked trout or mackerel, or Pot-au-Feu; and Sauce Tomate has an excellent flavour and can be used in many ways. It is particularly good with réchauffé dishes such as Pain de Boeuf and Rissoles. Sauce Vinaigrette needs no introduction; it is the perfect dressing for fresh green salads.

Sauce Raifort

Horseradish sauce

	Imperial	American
4 tbsp double cream	4 tbsp	4 tbsp
2 tsp grated horseradish	2 tsp	2 tsp
1 tsp sugar	1 tsp	1 tsp
1 tbsp wine vinegar	1 tbsp	1 tbsp
salt and pepper		

Stir the cream with the horseradish, then add the sugar, vinegar and seasoning to taste.

Sauce Tomate

Tomato sauce

	Imperial	American
500 g fresh tomatoes,	1 lb	1 lb
or 400 g can tomatoes	14 oz	14 oz
1 onion, sliced		
3 rashers or trimmings		
of lean streaky bacon		
1 clove garlic		
1 tsp sugar	1 tsp	1 tsp
a bouquet garni		
salt and pepper		

Chop the tomatoes roughly and place in a pan with the onion, bacon cut into strips, crushed garlic, sugar, bouquet garni and seasoning. Cook over a low heat for about 20 minutes or until the tomatoes are both soft and well-flavoured. Sieve, or put through a vegetable mill. Taste and season. Use as required.

Sauce Vinaigrette

French dressing

The oil used is again a matter of personal preference. Good quality olive oil is excellent for flavour, but arachide (groundnut oil) can be used with good results.

3 parts oil
1 part wine vinegar
salt
a pinch of sugar
a little made mustard
pepper

Place the ingredients in a bowl and whisk together. This sauce will separate when left to stand. Just give it another quick whisk before sending it to the table.

Tante Marie tip:
Chopped fresh herbs can be added to this sauce if desired.

Soups

The aroma of a good soup makes a promising start to a meal. Warming in winter or cool in summer, soups can be simple or exotic, to suit your menu or your mood.

Almost all soups need the basis of a good stock. This is simply a flavoured liquid made from bones – very often beef or veal – with vegetables and herbs. Salt is not added to it as it is more satisfactory to put this into the finished dishes, as their requirements can vary. You can use a stock cube when fresh stock is not available but this lacks the individuality of flavour that comes from making your own. Making stock is simple and not the time-consuming process that people sometimes imagine.

For the very best stock, which is needed for a consommé or for making aspic, use the poaching liquor from chicken or veal for a white stock, or from a Pot-au-Feu made with a joint of fresh beef for a beef stock.

Chicken and game stocks are made using the raw carcase and giblets (except the liver) which are left over when a bird is jointed. The cooked carcase can be used, though it gives a cloudy liquid instead of a clear one. It must not be boiled for too long – 1–2 hours is sufficent.

Fond de cuisine

Stock

White stock, beef stock, chicken stock, game stock.

	Imperial	American
1 kg veal *or* beef bones (do not use marrow bones as they are too fatty) or chicken, or game carcases and giblets	2 lb	2 lb
about 2 litres water	4 pt	10 cups
2 onions		
2–3 carrots		
1 leek, when available		
1–2 sticks celery		
a large bouquet garni		
about 6 peppercorns		

Clean the bones and improve their flavour by blanching. To do this place them in a pan with water to cover and bring slowly to the boil. Discard this water after it boils, as it has a strong flavour and an unpleasant scum. Rinse the bones, cover with fresh water and add the cleaned and peeled vegetables, bouquet garni and peppercorns. Cover, bring to the boil again and allow to simmer for 3–4 hours. Strain into a clean bowl and the stock is ready to use. If the stock has to be kept, cool it and place in the refrigerator. Remove any fat when set. It will keep for 2–3 days. For longer storage, freeze in a plastic box.

Fond brun

Brown stock

This is a dark brown stock which is used in some dishes. It is particularly useful for a Sauce Demi-glace, as it enriches both the colour and flavour of the sauce.

	Imperial	American
1 kg beef bones	2 lb	2 lb
2 onions		
2 carrots		
1 leek		
1 stick celery		
2 litres water	4 pt	10 cups
a bouquet garni		
6 peppercorns		

Place the bones in a roasting-pan and add a quartered onion and a carrot. Cook to a dark brown in a hot oven, Mark 6 (200°C/400°F), for about 30 minutes or until they are well coloured. Lift the bones and vegetables into a large saucepan or stock pot and pour on the water. Bring slowly to the boil. Add the rest of the prepared vegetables, bouquet garni and peppercorns and simmer over a very low heat for 4–5 hours. Strain, then refrigerate when cool.

Fumet de Poisson

Fish stock

A few fish bones or the head of a whole fish can be used to make a delicately flavoured stock to use in fish sauces and soups. Do not use plaice bones as they become bitter.

	Imperial	American
a few bones of white fish, e.g. sole, or a fish head		
1 onion, sliced		
1 carrot, sliced		
a bouquet garni		
1 litre water	2 pt	5 cups
300 ml dry white wine	$\frac{1}{2}$ pt	1 cup
a few black peppercorns		

Wash the bones or head well and place in a pan with all the other ingredients. Bring slowly to the boil, then simmer for 20 minutes. Strain and use as required.

Potage Vivier

A fish soup (serves 4)

An appetising soup from Brittany.

	Imperial	American
the head of a large fish, e.g. cod, conger eel or hake, or a medium-sized sea bream or a whiting		
2 cloves garlic		
$\frac{1}{4}$ tsp cumin seeds	$\frac{1}{4}$ tsp	$\frac{1}{4}$ tsp
salt		
8 black peppercorns		
2 tbsp oil	2 tbsp	2 tbsp
1 large onion, chopped		
1 large tbsp tomato purée	1 large tbsp	1 large tbsp
1 tbsp paprika pepper	1 tbsp	1 tbsp
1 stick celery		
a small bouquet garni		
a pinch of cayenne pepper		

To serve:
French bread

Pound the peeled garlic with the cumin, salt and peppercorns and moisten with a little oil to give a thick paste.

Cook the onion in the rest of the oil until golden. Add the tomato purée, paprika, and the pounded garlic and spices. Cook for 2 minutes over a low heat. Add 1 litre (1$\frac{3}{4}$ pt/4$\frac{1}{2}$ cups) of water and bring to the boil. Wash the fish head and add this with the celery and bouquet garni. Allow to simmer for 20 minutes.

Lift out the head and bones and pass the soup through a moderately fine vegetable mill, sieving the cooked flesh of the fish as well as the vegetables. Taste and season, adding a pinch of cayenne pepper. Serve hot with toasted slices of French bread handed separately.

Tante Marie tip:
If you are using shellfish such as prawns for another dish, add their shells to the stock for extra flavour.

Crème Jardinière

The gardener's wife's soup (serves 4–6)

A delicate cream of vegetable soup with a simple garnish.

	Imperial	American
1 medium carrot		
1 onion		
$\frac{1}{2}$ turnip		
1 medium leek		
1 cabbage or lettuce leaf		
40 g butter	$1\frac{1}{2}$ oz	3 tbsp
40 g plain flour	$1\frac{1}{2}$ oz	$\frac{1}{3}$ cup
1 litre white stock	$1\frac{3}{4}$ pt	4 cups
150 ml milk	$\frac{1}{4}$ pt	$\frac{2}{3}$ cup
salt and pepper		
2 tbsp double cream (optional)	2 tbsp	2 tbsp
finely chopped parsley or chives for garnish		

Prepare the vegetables, wash, and cut into julienne strips. Melt the butter in a saucepan. Soften the vegetables in this and cook over a gentle heat for 7–10 minutes, stirring all the time. They must not brown. Add the flour and cook for a moment. Pour the stock onto the vegetables. Bring to the boil, stirring well. Add the milk and 1 teaspoon of salt and cook gently until the vegetables are tender. Add the cream, if used. Taste and season. Serve in a hot tureen, sprinkled with a little finely chopped parsley or chives.

Tante Marie tip:
The vegetables used can be varied according to the season. Add peas or beans instead of cabbage in summer, or in winter add a Jerusalem artichoke.

Soupe à l'Oignon

French onion soup (serves 4–6)

This was the traditional fare of the porters at les Halles – the great market of Paris – where it was served at the bistros around the market and consumed with copious draughts of Beaujolais in the very early morning.

	Imperial	American
500 g onions, finely sliced	1 lb	1 lb
50 g butter	2 oz	$\frac{1}{4}$ cup
1 tsp sugar	1 tsp	1 tsp
2 tsp plain flour	2 tsp	2 tsp
1 litre beef or brown stock	$1\frac{3}{4}$ pt	$4\frac{1}{2}$ cups
salt and freshly ground black pepper		
French bread		
25–50 g Gruyère cheese, grated	1–2 oz	$\frac{1}{4}$–$\frac{1}{2}$ cup

Melt the butter in a heavy iron pan or thick saucepan over a moderate heat. Add the onions to the pan with the sugar. Stir frequently until the onions are golden brown. This must be done gently without burning the onions. It is a process which cannot be hurried and should take about 20 minutes. Sprinkle in the flour, stir until smooth. Pour in the stock gradually. Season well. Simmer gently for 15 minutes.

Cut the bread into slices. Cover with the cheese and brown under a hot grill. Pour the soup into a tureen and put the cheese-coated toast on top. Serve immediately.

Consommé au Céleri

Celery consommé (serves 4)

A clear soup with celery flavouring and garnish.

	Imperial	American
1 litre chicken stock	2 pt	$4\frac{1}{2}$ cups
1 carrot, finely diced		
1 onion, finely diced		
a bouquet garni		
4–5 peppercorns		
100 g lean leg or shin of beef, shredded	4 oz	$\frac{1}{2}$ cup
salt		
3–4 egg whites		
4 sticks celery		
3 tbsp sherry	3 tbsp	3 tbsp

Place the cold stock, carrot, onion, bouquet garni, peppercorns and meat in a large saucepan with salt to flavour. Break up the egg whites with a fork and stir into the pan. Reserve one or two sticks of the celery, chop the remainder and add this also. Cook gently over a low heat, stirring all the time with a wooden spoon, until it comes to simmering point. Allow to simmer very gently, without stirring, for about 1½–2 hours. During this time the liquid will become clear, and the solids will form a scum on the top. Do not break this up or stir it back into the liquid.

Cut the rest of the celery into julienne strips and cook in boiling salted water until tender. When the consommé is cooked, taste and add more salt if necessary. Put one or two spoons of the scum onto a damp linen cloth resting on a sieve over a clean bowl. Strain the soup gently through this. Drain the julienne of celery and put this in a soup tureen. Add the sherry to the consommé and pour this over the celery. Serve hot.

Tante Marie tip:
If a consommé has to be reheated, it may go cloudy if it is boiled again, so heat it in a bowl over a pan of hot water.

Crème Evita
Chilled tomato soup (serves 6–8)

	Imperial	American
1 kg ripe tomatoes	2 lb	2 lb
1 onion, finely chopped		
a bouquet garni		
4 peppercorns		
1 clove		
a strip of lemon rind		
1 litre chicken stock	2 pt	4½ cups
1 tsp lemon juice	1 tsp	1 tsp
a few drops of Tabasco sauce		
salt and pepper		

For the garnish:

4 tbsp double cream	4 tbsp	4 tbsp
fresh herbs, e.g. chives or mint		

Wipe the tomatoes, cut into quarters and place in a saucepan with the onion, bouquet garni, peppercorns, clove, lemon rind and stock. Cover and simmer gently until the tomatoes are tender. Pass through a fine sieve or vegetable mill. Add the lemon juice, Tabasco and seasoning to taste. Chill.

Serve in individual soup cups with the whipped cream spooned on top and sprinkled with chopped fresh herbs, or a sprig of mint.

Potage Niçoise
Tomato and green pepper soup
(serves 4–6)

	Imperial	American
½ green pepper		
1 onion		
225 g tomatoes	8 oz	8 oz
25 g butter	1 oz	2 tbsp
1 tbsp plain flour	1 tbsp	1 tbsp
1 litre stock	2 pt	4½ cups
a bouquet garni with several sprigs of tarragon		
1 clove garlic		
salt and freshly ground black pepper		
a pinch of sugar		

For the diablotin garnish:
Sauce Mornay (see page 27) made with:

150 ml milk	¼ pt	⅔ cup
20 g butter	¾ oz	2 tbsp
20 g plain flour	¾ oz	6 tsp
25 g cheese, grated	1 oz	¼ cup
French bread		
extra 25 g cheese, grated	1 oz	¼ cup

Remove the seeds and pith from the pepper and blanch it in boiling salted water for 5 minutes. Drain and dice. Chop the onion finely. Skin and pip the tomatoes and cut them into shreds.

Melt the butter in a thick saucepan, add the onion and cook slowly without allowing to brown. Sprinkle in the flour and cook gently for 2–3 minutes. Add the tomatoes, onion and pepper, stir carefully then pour in the stock. Add the bouquet garni and the garlic crushed with a little salt. Season with salt, pepper and a pinch of sugar. Simmer gently for 30 minutes. Taste and season.

For the diablotin make a thick Sauce Mornay. Cut the French bread into as many slices as there are soup cups. Put a good spoonful of the sauce on each slice. Sprinkle with the rest of the grated cheese. Place under a hot grill to brown.

Serve the soup in individual soup cups with a diablotin floating on each one.

Potage Fontanges

Pea soup (serves 4–6)

It can be difficult to obtain leeks when peas are in season, but this soup can also be made successfully with frozen peas. Sorrel is found growing wild in the summer, or you can grow a cultivated sorrel in the garden, to use for soups and as a vegetable.

	Imperial	American
225 g shelled or frozen peas	8 oz	8 oz
50 g butter	2 oz	$\frac{1}{4}$ cup
the white of 1 leek		
1 litre chicken stock	$1\frac{3}{4}$ pt	$4\frac{1}{2}$ cups
a bouquet garni		
salt and pepper		
25 g long grain rice	1 oz	2 tbsp
a few leaves of lettuce and sorrel		
1 egg yolk		
1 tbsp double cream	1 tbsp	1 tbsp
150 ml milk	$\frac{1}{4}$ pt	$\frac{2}{3}$ cup

Melt 25 g (1 oz/2 tablespoons) butter in a pan and add the peas and washed sliced leek. Sweat them for about 5 minutes over a low heat then add the stock, bouquet garni and seasoning. Bring to the boil and simmer until tender.

Meanwhile, boil the rice in salted water until tender, then drain and rinse. Slice the lettuce and sorrel to a chiffonade (see page 16). Melt 25 g (1 oz/2 tablespoons) butter in a small pan and simmer the chiffonade until just changed in colour.

Remove the bouquet garni. Sieve or liquidise the soup then bring to the boil and season. Mix the egg yolk and cream with the milk and add the soup to this, add the rice then reheat without boiling. Pour into a hot soup tureen and add the chiffonade of lettuce and sorrel.

Potage Crécy

Carrot and rice soup (serves 4)

King Edward III fought the first major battle of the Hundred Years' War on the fields of Crécy. In more peaceful times the fields are better renowned for the quality of their carrots – so much so that the word 'Crécy' used in the name of the dish indicates that it is made with them.

This soup is a simple but quickly made purée, thickened and garnished with rice.

	Imperial	American
1 onion, finely chopped		
2–3 rashers lean bacon, chopped		
25 g butter	1 oz	2 tbsp
500 g carrots	1 lb	1 lb
25 g rice	1 oz	2 tbsp
1 litre stock	2 pt	$4\frac{1}{2}$ cups
salt and pepper		

For the garnish:

	Imperial	American
25 g rice, cooked in stock	1 oz	2 tbsp
finely chopped parsley		

Melt the butter in a pan and soften the bacon and onion in this without allowing them to brown. Slice the carrots and add them with the rice and stock. Season and simmer gently for 30 minutes or until tender.

Cook the rice for the garnish in boiling salted stock for approximately 15 minutes or until tender.

Sieve the soup or put through a vegetable mill or liquidiser. It should be a thin creamy consistency. If it should be too thick, add more stock. Drain the rice garnish and add to the soup. Reheat and season. Serve hot, sprinkled with parsley.

Opposite: Potage aux Champignons (left), Potage Crécy (centre) and Potage Fontanges (right), with a choice of croûtons, French bread or melba toast.

Potage aux Champignons
Cream of mushroom soup (serves 4)

	Imperial	American
250 g mushrooms	8 oz	8 oz
50 g butter	2 oz	$\frac{1}{4}$ cup
25 g plain flour	1 oz	3 tbsp
600 ml milk	1 pt	$2\frac{1}{2}$ cups
salt and pepper		
150 ml chicken stock	$\frac{1}{4}$ pt	$\frac{2}{3}$ cup
150 ml single cream	$\frac{1}{4}$ pt	$\frac{2}{3}$ cup
2 egg yolks		

Wash the mushrooms and chop them finely. Melt the butter in a large pan, remove from the heat and stir in the flour. Replace over the heat and cook the roux for 2–3 minutes. Remove from the heat and add the milk gradually, stirring all the time. Add the mushrooms. Season and pour in the stock. Stir well. Bring to the boil and cook gently for 15 minutes.

Mix the cream with the egg yolks and stir in the hot soup. Return to the pan and reheat without boiling. Taste and season. Serve hot.

Tante Marie tip:
If you need to keep hot any soup which has been thickened with egg yolks, put it in a double saucepan or a bowl over a pan of hot water and keep on a low heat.

Potage Périgourdine
Périgord soup (serves 4)

A clear soup with a garnish of stuffed cabbage leaves.

	Imperial	American
1 litre best beef stock	2 pt	$4\frac{1}{2}$ cups

For the garnish:

	Imperial	American
3–4 cabbage leaves		
1 clove garlic		
1 shallot, chopped		
50 g minced cooked meat *or* ham	2 oz	$\frac{1}{2}$ cup
1 chicken liver, if available		
chopped herbs		
15 g breadcrumbs, soaked in a little milk	$\frac{1}{2}$ oz	$\frac{1}{4}$ cup
egg yolk		
salt and pepper		

Heat the stock in a large saucepan.

Wash the cabbage leaves and blanch for 1 minute in boiling water. Refresh and drain. Crush the garlic with a little salt and mix with the shallot, meat, chopped liver, herbs, breadcrumbs and egg yolk. Season well. Fill the cabbage leaves with this and roll up firmly. Tie with thread. Poach in the stock for 10 minutes. Cut the rolls into slices. Pour the soup into a tureen and float the slices of stuffed cabbage on top.

Pot-au-Feu
Boiled beef

Pot-au-Feu is a substantial dish of boiled beef cooked with vegetables. The bouillon is particularly good and is served first as the soup. This can be garnished with some of the chopped-up cooked vegetables and/or cooked noodles or, alternatively, grilled cheese toasts made from French bread can be floated on it. The meat and vegetables are then served next as the main course. The recipe for this will be found on page 97.

The bouillon is the best stock to use for consommé or aspic and these days it seems more economical to prepare this type of stock in this way, as you are also cooking meat for one or two other meals at the same time. Besides being eaten as suggested, remains can well be used for réchauffé dishes such as Pain de Boeuf.

Hors d'oeuvre

The tempting selection of dishes offered for the first course is a familiar feature of French meals. The hors d'oeuvre are often very simple but tasty and appetising. The choice is varied and depends upon the occasion, the time of year and the foods in season.

There are many delicacies which make an appetising start to a meal. In France you might be offered a single dish: perhaps some smoked trout, skinned and served with a creamy horse-radish sauce, or halves of beautifully ripened avocado with a spoonful of dressing in the hollow centre. At lunchtime an assorted selection of hors d'oeuvre is popular, and might include a variety of both raw and cooked vegetable salads, cold meats and sausages, fish and eggs.

A bowl of mussels served in a robustly flavoured sauce, or mackerel fillets in white wine, makes a pleasant change from the ubiquitous prawn cocktail.

A single fruit or vegetable which is at its prime can make a good start to both formal and in-formal meals. Asparagus, artichokes, tomatoes, avocados and melon can be served in many ways, both hot and cold.

Eggs, too, can make a pleasant start to a meal. Hard-boiled eggs in mayonnaise, poached eggs with a delicate sauce, or oeufs en cocotte are all delicious.

Pâtés make some of the most satisfactory 'starters'. They can be of different types: smooth liver pâtés, or rough-cut country terrines, made from pork, poultry or game.

Pâté de Foies de Volaille
A quick chicken liver pâté (serves 3–4)

This can be speedily prepared, using either a liquidiser or a vegetable mill. If you have other poultry liver available, add this in place of some of the chicken liver.

	Imperial	American
225 g chicken livers	8 oz	8 oz
2 shallots, finely chopped		
1–2 cloves garlic, crushed		
75 g butter	3 oz	6 tbsp
2 tbsp brandy	2 tbsp	2 tbsp
salt and pepper		
1 fresh bayleaf		
French bread for serving		

Remove the sinews from the chicken livers and rinse in cold water. Sauté the shallots and garlic in the butter until translucent. Add the livers and 1 tablespoon of brandy. Continue cooking until the livers are cooked through and the juices run clear.

Place the mixture, with the butter, in a liquidiser, add the remaining brandy and seasoning to taste. Blend on maximum speed until smooth, *or* pound together and then sieve.

Place the mixture in a small dish. Smooth the top and decorate with the bayleaf. Chill, then serve with French bread.

The next two recipes are for terrines which are traditionally cooked and served in special earthenware dishes.

Terrine Maison

Home-made terrine (serves 6–8)

	Imperial	American
approximately 8 rashers streaky bacon		
100 g pigs' or lambs' liver	4 oz	4 oz
100 g fresh pork	4 oz	4 oz
1 small onion		
1 tbsp finely chopped parsley	1 tbsp	1 tbsp
100 g sausagemeat	4 oz	4 oz
25 g breadcrumbs	1 oz	½ cup
a little milk		
salt and pepper		
a pinch of nutmeg		
2 tbsp brandy	2 tbsp	2 tbsp
a little beaten egg		
½ young rabbit		
1 fresh bayleaf		

To finish:

	Imperial	American
50 g butter, melted	2 oz	¼ cup
1 fresh bayleaf		

Line a terrine with the bacon, reserving one or two rashers for the top. Finely chop the liver and pork. Chop the onion and mix with the parsley. Add the liver, pork and sausagemeat and mix well. Soak the breadcrumbs in the milk, squeeze them out until almost dry, then beat them into the farce. Season well, adding the nutmeg, brandy and enough egg to make a slightly moist mixture. Cut the rabbit into thin slices, carefully removing all bones.

Spread a layer of the meat mixture in the bottom of the lined terrine and place a few slices of rabbit on the top. Cover again with more farce and the rest of the rabbit. Finish with a layer of farce. It is important to fill the mould as the meat shrinks during cooking. Place the remaining bacon rashers on the top and the bayleaf on these. Cover with greaseproof paper or aluminium foil, and a lid. Stand the terrine in a bain-marie or roasting-pan containing boiling water, and bake in a moderate oven, Mark 4 (180°C/350°F), for 1¼ hours. Remove from the oven and after 30 minutes cover with a saucer, with a weight of approximately 1 kg (2 lb) on it. Allow to cool, then chill in the refrigerator. Remove the bayleaf and pour over the melted butter. Garnish with the other bayleaf. This terrine can be kept for 7–8 days.

Tante Marie tip:
The quantity of brandy must not be reduced if the terrine is to be kept for several days. Chicken or game can replace the rabbit if desired. It is advisable not to put too heavy a weight on the top of the terrine. If it is over-weighted the juice will run over the top and the terrine will be dry and crumbly.

Pâté Lorraine

Lorraine meat loaf (serves 6)

	Imperial	American
2 joints of hare, either from the saddle or back legs		
100 g minced pork	4 oz	4 oz
100 g minced veal	4 oz	4 oz
approx 1 level tsp salt	1 tsp	1 tsp
a small pinch of cinnamon		
a pinch of cayenne pepper		
50 g lean bacon	2 oz	2 oz
1 onion, finely chopped		
1 tsp parsley	1 tsp	1 tsp
2 tbsp white wine	2 tbsp	2 tbsp
approximately 6 rashers streaky bacon		
50 g butter, melted	2 oz	¼ cup

Cut the flesh from the hare into thin strips. Chop any trimmings and mix these with the pork, veal, seasoning and spices.

Cut the lean bacon into strips and mix with the onion, parsley and wine. Season.

Line a terrine with the streaky bacon. Place half of the minced meat in the bottom and press down well with a fork. Cover with the strips of hare, then the onion and bacon mixture. Cover with the remaining minced meat and press down well. Place two or three bacon rashers on top.

Place in a roasting-pan containing boiling water and bake in a moderate oven, Mark 4 (180°C/350°F), for 2½ hours. Remove from the oven and allow to cool. Cover with a small plate or saucer with a weight of approximately 1 kg (2 lb) on it. When cold pour over the melted butter.

If you want to vary this recipe you can substitute other game for the hare.

Croustade de Pigeon

Pigeon pie (serves 4)

	Imperial	American
1 pigeon		
flaky pastry *or* puff pastry made with 175 g strong flour (*see page 208 or 210*)	6 oz	1½ cups
50 g minced veal	2 oz	2 oz
50 g minced pork	2 oz	2 oz
salt and pepper		
a pinch of cayenne pepper		
1 tbsp brandy	1 tbsp	1 tbsp
50 g soft liver pâté	2 oz	¼ cup
1 egg		
1 egg yolk for glazing		

Make the pastry as illustrated (see pages 208 or 210). Put in the refrigerator to relax for 20 minutes.

Remove the fillets from the breast of the pigeon and slice thinly. Chop the rest of the flesh and mix with the veal and pork. Season with salt, pepper and the cayenne. Add the brandy and mix together well.

Roll out the pastry on a lightly floured board. Cut into two circles, one 15 cm (6 in) and one 18 cm (7 in) in diameter. Place the smaller circle on the baking-tin and spread a layer of about half the farce on this, leaving a border all round the edge. Cover the farce with the fillets of pigeon and the liver pâté cut into slices or spread on. Season well and cover with the rest of the farce. Moisten the edges of the pastry and cover with the larger circle. Seal well and, using the back of a knife, knock up the edges and scallop in a decorative border. Put aside to relax in the refrigerator for 10 minutes. Brush over with beaten egg yolk then, using the back of a small knife, make a hole in the centre and a design of curved spokes radiating from this towards the edge. Place the croustade in a very hot oven, Mark 8 (230°C/450°F), for the first 10 minutes, then reduce the temperature to Mark 5 (190°C/375°F) and continue cooking for a further 50 minutes. Check that the pigeon is tender, then cool the pie on a wire rack.

Crudités

Vegetable salad hors d'oeuvre

Crudités are simply vegetables flavoured with dressing, and arranged either on platters or on hors d'oeuvre dishes in a colourful array. At least four vegetables are usually served, and accompanied by crusty French bread.

Tomatoes
Slice the tomatoes. Season with salt and black pepper and arrange on a dish or plate. Sauce Vinaigrette can be added, or the tomatoes can be served quite plain with chopped fresh herbs such as parsley, chives, basil or marjoram.

Cucumber
Slice the cucumber thinly. Sprinkle with salt and leave for 20 minutes. Rinse and drain, then macerate in a slightly sharp vinaigrette dressing.

Carrots
Grate the carrots finely. Add salt, black pepper and a little Sauce Vinaigrette. Allow to macerate for a while. Sprinkle with chopped parsley.

Celeriac
Cut the celeriac into julienne strips or grate it coarsely. Plunge into acidulated water immediately to prevent discoloration. Drain well and mix with a little mayonnaise.

Although 'crudités' means raw vegetables, cooked beetroot is usually served and sometimes cooked potatoes and blanched red cabbage.

Beetroot
Peel the cooked beetroot and cut into 1 cm (½ in) dice. Pour over a little Sauce Vinaigrette and allow to stand for a short while, turning the beetroot occasionally.

Potatoes
Cut the cooked new potatoes into small dice. Add Sauce Vinaigrette or mayonnaise and chopped chives.

Red cabbage
Shred the cabbage very finely, removing the hard centre core. Bring a pan of water to the boil and add 1-2 tablespoons of vinegar. Place the cabbage in the pan and blanch for ½-1 minute. Drain and refresh. Drain well again and macerate in vinaigrette dressing.

Hors d'oeuvre Variés
Assorted appetisers

This hors d'oeuvre is an exciting assortment of delicious 'bits and pieces'. The selection usually includes some meat, something fishy, vegetables, and perhaps some hard-boiled eggs which may be stuffed or simply coated in mayonnaise and garnished with anchovy.

Serve in a collection of small dishes, or in a sectioned hors d'oeuvre platter. A restaurant can offer a very wide selection, but in your own home a more modest collection, perhaps six items or so, may be more suitable.

The meat may be a home-made pâté, thinly sliced salami or garlic sausage, sliced ham or a little cooked chicken mixed with mayonnaise. For the fish, you might include some freshly peeled prawns, mackerel in white wine, mussels cooked à la marinière, cockles, whelks, rollmop herrings or other seafood.

Serve sliced or halved hard-boiled eggs coated with mayonnaise or stuffed with a herb or anchovy filling. Fresh bread rolls or a French loaf make a welcome accompaniment to the hors d'oeuvre.

The vegetables are similar to those suggested for Crudités. They can be served with a variety of cold dressings and are often flavoured with freshly chopped herbs. The selection depends very much on the season, and provides a good opportunity to enjoy the vegetables at their best. At any time of year there is a good choice available.

Mushrooms
Raw mushrooms can be thinly sliced and sprinkled with vinaigrette dressing or cooked à la Grecque.

Radishes
Whole radishes are washed and trimmed, leaving a little of the green stalk intact.

Mixed vegetables
Mixed cooked vegetables are stirred in a spoonful or two of mayonnaise and sprinkled with fresh herbs.

Beetroot
Serve with vinaigrette dressing as suggested above or with a mustard sauce made with 2 tablespoons of thick cream whisked with 1 teaspoon of French mustard, lemon juice and seasoning.

French beans
Cook the beans and serve in a thick tomato sauce with fresh herbs.

Aubergines
Cook as Caviare d'Aubergines, or Ratatouille.

Peppers
Slice thinly and decorate with black olives.

Hors d'Oeuvre Variés.

Assiette Anglaise
English platter

A visit to a delicatessen can provide the ingredients for a quickly prepared platter of cold meats. If you are not familiar with all the different types of garlic sausage, salami, liver sausage, smoked ham and other cold meats, this is a good time to experiment. Garnish the dish with olives, gherkins and parsley.

Artichauts
Globe artichokes

Artichokes make an attractive and refreshing hors d'oeuvre. Prepare them as described on page 160. Serve them hot with a Sauce Hollandaise spooned into the centre, or cold with Sauce Vinaigrette or Mayonnaise.

Opposite: Croustade de Pigeon. (see page 43)

Asperges, Sauce Hollandaise

Asparagus with Hollandaise sauce
(serves 4)

This is one of the best ways to serve asparagus during its all-too-short season which, in England, is from late spring to early summer.

	Imperial	American
1 kg asparagus	**2 lb**	**2 lb**
(*see page 162*)		
Sauce Hollandaise made		
with 2 egg yolks		
(*see page 32*)		

Trim the asparagus to even lengths. Scrape each stem very well and place in a bowl of cold salted water for 5–10 minutes.

Tie the asparagus into two bundles of even thickness and plunge into a pan of boiling salted water. Cook for 15–20 minutes according to the thickness of the asparagus. Remove from the pan and drain well. Remove the string and place the asparagus on a hot serving-dish. Serve immediately with the warm Sauce Hollandaise handed separately.

Cooked asparagus ready to serve with Sauce Hollandaise.

Avocats

Avocados

Not a long-standing tradition, but a fruit that has become extremely popular in France in recent years. The avocados must be perfectly ripe. Buy them when they are hard, then ripen them in a warm room or in the airing-cupboard. When ripe they can be kept in mild refrigeration for 3–4 days.

Avocats à la Vinaigrette

Avocados with French dressing
(serves 4)

2 ripe avocados
Sauce Vinaigrette
   (*see page 33*)

Mix the sauce and season it well. Cut the avocados in half lengthways, using a stainless-steel knife. Twist to loosen the stone and separate. Remove the stone.

Brush a little of the Sauce Vinaigrette over the cut surface of the avocados to prevent discoloration. Place in individual dishes and fill the centre with the dressing.

Tante Marie tip:
If you need to prepare the avocados a little in advance, brush the cut surfaces with the dressing and cover tightly with plastic clingfilm to prevent them from turning black.

Avocats aux Crevettes

Stuffed avocados with prawns (serves 6)

	Imperial	American
500 g fresh shrimps *or*	**1 lb**	**1 lb**
prawns,		
or **100 g frozen shrimps**	**4 oz**	**4 oz**
or **prawns**		
3 avocados		
2 hard-boiled eggs,		
finely chopped		
a little finely chopped		
parsley		
salt and pepper		
a pinch of cayenne pepper		
1 tbsp olive oil	**1 tbsp**	**1 tbsp**
2 tsp vinegar	**2 tsp**	**2 tsp**
lemon juice		
1 lettuce		
150 ml Sauce Vinaigrette	$\frac{1}{4}$ **pt**	$\frac{2}{3}$ **cup**
(*see page 33*)		

Peel the shrimps. Chop half of them finely. Cut the avocados in half and remove the stones. Scoop out the flesh and chop into large pieces. Mix this with the chopped shrimps, one of the hard-boiled eggs and some parsley. Season with the salt, pepper, cayenne, oil and vinegar. Fill each half of avocado with this mixture, piling it up into the centre. Sprinkle with the remaining chopped eggs, a little parsley, the remaining shrimps and the lemon juice. Cover the serving-dish with the lettuce and arrange the stuffed avocados on top. Serve chilled with well-flavoured Sauce Vinaigrette.

Melon aux Fruits de Mer

Melon with seafood (serves 4)

This appetiser makes a refreshing start to a meal on a hot day. Buy a slightly firm melon several days beforehand and ripen it at home in a warm place. A medium-sized melon will serve 4–6, or you can serve half a Charentais or Ogen melon per person.

	Imperial	American
1 melon		
225 g prepared shellfish, e.g. prawns, scampi, shrimps, etc	8 oz	8 oz
300 ml Sauce Verte (*see page 31*)	$\frac{1}{2}$ pt	$1\frac{1}{4}$ cups
salt and pepper		

To finish:
4 tomatoes, sliced
1 lemon, sliced
1 lettuce
6–8 whole prawns

Cut the top off the melon and put it on one side. Using a vegetable ball cutter, scoop the centre of the melon into balls. Allow to drain. Place the balls and the melon shell in the refrigerator to chill.

Make the Sauce Verte, taste and season. Stir the shellfish and melon balls into the Sauce Verte. Fill the melon shell with the mixture and replace the top.

Place on a serving-dish and surround with the tomatoes, lemon, crisp lettuce leaves and prawns.

Tante Marie tip:
Take care if you have to chill a melon. Unless it is well covered, the smell permeates other food stored in the refrigerator.

Concombre Farci Parisienne

Parisian stuffed cucumber (serves 4)

This dish of hot stuffed cucumber makes an interesting and well-flavoured start to a meal.

	Imperial	American
1 cucumber		
40 g butter	$1\frac{1}{2}$ oz	3 tbsp
$\frac{1}{2}$ onion, finely chopped		
$\frac{1}{2}$ tsp plain flour	$\frac{1}{2}$ tsp	$\frac{1}{2}$ tsp
1 clove garlic, crushed		
100 g mushrooms, chopped	4 oz	1 cup
1 tsp white breadcrumbs	1 tsp	1 tsp
25 g ham, finely chopped	1 oz	$\frac{1}{4}$ cup
1 tsp freshly chopped herbs	1 tsp	1 tsp
salt and pepper		
a little cheese, grated		
For the sauce:		
15 g plain flour	$\frac{1}{2}$ oz	$1\frac{1}{2}$ tbsp
$\frac{1}{2}$ tsp tomato purée	$\frac{1}{2}$ tsp	$\frac{1}{2}$ tsp
4 tbsp red wine	4 tbsp	4 tbsp
2 tbsp Madeira	2 tbsp	2 tbsp
6 tbsp stock	6 tbsp	6 tbsp

Cut the cucumber in half, then cut each piece in half lengthways. Melt the butter in a pan, add the onion and cook lightly. Add the flour, garlic, mushrooms, breadcrumbs, ham, herbs and seasoning. Cook for a few minutes. Scoop the seeds out of the cucumber and fill with the farce. Sprinkle with a little grated cheese.

Place the cucumber in a buttered heatproof dish and bake in a hot oven, Mark 6 (200°C/400°F), for 25 minutes. Remove from the oven and place in a clean, hot serving-dish. Sprinkle the flour for the sauce into the cooking-dish, stir well, then add the tomato purée, wine, Madeira and stock. Stir, then pour off into a saucepan and simmer for 3–4 minutes over a moderate heat. Season and pour round the cucumber. Serve hot.

Champignons à la Grecque

Marinated mushrooms (serves 3–4)

Mushrooms prepared in this way keep well in the refrigerator. Serve in small dishes as a single hors d'oeuvre or as part of an assortment.

	Imperial	American
250 g small button mushrooms	8 oz	8 oz
1 tomato		
12 small onions, peeled		
4 tbsp olive oil	4 tbsp	4 tbsp
4 tbsp white wine	4 tbsp	4 tbsp
150 ml white stock	$\frac{1}{4}$ pt	$\frac{2}{3}$ cup
juice of $\frac{1}{2}$ lemon		
1 bayleaf		
salt and pepper		
finely chopped parsley		

Wash the mushrooms immediately before cooking. Leave small ones whole, but cut larger ones into quarters. Chop the tomato coarsely. Place the mushrooms and tomato in a pan with the onions, oil, wine, stock, lemon juice and bayleaf and season well. Cover with a lid and cook quickly for 5 minutes. Allow the mushrooms to cool in the liquor. Remove the bayleaf and adjust the seasoning. Pour the vegetables and liquor into a serving-dish and sprinkle with very finely chopped parsley. Serve cold with the liquor.

Fenouil à la Provençale

Provençale-style fennel (serves 4)

Cooked in this way, root fennel can be served cold as part of a mixed hors d'oeuvre, or hot as a vegetable dish.

	Imperial	American
2 fennel roots		
1 onion		
350 g tomatoes	12 oz	12 oz
1 clove garlic		
150 ml stock	$\frac{1}{4}$ pt	$\frac{2}{3}$ cup
salt and pepper		

Wash the fennel and remove any discoloured outer leaves. Cut into quarters and blanch in boiling salted water for 15 minutes. Chop the onion finely, skin the tomatoes and cut into quarters. Place in a casserole with the crushed garlic, stock and seasoning. Arrange the fennel on top, cover with a lid and cook in a moderate oven, Mark 6 (200°C/400°F), for 1 hour or until tender.

Maquereaux au Vin Blanc

Mackerel in white wine (serves 4)

	Imperial	American
4 small mackerel		
150 ml white wine	$\frac{1}{4}$ pt	$\frac{2}{3}$ cup
150 ml water	$\frac{1}{4}$ pt	$\frac{2}{3}$ cup
1 carrot		
1 small onion		
2 bayleaves		
2 sprigs of fennel		
6–8 peppercorns		
salt		
1 tbsp lemon juice *or* wine vinegar	1 tbsp	1 tbsp

To finish:
chopped parsley and fennel

Place the wine, water, thinly sliced carrot and onion, bayleaves, fennel, peppercorns, salt and lemon juice or vinegar in a pan. Bring to the boil and simmer this court bouillon gently for 20 minutes.

Clean the mackerel and bone and fillet as illustrated on pages 66 and 67. Cut the fillets in half lengthways down the back. Place in a shallow dish, add the court bouillon, cover with a lid and cook in a moderately slow oven, Mark 3 (160°C/325°F), for 20 minutes. Cool in the liquor, then dish and serve with some of the liquor and a few slices of the vegetables. Sprinkle with the parsley and fennel.

Oeufs durs aux Tomates

Hard-boiled eggs with tomatoes (serves 4)

These attractively served eggs are often seen in French charcuteries.

	Imperial	American
4 tomatoes		
4 hard-boiled eggs		
4 tbsp Mayonnaise (*see page 30*)	4 tbsp	4 tbsp
finely chopped parsley		

Partly slice through the tomatoes, using a sharp serrated knife, leaving them joined at the base. Slice the eggs, using an egg slicer, and insert the slices into the tomato. Just before serving place a spoonful of creamy mayonnaise on each and sprinkle with finely chopped parsley.

Oeufs Tonnelier

The cooper's eggs (serves 4)

	Imperial	American
4 eggs		
4 anchovy fillets		
40 g butter	1½ oz	3 tbsp
2–3 tsp milk	2–3 tsp	2–3 tsp
salt and black pepper		
4 rounds of fried bread		

To finish:
anchovy fillets
capers
Aïoli (*see page 31*)

Hard-boil the eggs for 10 minutes. Plunge them into cold water and remove their shells. Cut a piece off one side (not the end) of each egg, then cut the eggs in half lengthways. Remove the yolks carefully and add them to the finely chopped anchovy fillets. Mix together and beat in the softened butter and milk. Taste and season. Fill one half of each egg with this mixture, heaping it up, but not so much that the other half of the egg will not fit neatly on the top. Cover with the second half. Spread the rounds of bread with the rest of the mixture, making a slight hollow in each to allow the egg to rest securely. Arrange the egg on the bread. Decorate with 2 strips of anchovy fillets and 3 capers to imitate the hoops on a barrel. Serve with Aïoli.

Caviar d'Aubergine

Poor man's caviare (serves 3–4)

	Imperial	American
1 large aubergine		
salt		
1 Spanish onion		
3 tbsp olive oil	3 tbsp	3 tbsp
1 small green pepper		
4 tomatoes		
a bouquet garni		
1 or more cloves garlic		
2 tbsp white wine	2 tbsp	2 tbsp
chopped parsley		
freshly ground black pepper		

Cut the aubergine in half. Cut across the surface and rub with salt. Drain for at least 20 minutes.

Squeeze the aubergine and dry on kitchen paper. Place, cut side down, in a buttered heatproof dish. Bake in a moderately hot oven, Mark 6 (200°C/400°F), for 45 minutes–1 hour. When tender, scrape out the flesh and chop it.

Chop the onion. Warm the oil in a pan, add the onion, cover with a lid and cook gently. Cut the pepper in half, remove the core and seeds, chop and add to the onion. Skin and chop the tomatoes, add to the pan, then add the chopped aubergine, bouquet garni and the clove of garlic, crushed with a little salt. Simmer gently until the mixture is tender and fairly thick. Remove the bouquet garni. Stir in the wine and parsley. Taste, and season with salt and pepper. Chill well, and serve as an hors d'oeuvre.

Tante Marie tip:
This freezes well, so you can make a supply for your deep freeze in the autumn, when all the vegetables are at their best.

Egg and Cheese Dishes

The thought of egg and cheese cookery brings to mind all sorts of delectable dishes: golden omelettes, dramatic soufflés, tasty quiches and a myriad of other good things. Some are quick and easy to make for a breakfast dish or a light snack, whilst others can grace your dinner table or a party buffet.

Good results depend, very often, on the skill of the cook in recognising the fact that eggs cook best at a moderate heat. They are never good when toughened by overcooking so attention to temperature and timing is all-important.

Oeufs à la Coque
Boiled eggs

Really fresh eggs are best for boiling. Place the eggs in boiling salted water and cook for 3–4 minutes according to taste. Serve immediately.

Oeufs Mollets
Soft-boiled eggs

Cook the whole eggs in boiling salted water for 6–7 minutes. Drain and rinse in cold water. Shell them carefully. Keep warm in a bowl of warm water for a short time, until served.

These can be garnished and served in many ways.

Oeufs Mollets à la Cressonière
Soft-boiled eggs with watercress (serves 4)

	Imperial	American
4 eggs		
1 bunch watercress		
25 g butter	1 oz	2 tbsp
300 ml Sauce Suprême	½ pt	1¼ cups
(*see page 28*)		
salt and pepper		
a little paprika pepper		

Before cooking the eggs, wash the watercress, trim the stalks, chop the leaves finely and stew in the butter for a few minutes. Make the sauce and soft-boil the eggs.

Season the watercress and place in a serving-dish, or divide between individual dishes. Place the eggs on top and spoon the sauce over. Sprinkle each egg with a little paprika.

Oeufs Mollets aux Fines Herbes
Soft-boiled eggs with herbs (serves 4)

	Imperial	American
4 soft-boiled eggs		
25 g butter, melted	1 oz	2 tbsp
juice of ½ lemon		
salt and pepper		
1 tbsp freshly chopped herbs, e.g. chives, parsley, chervil, tarragon	1 tbsp	1 tbsp

Toss the cooked, shelled eggs quickly in the melted butter and lemon juice. Season and add the herbs.

Oeufs Mollets Montrouge

Montrouge soft-boiled eggs (serves 4)

	Imperial	American
4 eggs		
150 g mushrooms	6 oz	6 oz
25 g butter	1 oz	2 tbsp
salt and pepper		
25 g plain flour	1 oz	3 tbsp
300 ml chicken stock	$\frac{1}{2}$ pt	1 cup
4 tbsp double cream	4 tbsp	4 tbsp
fleurons of fried bread		
parsley		

Remove the stalks from the mushrooms and chop with 50 g (2 oz/$\frac{1}{2}$ cup) of the whole mushrooms. Melt the butter, add the chopped mushrooms and cook gently for 2–3 minutes.

Brush the rest of the mushrooms with a little oil, add the seasoning, then grill.

Add the flour to the chopped cooked mushrooms and cook for 1 minute. Add the stock gradually, bring to the boil, then simmer for 5 minutes. Add the cream, taste and season. Meanwhile, soft-boil the eggs.

Arrange the grilled mushrooms on a heatproof dish and place the eggs on top. Coat with the sauce and garnish with fleurons of crisply-fried bread and parsley.

Oeufs Durs

Hard-boiled eggs

Place the eggs in boiling salted water and cook for 10 minutes, after which time both yolk and white will be completely set. Drain, then place in a bowl of cold water to cool.

To shell the eggs quickly, roll each one on a hard surface so the shell cracks all over. The shell will then peel off easily.

Oeufs durs, Sauce Mayonnaise

Hard-boiled eggs with mayonnaise (serves 4)

This is one of the simplest of all hors d'oeuvre.

4 eggs
lettuce
4 tbsp Mayonnaise
  (*see page 30*)
a little paprika pepper

Hard-boil the eggs, then cool and chill. Shell and serve either whole, or cut in half lengthways, on a bed of lettuce. Make the mayonnaise of a coating consistency, taste and season, then pour a spoonful over each egg. Sprinkle each egg with the paprika.

Oeufs durs à l'Aurore

Dawn eggs (serves 4)

	Imperial	American
4 eggs		
25 g butter	1 oz	2 tbsp
1–2 shallots, finely chopped		
a pinch of dry mustard		
1 tsp chopped parsley	1 tsp	1 tsp
2 tsp white wine	2 tsp	2 tsp
salt and pepper		
breadcrumbs		
300 ml Sauce Aurore	$\frac{1}{2}$ pt	1$\frac{1}{4}$ cups
(*see page 28*)		

Hard-boil the eggs, then shell them. Cut in half and scoop out the yolk. Melt half the butter, add the shallot and cook until tender. Mix this with the mustard, parsley, wine, seasoning and egg yolks. Fill each egg white with this mixture. Sprinkle the top of each one with breadcrumbs and dot with the remaining butter. Place in a shallow heatproof dish and brown quickly under the grill. Pour the hot Sauce Aurore around the eggs.

Oeufs Pochés

Poached eggs

Poached eggs are cooked in barely simmering water, and are not to be confused with steamed eggs cooked in an egg poacher.

It is essential that very fresh eggs are used.

Place about 1 litre (2 pt/4 cups) of water in a large pan and add 1 tablespoon of vinegar and 2 teaspoons of salt. Bring the water to the boil. Break the egg into a cup or small bowl. Keep the water below boiling point so that it is simmering and barely moving. Stir the water in a circle and gently drop the egg into the whirlpool movement of the water. If necessary, use a spoon to help bring the white in to gently envelop the yolk. When one egg starts to set, the next can be added. Cook for 2½–3 minutes. When the white is set and the yolk semi-liquid, lift out with a draining spoon. If the eggs are to be served hot, they can be kept for a short time in a bowl of warm water. To serve cold, chill in a bowl of cold water. Drain on kitchen paper or on a clean tea-towel. Trim off any ragged edges and serve according to the recipe.

Oeufs Pochés à la Bagrance

Bagrance poached eggs (serves 4)

4 poached eggs
2 very large *or* 4 medium
   tomatoes
2 tsp oil
salt and pepper
Sauce Béarnaise
   (*see page 32*)

Cut the tomatoes in half, arrange in a heatproof dish, brush with the oil and season. Bake in a moderately hot oven, Mark 5 (190°C/375°F), until tender. If only small tomatoes are available, cut into thick slices.

When the tomatoes are tender, place the poached eggs on top and cover with a spoonful of Sauce Béarnaise. Serve immediately.

Oeufs sur le plat

Eggs on the dish

Eggs cooked in this way are gently fried in the dish in which they will be served.

Use a shallow heatproof dish of a suitable size to hold 1 or 2 eggs. Prepare the ingredients to accompany them (see following recipes). Place a small nut of butter in the dish and place the dish over a very low heat. If necessary put a heat diffuser mat under the dish. Break the egg into a cup and slide gently into the butter. Keep the heat low so the white does not bubble. Season, then cook until the white is set. Add the garnish and serve immediately.

Oeufs sur le plat Rothomago

Rothomago eggs

Place 2 hot grilled slices of ham in the dish before adding the eggs. Gently cook the eggs as above. When cooked, garnish with grilled chipolata sausages.

Oeufs sur le plat Mirabeau

Mirabeau eggs

Blend a few drops of anchovy essence with the butter in the dish. Cook the eggs in this as above, then garnish with 2 anchovy fillets and about 4 stuffed olives.

Oeufs sur le plat à la Portugaise

Portuguese eggs

Skin and pip 2 or 3 tomatoes. Chop them and lightly cook in butter in the dish. Break the eggs on top, season and cook as above. Serve with a spoonful of tomato sauce on top.

Oeufs sur le plat Isoline

Isoline eggs

Slice and fry a chicken liver, and put on one side of the dish. On the other place 2 halves of Tomates à la Provençale (see page 181). Break the eggs in the centre and cook as above.

Oeufs sur le plat Isoline.

Oeufs en Cocotte aux Rognons.

Oeufs en Cocotte

Baked eggs

If you have to serve eggs to a number of people this is an easy and attractive method to use.

Choose dishes of a suitable size to hold an egg plus other ingredients. These may be individual glass or china ramequins or soufflé dishes. Butter the dishes and add the chosen mixture. Break an egg into each and season. Place the dishes in a roasting-pan and pour in boiling water to come halfway up the sides of the dishes. Bake in the oven until the white is just set but the yolk still soft (at Mark 5 [190°C/ 375°F] this takes 10 minutes). Lift the ramequins out of the water and arrange on a platter. Serve immediately.

Oeufs en Cocotte aux Rognons

Baked eggs with kidney

Sauté 1 chopped lamb's kidney per egg in a little butter. Season, place in the dish, add the egg and cook as above.

Oeufs en Cocotte à la Crème

Baked eggs with cream

Place 1 tablespoon of boiling cream in the dish, break in the egg and put a small knob of butter on the yolk. Cook as above.

Oeufs en Cocotte à la Reine

Queen's baked eggs

Place a little chopped cooked chicken with 2 teaspoons of cream in each dish. Add the egg and cook as above.

Oeufs Brouillés

Scrambled eggs

Allow 2 eggs per person, and about 15 g ($\frac{1}{2}$ oz/ 1 tablespoon) of butter. Melt the butter in a pan and add the lightly beaten eggs and seasoning. Cook over a low heat, stirring frequently, until the eggs are creamy. Remove from the heat slightly before they are ready as the heat of the pan will continue to cook them while they are being dished up.

The flavour can be altered very simply by the addition of other ingredients such as diced ham, garlic sausage, sliced mushrooms or shrimps.

This is a more substantial dish made with them.

Oeufs Brouillés à l'Arlesienne

Arlesienne scrambled eggs (serves 4–6)

When courgettes and tomatoes are in season this makes a good supper dish.

	Imperial	American
8 medium courgettes, *or* 1 small young marrow		
salt and pepper		
25 g butter	1 oz	2 tbsp
1 onion		
250 g tomatoes	8 oz	8 oz
1 clove garlic		
6 eggs		
a little Parmesan cheese, grated		
300 ml Sauce Tomate	$\frac{1}{2}$ pt	1$\frac{1}{4}$ cups
(*see page 33*)		

Cut the courgettes in half lengthways. If you use a small marrow instead of courgettes, halve it and scoop out the partly formed pips. Brush with a little melted butter, season and place in a heatproof dish. Cover with a lid and bake in a moderately hot oven, Mark 5 (190°C/375°F), for about 30 minutes or until tender. Melt the butter in a pan, chop the onion and cook gently in the butter. When it is nearly translucent, add the chopped tomatoes and crushed garlic. Simmer together until the tomatoes are cooked.

When the courgettes are tender, gently scoop out some of the flesh from each, chop and add this with the lightly beaten eggs to the tomato mixture. Season and cook like scrambled eggs. Fill the courgette shells with this mixture, sprinkle with the cheese and brown very quickly under the grill. Serve immediately with the hot Sauce Tomate.

Crêpes

Pancakes (serves 4)

	Imperial	American
150 g plain flour	5 oz	1¼ cups
1 egg		
1 egg yolk		
1 tbsp oil *or* melted butter	1 tbsp	1 tbsp
salt and pepper		
300 ml milk	½ pt	1¼ cups

Sift the flour into a bowl. Drop in the egg and yolk, oil or butter, seasonings and half of the milk. Whisk well together, or blend in an electric liquidiser. When smooth, add the rest of the milk. Stir again before using.

To cook the pancakes, heat the pan* with just enough oil to cover the bottom. When it is hot, pour it off into a heatproof bowl (i.e. china rather than plastic). Pour in sufficient batter to cover the base of the pan very thinly. Tilt the pan as you pour this in, so it is as thin as possible. When golden underneath and set on top, turn over with a palette knife, or toss with a quick flick of the wrist. Cook on the other side. Keep hot on a plate placed over a pan of hot water.

Ficelle de Picardie

Ham and cheese pancakes (serves 4)

A substantial ham and cheese pancake dish from St Omer in the Pas de Calais.

	Imperial	American
pancake batter as above		
For the filling:		
8 slices of ham		
300 ml Sauce Mornay (*see page 27*)	½ pt	1¼ cups
50 g Gruyère cheese, grated	2 oz	1 cup

Make 8 pancakes. Roll each one up with a slice of ham in the centre. Arrange the pancakes down the middle of a heatproof dish and pour over the Sauce Mornay. Sprinkle with the cheese and brown under the grill or in the top of a hot oven, Mark 7 (220°C/425°F).

*A crêpe pan is a thick iron pan with shallow sides. Use one of these or cook the pancakes in your omelette pan. You look after both pans in the same way (see page 57).

Crêpes au Camembert

Camembert pancakes (serves 4)

These savoury pancakes make a good hot first course. They can be prepared in advance and reheated and browned in the oven later.

	Imperial	American
pancake batter as above		
For the tomato sauce:		
1 tbsp oil	1 tbsp	1 tbsp
1 onion, finely chopped		
500 g ripe fresh *or* canned tomatoes	1 lb	1 lb
1 tsp tomato purée	1 tsp	1 tsp
salt and pepper		
a pinch of sugar		
For the filling:		
half a ripe Camembert cheese		
300 ml Sauce Béchamel (*see page 27*)	½ pt	1¼ cups
To finish:		
25 g cheese, grated	1 oz	½ cup

Make the pancake batter and allow it to stand.

To prepare the tomato sauce, warm the oil in a small pan, add the onion and cook gently without browning. Skin and pip the tomatoes, chop roughly and stir these in (or add the can of tomatoes with its juice). Add the tomato purée, seasoning and sugar. Cook for a few minutes until soft and well flavoured. Press through a sieve using a wooden spoon.

To make the filling, remove the rind from the Camembert and cream the cheese with a fork. Stir into the hot Béchamel sauce. Season.

Cook the pancakes and spread with the cheese filling. Roll up and place in a heatproof dish. Pour over the tomato sauce and sprinkle with the grated cheese. Brown under a hot grill or in the top of a hot oven, Mark 7 (220°C/425°F).

Omelettes

The reputation of the famous Mère Poularde restaurant on Mont St Michel was founded on the good lady's skill with an omelette pan and, indeed, many cooks have won a reputation in this way.

Nothing complicated is required to make an omelette – just eggs, butter and a good pan – but there is a certain knack in making them perfectly. First, make sure that you have a suitable pan: ideally, keep one just for omelettes and pancakes. You can choose a heavy iron pan or an aluminium one. Non-stick surfaces sound ideal, but great care is needed to ensure you do not scratch them. An iron or aluminium pan is soon made virtually non-stick, if you care for it. When it is new, half-fill the pan with oil and allow to stand for a day. Pour the oil off, then put the pan into use. When you have cooked your omelette, clean the pan by rubbing it round with salt on kitchen paper, then wiping it clean. Do not wash it at all as this spoils the lightly oiled surface.

Fresh eggs and butter are needed. Allow 2–3 eggs per person, and about 15 g ($\frac{1}{2}$ oz/1 tablespoon) butter. Make sure that plates are warm and fillings are prepared before you start. Beat the eggs with 1 teaspoon of water and seasoning. Heat the pan. When it is hot, add a nut of butter. Allow to melt, then pour in the egg mixture and stir rapidly over a good heat, using a fork to bring the egg mixture in from the edges to the centre. As soon as it is set over the base, spread the filling in the middle and fold over. Quickly slip a small nut of butter under the omelette, and give it a few seconds more on the heat: just enough to make it golden brown, but still soft and creamy in the centre. Turn out onto the plate, garnish and serve immediately. Keep a small omelette pan for single omelettes and a larger one for a big omelette to serve 2 or 3 people.

A plain omelette (Omelette Nature) is delicious, but omelettes can be garnished in a variety of ways, to suit all tastes.

Omelette à la Boulonnaise

Boulogne omelette (serves 1)

	Imperial	American
2–3 eggs		
15 g butter	$\frac{1}{2}$ oz	1 tbsp
salt and pepper		

For the filling:

	Imperial	American
1 herring roe		
15 g Beurre Maître d'Hôtel	$\frac{1}{2}$ oz	1 tbsp
(*see page 23*)		

Poach the roe or fry quickly in a little butter. Make the omelette as above. Place the roe in the centre with the Beurre Maître d'Hôtel. Fold over and serve.

Omelette à la Lyonnaise

Onion omelette (serves 1)

	Imperial	American
2–3 eggs		
15 g butter	$\frac{1}{2}$ oz	1 tbsp
salt and pepper		
1 tbsp chopped cooked onion	1 tbsp	1 tbsp
2 tsp chopped parsley	2 tsp	2 tsp
6 glazed onions		
(*see page 173*)		

Mix the chopped onion and parsley with the eggs. Make the omelette as above and garnish with the glazed onions.

Omelette à la Princesse

Princess omelette (serves 1)

	Imperial	American
2–3 eggs		
15 g butter	$\frac{1}{2}$ oz	1 tbsp
salt and pepper		
8 cooked asparagus tips		
3 tbsp Sauce Suprême	3 tbsp	3 tbsp
(*see page 28*)		

Make the omelette as above and fill with 4 of the asparagus tips. Garnish with the rest of the asparagus and the hot Sauce Suprême.

Omelette à la Fermière

The farmer's wife's omelette (serves 1)

	Imperial	American
2–3 eggs		
15 g butter	$\frac{1}{2}$ oz	1 tbsp
salt and pepper		
1 tbsp diced ham	1 tbsp	1 tbsp
1 tsp freshly chopped herbs	1 tsp	1 tsp

Mix the ham and herbs with the eggs before making the omelette as above.

Omelette à la Grandmère

Grannie's omelette (serves 1)

	Imperial	American
2–3 eggs		
15 g butter	½ oz	1 tbsp
salt and pepper		
1 tbsp fried diced croûtons	1 tbsp	1 tbsp
(see page 23)		
2 tsp chopped parsley	2 tsp	2 tsp

Mix the croûtons and parsley with the eggs before making the omelette as above.

Omelette aux Crevettes

Prawn omelette (serves 1)

	Imperial	American
2–3 eggs		
15 g butter	½ oz	1 tbsp
salt and pepper		
For the filling:		
2 tbsp shelled prawns	2 tbsp	2 tbsp
3 tbsp Sauce aux Crevettes	3 tbsp	3 tbsp
(see page 28)		
a few whole prawns		

Make the omelette as above. Mix the shelled prawns with the sauce, heat, then use to fill the omelette. Garnish with the whole prawns.

Omelette St Hubert

Game omelette (serves 1)

	Imperial	American
2–3 eggs		
15 g butter	½ oz	1 tbsp
salt and pepper		
For the filling:		
25 g mushrooms	1 oz	¼ cup
15 g butter	½ oz	1 tbsp
2 tbsp minced cooked game, e.g. venison or pheasant	2 tbsp	2 tbsp
3 tbsp Sauce Demi-glace (see page 29), or gravy from the cooking of the game	3 tbsp	3 tbsp

Slice the mushrooms and sauté lightly in the butter. Warm the minced game with 1 tablespoon of the sauce. Make the omelette as above and fill with the game mixture. Fold and serve. Garnish the top with the mushrooms and pour the rest of the hot sauce at the side.

Soufflé au Fromage

Cheese soufflé (serves 4)

A soufflé cannot be kept waiting, so plan the timing carefully and see that your guests are ready and waiting for it.

The sauce can be prepared some time in advance, so that you have only to beat the egg whites, fold them in, and put the soufflé into the oven. Then time the cooking carefully and, when the soufflé is ready, put it on a plate and take it to the table immediately.

	Imperial	American
25 g butter	1 oz	2 tbsp
25 g plain flour	1 oz	3 tbsp
225 ml milk	7½ fl oz	1 cup
4 eggs, separated		
25 g Parmesan cheese, grated	1 oz	¼ cup
25 g hard cheese, e.g. Cheddar, grated	1 oz	½ cup
salt and pepper		

Melt the butter in a saucepan, add the flour and cook for 2–3 minutes. Remove from the heat and add the milk gradually, stirring well. Bring to the boil, stirring all the time, then simmer for 4–5 minutes. Remove from the heat and mix in the egg yolks and grated cheeses. Taste and season. Pour into a bowl.

Grease an 18 cm (7 in) diameter soufflé dish with butter and dust with grated Parmesan. Whisk the egg whites until they stand up in stiff peaks. Fold lightly into the cheese sauce, about a third at a time. Pour into the dish and bake in a moderately hot oven, Mark 5 (190°C/375°F), for 25 minutes. Serve immediately.

Right: Omelette aux Crevettes.

Fondue au Jambon

Ham and cheese cream (serves 4)

Eggs and cheese are used to make this attractive dish. The word fondue brings to mind a picture of a cheese fondue bubbling over a heater, but the word also means soft and is used in this sense to describe this delicate mould.

	Imperial	American
25 g butter	1 oz	2 tbsp
25 g plain flour	1 oz	3 tbsp
225 ml milk	7½ fl oz	1 cup
2 eggs		
3 egg yolks		
100 g Gruyère cheese, grated	4 oz	2 cups
100 g ham, finely chopped	4 oz	1 cup

For the sauce:

	Imperial	American
25 g butter	1 oz	2 tbsp
25 g plain flour	1 oz	3 tbsp
300 ml milk	½ pt	1¼ cups
salt and pepper		
1 tbsp tomato purée	1 tbsp	1 tbsp
75 g cheese, grated	3 oz	1½ cups

Melt the butter in a pan over a gentle heat. Remove from the heat and stir in the flour. Cook for 2–3 minutes, then add the milk. Stir quickly until a fairly thick sauce is obtained. Remove from the heat and beat in the eggs and yolks, one by one. Continuing to beat, add the Gruyère cheese and ham. Pour into a greased 1 litre (2 pt/4 cups) mould and place in a bain-marie or roasting-pan containing boiling water. Bake in a moderately hot oven, Mark 5 (190°C/375°F), for 45 minutes. When cooked, unmould onto a round plate and have the sauce ready to pour over.

To make the sauce, melt the butter in a pan, remove from the heat and stir in the flour. Replace over a gentle heat and cook for 2–3 minutes, stirring all the time. Add the milk and bring to the boil, stirring all the time. Season to taste and boil for at least 5 minutes. Remove from the heat and stir in the tomato purée and grated cheese. Pour the sauce over the fondue and serve at once.

Tante Marie tip:
Make this in individual moulds for a tasty hot hors d'oeuvre.

Mousse au Camembert

Camembert mousse (serves 8)

An interesting addition to the table for a wine and cheese party.

	Imperial	American
1 ripe Camembert cheese		
7 g gelatine	¼ oz	½ pkt
25 g butter	1 oz	2 tbsp
25 g plain flour	1 oz	3 tbsp
300 ml milk	½ pt	1¼ cups
25 g Parmesan cheese, grated	1 oz	¼ cup
salt and pepper		
a pinch of cayenne pepper		
1 heaped tsp French mustard	1 tsp	1 tsp
1 heaped tsp tomato purée	1 tsp	1 tsp
2 eggs, separated		
25 g blanched almonds	1 oz	⅓ cup
25 g butter for frying the almonds	1 oz	2 tbsp

Remove the rind from the Camembert and cream the cheese. Soften the gelatine in cold water (see page 191). Melt the butter in a pan, stir the flour and cook for a moment or two over a low heat. Add the milk gradually. Bring to the boil, then simmer for 5 minutes. Add both the cheeses, seasonings, mustard, tomato purée, gelatine and egg yolks. Cook over a very low heat, stirring all the time until the mixture thickens without boiling.

Pour the mixture into a bowl and allow to cool. Put a band of greaseproof paper around an 11 or 12.5 cm (4½ or 5 in) soufflé dish. Fry the halved almonds in the butter, then drain and salt them. Keep aside about 8–10 almonds for the decoration and chop the rest.

When the mixture is on the point of setting, whisk the egg whites until very stiff and fold into it. Pour into the soufflé dish to come 12–25 mm (½–1 in) above the top. Leave in a cool place to set. When firm, remove the greaseproof paper and decorate the edge with chopped salted almonds. Arrange the halved nuts in a pattern in the centre.

Pissaladière à la Mènagère

Onion and anchovy bread (serves 5–6)

This French version of the Italian pizza is popular. It freezes extremely well.

	Imperial	American
150 g plain flour	5 oz	1¼ cups
¼ tsp salt	¼ tsp	¼ tsp
40 g butter	1½ oz	3 tbsp
15 g fresh yeast,	½ oz	1 tbsp
or 7 g dried yeast	¼ oz	2 tsp
a little tepid water		
1 egg		

For the filling:

	Imperial	American
3–4 tbsp oil	3–4 tbsp	3–4 tbsp
500 g onions, thinly sliced	1 lb	1 lb
2 tomatoes, skinned and		
sliced		
salt and pepper		
1 clove garlic (*optional*)		

For the garnish:
1 small can anchovy fillets,
  drained
black olives

Sift the flour and salt into a bowl. Cut the butter into pieces and rub it into the flour. Dissolve the yeast in 2 tablespoons of tepid water. Make a well in the centre of the flour and drop in the egg and yeast. Work to a dough, adding more water as required. Cover and allow to rise in a slightly warm place for 1–2 hours.

Meanwhile, make the filling. Heat the oil in a frying-pan and cook the onions gently until soft but not coloured. Add the tomatoes, seasoning and crushed garlic, if used. Continue cooking until the liquid has evaporated. Season well and allow to cool.

When the dough has risen, knock it back and knead into a ball. Place in the centre of a greased 22 cm (9 in) flan tin and press out to fill the circle. Cover with the filling.

Garnish with a lattice of anchovies and place olives in between. Allow to rise for 15 minutes. Bake in the centre of a preheated moderately hot oven, Mark 6 (200°C/400°F), for 20 minutes. Reduce the temperature to Mark 4 (180°C/350°F) and cook for a further 20 minutes.

Tourte Poitevine

Cheese tart (serves 4)

This cheese flan from the region of Poitiers is excellent for a light luncheon dish or for picnics.

	Imperial	American
For the pastry:		
225 g plain flour	8 oz	2 cups
a pinch of salt		
100 g butter	4 oz	½ cup
cold water to mix		
For the filling:		
225 g curd cheese	8 oz	8 oz
1 egg		
50 g Gruyère cheese,	2 oz	1 cup
grated		
75 g gammon rasher, diced	3 oz	3 oz
salt and freshly ground		
black pepper		
1 tbsp chopped chives	1 tbsp	1 tbsp
1 tsp chopped chervil	1 tsp	1 tsp
beaten egg to glaze		

To make the pastry, sift the flour and salt into a bowl. Cut the butter into pieces and rub it into the flour with the fingertips. Add approximately 2 tablespoons water to just bind together. Wrap and chill.

To make the filling, mix the curd cheese with the egg, Gruyère cheese and gammon. Season with pepper and a little salt, if needed. Stir in the herbs.

Line an 18 cm (7 in) flan ring with two-thirds of the pastry (see page 212). Spoon in the filling and damp the edge of the pastry. Roll the rest of the pastry into a circle and place on top. Press the edges gently together and trim. Brush over with beaten egg and make two cuts in the top. Bake in a moderately hot oven, Mark 6 (200°C/400°F), for 30 minutes or until golden brown. Serve hot or cold.

Tarte Basquaise

Basque tart (serves 5–6)

	Imperial	American
flaky pastry made with 100 g plain flour (*see pages 208–209*)	4 oz	1 cup

For the filling:
1 green pepper

225 g ripe tomatoes	8 oz	8 oz
25 g butter	1 oz	2 tbsp

salt and pepper
a good pinch of cayenne
   pepper
4 rashers lean bacon
1 egg
1 egg yolk

150 ml double cream	$\frac{1}{4}$ pt	$\frac{2}{3}$ cup

Make the pastry, wrap and put aside to chill.

Cut the green pepper into large dice, halve the tomatoes, scoop out the pulp and chop roughly. Melt the butter in a pan. When it is hot, add the green pepper, tomatoes, seasonings and bacon cut into strips. Cover with greaseproof paper and a lid and cook over a very gentle heat for 30 minutes.

Meanwhile, roll out the pastry on a lightly floured board and line into a 22 cm (9 in) flan ring (see page 212). Prick the base well, cover with a piece of greaseproof paper and baking-beans and bake 'blind' in a moderately hot oven, Mark 6 (200°C/400°F), for 20 minutes. Remove the greaseproof paper and the beans and return to the oven for a further 5–10 minutes to dry out.

Meanwhile, lightly whisk together the egg, egg yolk and cream. Stir this into the vegetable mixture and fill the flan. Reduce the temperature to Mark 4 (180°C/350°F) and return the flan to the oven to cook for a further 20 minutes or until set. Serve hot.

Tarte Basquaise.

Tartelettes au Roquefort
Roquefort tartlets (makes 12)

These tartlets with their soufflé-like filling are good to serve hot with drinks.

	Imperial	American
Pâte Brisée made with		
125 g plain flour	4½ oz	1 cup
(*see page 207*)		

For the filling:

	Imperial	American
25 g butter	1 oz	2 tbsp
1 tsp grated onion	1 tsp	1 tsp
25 g plain flour	1 oz	3 tbsp
125 ml milk	¼ pt	⅔ cup
1 egg, separated		
1 tbsp Madeira wine	1 tbsp	1 tbsp
75 g Roquefort cheese	3 oz	½ cup
salt and pepper		

For the garnish:
**stuffed olives, *or* chopped
   parsley**

Make the pastry, wrap and put aside to relax until well chilled.

Roll out the pastry on a lightly floured board and line into a dozen or so greased tartlet tins. Prick well, cover each with a piece of greaseproof paper and fill with baking-beans. Bake 'blind' in a moderately hot oven, Mark 6 (200°C/400°F), for 15 minutes. Remove the greaseproof paper and beans and return to the oven for about 5 minutes to dry out.

To make the filling, melt the butter in a pan, add the onion and cook until soft. Stir in the flour and cook for 2–3 minutes, then remove from the heat and add the milk gradually, stirring all the time. Return to the heat and bring to the boil, stirring all the time, until a thick smooth sauce is obtained. Remove from the heat and stir in the egg yolk, Madeira and softened cheese. Taste and season. Whisk the egg white until stiff then fold in lightly. Place one heaped teaspoon of this mixture in each pastry case and bake in a hot oven, Mark 7 (220°C/425°F), for 20 minutes or until lightly brown.

Serve very hot, garnished with a slice of stuffed olive or sprinkled with chopped parsley.

Tante Marie tip:
If Roquefort cheese is not available, substitute another blue-vein cheese such as Stilton or Gorgonzola.

Quiche Lorraine
Bacon and egg flan (serves 4)

This famous flan is seen in many parts of France besides Lorraine these days, and is a great favourite in Britain.

Gruyère cheese is ideal, but if it is not available use another cheese such as grated Cheddar or Lancashire.

	Imperial	American
Pâte Brisée made with		
100 g plain flour	4 oz	1 cup
(*see page 207*)		

For the filling:

	Imperial	American
50 g lean bacon *or* ham		
50 g Gruyère cheese	2 oz	1 cup
2 eggs		
150 ml single cream	¼ pt	⅔ cup
or creamy milk		
salt and pepper		

Make the pastry, wrap and put aside to chill for 15–20 minutes.

Roll out the pastry on a lightly floured board and carefully line into an 18 cm (7 in) flan ring. Cut the bacon or ham into strips and sprinkle over the base of the pastry case. Cut the cheese into wafer-thin slices and arrange on top of the bacon or ham. Whisk the eggs lightly and add the cream or milk. Whisk again. Season, then strain the mixture into the flan case. Cook in a moderately hot oven, Mark 6 (200°C/400°F), for approximately 30–35 minutes. Serve warm.

Tante Marie tip:
If the bacon is too salty, blanch it in boiling water for 2 minutes, then drain.

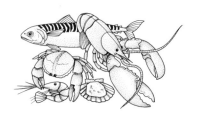

Seafood

Standing on a quayside, shopping basket on arm, watching the fish being landed and brought straight to the fish stall, is one of the delights of shopping in France.

The unglamorous, hard-working boats line the quayside, and the stalls offer boxes of different varieties of oysters, clams, sea-urchins, crabs, large sad-looking grey or black lobsters, red mullet, whiting, sea bream, conger eel and often some unfamiliar fish, such as John Dory, rascasse, roussette or fresh tuna. It is not difficult to judge the freshness of the fish in these conditions. When buying from a more prosaic fishmonger's you need to be able to look at the eyes; they should be bright and clear, not sunken and dull. The gills should be red, the tails stiff and the flesh firm and, of course, the smell should be fresh.

Fish is one of the most delicious of foods and this is evident from the hundreds of different ways in which it is served by French chefs and housewives. The complex and skilled dishes of the 'haute cuisine', such as Filets de Sole à la Suchet, with its delicate wine sauce, contrast with the robust regional Potage Vivier, Maquereaux Mirelle, Mulet à la Provençale and other flavoursome dishes. There is such a wide variety of fish, whether from sea or fresh water, that the choice can seem almost bewildering until you remember that there is only a limited number of methods of preparing and cooking each one so, once you have mastered the skills, you can cook any recipe that you choose.

The fishmonger is a good friend and will quickly clean and fillet fish for you. If, however, he is too busy or if you have freshly caught fish to prepare yourself, the picture guides will help you with any problems you may encounter in preparing round fish, flat fish and crabs.

Harengs à la Diable
Devilled herrings (serves 4)

Mustard sauce provides a sharp accompaniment to grilled herrings.

	Imperial	American
4 herrings		
salt and pepper		
a few white breadcrumbs		

For the mustard sauce:

	Imperial	American
1½–2 level tbsp Dijon mustard	1½–2 tbsp	1½–2 tbsp
100 g butter	4 oz	½ cup
1 tbsp wine vinegar	1 tbsp	1 tbsp

For the garnish:
1 bunch watercress

Clean and scale the herrings and cut off the fins (see pages 66–67). Slash a few diagonal knife cuts across the body. Season with salt and pepper, and sprinkle with the breadcrumbs. Grill slowly until golden brown on both sides. If there are roes, grill these too.

Meanwhile, make the sauce. Place the mustard in a bowl over a pan of warm water and whisk in half the butter gradually, beating with a sauce whisk. Remove from the heat, whisk in the rest of the butter, then add the vinegar and seasoning to taste.

Place the herrings in a serving-dish, garnish with the watercress and hand the sauce separately.

Turban de Colin

Hake ring (serves 4)

This light fish mousse with mushroom sauce can also be made with cod or other kinds of white fish.

	Imperial	American
For the court bouillon:		
300 ml water	$\frac{1}{2}$ pt	$1\frac{1}{4}$ cups
1 tbsp tarragon vinegar	1 tbsp	1 tbsp
a bouquet garni including 4 *or* 5 parsley stalks		
1 medium carrot, sliced		
1 medium onion, sliced		
5–6 peppercorns		
salt		
For the ring mould:		
500 g hake *or* other white fish	1 lb	1 lb
50 g bread	2 oz	1 cup
150 ml milk	$\frac{1}{4}$ pt	$\frac{2}{3}$ cup
salt and pepper		
75 g cheese, grated	3 oz	$1\frac{1}{2}$ cups
2 egg whites		
melted butter		
a few sieved, lightly browned breadcrumbs		
For the mushroom sauce:		
100 g mushrooms	4 oz	4 oz
50 g butter	2 oz	$\frac{1}{4}$ cup
salt and pepper		
25 g plain flour	1 oz	3 tbsp
150 ml court bouillon in which the fish was cooked	$\frac{1}{4}$ pt	$\frac{2}{3}$ cup
300 ml milk	$\frac{1}{2}$ pt	$1\frac{1}{4}$ cups
2 egg yolks		

To make the court bouillon, place the water and vinegar in a pan, add the bouquet garni, carrot, onion and seasoning and bring to simmering point. Add the fish and cook gently for 10–15 minutes or until cooked. Cut the bread into small dice and place in a pan with the hot milk, $\frac{1}{2}$ teaspoon of salt and a good pinch of pepper. Stir it over the heat until a thick sauce consistency is obtained, then beat vigorously with a wooden spoon.

When the fish is cooked, drain well, retaining the court bouillon. Remove the skin and bones and flake the fish, using two forks so that it is lightly fluffed up.

Place the bread and milk mixture in a bowl and stir in the grated cheese. Mix in the fish and season well. Separate the eggs, whisk the whites very stiffly, then fold them into the fish mixture as lightly as possible.

Grease a 20 cm (8 in) ring mould with the melted butter. Dust out with the breadcrumbs. Fill the mould with the fish mixture, dropping it in with a spoon. Do not press it down too firmly or the result will be a heavy texture. Smooth the surface with a palette knife. Stand the mould in a roasting-pan containing boiling water and cook in a moderately hot oven, Mark 6 (200°C/400°F), for 20–30 minutes or until firm.

Meanwhile, wipe and slice the mushrooms. Melt 25 g (1 oz/2 tablespoons) of butter in a pan, add the mushrooms, season and cover with greaseproof paper and a lid. Cook for 3–4 minutes, shaking the pan from time to time.

Melt the rest of the butter in another pan, remove from the heat and stir in the flour. Return to the heat and cook for 2–3 minutes, keeping the roux well stirred. Strain on 150 ml ($\frac{1}{4}$ pt/$\frac{2}{3}$ cup) of the court bouillon in which the fish was cooked, add the milk and bring to the boil. Season well and simmer for 5 minutes, keeping well stirred. Add the mushrooms and the butter in which they were cooked. Remove from the heat and whisk in the egg yolks. Cook over a very gentle heat until the mixture thickens without boiling, stirring all the time. Taste and season. Remove the mould from the oven, run a knife round the edges and wipe off any moisture on the outside of the mould. Invert it onto a hot serving-dish, allow to stand for 30 seconds, then unmould carefully. Fill the centre with the mushroom sauce. Serve any extra sauce in a sauce-boat.

Tante Marie tip:
If you have a non-stick siliconised ring mould you will find it ideal to use.

Preparation of Round Fish such as Trout, Herring, Mackerel and Whiting

2. Remove the gut (do this on a newspaper, so it is easy to clean up afterwards) and rinse well.

1. Cut the fish open from gills to vent, using a sharp knife.

3. Cut off the fins, using a pair of kitchen scissors.

4. Fish which are in good condition have plenty of scales. Hold the fish firmly by the tail then remove the scales by scraping from tail to head with a sharp knife. Wash in a bowl of cold water.

6. To remove the backbone, open the fish out so it is flat on the board, then press on the backbone to loosen it. Turn the fish over and loosen the small bones from the flesh.

5. Eyes look very unappetising if left when the fish is served. Remove them, using the handle of a tea-spoon to slide them out.

7. Lift out the backbone and cut it off at each end, using scissors or a knife.

Mulet à la Provençale

Provençale-style grey mullet (serves 3–4)

This attractively marked fish is excellent for cooking. The flesh has a pleasant texture, reminiscent of mackerel, but the flavour is much more delicate. It can be cooked in a variety of ways: stuffed and baked, poached or fried.

	Imperial	American
1 grey mullet (about 750 g)	1½ lb	1½ lb
2 tbsp oil	2 tbsp	2 tbsp
1 onion, chopped		
500 g tomatoes, skinned and chopped	1 lb	1 lb
1–2 cloves garlic		
4 tbsp dry white wine	4 tbsp	4 tbsp
salt and pepper		
finely chopped parsley		

Heat the oil in a pan, add the onion and sauté lightly. Add the tomatoes, crushed garlic, wine and seasoning. Simmer gently for 10 minutes.

Meanwhile, prepare the fish. Cut off the head, tail and fins. Clean it as shown on pages 66–67, taking care to remove all the scales, then wash well. Cut into 5 cm (2 in) slices. Add to the tomato mixture, cover with a lid and cook slowly for a further 20 minutes. Lift the fish into a warm serving-dish and add 1 teaspoon of parsley. Taste and season the sauce. Pour over the fish and sprinkle with a little more parsley. Serve hot.

Above: Grey mullet.
Below: Mulet à la Provençale.

Grillade au Fenouil

Grilled red mullet with fennel (serves 4)

Look at a campsite in France on a warm summer evening and you will see a blue haze from all the barbecues cooking supper, and smell the steaks and fish grilling. This fennel-flavoured fish can be barbecued in this way or grilled in the kitchen.

	Imperial	American
4–8 red mullet (depending on size)		
salt and pepper		
a little oil		
a sprig of fennel		
For the Beurre au Fenouil:		
2 tbsp chopped fennel	2 tbsp	2 tbsp
6 peppercorns		
4 tbsp white wine	4 tbsp	4 tbsp
1 tbsp wine vinegar	1 tbsp	1 tbsp
1 egg yolk		
100 g butter	4 oz	$\frac{1}{2}$ cup

Prepare the fish as shown on pages 66–67. Score the flesh, season, and brush with the oil.

To make the Beurre au Fenouil, place half the fennel in a small pan with the crushed peppercorns, wine and vinegar. Boil until reduced to a teaspoonful. Strain into a bowl and add the egg yolk. Whisk over hot water until the mixture thickens. Remove from the heat and whisk in the butter. Season and stir in the rest of the fennel.

If you are cooking on a barbecue, put a layer of fennel on top of the hot charcoal before grilling the fish. Grill until cooked on each side, or place a bunch of *dried* fennel underneath. Set light to the fennel and, as it burns, turn the fish so that each side is flavoured. If you are using a conventional grill in the kitchen, grill the fish until cooked. Arrange the fish in a hot serving-dish and serve with the fennel-flavoured sauce.

Tante Marie tip:
Mackerel, John Dory, or sea bream can also be cooked in the same way.

Maquereaux

Mackerel

Buy mackerel when they are really fresh, with a satiny sheen on the skin. Grilling and frying are both good ways to cook them. As they have some natural oils in the flesh, use only a little butter or oil for cooking. For a main course 275–350 g (10–12 oz) is an average weight for a mackerel.

Maquereaux Farcis

Stuffed mackerel (serves 4)

	Imperial	American
4 mackerel		
25 g butter	1 oz	2 tbsp
1 onion, finely chopped		
100 g mushrooms	4 oz	4 oz
1 tbsp chopped parsley	1 tbsp	1 tbsp
2 cloves garlic		
salt and pepper		
1 lemon		
sprigs of parsley		
300 ml Sauce au Fines Herbes (*see page 28*)	$\frac{1}{2}$ pt	$1\frac{1}{4}$ cups

Prepare the fish as shown on pages 66–67, removing the backbone. Melt the butter in a pan, add the onion and cook gently until transparent. Stir in the finely sliced mushrooms, parsley and crushed garlic. Season well. Fill the mackerel with this mixture and press back in shape. Slash each side of the fish with 3 shallow diagonal cuts and grill for 10–12 minutes, turning them once after the first side is browned. The skin should be golden brown.

Arrange on a serving-dish. Garnish with the lemon and parsley and hand the sauce separately.

Maquereaux Mirelle

Fried mackerel with mushrooms and tomatoes (serves 4)

	Imperial	American
4 mackerel		
salt and pepper		
3–4 tbsp plain flour	3–4 tbsp	3–4 tbsp
oil for frying		
1 shallot, finely chopped		
1 onion, finely chopped		
100 g mushrooms, finely chopped	4 oz	1 cup
1 clove garlic		
4 tomatoes		

To finish:

	Imperial	American
1 tbsp finely chopped fresh herbs	1 tbsp	1 tbsp

Clean and bone the fish as shown on pages 66–67. Open flat, season and dip in the flour. Place 2–3 tablespoons of oil in a sauté pan. When it is very hot, add the fish and brown them on both sides, allowing about 10 minutes in all.

Meanwhile, heat about 1 tablespoon of oil in a small pan, add the shallot and onion and cook until soft, taking care not to let them brown. Add the finely chopped mushrooms and the garlic crushed with a little salt. Cook for 2–3 minutes, stirring well. Remove the mixture from the heat and keep hot. Dip the tomatoes into boiling water, remove their skins, cut into quarters and heat them through in a little oil.

Arrange the fish on a hot serving-dish. Cover each with a layer of mushroom mixture and arrange the tomatoes around the sides of the fish. Sprinkle the herbs over the fish.

Galette de Morue à la Niçoise

Niçoise fish flan (serves 4)

This recipe, which should be made with salt cod, makes the fish very palatable. The cod is soaked for 24 hours, changing the water at intervals, before cooking. Salt cod is not obtainable everywhere, but smoked haddock is very good used as a substitute. Smoked haddock does not, of course, need to be soaked.

	Imperial	American
100 g salt cod, soaked as described above	4 oz	4 oz
Sauce Tomate made with 350 g tomatoes (*see page 33*)	12 oz	12 oz
flaky pastry made with 100 g strong flour (*see pages 208–209*)	4 oz	1 cup
2 eggs		
6 anchovy fillets		
12 black olives, stoned		
freshly ground black pepper		

Poach the fish in simmering water until tender. Do not add salt. Make the Sauce Tomate and put aside to get cold. Make the pastry and place in the refrigerator to chill.

Whisk the two eggs lightly together and stir into the Sauce Tomate. Roll out the pastry on a lightly floured board and line into an 18 cm (7 in) flan ring as shown on page 212.

Remove the skin and bones and flake the fish. Place the fish in the pastry case with the anchovies, cut into pieces, and the olives. Sprinkle with the pepper, then pour over the sauce. Cook in a moderately hot oven, Mark 6 (200°C/400°F), for 25–30 minutes or until the pastry is golden and the filling set.

Sole

Sole is a white fish which is needed in many recipes. These are three types most commonly found.

Lemon sole

These fish have a yellowish-grey skin, and are wider in shape than the Dover sole. The flesh is a little softer in texture, but can be very palatable when well cooked. The French name is sole-limande.

Dover sole

This firm-fleshed fish is ideal for all the classic ways of serving sole. It has the great virtue of being easily skinned whole – an essential feature in the preparation of Sole Meunière and Sole Farci. It can be served on the bone or filleted. It is easy to recognise from its shape and the dark grey, blotched skin.

Slip soles are small ones weighing 175–225 g (6–8 oz). The sole can vary from this size up to 700 g (1½ lb). If you are serving whole fish allow one of 350–450 g

(12 oz–1 lb) per person. Fillets should be cut from fish of 450 g (1 lb) upwards. Allow 1 or 2 fillets per person, depending on the size of the fish and the number of courses in the meal.

Witch sole

This is sometimes known as Torbay or grey sole. Again, the shape is recognisably different. The skin is light grey and the fins have a ragged appearance. Like the lemon sole it can be excellent value, though it is not as good as the Dover sole.

Filets de Sole Cubat

Fillets of sole with mushroom purée
(serves 4)

As this dish is browned with cheese on top it is easy for the hostess to prepare early in the day and reheat later.

	Imperial	American
8 fillets of sole, skinned		
salt and pepper		
a little butter		
1 carrot, sliced		
1 onion, sliced		
a bouquet garni		
6 peppercorns		
150 ml white wine	$\frac{1}{4}$ pt	$\frac{2}{3}$ cup
about 150 ml water	$\frac{1}{4}$ pt	$\frac{2}{3}$ cup

For the mushroom sauce:

	Imperial	American
100 g mushrooms	4 oz	4 oz
40 g butter	$1\frac{1}{2}$ oz	3 tbsp
15 g plain flour	$\frac{1}{2}$ oz	$1\frac{1}{2}$ tbsp
150 ml milk	$\frac{1}{4}$ pt	$\frac{2}{3}$ cup

For the Sauce Velouté:

	Imperial	American
25 g butter	1 oz	2 tbsp
25 g plain flour	1 oz	3 tbsp
300 ml liquor from cooking the fish	$\frac{1}{2}$ pt	$1\frac{1}{4}$ cups
2 tbsp double cream	2 tbsp	2 tbsp
40 g cheese, grated	$1\frac{1}{2}$ oz	$\frac{3}{4}$ cup

To finish:

	Imperial	American
a few browned breadcrumbs		
25 g cheese, grated	1 oz	$\frac{1}{2}$ cup

Buy fillets of fish, or fillet whole fish as shown on pages 72–73. Wash and trim the skinned fillets, season and fold into three. Place in a buttered heat-proof dish and arrange the carrot and onion around the sides. Tuck the bouquet garni well down in the dish and add the peppercorns and salt. Add the wine and enough water to cover the fish. Cover with greaseproof paper and a lid. Poach in a moderate oven, Mark 4 (180°C/350°F), for 20 minutes or until the fish is cooked.

Meanwhile, rinse the mushrooms and put them through the coarse grid of a vegetable mill or chop them finely in a blender or food processor. Melt the butter in a pan, add the mushrooms and cook gently over a low heat, stirring frequently until tender. Remove the pan from the heat, sprinkle in the flour and mix thoroughly. Blend in the milk. Return to the heat and bring to the boil, stirring all the time. Season, then simmer for 5 minutes.

Make the Sauce Velouté (see page 27). For the stock, strain the liquor in which the fish was cooked (if there is less than 300 ml ($\frac{1}{2}$ pt/$1\frac{1}{4}$ cups), add a little extra milk) and add it to the pan. Bring to the boil and simmer for 5 minutes, stirring all the time. Add the cream. Remove the pan from the heat and whisk in the cheese. Taste and season.

Place the mushroom mixture in the bottom of a hot serving-dish and arrange the sole fillets on top. Pour over the sauce. Dust with the breadcrumbs and cheese. Brown under a hot grill or in the top of a hot oven, Mark 7 (220°C/425°F).

Left to right: Lemon sole, Dover sole and witch sole.

To Skin and Fillet Dover Sole

About 550 g (1¼ lb) is the best size for filleting.

2. With a knife, ease the skin away from the flesh at the tail end. Dab a little salt on your fingers to help get a firm grip and pull briskly from tail to head, removing the skin completely. Turn over and repeat on the other side.

1. Use a sharp knife to make a cut down each side of the fish between the fins and the flesh, and across the tail. Loosen the skin by running the thumb under the flap of skin.

3. Cut off the fillets of fish. First make a central cut right down the backbone of the fish using a flexible-bladed filleting-knife.

4. Cut the fillets off the bone in two or three smooth strokes. Trim off any untidy edges and wash the fillets.

5. Here you see four different ways of using the fillets. Fold in half or thirds, or roll into paupiettes. For fried fish they can be used flat or decoratively cut and plaited en ruban.

Filets de Sole aux Crevettes

Fillets of sole with prawns (serves 4)

Poached sole served with a wine sauce, and garnished with carrot and prawns.

	Imperial	American
8 fillets of sole, skinned		
1 small onion		
4 tbsp dry white wine	4 tbsp	4 tbsp
150 ml fish stock	$\frac{1}{4}$ pt	$\frac{2}{3}$ cup
(*see page 35*)		
6 black peppercorns		
salt		
1 medium carrot		
20 g butter	$\frac{3}{4}$ oz	$1\frac{1}{2}$ tbsp
20 g plain flour	$\frac{3}{4}$ oz	2 tbsp
4 tbsp single cream	4 tbsp	4 tbsp
50 g shelled prawns	2 oz	2 oz

For the garnish:
4 whole prawns
1 lemon
parsley

Buy fillets of fish, or fillet whole fish as shown opposite. Cut the onion into thick slices and place in a heatproof dish. Wash and trim the skinned fillets, fold into three, and place them in the dish. Pour over the wine and fish stock. Add the peppercorns and salt, cover with a lid, and poach in a moderate oven, Mark 4 (180°C/350°F), for approximately 20–25 minutes or until cooked.

Cut the carrot into julienne strips and cook in boiling salted water until tender.

Melt the butter in a pan, add the flour and cook for 2–3 minutes. Remove the pan from the heat. When the fish is cooked, drain off the liquor and stir into the roux. Bring to the boil, then simmer for 5 minutes, stirring frequently. Add the cream, and stir in the carrots and prawns. Taste and season.

Arrange the fish on a warm serving-dish. Pour over the sauce and garnish with the prawns, slices of lemon and parsley.

Tante Marie tip:
When prawns are used for a garnish the heads are left on, but the shell can be removed from the body to make them easier to eat.

Filets de Sole à la Florentine

Poached sole with spinach and cheese sauce (serves 4)

The word Florentine in a recipe name indicates that the dish contains spinach.

	Imperial	American
8 fillets of sole, skinned		
salt and pepper		
150 ml dry white wine	$\frac{1}{4}$ pt	$\frac{2}{3}$ cup
2–3 shallots, *or* 1 small onion		

For the Sauce Béchamel:

	Imperial	American
40 g butter	$1\frac{1}{2}$ oz	3 tbsp
40 g plain flour	$1\frac{1}{2}$ oz	$\frac{1}{3}$ cup
300 ml milk	$\frac{1}{2}$ pt	$1\frac{1}{4}$ cups

	Imperial	American
1 kg fresh spinach,	2 lb	2 lb
or 500 g frozen spinach	1 lb	1 lb
2 tbsp double cream	2 tbsp	2 tbsp
50 g cheese, grated	2 oz	1 cup
a few breadcrumbs		

Buy fillets of fish, or fillet whole fish as shown on pages 72–73. Wash and trim the skinned fillets and fold into three. Place in a heatproof dish, season and pour over the wine. Add the thickly sliced shallots or onion. Cover with buttered paper and a lid. Poach in a moderate oven, Mark 4 (180°C/350°F), for approximately 20 minutes.

Make the Sauce Béchamel (see page 27).

Wash the spinach thoroughly and cook in a very little boiling salted water for about 10 minutes or until tender. Drain very well, chop, taste and season.

Strain off the liquor in which the fish was cooked. Reduce it over a good heat until only half the quantity remains. Add to the sauce. Stir in the cream and half of the cheese. Season well. If the consistency is too thick, add a little more milk.

Pour a thin layer of the sauce into the bottom of a buttered heatproof serving-dish. Cover with the spinach, place the fillets on top and coat evenly with the rest of the sauce. Mix the rest of the cheese with the breadcrumbs and sprinkle on the top. Brown under a hot grill.

Tante Marie tip:

When you want a more substantial and less ex- pensive dish, use smoked haddock in place of the sole or, for a milder flavour, fresh haddock.

Filets de Sole à la Suchet

Suchet fillets of sole (serves 4)

This is a dish in the classic tradition. The fish is poached in wine with herb and vegetable flavourings. A smooth wine sauce is made from the liquor and the dish is garnished attractively with a piped potato border.

	Imperial	American
8 fillets of sole, skinned		
Pommes de Terre Duchesse made with 750 g potatoes (*see page 179*)	$1\frac{1}{2}$ lb	$1\frac{1}{2}$ lb
1 small onion, thickly sliced		
a few parsley stalks		
1 bayleaf		
5–6 peppercorns		
salt and pepper		
150 ml dry white wine	$\frac{1}{4}$ pt	$\frac{2}{3}$ cup
150 ml water	$\frac{1}{4}$ pt	$\frac{2}{3}$ cup
350 g carrots	12 oz	12 oz
40 g butter	$1\frac{1}{2}$ oz	3 tbsp
20 g plain flour	$\frac{3}{4}$ oz	2 tbsp
4 tbsp single cream	4 tbsp	4 tbsp
beaten egg for glazing		

Buy fillets of fish, or fillet whole fish as shown on pages 72–73.

Cook the potatoes for the Pommes de Terre Duchesse. Wash and trim the skinned fillets and fold into three, with the skinned side inwards. Place in a heatproof dish with the onion, parsley stalks, bayleaf, peppercorns and a sprinkling of salt. Pour over the wine and water. Cover with the skeleton and skin of the fish, or with a piece of greaseproof paper. Cover with a lid, and poach in a moderate oven, Mark 4 (180°C/350°F) for 25–30 minutes or until the fish is white in colour and firm to the touch.

Meanwhile, peel or scrape the carrots, rinse well, and cut into julienne strips the size of matchsticks. Melt the butter in a small pan with 4 tablespoons water. Add the carrots, season, cover with a lid and cook gently until tender (usually about 15 minutes).

Complete the Pommes de Terre Duchesse mixture and place in a 30 cm (12 in) forcing bag with a large

Filets de Sole à la Suchet.

rosette pipe. Butter the edge of a heatproof serving-dish and pipe the potato in a border around the edge. Place under a hot grill or in the top of a hot oven, Mark 7 (220°C/425°F), and cook until set. Brush lightly with a little beaten egg and allow to brown.

When the carrots are cooked, boil off the water so that only the butter remains. Melt 25 g (1 oz/2 tbsp) of butter in another pan, sprinkle in the flour and stir gently, then add the strained liquor in which the fish was poached. Bring to the boil, stirring all the time, then simmer for 5 minutes. Remove from the heat and add the cream. Beat in 15 g ($\frac{1}{2}$ oz/1 tbsp) of butter gradually, using a sauce whisk to give a gloss to the sauce. Add the carrots. Taste and season, and adjust the consistency if necessary. Drain the fish

thoroughly and arrange in the centre of the serving-dish. Pour over the sauce and serve hot.

Tante Marie tip:
Witch sole is good for this, as well as the more expensive Dover sole. Plaice can be substituted; or neatly cut slices of fresh haddock, blue ling, or other white fish can be used.

Sole Meunière

Fried sole (serves 4)

Dover sole are best for this recipe if you want to serve whole fish. If you want to cook other types of sole or plaice in this way, fillet them first.

	Imperial	American
4 Dover soles (350 g each)	12 oz each	12 oz each
a little milk		
seasoned flour		
75–100 g butter	3–4 oz	½ cup
2 lemons		
finely chopped parsley		
salt and pepper		

Clean, skin and wash the whole fish as shown on pages 72–73. Dip them in the milk and then into seasoned flour.

Heat half the butter in a frying-pan. When it is bubbling hot, place the fish in the pan and sprinkle with a little salt. Cook until the underside of the fish is golden, then turn quickly in the pan, supporting the fish with a palette knife or spatula. Cook the other side.

When golden brown, lift onto a hot dish. Wipe the pan with kitchen paper. Add the rest of the butter and heat it quickly until it turns a nut-brown colour. Add the strained juice of 1 lemon together with some of the parsley. Season, then pour over the fish. Garnish the dish with thin slices of lemon cut from the second lemon.

Tante Marie tip:
An oval fish frying-pan is ideal for cooking whole fish.

Sole Farci

Sole stuffed with prawns (serves 1)

Deep-fried sole stuffed with prawns and mushrooms.

	Imperial	American
1 Dover sole (225–350 g)	8–12 oz	8–12 oz
seasoned flour		
1 egg		
sieved fresh *or* dried white breadcrumbs		
50 g mushrooms	2 oz	2 oz
15 g butter	½ oz	1 tbsp
salt and pepper		
a little lemon juice		
25 g shelled prawns	1 oz	¼ cup
fat for deep frying		
finely chopped parsley		
1 lemon		

Cut the fins off the fish. Skin it, removing both the black and the white skin as shown on pages 72–73. Wash and dry the fish. Make a cut down the centre of one side of the fish, and loosen the flesh so that it can be rolled back from the centre. Use a pair of kitchen scissors to snip through the backbone at each end of the cut and once or twice in the middle. Coat the fish with the seasoned flour, egg and breadcrumbs. Slice the mushrooms and cook in the butter with the seasoning and lemon juice. Add the prawns to warm through.

Heat a deep pan of fat to 190°C (375°F), add the fish and fry until golden brown. Drain on kitchen paper. Lift out the backbone.

Place the fish on a hot serving-dish, and fill the centre of the fish with the prawns and mushrooms sprinkled with the parsley. Garnish with lemon.

Soufflé de Turbot Royale
Royal turbot soufflé (serves 4)

This cheese soufflé layered with turbot makes an impressive party piece.

	Imperial	American
500 g turbot	1 lb	1 lb
150 ml wine	$\frac{1}{4}$ pt	$\frac{2}{3}$ cup
150 ml water	$\frac{1}{4}$ pt	$\frac{2}{3}$ cup
1 small onion		
1 carrot		
a bouquet garni		
salt and pepper		
a little butter		
a few white breadcrumbs		
50 g butter	2 oz	$\frac{1}{4}$ cup
50 g plain flour	2 oz	$\frac{1}{2}$ cup
300 ml milk	$\frac{1}{2}$ pt	$1\frac{1}{4}$ cups
40 g Parmesan cheese, grated	$1\frac{1}{2}$ oz	$\frac{1}{3}$ cup
40 g Cheddar cheese, grated	$1\frac{1}{2}$ oz	$\frac{3}{4}$ cup
2 egg yolks		
4 egg whites		

Place the wine, water, onion, carrot, bouquet garni and seasoning in a pan. Bring to the boil, then simmer for 20 minutes, then add the turbot and simmer very gently for a further 15 minutes. Drain the fish, and boil the liquor until reduced to a glaze. Remove the fish from the bone and flake into large pieces, then toss these in the glaze.

Prepare an 18 cm (7 in) soufflé dish by greasing well with butter and dusting with breadcrumbs. Melt the butter in a pan, remove from the heat and stir in the flour. Return to the heat and cook for 2–3 minutes, stirring well. Remove from the heat and stir in the milk gradually. Replace over the heat and bring to the boil, stirring all the time, then boil for 5 minutes. Remove from the heat and whisk in the cheeses and beaten egg yolks. Taste and season. Whisk the egg whites until stiff, then fold into the sauce. Spread a layer of the mixture on the bottom of the soufflé dish. Cover with a layer of fish, and continue in this way, finishing with a layer of soufflé mixture.

Place in the centre of a moderately hot oven, Mark 5 (190°C/375°F) and cook for 10 minutes, then increase the temperature to Mark 6 (200°C/400°F) and continue cooking for a further 15 minutes. Serve immediately.

Filets de Merlan à la Toulonnaise
Toulon style fillets of whiting (serves 4)

In this recipe aubergine and tomatoes give a colourful garnish to crisply fried whiting.

	Imperial	American
4–8 fillets of whiting		
1 aubergine (about 225 g)	8 oz	8 oz
salt and pepper		
1 onion		
1 tbsp oil	1 tbsp	1 tbsp
500 g tomatoes	1 lb	1 lb
1 clove garlic		
seasoned flour		
1 egg		
fresh white breadcrumbs		
oil for frying		
1 lemon		

Cut the aubergine into moderately large dice, sprinkle with salt and leave to drain for 20–30 minutes. Peel the onion and chop finely. Heat the oil in a pan, add the onion and cook gently until tender. Skin the tomatoes and chop them roughly. Add to the pan with the crushed garlic and seasoning. Simmer gently until the vegetables are tender and a thick purée is obtained.

Wash the fish and remove any small bones left on the flesh. Dip in the seasoned flour, then in the beaten egg, then in the breadcrumbs. Pour sufficient oil into a frying-pan to cover the base. Heat, add the fillets and cook until golden brown on both sides. Remove and drain. Keep hot.

Pat the aubergines dry on kitchen paper. Toss in 1 tablespoon of seasoned flour, then fry in the oil until golden brown and tender.

To serve, pour the tomato fondue onto the dish, arrange the aubergines around the sides and place the fillets of fish in the centre. Garnish with slices of lemon.

Truites

Trout

Fresh trout are one of the most popular fresh-water fish. They can be grilled, poached, fried in butter, or baked in foil.

Use fresh trout from early spring to late summer, or frozen ones at any time. For a first course choose small ones weighing approximately 150–175 g (5–6 oz). For a main course a larger one 200–250 g (7–9 oz) might be more appreciated.

Truites à la Grenobloise

Grenoble trout (serves 4)

	Imperial	American
4 trout		
2 tbsp fresh white breadcrumbs	2 tbsp	2 tbsp
1 tbsp finely chopped fresh herbs, e.g. parsley and tarragon	1 tbsp	1 tbsp
100 g butter	4 oz	$\frac{1}{2}$ cup
salt and pepper		
beaten egg to bind		
2 tbsp seasoned flour	2 tbsp	2 tbsp
2 lemons		
2 tbsp capers	2 tbsp	2 tbsp
chopped parsley		

Clean the fish and remove the backbones as shown on pages 66–67. Mix the breadcrumbs with the herbs, 15 g ($\frac{1}{2}$ oz/1 tbsp) melted butter and seasoning. Add sufficient egg to bind together. Fill the fish with this stuffing, then dip in the seasoned flour. Melt the rest of the butter in a frying-pan, add the fish and fry until golden brown on both sides. Place on a serving-dish and keep warm. Add the juice of 1 lemon to the butter in the pan and swill around. Stir in the capers and pour over the fish. Cut the rind from the remaining lemon, then slice it thinly. Garnish each fish with 1–2 lemon slices and sprinkle with the parsley.

Truites Caprice de Buffon

Stuffed trout (serves 4)

	Imperial	American
4 trout		
1 tbsp finely chopped fresh herbs, e.g. parsley, thyme and chervil	1 tbsp	1 tbsp
3 tbsp fresh breadcrumbs	3 tbsp	3 tbsp
salt and pepper		
beaten egg to bind		
2 tbsp seasoned flour	2 tbsp	2 tbsp
75 g unsalted butter	3 oz	6 tbsp
juice of 1 lemon		
juice of 1 orange		
1 tbsp chopped parsley	1 tbsp	1 tbsp

For the garnish:
1 lemon
1 orange
2 bananas

Prepare the fish as shown on pages 66–67. Prepare the garnish of thin slices of orange and lemon, decorated with a canelle knife (see page 12). To make the stuffing, mix the herbs with the breadcrumbs and seasoning. Add sufficient egg to bind together.

Fill the fish with this mixture. If you are preparing a special meal, this stage can be completed in the morning, and the fish can be covered with plastic clingfilm or foil and left in the refrigerator until you are ready to fry them.

Before cooking, toss the fish in the seasoned flour. Melt 50 g (2 oz/$\frac{1}{4}$ cup) of butter in a frying-pan. When it is foaming, add the fish and cook until golden brown underneath. Turn them over, supporting them on a palette knife or fish slice, and cook until golden brown on the other side.

Meanwhile, arrange most of the orange and lemon slices around the edge of a serving-dish. Lift the cooked fish onto the dish, then peel the bananas and cut in half lengthways. Add the rest of the butter to the pan and fry the bananas. Place half a banana on each trout. Add the lemon and orange juices and parsley to the pan, swill around, season, then pour over the fish. Garnish with the remaining slices of orange and lemon and serve hot.

1. Ingredients for Truites Caprice de Buffon.

2. Fill the fish with the herb mixture.

3. Truites Caprice de Buffon.

Truites à l'Estragon

Trout in tarragon sauce (serves 4)

	Imperial	American
4 trout		
salt and pepper		
150 ml white wine	$\frac{1}{4}$ pt	$\frac{2}{3}$ cup
150 ml water	$\frac{1}{4}$ pt	$\frac{2}{3}$ cup
a slice of onion		
1 carrot, sliced		
1 handful tarragon		
40 g butter	$1\frac{1}{2}$ oz	3 tbsp
25 g plain flour	1 oz	3 tbsp
150 ml double cream	$\frac{1}{4}$ pt	$\frac{2}{3}$ cup
salt and pepper		

Clean the trout and remove the eyes and fins as shown on pages 66–67. Season inside and out, then place in a heatproof dish. Add the wine and water to cover the fish. Add the onion, seasoning, carrot and a sprig of tarragon. Cover with a lid and poach in a moderately hot oven, Mark 5 (190°C/375°F), for 20 minutes or until cooked. At the end of this time, remove the trout, drain, arrange them on the serving-dish and keep hot.

Strain the liquor in which the fish was cooked into a saucepan and boil to reduce by half. Use a fork to blend the butter with the flour, and whisk this into the boiling liquid. Add the cream and boil the sauce gently for 4–5 minutes. Add 2–3 tablespoons chopped tarragon, season to taste and adjust the consistency if necessary. Pour smoothly over the fish and garnish each fish with whole tarragon leaves.

Saumon

Salmon

Saumon Poché au Beurre Blanc

Poached salmon with butter sauce (serves 4)

In the past, pike was traditionally served in this way with the Beurre Blanc sauce, but salmon is often used too: even in the Loire Valley where the recipe originated. It can also be successfully adapted to mild-flavoured sea-fish such as hake or halibut.

	Imperial	American
4 salmon cutlets		
1 onion, sliced		
1 carrot, sliced		
a bouquet garni		
salt and 2 *or* 3 peppercorns		
4 tbsp white wine	4 tbsp	4 tbsp
600 ml water	1 pt	$2\frac{1}{2}$ cups
For the Sauce Beurre Blanc:		
6 shallots		
150 ml dry white wine	$\frac{1}{4}$ pt	$\frac{2}{3}$ cup
175 g unsalted butter	6 oz	$\frac{3}{4}$ cup
1 tbsp double cream	1 tbsp	1 tbsp
For the garnish:		
lemon		
parsley		

Place the onion, carrot, bouquet garni, seasoning, water and wine in a pan. Bring to the boil, then simmer for 20 minutes. Strain, pour the liquid into a pan, add the salmon, cover with a lid and poach for 15–20 minutes.

Meanwhile, make the sauce. Chop the shallots finely and place in a pan with the wine and 3 tablespoons of fish liquor. Reduce this until the shallots are tender and about 2 tablespoons of liquor remain. Whisk in the softened butter gradually, then the cream. Whisk this in without boiling. Season with salt.

Drain the salmon, skin, and arrange on a serving-dish. Place a spoonful of sauce on each cutlet and garnish with the lemon and parsley. Serve the rest of the sauce in a bowl or sauce-boat.

Truite Saumonée

Salmon trout or sea trout

Called sea trout by the fisherman and salmon trout by the fishmonger, this fish is undeniably one of the delights of summertime. In British fishmongers' shops it is most often seen in May and June, although the fishing season actually extends from March to September.

Truite Saumonée, Sauce Verte

Salmon trout with herb mayonnaise (serves 8)

This makes an attractive centre-piece for a buffet. Quantities are for a medium-sized salmon trout and can be adjusted as necessary.

	Imperial	American
1 salmon trout (1.5 kg)	$3\frac{1}{4}$ lb	$3\frac{1}{4}$ lb
For the court bouillon:		
2 litres water	4 pt	9 cups
300 ml white wine	$\frac{1}{2}$ pt	$1\frac{1}{4}$ cups
1 onion		
2 carrots		
1 stick celery		
a bouquet garni		
6 peppercorns		
salt		
300 ml Sauce Verte (*see page 31*)	$\frac{1}{2}$ pt	$1\frac{1}{4}$ cups
For the garnish:		
$\frac{1}{2}$ cucumber		
500 g tomatoes	1 lb	1 lb
4 lemon baskets		
finely chopped herbs		

Place all the ingredients for the court bouillon in a pan, cover with a lid and simmer gently for 30 minutes. Allow to cool. Clean the fish as shown on pages 66–67. Wrap it in greaseproof paper, foil or muslin. Pour the liquid into a fish-kettle or large roasting-pan, add the fish and cover with a lid or foil. Bring slowly to simmering point, then simmer very gently for 35–45 minutes. Allow the fish to cool in the liquid. Drain well and remove the skin.

Make the Sauce Verte. To prepare the garnish, slice the cucumber, arrange the slices on a wire rack and sprinkle with a little salt. Allow to drain for about 30 minutes. Rinse off the salt before using. Skin the tomatoes. Cut 4 of them in half, remove the pulp carefully, chop roughly and season.

To make a lemon basket, firstly roll the lemon on its side to determine the flattest possible base. If necessary, remove a very thin slice of peel to enable it to sit firm. With the point of a small sharp knife, cut through the rind along the top of the lemon, on either side of a small strip which will form the handle. Continue each cut from the pointed to the stem end. Then cut along the length of each lemon just above the middle. Carefully enlarge these cuts to remove a wedge from each side. Using a grapefruit knife, remove all the flesh from inside the rest of the lemon and from under the handle. With a small pair of scissors, vandyke the edge of the basket (cut the edge into small decorative points). Fill the lemon baskets with the chopped tomato and decorate with the herbs. Place 2 lemon baskets at each end of an oval serving-dish. Slice the remaining tomatoes thinly.

Lift the fish carefully onto the serving-dish. Coat with the sauce and decorate the dish with the sliced tomato and cucumber.

Shellfish

Crabe

Crab

Fresh crabs are available all the year round, but are at their best in the summer. Buy one which is fresh, and relatively heavy for its size.

Crabe Garni au Fenouil

Hot crab with fennel (serves 1–2)

	Imperial	American
1 medium crab		
25 g butter	1 oz	2 tbsp
$\frac{1}{2}$ onion, finely chopped		
1 tsp plain flour	1 tsp	1 tsp
2 tbsp white wine	2 tbsp	2 tbsp
1 tbsp double cream	1 tbsp	1 tbsp
2 tsp chopped fennel	2 tsp	2 tsp
salt and pepper		
25 g Gruyère cheese	1 oz	$\frac{1}{2}$ cup

Shellfish

How to Prepare a Crab

3. Just behind the eyes you find the bony stomach sac. Remove this and discard it.

1. Separate the two halves by pressing on the tail end and opening it sideways.

4. All the rest of the flesh can be eaten. Using the handle of a teaspoon, loosen the flesh under the shell and scoop it into a bowl.

2. Take out and discard the 'dead men's fingers' or gills.

5. If you are planning to use the shell, tap around the 'false' shell line and lift off the inner section. Scrub the shell thoroughly.

6. Hold each leg firmly in turn and twist to remove.

9. Crack the large claws, using a kitchen weight or a clean hammer.

7. The body contains white meat. Cut it in half, using firm pressure on a heavy knife.

10. Lift off the pieces of shell and separate the flesh.

8. Scoop out the white meat, using a skewer to get into the hollows of the body. Discard all shell.

11. Crack the small legs, using claw crackers or a weight. Remove shell and scrape out the flesh. Reserve the tips for garnishing.

Prepare the crab as shown on pages 82–83. Melt the butter, add the onion and cook until transparent. Add the flour and cook for 1 minute, then stir in the wine and cream. Bring to the boil, stirring all the time, and cook for 3–4 minutes. Add the crab meat and fennel and season to taste. Fill the shell with this mixture, sprinkle with the cheese and brown under a hot grill.

Crabe Omaha

Crab salad (serves 4–6)

	Imperial	American
1 medium *or* large crab		
4 tomatoes		
½ cucumber		
salt and pepper		
2 hard-boiled eggs		
2 tbsp Mayonnaise	2 tbsp	2 tbsp
(*see page 30*)		
Tabasco sauce, *or* tomato		
purée *and* cayenne pepper		
1 tbsp chilli vinegar	1 tbsp	1 tbsp
1 tbsp chopped tarragon	1 tbsp	1 tbsp
2 tsp made mustard	2 tsp	2 tsp
1 tbsp double cream	1 tbsp	1 tbsp

To finish:
1 lettuce

Prepare the crab as shown on pages 82–83. Skin and pip the tomatoes and chop them roughly. Do not skin the cucumber, but cut it in half, remove the seeds, then cut into small dice. Sprinkle with salt and allow to drain for 20 minutes. Rinse off the salt before using. Chop the crab meat and eggs and mix them well together. Place the mayonnaise in a large bowl with the Tabasco, vinegar, tarragon, mustard and cream. Season, and blend together. Stir in the fish mixture, tomato and cucumber. Line a glass bowl with lettuce leaves and pile the crab mixture in the centre.

Tante Marie tip:
If you serve this for a buffet party, scrub the crab shell thoroughly and brush the back of the shell with oil. Use this to decorate a flat serving-dish and arrange the salad around it.

Crabe Garni au Fenouil.

Homard

Lobsters

Lobsters are delicious but must be cooked gently, since shellfish can be tough if overdone. To prepare the lobster, cut it in half lengthways and remove the stomach sac from the head. Take out the black line of the intestine which runs down the length of the body, and the gills, often known as 'dead men's fingers'. The rest is all edible.

Homard à la Thermidor

Lobster Thermidor (serves 2)

	Imperial	American
1 lobster (about 750 g)	$1\frac{1}{2}$ lb	$1\frac{1}{2}$ lb
65 g butter	$2\frac{1}{2}$ oz	5 tbsp
1 tbsp oil	1 tbsp	1 tbsp
salt and pepper		
2 shallots, finely chopped		
150 ml dry white wine	$\frac{1}{4}$ pt	$\frac{2}{3}$ cup
300 ml Sauce Béchamel	$\frac{1}{2}$ pt	$1\frac{1}{4}$ cups
(see page 27)		
1 tbsp chopped chervil and tarragon	1 tbsp	1 tbsp
1 heaped tsp made mustard	1 tsp	1 tsp
25 g Parmesan cheese, grated	1 oz	$\frac{1}{4}$ cup

Cut the lobster in half from head to tail. Remove all meat from the shells and claws and cut the tail flesh into dice.

Melt 25 g (1 oz/2 tbsp) of butter with the oil in a pan. Add the lobster meat and heat through. Season to taste. Remove from the pan and put on one side. Add the shallot to the pan with more butter as needed, and soften it gently. Add the wine, increase the heat to reduce it by half, stir in the Sauce Béchamel and add the herbs and mustard. Taste and adjust the seasoning. Remove from the heat and whisk in the remaining butter gradually. Spread a layer of this sauce in the bottom of the lobster shells, then arrange the lobster meat on top. Cover again with the rest of the sauce. Sprinkle with the cheese and brown under a hot grill, or in the top of a hot oven, Mark 7 (220°C/425°F). Serve at once.

Top: Ingredients for Homard à la Thermidor.
Bottom: Homard à la Thermidor.

Coquilles St Jacques

Scallops

Fresh scallops can be available in Britain from about November to April. Wash them well to remove sand, and remove all black parts. The orange coral is delicious and is cooked with the white meat.

1. Fork the rice into a lightly oiled ring mould.

2. Pat it down gently.

Couronne de Coquilles St Jacques

Creamy scallop ring (serves 4)

	Imperial	American
175 g long grain rice	6 oz	$\frac{3}{4}$ cup
1 clove garlic		
6 large scallops,		
or 225 g small ones	8 oz	8 oz
4 tbsp white wine	4 tbsp	4 tbsp
a slice of onion		
a slice of carrot		
a bouquet garni		
40 g butter	$1\frac{1}{2}$ oz	3 tbsp
40 g plain flour	$1\frac{1}{2}$ oz	$\frac{1}{3}$ cup
225 ml milk	$7\frac{1}{2}$ fl oz	1 cup
1 tbsp tomato purée	1 tbsp	1 tbsp
4 tbsp double cream	4 tbsp	4 tbsp
4 tbsp sherry	4 tbsp	4 tbsp
salt, pepper, paprika and		
cayenne pepper		

For the garnish:
lemon and parsley

Wash the rice, then cook in boiling salted water with the clove of garlic until just tender. Drain, remove the garlic and rinse the rice under hot water. Drain thoroughly. Place in a heatproof dish to dry in a low oven for 30 minutes.

Wash the scallops and cut them into pieces. Place in a pan with the wine, onion, carrot and bouquet garni and poach gently for 5–7 minutes. Remove the onion, carrot and bouquet garni.

To make the sauce, melt the butter in a pan, add the flour and cook for 2–3 minutes. Remove from the heat and stir in the milk and the liquor in which the scallops were cooked. Bring to the boil, stirring all the time, then simmer for 5 minutes. Add the tomato purée, cream, sherry, seasoning, paprika and cayenne pepper. Taste and adjust the seasoning. Butter a ring mould and press the cooked rice lightly into it, using a fork. Turn out the rice ring onto a round serving-dish and place the scallops in the centre. Fill the centre of the mould with the sauce and pour the remainder around the edge or hand it separately. Garnish with the lemon and parsley.

3. Turn out onto a plate.

4. The finished Couronne de Coquilles St Jacques, garnished with lemon and parsley.

Coquilles St Jacques à la Nantaise

Nantes scallops (serves 4)

	Imperial	American
4 large scallops,		
or 225 g small scallops	8 oz	8 oz
150 ml white wine	$\frac{1}{4}$ pt	$\frac{2}{3}$ cup
a slice of carrot		
a slice of onion		
$\frac{1}{2}$ bayleaf		
2 peppercorns		
75 g mushrooms	3 oz	3 oz
40 g butter	$1\frac{1}{2}$ oz	3 tbsp

For the Sauce Vin Blanc:

25 g butter	1 oz	2 tbsp
25 g plain flour	1 oz	3 tbsp
300 ml fish stock	$\frac{1}{2}$ pt	$1\frac{1}{4}$ cups
(*see page 35*)		
1 egg yolk		
1 tbsp double cream	1 tbsp	1 tbsp
salt and pepper		

Cut the scallops from their shells, wash them well and remove the black parts. Slice the white flesh into rounds and cut the coral into two or three pieces.

Pour the wine into a pan and add the scallops, carrot, onion, bayleaf and peppercorns. Poach gently for 5 minutes, then remove the scallops and reduce the liquor in which they were cooked to half its original quantity.

Slice the mushrooms. Melt the butter in a small pan and add the mushrooms. Cover with greaseproof paper and a lid and cook over a gentle heat until the mushrooms are soft.

To make the sauce, melt the butter in a small pan. Remove from the heat and stir in the flour. Replace over the heat and cook for 2–3 minutes, stirring all the time. Strain on the fish stock and the scallop liquor, bring to the boil, stirring well, then simmer for 5 minutes. Beat the egg yolk with the cream and add this to the sauce. Whisk it in and reheat without boiling. Taste and adjust the seasoning.

Divide the scallops between four well-scrubbed shells and spoon the sliced mushrooms over. Coat with the sauce and glaze quickly under a hot grill.

Tante Marie tip:
Muscadet is the wine for both cooking scallops and for serving with them in this part of France.

Moules

Mussels

When you are planning to use mussels, buy them the day before they are needed. Put them in a bucket of sea water, or fresh water with a little salt added. Mix in a rounded tablespoon of flour. The mussels will feed on this and become plump and tender. In the process they also clean themselves of sand.

Any broken mussels must be discarded. If you have one which is open, give it a sharp tap. If it does not close, then the mussel is dead and must not be used as it could cause food poisoning.

When you are ready to cook the mussels, wash them very well in several changes of cold water. Scrape off the barnacles with an old knife and also scrape off the beard of the mussel, i.e. the black threads which you see on the flat hinge side of the shell. When you have finished, cook them immediately.

Mussels should be in good supply in Britain from early autumn to early spring.

Moules à la Marinière

Mussels in wine (serves 3–4)

	Imperial	American
2 kg mussels	4 lb	4 lb
2 shallots, finely chopped		
1 onion, finely chopped		
50 g butter	2 oz	$\frac{1}{4}$ cup
a bouquet garni made with 6 parsley stalks and sprigs of thyme		
150 ml dry white wine	$\frac{1}{4}$ pt	$\frac{2}{3}$ cup
black pepper		
finely chopped parsley		

Prepare the mussels as described above. Place the shallots, onion, butter, bouquet garni, wine, a sprinkling of pepper and the mussels in a large strong pan. Cover with a lid. Shake the pan over a good heat for 5 minutes or until all the mussels are open. Remove them and pile up in warmed individual bowls. Pour over the liquor in which they were cooked and sprinkle generously with the parsley. Serve at once.

Moules à la Marinière.

Calmar ou Encornet

Squid

Squid are known as calmar or encornet in France. In Britain they are available either fresh or frozen. Select medium or small ones. If they are large, weighing over 500 g (1 lb) each, they are inclined to be tough.

To prepare for cooking:

1. Pull the head and tentacles away from the tail section.

2. The ink sac is found in the soft part of the body attached to the head. Look for this and remove it. The sac is used in some recipes.

3. Cut the tentacles away from just above the eyes. Keep the tentacles, but discard the rest of the eye and internal body section.

4. There is a small round cartilage near the base of the tentacles. Squeeze out and discard.

5. Inside the tail there is a thin flat icicle-like cartilage. Discard this too.

6. Tear the fins from the tail and keep ready to use.

7. Remove as much as possible of the thin pinkish membrane from the tail, fins and tentacles. Rinse the squid well. Unless it is going to be stuffed whole, cut the end off the sac so that you can wash the inside easily. The squid is now ready to cook.

Calmar à l'Armoricaine

Squid Armorica (serves 4–6)

Armorica is the old name for Brittany. Homard à l'Armoricaine is a traditional speciality of the Breton fishermen. In this recipe squid is cooked in a similar way.

	Imperial	American
1 kg squid	2 lb	2 lb
2 tbsp oil	2 tbsp	2 tbsp
25 g butter	1 oz	2 tbsp
1 carrot, grated		
2 shallots, finely chopped		
1 onion, finely chopped		
1 clove garlic		
a bouquet garni with a sprig of tarragon		
3–4 tbsp tomato purée	3–4 tbsp	3–4 tbsp
a pinch each of saffron, cayenne pepper and curry powder		
salt and pepper		
300 ml dry white wine	$\frac{1}{2}$ pt	$1\frac{1}{4}$ cups
1 tbsp brandy	1 tbsp	1 tbsp
1–2 tbsp double cream (*optional*)	1–2 tbsp	1–2 tbsp

For the saffron rice:

225 g long grain rice	8 oz	1 cup
a pinch of saffron		

Prepare the squid as above. Cut into rings, rinse well and drain. Heat the oil and butter, add the squid and sauté quickly until just set. Remove the squid and add the carrot, shallot, onion and crushed garlic. Cover with a lid and cook gently over a low heat for 5 minutes. Add the bouquet garni, tomato purée, saffron, cayenne pepper, curry powder and seasoning. Stir in the wine and brandy. Replace the squid and simmer gently, uncovered, for 45 minutes or until tender.

Meanwhile, wash the rice, then cook with the saffron in plenty of boiling salted water for 15–20 minutes or until tender. Drain well in a colander. Place in a buttered casserole, cover with a lid and keep warm in a slow oven, Mark $\frac{1}{2}$ (120°C/250°F), until required.

Add the cream to the squid mixture, taste and season. Serve with the saffron rice.

Meat

One of the nicest things about French meat cookery is the wide variety of flavours you can produce from classic or country recipes in which local ingredients have a great influence. The local wine or cider adds its own special character. Côtes de Porc aux Pruneaux from the Loire and Côtes de Porc à la Vallée d'Auge from Normandy are good examples.

In the south, tomatoes and olives give a distinctive flavour to dishes from Provence and the surrounding regions. Paupiettes de Boeuf à la Vauclusienne conjure up images of sultry heat and magnificent scenery.

Veal is a popular meat cooked in many ways. Blanquette de Veau is a traditional recipe, while Escalope de Veau à la Viennoise is a country dish from Austria which the French have elaborated into a classic one of their own.

Lamb from the salt marshes of Brittany has its own special flavour. It may be roasted with a simple garnish as in Carré d'Agneau aux Courgettes, or combined with rosemary and garlic as in Gigot d'Agneau au Romarin. Cutlets, noisettes, stews and braises all provide variety. In the south, young goat is often cooked and served in a similar way to lamb.

Charolais cattle are a feature of the countryside. The flesh has an excellent flavour and there are recipes to suit all occasions. Recipes which the French housewife might prepare for her family include l'Estouffat Gascon, Pot-au-Feu or Boeuf Braisée. Steaks are always popular, whether served with a classic garnish, or grilled in the open air with a sprinkling of herbs on the embers to scent the air and flavour the meat.

French meat cookery embraces all methods of cooking, and recipes which can be served in many different ways. There is always a recipe to inspire the cook and delight her family or guests.

Le Boeuf
Beef

For good flavour and tenderness, beef is usually hung for 7–10 days after slaughter. The colour of the flesh will depend on the breed of the animal and various other factors. The rules regarding this vary considerably these days. However, the meat should have a good quantity of marbling, i.e. there should be fine fatty streaks in the flesh and the fat should be creamy white. The fat on older animals and some dairy breeds is usually a darker yellow. A side of beef weighs 100–200 kg (200–400 lb). Because of the weight and size of the carcase, it is cut into two to facilitate handling. A hindquarter weighs approximately 50–100 kg (100–200 lb), and a forequarter weighs approximately 45–70 kg (90–140 lb). The size of the carcase also means that each cut is much larger than is needed for normal domestic uses and so the housewife, unless buying meat for the freezer, buys the weight she requires.

HINDQUARTER
Jambe de Derrière (*Leg of beef*)
This is the lower part of the leg below the knee. It contains thick sinews, which need to be cut out, and a large amount of connective tissue. It therefore needs long, slow cooking, such as stewing. It is also used for clarification of consommé.

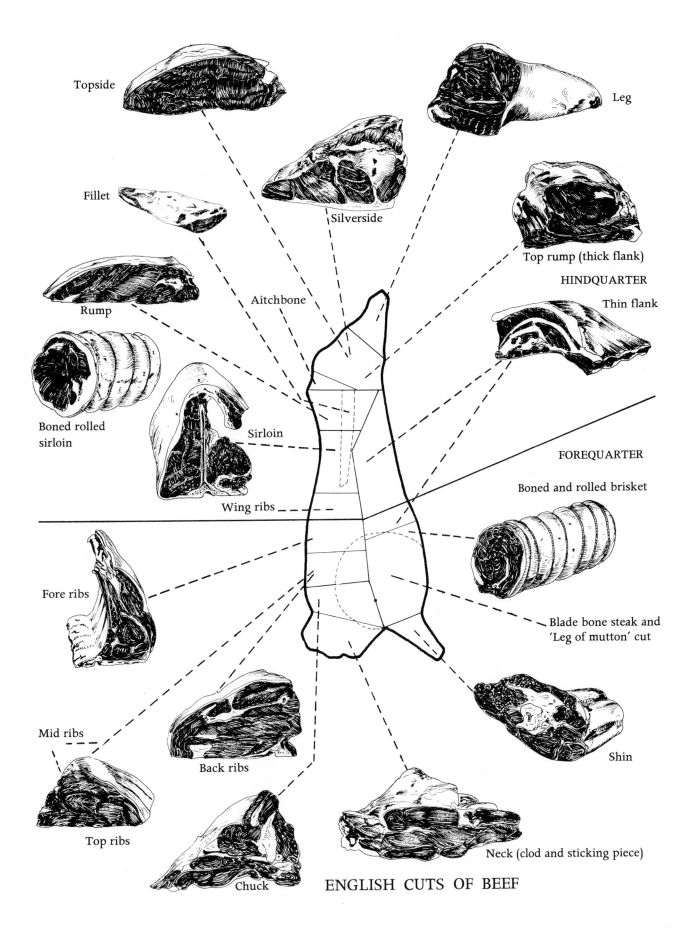

Topside

Leg

Fillet

Silverside

Top rump (thick flank)

Rump

HINDQUARTER

Aitchbone

Thin flank

Boned rolled
sirloin

Sirloin

FOREQUARTER

Boned and rolled brisket

Wing ribs

Fore ribs

Blade bone steak and
'Leg of mutton' cut

Mid ribs

Back ribs

Shin

Top ribs

Chuck

Neck (clod and sticking piece)

ENGLISH CUTS OF BEEF

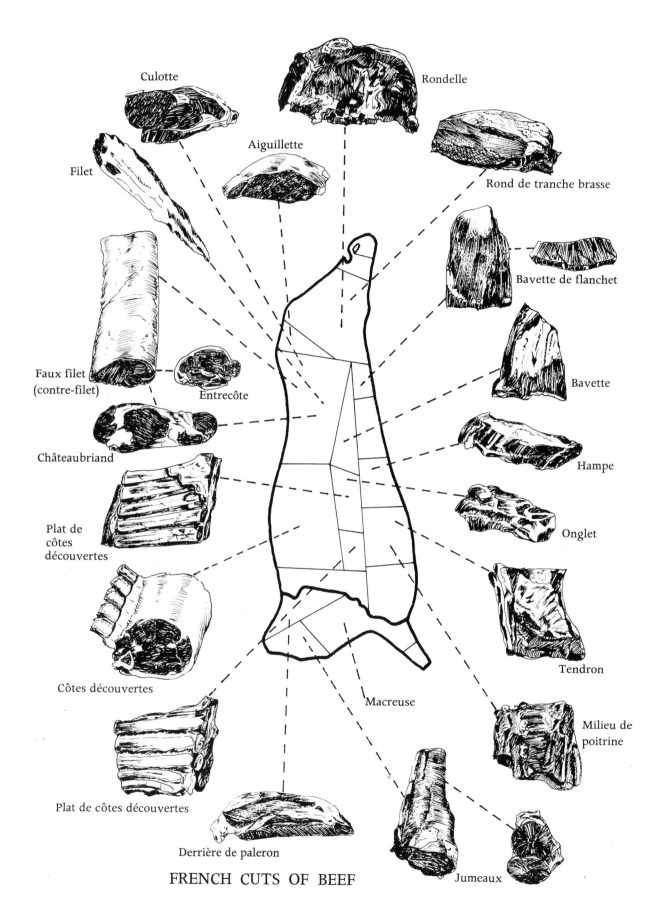

Culotte

Rondelle

Aiguillette

Filet

Rond de tranche brasse

Bavette de flanchet

Faux filet
(contre-filet)

Entrecôte

Bavette

Châteaubriand

Hampe

Plat de
côtes
découvertes

Onglet

Côtes découvertes

Tendron

Macreuse

Milieu de
poitrine

Plat de côtes découvertes

Derrière de paleron

Jumeaux

FRENCH CUTS OF BEEF

Tendre de Tranche, Rondelle, Gîte à la Noix (*Topside*, *Silverside* and *Top rump*)

These three joints are all cut from the upper part of the leg.

Tendre de Tranche (*Topside*)

This cut lies down the inside of the leg. When the butcher puts the whole leg on the block, this cut is uppermost and, for this reason, is called topside. It is the best cut from the leg and is suitable for roasting, braising and stewing. It can also be boiled – see Pot-au-Feu (page 97).

It is usually cut into two or three down the length and wrapped in extra fat to keep it moist during cooking. It can then be cut into smaller joints to suit the housewife.

Rondelle (*Silverside*)

This cut lies behind the topside, on the outside of the leg. It gets its name from the silver sheath which covers one side. This is also divided down the length and cut into smaller joints. It can be roasted, braised or boiled. The grain of the meat has an open texture which enables it to absorb brine easily. For this reason, it is often pickled in brine and boiled as salt beef in Britain.

Gîte à la Noix (*Top rump*; also known as *thick flank*)

This comes from the front of the leg. It can be roasted, braised or stewed.

Aiguillette (*Aitchbone*)

A coarse-grained cut of meat, sold in some areas as a joint for roasting or braising.

Culotte; also known as **Romsteck** when sliced (*Rump*)

See Steaks (page 99).

L'Aloyeau; also known as **Contre-filet** when boned (*Sirloin*)

A tender succulent cut which can be cooked on the bone or boned and rolled. It is a first class roasting joint. (See also Steaks – page 99.)

Côtes d'Aloyeau (*Wing ribs*)

These are the first three ribs. The meat is very tender and sweet and makes a prime roasting joint. It can also be cut into steaks (see page 99).

Bavette de Flanchet (*Thin flank*)

Thin flank is the under-belly of the carcase. It is suitable for stewing but the quality is rather poor. It is often made into sausages. (See also Skirt.)

FOREQUARTER

Côtes de Premier (*Fore ribs*)

These are the four ribs next to the wing ribs. They have a little more fat, but are tender and have a good flavour and are suitable for roasting.

Côtes Découvertes (*Mid ribs*)

Sometimes they are referred to as top, back and flat ribs (plat de côtes découvertes). The meat is lean but slightly coarser than the fore ribs and is therefore more suitable for braising, pot-roasting or stewing.

Côtes de Collier (*Chuck ribs*)

These provide good quality stewing steak.

Paleron, Jumeaux and Macreuse (*Clod* and *sticking piece*)

This can be used for stewing but, because it is the neck, where the animal is bled, it is a rather bloody joint and not often seen. It can be minced or made into sausages.

Poitrine (*Brisket*)

The front part of the belly. It is often pickled in brine and boiled, or it can be pot-roasted.

Bavette de Flanchet (*Thin flank*)

See Hindquarter (above).

'Leg of Mutton' cut and blade bone

These first-class stewing steaks are cut from the front leg. They are typically English cuts of meat and there is no French equivalent.

Jambe de Devant (*Shin*)

This is similar to leg of beef but is cut from the front leg.

Bavette (*Skirt*)

Although in France this is also called bavette, it is a much better quality than thin flank (bavette de flanchet) and comes from the internal connective muscles. It has a particularly coarse grain but is very good for stewing and has an excellent flavour.

Stewing

Chuck, blade bone and leg of mutton are all good stewing cuts. Make sure the meat is lean and marbled. Allow 100 g (4 oz) prepared meat or approximately 125 g (5 oz) untrimmed meat per person.

Carbonnade de Boeuf à la Flamande

Flemish beef stew (serves 4)

Dishes called à la Flamande are traditionally French in spite of their name. They come from the north-eastern part of France and, made with beer, are typical of the homely cooking from that area.

	Imperial	American
750 g chuck *or* blade bone steak	1½ lb	1½ lb
50 g butter *or* dripping	2 oz	¼ cup
750 g onions, thinly sliced	1½ lb	1½ lb
1 tbsp brown sugar	1 tbsp	1 tbsp
1 tbsp seasoned flour	1 tbsp	1 tbsp
1 clove garlic		
600 ml brown ale	1 pt	2½ cups
salt and pepper		

Trim the meat and cut into 2½ cm (1 in) cubes. Heat the butter in a heavy pan and add the onions and brown sugar. Cook until they are lightly browned then remove from the pan. Toss the meat in the seasoned flour. Reheat the butter and fry the meat until it is sealed and brown. Return the onions to the pan and add the crushed garlic. Pour on the beer, season, bring to simmering point and cover with greaseproof paper and a lid. Cook in a moderate oven, Mark 4 (180°C/350°F), for 2½–3 hours or until the meat is tender.

Remove the meat from the pan and place on a hot dish. Bring the sauce to the boil and allow it to reduce by about one-third. Pour over the meat and serve.

Sauté de Boeuf au Chinon

Chinon beef casserole (serves 4)

A savoury beef casserole which takes its name from Chinon in the Loire Valley. The local red wine is used in this area for cooking the dish but any other medium dry red wine can be substituted with pleasing results.

	Imperial	American
750 g chuck steak	1½ lb	1½ lb
300 ml red Chinon wine	½ pt	1¼ cups
150 ml water	¼ pt	⅔ cup
1 carrot, diced		
1 onion, sliced		
6–8 peppercorns		
a bouquet garni		
40 g dripping	1½ oz	3 tbsp
10–12 button onions		
2 tbsp plain flour	2 tbsp	2 tbsp
1 tsp tomato purée	1 tsp	1 tsp
1 clove garlic		
salt and pepper		
100 g mushrooms	4 oz	4 oz
2 slices bread		
25 g butter	1 oz	2 tbsp
oil		
chopped parsley		

The day before making this dish the meat is marinaded to flavour and tenderise it. Trim the meat and cut into about 2½ cm (1 in) cubes. Place these in a bowl with the wine, water, carrot and onion. Add the peppercorns and bouquet garni. Leave in a cool place to soak. Turn over once or twice.

At the end of this time lift out the meat and vegetables. Discard the peppercorns and keep the liquid and bouquet garni.

Melt the dripping in a saucepan and brown the whole button onions, then remove them and brown the meat quickly, adding more fat if required. Reduce the heat and sprinkle in the flour. Stir until lightly browned, then add the liquid and vegetables from the marinade, the onions, bouquet garni, tomato purée and the clove of garlic crushed in a teaspoon of salt. Bring to the boil, stirring well, and simmer gently over a very low heat on the hob or put in a casserole in the oven at Mark 3 (160°C/325°F) for 2½ hours or until tender. Do not allow to boil fast. Fifteen minutes before the end of this time, add the mushrooms.

Cut the bread into crescent shapes to make croûtons. Heat the butter with sufficient oil to cover the bottom of the frying-pan and fry the bread on both sides until golden brown. Drain on kitchen paper and allow to get cold.

When the meat is tender, remove the bouquet garni. Place the meat on a serving-dish with the vegetables. Reduce the sauce if necessary then taste and season. Remove any grease with kitchen paper and pour the sauce over the meat. Garnish with the croûtons. Sprinkle with parsley.

Above: Ingredients for l'Estouffat Gascon, including slices of chuck steak – a cut ideal for stewing.
Below: L'Estouffat Gascon.

L'Estouffat Gascon

Gascon beef casserole (serves 6–8)

Red wine stews are always popular and this one cooked with haricot beans should prove a great favourite with all the family.

	Imperial	American
225 g haricot beans, soaked overnight	8 oz	1 cup
1 kg lean stewing steak, e.g. chuck steak	2 lb	2 lb
100 g streaky bacon	4 oz	4 oz
75 g lean ham	3 oz	3 oz
75 g dripping	3 oz	6 tbsp
10 button onions, peeled, or 2 larger onions, chopped		
3-4 cloves garlic		
600 ml red wine	1 pt	2½ cups
salt and pepper		
a bouquet garni		
3-4 tomatoes		
1 onion, finely chopped		
1-2 carrots, diced		
a little stock		

Drain the beans and place them in a pan of cold water. Bring to simmering point, and cook gently for 1¼ hours. Do not add salt as this tends to harden the beans.

Trim any fat or gristle from the meat and cut into moderate-sized cubes. Cut the bacon and the ham into short strips. Melt 50 g (2 oz/¼ cup) of dripping in a pan and add the bacon and ham. Cook for a couple of minutes then, when the fat is hot, add the beef and brown it well all over, keeping a good heat under the pan. Lower the heat and add the onions, crushed garlic, wine, seasoning and bouquet garni. Skin and pip the tomatoes, cut into shreds and add these too. Cover with a lid and cook gently for 1½ hours. Meanwhile, melt the rest of the dripping in a pan and fry the onion and carrot. When the beans have cooked, drain them and add them to the pan and stir with the vegetables.

When the beef has been cooking for 1½ hours stir in the bean and vegetable mixture. Add a little more stock if necessary and cook for another hour, or until the beans and meat are tender. Taste and add salt and pepper if required. Remove the bouquet garni and pile the stew into a hot casserole.

Paupiettes de Boeuf

Beef rolls

Thin slices of topside are the best. Slices of silverside, top rump or buttock steak can be used but the latter will require longer cooking time. Slices weighing 75 g (3 oz) are adequate for each person.

Paupiettes de Boeuf à la Vauclusienne

Vaucluse beef rolls (serves 4)

This dish comes from Vaucluse: a district in Provence in the south of France.

	Imperial	American
4 thin slices of topside _or_ **silverside (75 g each)**	3 oz	3 oz
1 clove garlic		
salt and pepper		
1 tbsp chopped parsley	1 tbsp	1 tbsp
a small sprig of thyme, chopped		
1 medium onion, finely chopped		
2 tbsp oil	2 tbsp	2 tbsp
2 slices ham, chopped		
3 tbsp white breadcrumbs	3 tbsp	3 tbsp
150 ml white wine	$\frac{1}{4}$ pt	$\frac{2}{3}$ cup
150 ml Sauce Tomate (_see page 33_)	$\frac{1}{4}$ pt	$\frac{2}{3}$ cup
a little arrowroot		
20 black olives		

Crush the clove of garlic with a little salt. Mix it with the chopped herbs and onion. Heat the oil in a pan, add the onion mixture and cook gently until the onion is soft. Add the ham and breadcrumbs. Season well. Spread this mixture on each steak, pressing it on well. Roll each steak up and tie with thin string at each end and in the centre.

Place the paupiettes in a pan with a little hot oil and brown on all sides. Pour in the wine and the Sauce Tomate, adding a little water if necessary, so that the paupiettes are sufficiently covered. Place a piece of greaseproof paper on top and cover with a lid. Cook in a moderate oven, Mark 4 (180°C/350°F), for $1\frac{1}{2}$–2 hours. At the end of this time, lift out the paupiettes carefully, remove the string and keep them hot. Remove the excess grease from the cooking liquor. Increase the heat and reduce the liquor thoroughly. (If liked, it can be thickened with a little arrowroot slaked in a spoonful of cold water.) Add the stoned olives and season well. Heat the sauce through. Place the paupiettes on a hot serving-dish. Pour over the sauce and serve very hot.

Tante Marie tip:
This dish is very satisfactory for freezing. Prepare completely but do not add the olives before freezing. These can be added after thawing, then reheated with the dish.

Braising and Boiling

Topside, silverside, top rump or top and back ribs are all suitable. The meat must be lean with plenty of marbling. Choose joints which are neat and compact in shape as these cook evenly. A joint weighing 1.5 kg (3½ lb) will feed 5-6 people. (Very small joints are uneconomic as they shrink too much during cooking.)

Pot-au-Feu

Boiled beef (serves 4–6)

This way of cooking beef is one of the mainstays of the French kitchen. Long slow cooking ensures that any cut can be made tender.

	Imperial	American
1.5–2 kg topside, silverside, top rump, or back or top ribs	3–4 lb	3–4 lb
a few beef bones		
giblets from 1 chicken		
salt		
a bouquet garni		
1 clove garlic		
4–6 peppercorns		
3–4 medium carrots		
2–3 medium turnips		
2 medium parsnips		
2 sticks celery		
2 leeks		

For serving:
freshly boiled potatoes, coarse salt, gherkins, horseradish sauce and mustard

Place the meat and bones in a large pan and add water to cover – about 4 litres (6½ pt/16 cups) (2 litres per 1 kg of meat) and 2 teaspoons of salt. Bring slowly to the boil and remove the scum. Reduce the heat, then turn it up to boil again. This will bring the scum to the top so that you can lift off the rest of it.

Add the bouquet garni, the whole clove of garlic and the peppercorns. Cover with a lid and simmer gently for 1 hour. Meanwhile, prepare the vegetables, leaving them whole. After the hour, add these and continue to simmer very gently for another 3½–4 hours or until the meat is extremely tender.

The soup course

Place some of the vegetables cut into dice in each soup bowl and pour over a ladleful of the bouillon. Put a slice of toasted French bread grilled with Gruyère cheese on each one.

The meat course

Lift the meat onto the dish and slice it either in the kitchen or at the table. Arrange the vegetables around it, adding some freshly boiled potatoes. Serve it with freshly ground sea salt, gherkins, creamy horseradish sauce and mustard.

It is very easy to cook for more than one meal with this dish. Any leftover bouillon can be used to make consommé, aspic or well-flavoured soups. The meat can be used cold, or hot in réchauffé dishes such as Pain de Boeuf or Rissoles.

Boeuf Braisé

Braised beef (serves 5–7)

This is an ideal method of cooking lean joints which are, perhaps, not tender enough for roasting. The flavour is superb and the dish needs little attention while it is cooking. Try it also with boned and rolled shoulder or leg of lamb or with veal, or a whole liver using white wine instead of red. The wine, of course, adds to the flavour and helps to tenderise the meat, but for economy a well-flavoured stock can be used with pleasing results.

	Imperial	American
1.5–2 kg topside *or* **top rump**	$3\frac{1}{2}$–4 lb	$3\frac{1}{2}$–4 lb
100 g piece of larding bacon	4 oz	4 oz
1 large onion		
2 carrots		
2 sticks celery		
1 leek		
25–50 g dripping *or* **butter**	1–2 oz	2–4 tbsp
600 ml stock,	1 pt	$2\frac{1}{2}$ cups
or **300 ml stock**	$\frac{1}{2}$ pt	$1\frac{1}{4}$ cups
and **300 ml red wine**	$\frac{1}{2}$ pt	$1\frac{1}{4}$ cups
a bouquet garni		
salt and pepper		

To finish:

1–2 tsp arrowroot	1–2 tsp	1–2 tsp
chopped parsley		

Cut the larding bacon into strips approximately 12 mm ($\frac{1}{4}$ in) square and 5 cm (2 in) long and place in iced water for 30 minutes. This stiffens the fat and makes it easier to use.

Remove all the fat around the meat and, with a larding needle, either thread the lardons down the length of the meat or loop them along the top.

Chop the vegetables. Heat the dripping or butter in a heavy pan or heatproof casserole and brown the meat all over. Remove from the pan and reduce the heat. Add the vegetables, cover with greaseproof paper and a lid and cook until they are tender and lightly coloured. (For white meats do not colour the vegetables.)

Replace the meat and add the stock, wine (if used), bouquet garni and seasoning. (Season sufficiently well to flavour the meat but do not overseason as the sauce will be reduced at the end of the cooking time.) Bring to the boil and place in a preheated oven, Mark 4 (180°C/350°F), for approximately 2–$2\frac{1}{2}$ hours or until the meat is tender.

When the meat is cooked, remove it from the pan and slice it evenly. Arrange down the centre of a large serving-dish, cover with greaseproof paper to prevent it drying out and keep hot.

Strain the braising liquor into a clean pan. To remove the excess fat from the surface, bring to the boil and move the pan slightly off the heat to force the resultant scum to one side. Skim this off with a large spoon. Repeat if necessary, to remove all the fat from the surface of the liquor.

The sauce can now be finished in either of the following ways:

(a) Reduce the sauce by boiling until it is thick and syrupy. Check the seasoning and pour over the meat; *or*

(b) Slake the arrowroot with a little water and add to the braising liquor. Bring to the boil, stirring all the time. Check the seasoning. Pour a little over the meat and serve the rest separately.

This dish is usually served with a selection of vegetables, e.g. button onions, peas, lozenges of French beans, carrots, mushrooms, new potatoes or Pommes de Terre Château. The vegetables are cooked separately and are then tossed in butter and arranged in decorative piles around the meat.

Steaks

Steaks must be prime cuts of meat so that they can be subjected to the fierce heat of grilling and frying and still be tender and succulent to eat. In any animal the muscles which do the most work are tough and contain a lot of sinew. Those which do little work are tender and these are the ones which are used for steaks. This is why stewing meats come mainly from the front part of the animal and the steaks from the centre and the back, i.e. the wing rib, sirloin, rump and fillet.

The names of steaks can vary according to custom and locality but the following definitions are those most generally used.

Sirloin steaks
These are tender and have a good flavour. They are cut from the sirloin and the wing rib. The fillet is removed and the meat is boned. The steaks are cut 2–3 cm ($\frac{3}{4}$–1 in) thick and weigh 175–275 g (6–10 oz).

In France this is sold as faux-filet. The same cut of meat trimmed for roasting is a contre-filet.

Entrecôte steaks
Entrecôte means 'between the ribs' and at one time was a slice of meat cut from between the bones on a wing rib. Nowadays, it is a slice from the sirloin or wing rib and is just another name for a sirloin steak.

Fillet steak is sometimes incorrectly sold as entrecôte as it is mistakenly interpreted 'below the ribs'.

Porterhouse and T-Bone steaks
These are cut from the unboned sirloin including the fillet and look like an outsize chop. They weigh 500 g–1.50 kg (1$\frac{1}{4}$–3 lb).

In some areas in Britain, porterhouse is also another name for a sirloin or entrecôte steak.

Rump steak
Rump steak is the cut of meat between the top of the leg and the sirloin. Because the muscles have been used more than the sirloin or fillet it has an exceptionally good flavour, but may not be quite as tender. The point end of each slice is the tenderest and tastiest.

It should be cut about 2.5 cm (1 in) thick to the weight you choose, usually 175–225 g (6–8 oz).

Fillet
The fillet is an internal muscle which lies under the bones of the sirloin and rump and for this reason is often called the undercut. Because of its position in the animal, it does little work and is therefore very tender.

A whole fillet weighs 1.75–2.75 kg (4–6 lb) and can be roasted or cooked 'en croûte' (wrapped in pastry in a similar way to Gigot en Croûte – see page 105).

Châteaubriand
This is cut from the thicker end of the fillet. It should be approximately 7.5 cm (3 in) thick and weigh 500–750 g (1$\frac{1}{4}$–1$\frac{3}{4}$ lb). It is usually cooked for 2 people.

Tournedos and fillet steaks

These are cut from the middle of the fillet.

Tournedos are trimmed of all sinew and fat. A thin piece of pork fat is wrapped around the outside and they are tied to keep a good shape whilst cooking. The string and fat are removed before serving.

They should be 3–4 cm (1$\frac{1}{2}$–1$\frac{3}{4}$ in) thick and weigh about 175 g (6 oz). Fillet steaks are untrimmed and weigh about 175–225 g (6–8 oz).

Minute steaks
These are thin slices of fillet or entrecôte steaks. They are cooked very quickly on both sides as their name suggests.

Filet mignon
A true filet mignon is the fillet from lamb. However, this is rarely obtainable and the tail end of the fillet of beef is used instead. It is used for flambé dishes.

Cooking methods and times
Whether grilling or frying, for good juicy results make certain that the grill is preheated for about 10 minutes or that the butter is sizzling hot in the frying-pan before starting to cook your steaks. The meat is then sealed immediately it comes in contact with the heat. This ensures that the juices remain in the meat so that it does not become dry.

When the steak is browned, turn it over and cook the other side in the same way. Then reduce the heat to cook it for as long as required.

The French maintain that the longer a good cut of meat is cooked, the tougher it is likely to become. The general taste in Britain is more conservative so that 'medium rare' steaks are cooked for longer than is normal anywhere in France.

French terms		2.5 cm (1 in)	3–4 cm (1¾ in)
		cooking times for each side	
bleu	very bloody	seared very quickly on both sides	
saignant (bloody)	very rare	½–1 min	1 min
à point	sealed well but still underdone to British taste	1–1½ min	2 min
bien cuit (well done)	well cooked on the outside, very red on the inside	2 min	3 min
très bien cuit	well cooked on the outside, red on the inside	3 min	4 min
English terms			
rare	sealed well, red on inside	1–4 min	2–5 min
medium rare	pink on the inside	5–6 min	7–8 min
well done	cooked right through	7–8 min	8–10 min

You will generally find that in France steaks are cut thinner and weigh less than British ones, and cooking times will vary according to the size and thickness of the steak.

Garnished Steak Dishes

Entrecôte Henri IV (*Henri IV sirloin steak*)
Fried entrecôte steak garnished with Pommes de Terre Pont Neuf, Sauce Béarnaise and watercress.

Tournedos à la Choron (*Choron fillet steak*)
Fried tournedos set on croûtes of fried bread, garnished with artichoke bases filled with peas, Pommes de Terre Noisette and Sauce Choron.

Steak Vert Pré (*Steak with straw potatoes*)
Entrecôte or rump steak grilled and garnished with Pommes de Terre Paille and watercress.

Steak à Cheval (*Steak with eggs*)
Entrecôte or rump steak grilled and served with one or two fried eggs on top of the steak.

Steak au Poivre (*Peppered steak*)
Rump steak coated in crushed peppercorns and fried in butter. The pan is déglaced with brandy. White wine and cream are added, heated through gently and the sauce poured over the steak.

Châteaubriand

Roast fillet steak (serves 2)

A special dinner dish for 2 people.

	Imperial	American
450–750 g piece of fillet steak	1–1½ lb	1–1½ lb
25–50 g butter	1–2 oz	2–4 tbsp
Pommes de Terre Château made with 500 g potatoes (*see page 179*)	1 lb	1 lb
Sauce Béarnaise (*see page 32*)		
1 bunch watercress		

Prepare the Pommes de Terre Château. While they are cooking, trim the fillet and tie to a neat shape. Heat the butter in a pan and fry the fillet well on all

1. Bard the steaks for Tournedos Rossini with strips of pork fat.

sides to brown and to seal in the juices. Then place it in a preheated oven, Mark 6 (200°C/400°F), for 15–20 minutes to finish cooking. The time will depend on the size and shape of the fillet. When cooked the meat should be rare, so you must allow a longer cooking time if you like your steak well done.

Make the Sauce Béarnaise. When the meat is cooked, slice it and arrange on a hot dish. Garnish with the Pommes de Terre Château and the watercress. Serve the Sauce Béarnaise separately.

Tournedos Rossini

Steak Rossini (serves 4)

This is one of the most luxurious ways of serving steak. It should be garnished with pâté de foie gras and truffle, but as these put the dish into the millionaire class you may prefer to use a less expensive pâté de foie and garnish the top with cooked mushrooms. It will nevertheless still be very good indeed.

	Imperial	American
4 tournedos, 3–4 cm thick	$1\frac{1}{2}$–$1\frac{3}{4}$ in	$1\frac{1}{2}$–$1\frac{3}{4}$ in
larding bacon *or* pork fat		
4 slices bread		
50 g butter	2 oz	$\frac{1}{4}$ cup
2 tbsp oil	2 tbsp	2 tbsp
75 g pâté de foie	3 oz	3 oz
300 ml Sauce Madère	$\frac{1}{2}$ pt	$1\frac{1}{4}$ cups
(*see page 29*)		
1 truffle, *or* 4 cooked mushrooms		

Trim the tournedos of all fat and gristle. Cut a strip of larding bacon *or* pork fat the same depth as the tournedos and long enough to tie around each piece of steak. Secure with string in a neat circular shape. Cut four circles of bread the same diameter as the steaks. Fry in the butter and oil until golden brown.

Cut the pâté into 4 slices. Fry the tournedos over a good heat allowing 2 minutes on each side. Remove the string and strips of fat from the steaks.

Arrange the croûtes on a serving-dish, place a tournedo on each and top with a slice of pâté. Coat each steak with hot Sauce Madère and hand the rest in a sauce boat. Garnish each one with a slice of truffle or a cooked mushroom.

2. When cooking the tournedos, turn them carefully with tongs so you do not pierce the meat and allow the juices to escape.

3. Tournedos Rossini.

L'Agneau

Lamb

British and New Zealand lamb is available in Britain. British lamb is at its best and cheapest from August to November and New Zealand from January to May. British lambs are larger and therefore the joints weigh more. The meat should be pinkish-red. New Zealand lamb sometimes has a slightly darker flesh. This is caused by storage during shipping but with the latest improved conditions it should look similar to British lamb. The fat on British lamb is creamy white, and on New Zealand lamb is a slightly darker colour. The fat on both should be firm.

Le Gigot (*Leg*)

A leg of British lamb will weigh 2.25–3.25 kg (5–7 lb) and a New Zealand leg 1.50–2.25 kg (3½–5 lb). Both can be cut in half to provide smaller joints (knuckle end and fillet end). Allow 280–350 g (10–12 oz) meat on the bone per person. This will give enough for a good portion each with some left over.

La Longe or le Filet d'Agneau (*Loin*)

This is the part of the carcase between the leg and the ribs. A complete loin consists of the chump and the loin and this can be cooked as one joint, or if large it can be cut into separate joints. The chump can also be cut into chops and the loin into chops or noisettes. (For cutting noisettes, see Noisettes d'Agneau Chasseur – page 108).

A saddle (la selle) is the two sides of the loin, chump and the tail left in one piece. The baron (le baron) is the whole hind section of the saddle with the legs. The loin is an ideal roasting joint and can be cooked on the bone or boned, stuffed and rolled. Noisettes are usually fried. Chops can be grilled or fried.

To make carving or boning easier ask your butcher to chine the joint for you, i.e. cut through the base of the bones near the spinal column.

The tough outer skin called the 'bark' should also be removed from joints or chops before cooking.

Approximate average weights

			Serves
LOIN			
British	1.75–2.25 kg	4–5 lb	5–6
New Zealand	1.50–2 kg	3–4 lb	4–5
CHUMP CHOPS			
British	225–275 g	8–10 oz each	
New Zealand	175–225 g	6–8 oz each	
LOIN CHOPS			
British	100–175 g	4–6 oz each	
New Zealand	75–100 g	3–4 oz each	
SADDLE			
British	4–5 kg	8–10 lb	10–12
New Zealand	2–3.50 kg	6–7 lb	8–10

Le Carré d'Agneau (*Best end of neck*)

Best end of neck consists of the ribs between the loin and the shoulder, and can also be cut into cutlets (côtelettes) (usually seven) or into noisettes. It is sometimes called a rack of lamb. A pair of best ends can be trimmed and tied together to form a guard of honour (Garde d'Honneur) or a crown roast (Couronne d'Agneau).

The best end is very suitable for roasting and, like loin, can be cooked on the bone or boned, stuffed and rolled. Cutlets can be grilled, fried or casseroled. The 'bark' must be removed and chining makes carving and boning easier.

Approximate average weights

			Serves
British	1–1.25 kg	2–2½ lb	3–4
New Zealand	500–800 g	1¼–1¾ lb	3

Cutlets weigh 75–150 g (3–5 oz) each. Allow 2 per person.

l'Epaule (*Shoulder*)

This can be cooked whole or cut into two smaller joints: the blade bone and the knuckle end. It can also be boned, stuffed and rolled. It is a good roasting or braising joint and the meat can be cut up and used for a stew such as Navarin d'Agneau Printanier. A shoulder is a very tender and sweet joint but it can be fatty. Your butcher will bone it for you provided you ask him in good time. Ask him to leave it untied so that you can cut out any excess fat and use the stuffing of your choice.

Approximate average weights

			Serves
British	1.75–2.75 kg	4–6 lb	6–7
New Zealand	1.50–1.75 kg	3½–4 lb	5–6

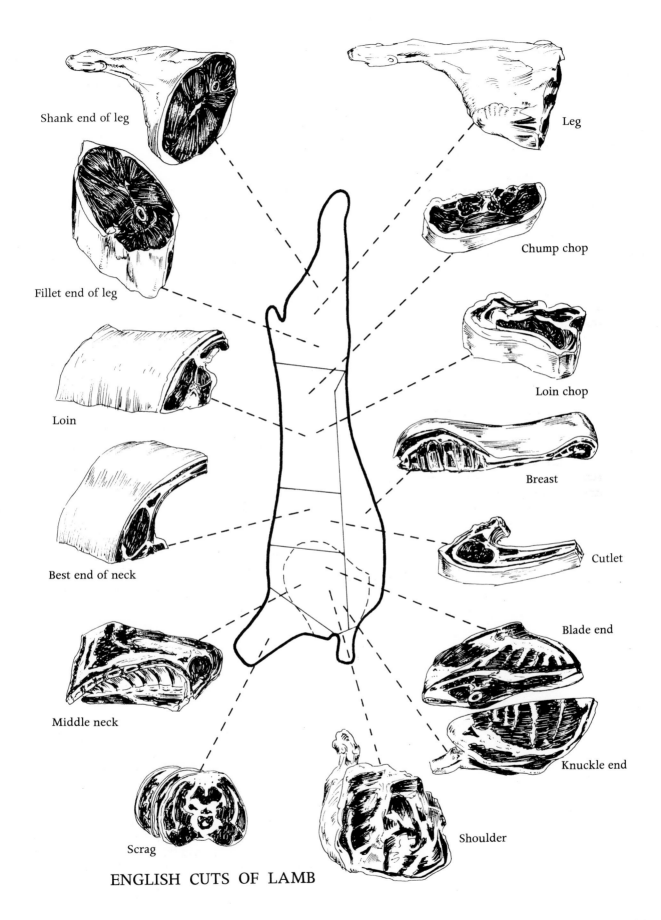

Shank end of leg

Leg

Fillet end of leg

Chump chop

Loin

Loin chop

Best end of neck

Breast

Cutlet

Middle neck

Blade end

Knuckle end

Scrag

Shoulder

ENGLISH CUTS OF LAMB

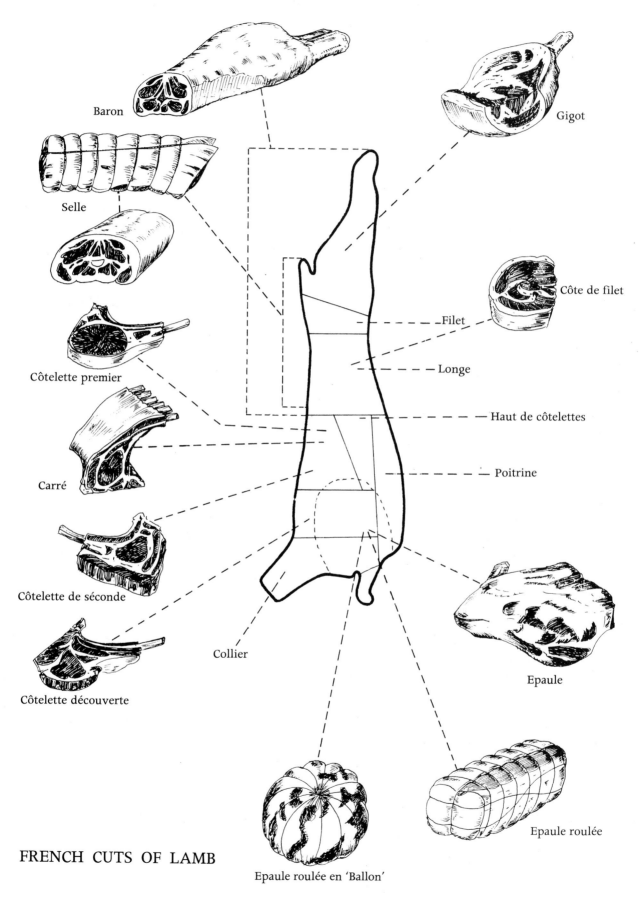

Baron

Gigot

Selle

Côtelette premier

Côte de filet

Carré

Filet

Longe

Haut de côtelettes

Côtelette de séconde

Poitrine

Côtelette découverte

Collier

Epaule

Epaule roulée

FRENCH CUTS OF LAMB

Epaule roulée en 'Ballon'

Les Côtelettes Découvertes, le Collier (*Middle neck and scrag*)

These cuts are used for stews or soups. The meat is tender but there is a large proportion of bone. The cut sold as fillet of lamb is the meat cut from the middle neck and scrag.

La Poitrine (*Breast*)

This is a fatty piece of meat but can be tasty if boned, stuffed and slow or pot roasted. If used for a stew, it is advisable to cook it the day before it is needed so that the fat will set on the surface and can be skimmed off quite easily.

Gigot en Croûte

Leg of lamb in pastry (serves 6)

One of the best ways to prepare a leg of lamb is to bake it en croûte. The meat retains its juices and becomes very tender inside the light crust of pastry. Flaky pastry is very good, but for perfection make your own puff pastry.

	Imperial	American
1.5 kg leg of lamb	3½ lb	3½ lb
50 g butter	2 oz	¼ cup
salt and pepper		
puff pastry *or* flaky pastry made with 350 g plain flour (*see page 208 or 210*)	12 oz	3 cups
1 egg for glazing		
Sauce Soubise (*see page 27*)		

Spread the butter over the meat and season well. Place in a roasting-pan and roast in a moderately hot oven, Mark 6 (200°C/400°F), for 30–40 minutes. Remove and allow to cool.

Make the pastry and place in the refrigerator to chill for at least 20 minutes. Roll out the pastry on a floured board. Put the meat in the centre of the pastry. Wrap the pastry round the meat and seal neatly, moistening the edges with beaten egg to ensure that it is perfectly sealed. From the trimmings of the pastry, cut leaves and crescents. Brush the pastry over with beaten egg. Arrange the leaves and crescents in a design and brush them with egg too. Place on a baking tray and cook in a hot oven, Mark 7 (220°C/425°F), for 20–30 minutes, then reduce the temperature to Mark 4 (180°C/350°F) and continue to bake so that it has 1¼ hours in all. If it tends to become too brown, cover with a piece of foil or buttered greaseproof paper.

Whilst it is cooking, make the Sauce Soubise.

To serve, lift the meat onto a hot serving-dish. Carve in the same way as an ordinary roast leg of lamb, serving some pastry with each portion. Hand the sauce separately.

Tante Marie tip:
If using puff pastry, start the cooking at Mark 8 (230°C/450°F).

Gigot d'Agneau au Romarin

Leg of lamb with rosemary (serves 6–8)

	Imperial	American
1 leg of lamb		
2 cloves garlic		
salt and pepper		
3 tbsp finely chopped parsley	3 tbsp	3 tbsp
2 tbsp fresh rosemary, *or* 2 tsp dried rosemary	2 tbsp / 2 tsp	2 tbsp / 2 tsp
3 tbsp olive oil	3 tbsp	3 tbsp
450 ml stock or water	¾ pt	1¾ cups
8 tomatoes		
2 green peppers		
2 tsp anchovy essence	2 tsp	2 tsp

Crush the garlic with 1 teaspoon salt, and mix with the parsley, rosemary and 1 tablespoon of the oil. With a small sharp knife, make some deep cuts in the thick part of the meat and spread the herb mixture into the cuts and over the surface.

Place in a roasting-pan with the stock or water and cook in a moderate oven, Mark 4 (180°C/350°F), for 35 minutes per 500 g (1 lb) plus 35 minutes over, basting frequently.

Cut the tomatoes in half and scoop out the pips. Remove the core and seeds from the peppers, cut into dice and blanch in boiling salted water for 2–3 minutes. Drain and refresh. Warm the rest of the oil in a pan and cook the peppers gently in this. Place the tomato halves in the oven and cook gently for about 5–10 minutes until tender. Fill with the green peppers.

Lift the meat onto a warm serving-dish. Add the

anchovy essence to the gravy and cook until it thickens slightly. Pour around the meat and garnish with the tomatoes.

Longe d'Agneau Persillé
Stuffed loin of lamb (serves 4–6)

A savoury parsley and garlic stuffing and topping makes this an extra special dish.

	Imperial	American
1 loin of lamb, boned		
3–4 tbsp chopped parsley	3–4 tbsp	3–4 tbsp
4–6 tbsp breadcrumbs	4–6 tbsp	4–6 tbsp
1 large clove garlic		
salt and pepper		
50 g butter,	2 oz	$\frac{1}{4}$ cup
or 25 g butter *and*	1 oz	2 tbsp
25 g dripping	1 oz	2 tbsp
2 tbsp French mustard	2 tbsp	2 tbsp
150 ml stock	$\frac{1}{4}$ pt	$\frac{2}{3}$ cup

Mix together the parsley, breadcrumbs, garlic crushed with a little salt and seasoning. Spread half of this mixture over the meat. Roll up and tie securely with string. Season the meat and place in a roasting-pan. Spread 25 g (1 oz/2 tbsp) of butter or dripping over the surface and roast in a very hot oven, Mark 8 (230°C/450°F), for the first 20 minutes. Reduce the temperature to Mark 6 (200°C/400°F) and continue to cook at this temperature for the required time, allowing 20 minutes per 500 g (1 lb) and 20 minutes over. Remove the joint from the oven 20 minutes before the end of the cooking time. Spread it thickly with the French mustard and cover it in the rest of the farce mixture. Place the remaining 25 g (1 oz/ 2 tbsp) butter in knobs on the top. Return to the oven to brown.

To serve, strain off the fat and leave the juices in the pan. Déglace the pan with the stock. Reheat and adjust the seasoning. Carve the meat into fairly thick slices and arrange, overlapping, down the centre of a hot serving-dish. Spoon over the gravy.

Tante Marie tip:
To make carving easier, remove the string before spreading the mustard on the meat.

Côtes d'Agneau Champvallon
Champvallon lamb chops (serves 4)

A tasty lamb hot-pot.

	Imperial	American
4 lamb chops from the chump or loin		
25 g butter	1 oz	2 tbsp
150 ml stock	$\frac{1}{4}$ pt	$\frac{2}{3}$ cup
150 ml white wine *or* dry cider	$\frac{1}{4}$ pt	$\frac{2}{3}$ cup
3 tsp tomato purée	3 tsp	3 tsp
1 onion, finely chopped		
salt and pepper		
2 tbsp chopped parsley	2 tbsp	2 tbsp
350 g potatoes, sliced	12 oz	2 cups

Trim most of the fat from the chops. Heat the butter in a frying-pan and, when it is sizzling hot, add the chops and brown them quickly on each side. Remove the chops from the pan and place them in a casserole. Pour off the excess fat. While the pan is still hot, pour in the stock, wine or cider and tomato purée and stir. Boil them together, then pour over the chops.

Sprinkle with the onion, seasoning and one tablespoon finely chopped parsley. Arrange the sliced potatoes in a layer on top. Cover with a lid and bake in a moderately hot oven, Mark 5 (190°C/375°F), for 1–1$\frac{1}{4}$ hours. Remove the lid for the last 20 minutes to allow the potatoes to brown.

Sprinkle with the rest of the parsley just before serving.

Tante Marie tip:
Use middle neck cutlets for economy. Remove the spinal cord, the gristle and fat at the top of each cutlet. Allow two per serving.

Côtelettes d'Agneau en Cuirasse
Lamb cutlets in armour (serves 4)

These cutlets are covered with a light crisp flaky pastry, so do not let the title mislead you!

	Imperial	American
4 lamb cutlets		
flaky pastry made with		
225 g plain flour	8 oz	2 cups
(*see pages 208–209*)		
50 g butter	2 oz	$\frac{1}{4}$ cup
100 g mushrooms	4 oz	4 oz
1 small onion		
2 shallots		
salt and pepper		
a pinch of nutmeg		
1 tbsp olive oil	1 tbsp	1 tbsp
4 thin slices ham		
1 egg for glazing		
300 ml Sauce Tomate	$\frac{1}{2}$ pt	$1\frac{1}{4}$ cups
(*see page 33*)		

Make the pastry and put aside to relax. Trim the cutlets and remove any excess fat. Melt half the butter in a frying-pan and fry the cutlets until brown on both sides. Put them aside to get cold.

Make the duxelle with the mushrooms: chop the mushrooms finely, squeeze them in kitchen paper so that as much of their moisture is extracted as possible. Finely chop the onion and shallots. Heat the oil and the remaining butter in a pan, add the onion and shallots and lightly brown. Then add the mushrooms, seasoning and nutmeg. Cook over a good heat, stirring all the time until all the moisture from the mushrooms has evaporated. Lift onto a plate to cool and then divide into eight. Cut each slice of ham into two.

Roll out the pastry thinly on a lightly floured board. Cut into eight squares and brush the edges with water. Place a slice of ham, one portion of the duxelle and a cutlet on each piece of pastry. Cover with another portion of the duxelle and slice of ham and finally the second piece of pastry. Seal well and trim to shape. Allow the bone to project. Knock up and flute the sides. Decorate each one with three leaves cut from the pastry trimmings. Brush over with beaten egg and bake in a hot oven, Mark 7 (220°C/425°F), for about 20 minutes. Serve hot accompanied by Sauce Tomate.

Côtelettes d'Agneau Dubarry
Dubarry lamb cutlets (serves 4)

A dish named Dubarry indicates that cauliflower is used as a main ingredient or garnish. It is named after Madame du Barry, the mistress of Louis XV.

	Imperial	American
4 or 8 lamb cutlets		
1 cauliflower		
salt and pepper		
40 g butter	$1\frac{1}{2}$ oz	3 tbsp
300 ml Sauce Mornay	$\frac{1}{2}$ pt	$1\frac{1}{4}$ cups
(*see page 27*)		
50 g cheese, grated	2 oz	1 cup
150 ml white wine	$\frac{1}{4}$ pt	$\frac{2}{3}$ cup

Wash the cauliflower and divide into florets. Cook in boiling salted water until tender.

While the cauliflower is cooking, trim the cutlets. Melt the butter in a frying-pan. When it is hot, add the cutlets and fry first on one side and then on the other for 7–8 minutes. When cooked, keep hot and retain the fat and juices in the pan.

Make the Sauce Mornay.

Drain the cauliflower well and arrange around a heatproof dish. Coat with the Sauce Mornay and sprinkle with the cheese. Brown under a hot grill.

Place the cutlets in the centre of the dish. Pour off all but 2 tablespoons of the fat and reheat. Déglace the pan with the wine, boil, season and pour over the cutlets.

Epaule d'Agneau aux Navets
Shoulder of lamb with turnips (serves 6)

Braising gives a good flavour and a moist joint with a marvellous sauce. A boned shoulder is a good cut of meat to use for this. It can be stuffed and either rolled and tied in a sausage shape, or en ballotine (tied in a round).

	Imperial	American
1 shoulder of lamb, boned		
100 g mushrooms	4 oz	4 oz
1 medium onion		
225 g sausagemeat	8 oz	8 oz
2–3 tbsp finely chopped parsley	2–3 tbsp	2–3 tbsp
salt and pepper		
150 ml stock	$\frac{1}{4}$ pt	$\frac{2}{3}$ cup
150 ml dry white wine	$\frac{1}{4}$ pt	$\frac{2}{3}$ cup
1 tsp arrowroot	1 tsp	1 tsp

For the garnish:

	Imperial	American
500 g small turnips	1 lb	1 lb
250 g small onions	8 oz	8 oz
350 g small carrots	12 oz	12 oz
50 g butter	2 oz	$\frac{1}{4}$ cup
finely chopped parsley		

Prepare the stuffing as follows: chop the mushrooms and onion finely and mix with the sausagemeat and parsley. Season very well. Spread this mixture inside the boned meat. Close the edges together and fasten securely with thin string. Place in a roasting-pan, add the stock and wine and cover with foil. Braise in a hot oven, Mark 6 (200°C/400°F), for 30 minutes per 500 g (1 lb), plus 30 minutes over. Thirty minutes before the end of the cooking time, remove the foil to allow the meat to brown.

Meanwhile, peel the turnips and onions and scrape or peel the carrots. If the turnips are large, cut them into barrel shapes the size of a large olive, or into dice. Place all three vegetables in separate pans of boiling salted water and cook until just tender. Remove and toss them through in melted butter, sprinkle with finely chopped parsley and season well.

Lift the meat onto a hot dish, remove the string and surround with the garnish of vegetables. Slake the arrowroot in a little water, skim the fat from the stock and add the arrowroot. Bring to the boil, then simmer for 1–2 minutes. Taste and season. Strain and serve the gravy separately.

Noisettes d'Agneau Chasseur
Hunter's lamb (serves 4)

Noisettes of lamb with a mushroom sauce.

	Imperial	American
750 g–1 kg best end of neck of lamb	1$\frac{3}{4}$–2 lb	1$\frac{3}{4}$–2 lb
25 g butter	1 oz	2 tbsp
1 clove garlic		
1 small onion, finely chopped		
100 g mushrooms, finely chopped	4 oz	4 oz
2 tsp plain flour	2 tsp	2 tsp
1 tsp tomato purée	1 tsp	1 tsp
4 tbsp white wine	4 tbsp	4 tbsp
150 ml stock	$\frac{1}{4}$ pt	$\frac{2}{3}$ cup
salt and pepper		
chopped parsley		
heart-shaped croûtons		

Remove the 'bark' from the meat and bone the best end. Cut off any excess fat and roll the meat up. Tie with string at 2.5 cm (1 in) intervals and cut the meat through, between each string.

Melt the butter in a frying-pan. When it is hot, add the meat and brown on both sides, then cook gently until tender (this should take 15–20 minutes).

Crush the garlic. Pour off any excess fat, leaving about 2 tablespoons in the pan, add the onions and cook until soft and golden brown. Add the mushrooms and cook for 1–2 minutes. Stir in the flour and mix well. Add the tomato purée, wine, stock and crushed garlic. Cook gently for 5 minutes. Taste and season and pour over the noisettes. Sprinkle with chopped parsley and arrange heart-shaped croûtons around the edge of the dish.

Right: Noisettes d'Agneau Chasseur, shown with the boned and rolled best end (right) ready to cut into slices.

Carré d'Agneau aux Courgettes

Best end of neck of lamb with courgettes (serves 3–4)

Tender courgettes provide a delicate contrast to the savoury filling in the lamb.

	Imperial	American
1 best end of neck of lamb, chined		
2 tbsp oil	2 tbsp	2 tbsp
1 onion, finely chopped		
3 cloves garlic		
1 lemon		
6 anchovy fillets		
salt and pepper		
450 g courgettes	1 lb	1 lb
300 ml stock	½ pt	1¼ cups
chopped parsley		

Heat the oil in a pan, add the onion and fry without browning. Crush the garlic with a little salt and add to the pan. Grate the yellow zest of the lemon and chop the anchovies. Add these as well.

Remove the 'bark' or skin from the meat, then bone it. Season and spread with the savoury onion filling. Roll up tightly and tie with string.

Place the meat in a roasting-pan with 1 tablespoon of oil and roast in a moderately hot oven, Mark 6 (200°C/400°F), for approximately 1 hour or until golden brown and tender. Baste from time to time.

Meanwhile, wash the courgettes, cut off the ends and cut into large sticks about 5 cm (2 in) in length. Cook in boiling salted water for 12 minutes or until tender. Drain well.

Ten minutes before the meat is cooked place the courgettes in the roasting-pan and baste with the meat juices.

To serve, carve the meat in slices and arrange down the centre of a platter. Surround with the courgettes.

Remove excess fat from the roasting-pan and pour in the stock. Boil well to reduce. Taste and season. Pour over the meat and, just before serving, sprinkle lavishly with chopped parsley.

Navarin Printanier

Spring stew (serves 4)

This appetising brown lamb stew with spring vegetables is a complete meal in itself. Shoulder, best end of neck or fillet can be used for this dish.

	Imperial	American
1 kg lamb on the bone,	2 lb	2 lb
or 600 g lean boneless lamb	1¼ lb	1¼ lb
¼ tsp sugar	¼ tsp	¼ tsp
40 g dripping	1½ oz	3 tbsp
40 g plain flour	1½ oz	⅓ cup
1 clove garlic		
1 tsp tomato purée	1 tsp	1 tsp
a bouquet garni		
salt and pepper		
600 ml stock	1 pt	2½ cups
125 ml dry white wine	¼ pt	⅔ cup
350 g small turnips	12 oz	12 oz
250 g small onions	8 oz	8 oz
250 g small new carrots	8 oz	8 oz
500 g small new potatoes	1 lb	1 lb
100 g French beans	4 oz	4 oz
100 g shelled peas	4 oz	4 oz

Cut the meat into cutlets or into moderately large pieces. Sprinkle with the sugar. Melt the dripping in a heavy pan. When hot, add the meat and cook until well browned. Sprinkle in the flour and allow this to brown more gently. Add the crushed garlic, tomato purée, bouquet garni and seasoning. Pour on the stock and wine. Bring to the boil and simmer for 30 minutes, or cook in the oven at Mark 3 (160°C/325°F).

Add the turnips, onions, carrots and potatoes. These should be small young ones – if they are at all large 'turn' them to the size of large olives. Continue cooking for a further 30 minutes, then add the beans and, after a further 5–10 minutes, the peas. If necessary, add a little more stock during the cooking time.

When all the meat and vegetables are cooked and tender, serve the meat and vegetables in a deep dish. Adjust the sauce to a coating consistency, remove any grease and pour over the dish.

Le Porc

Pork

All British pork is home produced and is available throughout the year. The meat should be clear pink and the fat white. An opalescent or yellow sheen indicates poor quality.

A side of pork weighs approximately 22–25 kg (50–55 lb).

All pork must be well cooked as it is possible for the meat to contain parasitic cysts (*Trichinae*) and these are destroyed by heat.

Le Jambon (*Leg of pork*)
A large joint weighing about 5.50–6.50 kg (12–14 lb) can be cut into two or three joints. Excellent for roasting and it can be braised.

Le Filet et le Carré (*Loin*)
This consists of the chump, loin and ribs and is cut into suitably sized joints, chops or cutlets. A whole loin weighs 3.00–5.50 kg (7–12 lb). Joints can be roasted and chops and cutlets fried, grilled, stewed or casseroled.

The French refer to the chump end of the loin as well as the fillet itself as 'le filet'. In Britain and America fillet refers only to the undercut of the loin from large pigs and it is bought by the weight required. It is very suitable to sauté, stew, fry and roast.

L'Epaule (*Shoulder*)
This can be bought boned and rolled and cut into joints, but is frequently divided into the blade bone, spare rib and hand and spring.

Weight: 4.50–6.50 kg (10–14 lb).

Suitable to stew and sauté. Also makes good economical roasting joints.

La Palette (*Blade bone*)
A lean semi-circular piece of meat which is the top part of the shoulder blade.

Weight: 1.00–1.50 kg (2–3 lb).

Suitable to stew or sauté. Also a good economical roasting joint.

L'Echine (*Spare rib*)
May be cut into two or into spare rib cutlets.

Weight of complete spare rib: 1.75–2.25 kg (4–5 lb).

Suitable to stew or sauté and is another economical roasting joint.

Le Plat de Côtes (*Hand and spring*)
This is the lower part of the shoulder and the front leg of the pig. It has a coarser grained flesh than other cuts but is lean.

Weight: 2.25 kg (5 lb).

Suitable to stew, sauté and roast.

La Poitrine (*Belly*)
The thick end of belly is a lean, sweet-tasting piece of meat which can be roasted or stewed. The rest of the belly is streaky and, although tasty, may be too fat for some tastes. It is excellent used in choucroûte garni and can also be roasted or sliced and grilled.

La Tête (*Head*)
Half a head weighs approximately 2.25 kg (5 lb) and can be used for making brawn or hure de porc (potted head of pork).

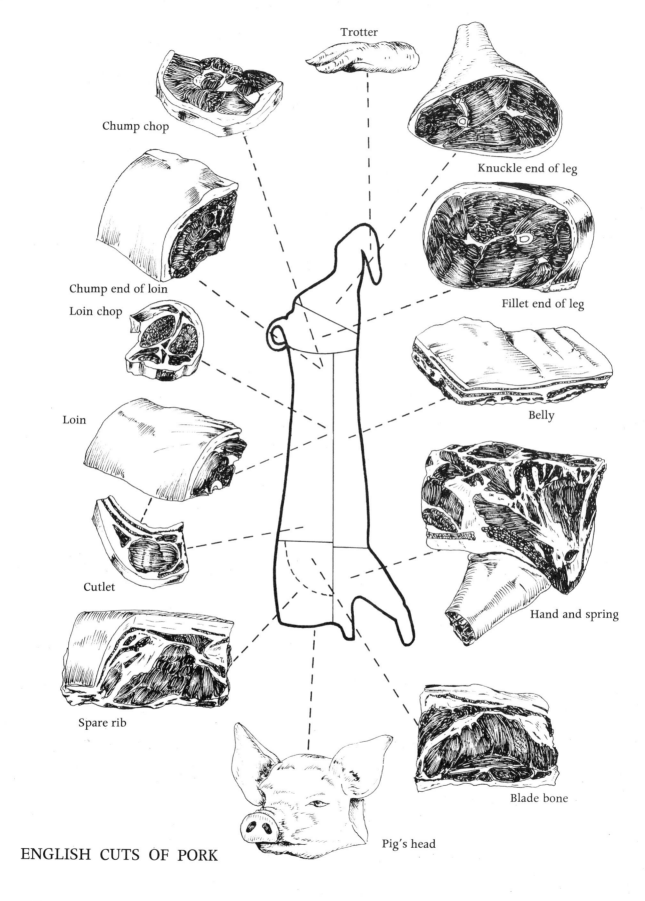

Trotter

Chump chop

Knuckle end of leg

Chump end of loin

Loin chop

Fillet end of leg

Loin

Belly

Cutlet

Hand and spring

Spare rib

Blade bone

Pig's head

ENGLISH CUTS OF PORK

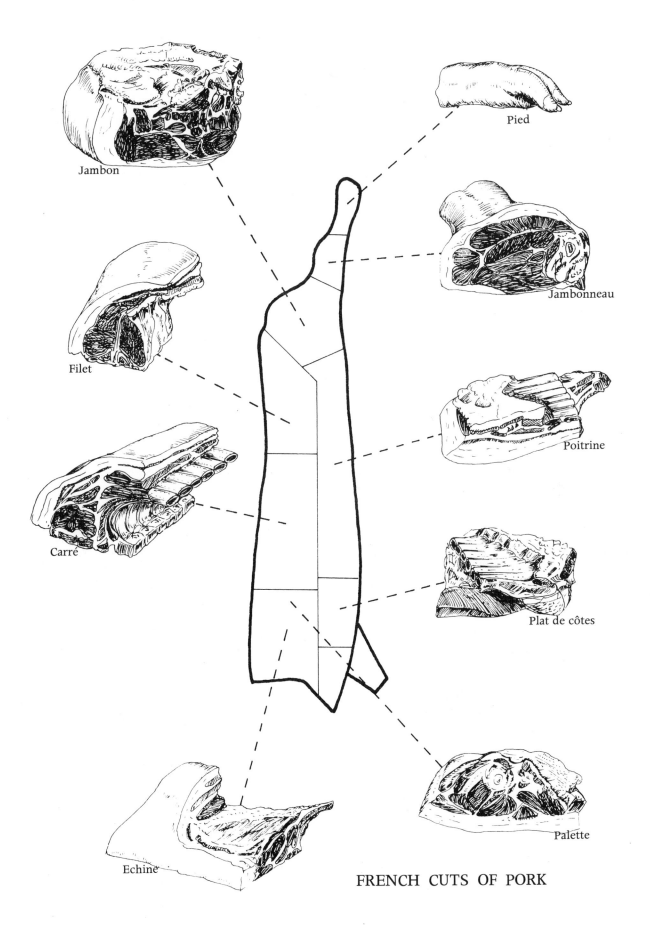

Pied

Jambon

Jambonneau

Filet

Poitrine

Carré

Plat de côtes

Echine

Palette

FRENCH CUTS OF PORK

Carré de Porc à l'Ananas

Roast pork with pineapple (serves 6)

This is an attractive and uncomplicated dish. The sharp flavour of fresh pineapple contrasts well with the richness of the meat.

	Imperial	American
2 kg loin of pork	4 lb	4 lb
oil		
salt and pepper		
2 tsp plain flour	2 tsp	2 tsp
150 ml red wine	$\frac{1}{4}$ pt	$\frac{2}{3}$ cup
300 ml stock made from the pork bones	$\frac{1}{2}$ pt	$1\frac{1}{4}$ cups
1 medium pineapple		

Have the meat boned, rolled, and tied, with the crackling scored in narrow strips. Rub salt into the cuts, and brush with oil. Roast in a moderately hot oven, Mark 6 (200°C/400°F), allowing 30 minutes per 500 g (1 lb) plus 30 minutes over. Reduce the temperature towards the end if the meat is getting over-browned.

Cutting the pineapple for Carré de Porc à l'Ananas.

This is an excellent joint for spit roasting, so it can be cooked in this way if you prefer. Put the meat on the spit with the prongs pressed well into it. Cook on a high heat for 10 minutes, then reduce to a moderate temperature and cook for a further 35–40 minutes per 500 g (1 lb)

While the meat is cooking, prepare the pineapple (see below). Cut in half lengthways, then cut the fruit out of each half, using a curved grapefruit knife. Remove the hard centre core, and slice the fruit thinly. Return to the pineapple halves.

When the meat is cooked, lift it onto a serving-dish and keep warm while the gravy is made. Pour off most of the fat from the roasting-pan or drip tray and sprinkle the flour into the pan, stir and cook gently until browned. Stir in the wine and stock and simmer for 5 minutes. Season, then strain into a sauce-boat.

To serve, place the pineapple at each end of the serving-dish. Carve the meat at the table, or, if preferred, carve it into slices in the kitchen, then arrange on the serving-dish with the pineapple garnish.

Carré de Porc à l'Ananas.

Rôti de Porc à l'Ail

Garlic flavoured roast pork (serves 5–6)

This dish, from Languedoc in south-west France, not only tastes good, but smells mouthwatering whilst it is cooking.

	Imperial	American
1.5 kg loin or leg of pork	3½ lb	3½ lb
2–3 cloves garlic		
salt and freshly ground black pepper		
2 tbsp oil	2 tbsp	2 tbsp
1 carrot		
1 onion		
1 tsp plain flour	1 tsp	1 tsp
300 ml stock	½ pt	1¼ cups

Twelve hours before roasting the meat, remove the skin from the cloves of garlic and cut them into strips. Insert under the rind and in the flesh of the pork. Season well with salt and pepper and sprinkle with the oil.

Place the meat in a roasting-pan with the carrot and onion and cook in a moderately hot oven, Mark 6 (200°C/400°F), for 30 minutes per 500 g (1 lb) and 30 minutes over.

Côtes de Porc Charcutière.

When the meat is cooked, lift onto a hot serving-dish. Strain off the fat from the pan, retaining the juices. Add the flour, replace over the heat and cook until well browned. Add the stock gradually, mixing in all the residue from the sides of the pan. Bring to the boil, season to taste and strain. Serve separately.

Côtes de Porc Charcutière

Piquant pork chops (serves 4)

The spicy sauce complements the richness of the pork. A cool white wine is an excellent accompaniment to this dish.

	Imperial	American
4 pork chops		
25 g butter	1 oz	2 tbsp
25 g plain flour	1 oz	¼ cup
2 tbsp tomato purée	2 tbsp	2 tbsp
450 ml water	¾ pt	2 cups
2 tbsp chopped gherkins	2 tbsp	2 tbsp
2 tbsp chopped cocktail onions	2 tbsp	2 tbsp
1 tbsp chopped capers	1 tbsp	1 tbsp
1 tbsp French mustard	1 tbsp	1 tbsp
1 tsp vinegar	1 tsp	1 tsp
salt and pepper		

For the garnish:
4 gherkins

Trim the excess fat from the chops. Plunge them into a pan of boiling water for 5 minutes, then remove and drain.

Make the sauce in a pan large enough to easily contain the chops. Melt the butter then add the flour. Stir together and cook over a gentle heat for 2–3 minutes. Remove from the heat and stir in the tomato purée and water. Add the gherkins, onions and capers and bring to simmering point, stirring all the time. Add the chops to the sauce and cover with a piece of greaseproof paper and a lid. Cook over a gentle heat for 30–40 minutes.

Just before serving, stir in the mustard and vinegar. Lift the chops out of the sauce and arrange, overlapping, down the centre of the serving-dish. Check the seasoning then pour over the sauce. Cut the gherkins into fans and garnish each chop with these.

Côtes de Porc aux Pruneaux

Pork chops with prunes (serves 4)

If you are a visitor to the historic town of Tours in the Loire Valley, do look out for this dish which is a speciality of the restaurants in this region.

	Imperial	American
16–20 prunes		
300 ml white wine	$\frac{1}{2}$ pt	$1\frac{1}{4}$ cups
4 pork chops		
2 tbsp seasoned flour	2 tbsp	2 tbsp
50 g butter	2 oz	$\frac{1}{4}$ cup
salt and pepper		
2 tsp redcurrant jelly	2 tsp	2 tsp
2 tbsp double cream	2 tbsp	2 tbsp

Place the prunes in the wine and allow to soak overnight. The next day, simmer the prunes and wine in a covered pan for 8–10 minutes or until tender.

Trim the chops, removing any excess fat, and pass them through the seasoned flour. Melt the butter in a frying-pan. When it is hot, add the chops and turn them so they brown well on both sides. (Allow 7–10 minutes on each side.) Season well. Pork must be well cooked, so check that no red line is visible down the side of the bone and that no blood is seeping from the chine bone. When satisfied that the chops are sufficiently cooked, lift them onto a hot serving-dish and arrange the prunes down each side. Pour off all but 2 tablespoons of the fat in the frying-pan, pour on the wine from the prunes and reduce it quickly over a good heat to half its quantity. Stir in the redcurrant jelly, mixing it well, then add the cream. Taste and season. Pour the sauce over the chops and serve very hot.

Tante Marie tip:
Vouvray is the local wine traditionally recommended for use in this dish but, in view of the cost of this wine outside France, we suggest you use another dry or semi-sweet white wine and drink the chilled Vouvray with the pork. For economy, cook in dry cider.

Côtes de Porc à la Vallée d'Auge

Normandy pork chops (serves 4)

This dish comes from Normandy and makes full use of the local ingredients. Fillet of pork, chicken or pheasant can also be cooked in this way.

	Imperial	American
4 lean pork chops		
50 g butter	2 oz	$\frac{1}{4}$ cup
1–2 tbsp calvados *or* brandy (*optional*)	1–2 tbsp	1–2 tbsp
2 small cooking apples		
1 tbsp plain flour	1 tbsp	1 tbsp
300 ml cider	$\frac{1}{2}$ pt	$1\frac{1}{4}$ cups
a bouquet garni		
salt and pepper		
2–3 firm dessert apples		
150 ml double cream	$\frac{1}{4}$ pt	$\frac{2}{3}$ cup

For the garnish:
diced fried croûtons
finely chopped parsley

Cut the rind from the chops and trim them neatly, leaving a little fat on each. Remove the spinal cord. Melt 25 g (1 oz/2 tbsp) of butter in a pan. When it is hot, add the chops and fry on both sides until golden brown and well sealed. Flame them with the calvados or brandy (if used), then remove from the pan. Peel, core and slice the apples and cook them gently in the pan for a few minutes. Sprinkle in the flour and cook for 1–2 minutes, then add the cider, bouquet garni and seasoning. Return the chops to the pan, cover with greaseproof paper and a lid and cook in a moderate oven, Mark 4 (180°C/350°F) for 35–40 minutes or until the chops are tender.

While the chops are cooking, fry the croûtons, then peel and core the dessert apples and cut each into 4 rings. Fry them gently in the remaining butter until golden brown and tender. Keep hot.

Place the chops on a hot dish. Bring the sauce to the boil, pour in the cream, reheat and adjust the seasoning. Pour over the chops and arrange the apple rings down each side of the dish. Sprinkle the fried croûtons and parsley over the surface and serve.

Saucisses à la Ménagère

Home-style sausages (serves 4)

French sausages are made entirely with meat but this recipe can be made very successfully with English-type sausages or chipolatas.

	Imperial	American
500 g pork sausages	1 lb	1 lb
25 g butter	1 oz	2 tbsp
65 g lean bacon	2½ oz	2½ oz
6 shallots, or 1 onion		
2 tsp plain flour	2 tsp	2 tsp
250 ml stock	8 fl oz	1 cup
75 ml red wine	2½ fl oz	⅓ cup
1 bayleaf		
salt and pepper		
100 g mushrooms	4 oz	4 oz
1 cooked turnip		

For the garnish:

Pommes de Terre Duchesse made with 750 g potatoes	1½ lb	1½ lb
(*see page 179*)		
fried triangular-shaped croûtons		
finely chopped parsley		

Prick the sausages well with a fork. Heat the butter in a frying-pan. When it is hot, add the sausages and cook slowly until well browned. Cut the bacon into strips and finely chop the shallots or onion. Remove the sausages from the pan and cook the bacon and onion together. When they are tender, sprinkle in the flour and cook for 2–3 minutes, stirring all the time. Pour on the stock and wine, add the bayleaf and seasoning. Bring gently to simmering point, return the sausages to the pan, cover with grease-proof paper and a lid and cook for 10 minutes. Add the mushrooms and continue to cook gently for a further 10–15 minutes. Add the turnip to the sausage mixture and heat through thoroughly. Adjust the consistency of the sauce and check the seasoning. Remove the bayleaf.

Meanwhile, prepare the Pommes de Terre Duchesse and season well. Place the potatoes in a forcing bag with a large rosette pipe. Lightly grease a hot serving-dish and pipe a border of potato around it. Fry the croûtons.

Fill the centre of the dish with the sausage mixture, garnish with the croûtons and sprinkle with the parsley.

Sauté de Porc aux Aubergines

Pork and aubergine casserole (serves 3–4)

An uncomplicated casserole with an excellent flavour.

	Imperial	American
500 g lean pork, e.g. hand *or* blade bone *or* spare rib	1 lb	1 lb
500 g aubergines	1 lb	1 lb
salt and pepper		
2 tbsp oil	2 tbsp	2 tbsp
2 onions, chopped		
150 ml stock	¼ pt	⅔ cup
2 cloves garlic		
a pinch of cayenne pepper		
2 tbsp chopped parsley	2 tbsp	2 tbsp

Cut the aubergines into chunks. Sprinkle with salt and leave for 30 minutes.

Cut the meat into cubes, removing any fat. Heat the oil in a pan. When it is hot, add the meat and brown quickly. Add the onions, cover with a lid and cook gently for 10 minutes, then add the stock. Crush the garlic in a little salt, and stir this in. Cover and cook gently. Rinse the aubergines in cold water. Add these after the meat has been cooking for 1 hour, and continue cooking for a further 45 minutes. Season to taste with salt, pepper and cayenne. Sprinkle with parsley and serve.

Le Veau

Veal

Veal is the meat of a young calf which is not more than four months old. The best veal available in Britain comes from Holland where it is fed on milk concentrates. Home-grown veal can be fed with milk or cereals. Milk-fed veal is lighter in colour and has a more delicate flavour.

Prime-quality veal has a light pink flesh and firm pinkish-white fat. Yellow-tinged or blotchy flesh is poor quality or stale. There should be a good proportion of meat to bone and the cuts should be moderate in size. Chops, for instance, should be no bigger than small pork chops. If they are too big the animal may have been 'young beef' by the time it was killed and may need long slow cooking. Very small veal comes from young 'bobby' calves: the calves of dairy herds, possibly only a week or two old. It has little flavour and is uneconomic to buy as there is little meat on most of the carcase.

Veal is butchered in a similar way to lamb, but may be used differently. A side of veal will weigh 20-100 kg (40-200 lb). As the size of the carcase varies so much it is usual to buy joints by the weight required.

La Cuisseau (*Leg*)
A leg from a small side of veal will weigh about $6\frac{1}{2}$ kg (14 lb). It can be cut into two or three joints and roasted or braised. However, it is the fleshiest part of the animal and so usually cut into escalopes. A good butcher will divide the three muscles in the top of the leg into the following cuts:

Noix de Veau (*Top side*)

Sous Noix (*Silverside*)

Quasi (*Top rump*)

Even slices of meat can then be cut which keep their shape. A thin slice cut obliquely through the grain will hold its shape during cooking. A thick slice cut across the grain and beaten out will shrink back when placed in a hot pan. A slice cut through the whole of the leg tends to fall apart along the natural seam lines of the meat and makes good presentation difficult. Escalopes should weigh 90-125 g (3-4 oz) each.

Le Filet et La Longe (*Chump end* and *loin of veal*)
Veal can be roasted, particularly if boned and stuffed with moist filling, but tends to be dry if not barded or larded. Braising is an ideal method of cooking this meat and the chump end or the loin provide compact joints which can be sliced neatly after cooking. Veau Braisé Bouquetière is an attractive and tasty recipe for these cuts. Chops can also be cut from the loin.

Le Carré (*Best end*)
This can be cut as a separate joint or into cutlets. More usually the front part of the carcase - the shoulder, best end and middle neck - is boned and can be rolled and cut into joints which can be braised or roasted. This is often called the oyster. It can also be minced or cut up for stewing veal (see Blanquette de Veau - page 123).

La Poitrine (*Breast*)
This can be boned, stuffed and slow roasted or braised. It is a very good cut to use for a ballotine de veau and it can also be cut up and stewed.

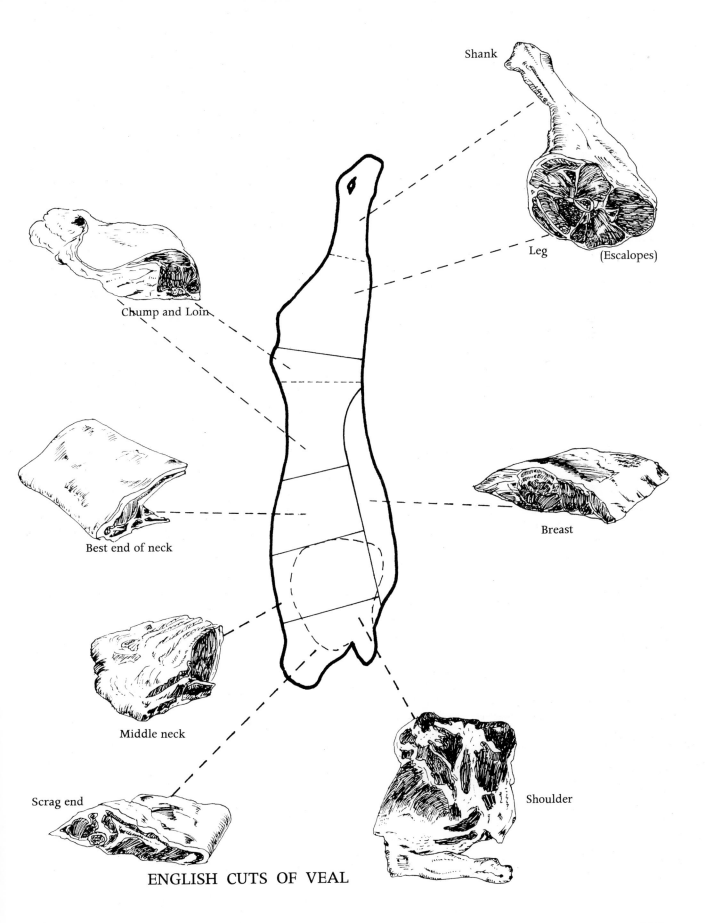

Shank

Leg   (Escalopes)

Chump and Loin

Best end of neck

Breast

Middle neck

Scrag end

Shoulder

ENGLISH CUTS OF VEAL

119

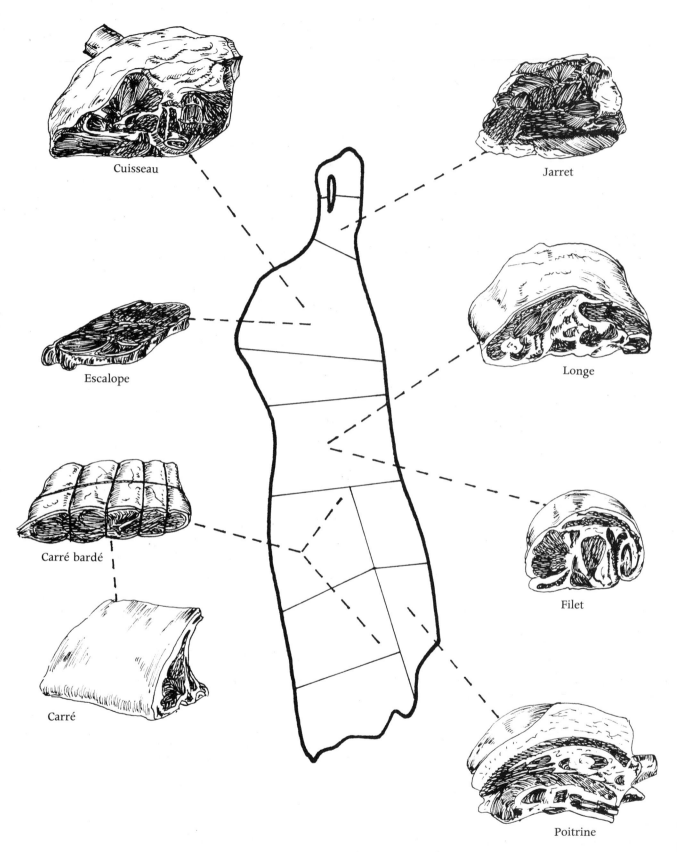

Cuisseau

Jarret

Escalope

Longe

Carré bardé

Filet

Carré

Poitrine

FRENCH CUTS OF VEAL

Escalopes de Veau à la Viennoise

Viennese veal escalopes (serves 4)

A French version of the famous Austrian Wiener Schnitzel.

	Imperial	American
4 veal escalopes (75–100 g each)	3–4 oz each	3–4 oz each
3–4 tbsp seasoned flour	3–4 tbsp	3–4 tbsp
2 eggs, beaten		
3 tbsp oil	3 tbsp	3 tbsp
sieved white breadcrumbs		
2 hard-boiled eggs		
2–3 lemons		
4 anchovy fillets		
chopped parsley		
75 g unsalted butter	3 oz	6 tbsp
1–2 tbsp capers	1–2 tbsp	1–2 tbsp
salt and pepper		

Trim the escalopes. Place them between two sheets of thin plastic or strong paper and flatten with a meat mallet or rolling-pin.

Prepare the ingredients for coating and put each one on a deep plate or a small food tray, in the order in which they will be used: seasoned flour, eggs beaten with 1 tablespoon oil, and sieved white breadcrumbs. Dip each escalope into each tray in turn and then pat smooth with a palette knife.

To prepare the garnish, separate the hard-boiled eggs and chop the whites finely, using a stainless-steel knife, and sieve the yolks. One lemon is going to be used as a garnish, so decorate this with a canelle knife (see page 24) if you like to, and cut into thin slices, removing any pips. Take four lemon slices and decorate with a rolled anchovy fillet surrounded by a ring of chopped parsley.

To arrange the garnish on the serving-dish, place the chopped egg whites, sieved yolks and parsley in lines around the dish, then the half slices of lemon

Escalopes de Veau à la Viennoise.

around the outside edge. Cover with cling-film plastic if it is not going to be served immediately.

Escalopes are quite large and frying a number of them can take time. It is often easier to cook them in two frying-pans. They can be kept satisfactorily hot by placing them, uncovered, in a slow oven after frying. Heat the butter and 2 tablespoons of oil in the frying-pan. When hot, add the escalopes and fry on both sides until golden brown and tender. Each escalope takes about 8–10 minutes to cook.

About 10 minutes before the escalopes are cooked, remove the plastic covering from the garnished serving-dish and place the dish over a pan of hot water to warm. When you are ready to serve, arrange the escalopes, overlapping, down the centre of the dish and scatter a few capers over. Reheat the butter in the pan (add more if necessary) and, when hot, add the lemon juice. Boil fiercely for a moment, season and pour over the escalopes. Arrange the garnished lemon slices on the escalopes and serve immediately.

Veau Braisé Bouquetière

Braised veal (serves 5–6)

This dish has a garnish of young carrots, potatoes and French beans around the meat. If you like more vegetables you can use the classic bouquetière garnish which also includes peas, turned turnips and sprigs of cauliflower.

	Imperial	American
1.5 kg chump end of loin, boned and rolled	3½ lb	3½ lb
100 g piece of bacon fat	4 oz	4 oz
salt and pepper		
3 tbsp oil	3 tbsp	3 tbsp
2 onions		
3 shallots		
1 carrot		
2 cloves garlic		
300 ml white wine	½ pt	1¼ cups
300 ml white stock	½ pt	1¼ cups
a bouquet garni		
2 tsp tomato purée	2 tsp	2 tsp
2 tsp paprika pepper	2 tsp	2 tsp
1 tsp arrowroot	1 tsp	1 tsp

For the garnish:

500 g new carrots	1 lb	1 lb
25 g butter	1 oz	2 tbsp
a pinch of sugar		
500 g even-sized new potatoes	1 lb	1 lb
250 g French beans	8 oz	8 oz
chopped parsley		

Cut the larding bacon fat into strips and season with salt and pepper. Lard the veal with these strips and tie into a neat shape. Heat the oil in a sauté pan, add the veal and brown well on all sides. Remove from the pan.

Peel and slice the onions, shallots and carrot. Brown these in the fat, then add the crushed garlic, wine, stock, bouquet garni, seasoning, tomato purée and paprika. Replace the meat in the pan with any juice that has run out of it, cover with a lid and cook at Mark 4 (180°C/350°F) for 1½ hours.

Meanwhile, prepare the vegetables for the garnish. Peel the carrots, trim to neat shapes and cook in boiling salted water with the butter and sugar. When they are tender allow the liquid to reduce until they are glazed. Wash the potatoes and cook in boiling salted water until tender. Peel and keep hot in a steamer. Top and tail the beans, break into two or three pieces and cook in boiling salted water, then drain.

To serve, lift the veal out of the pan when tender and carve in slices. Arrange on the serving-dish and cover with foil, then place in a slow oven to keep hot while the sauce is made. Strain the sauce, bring to the boil and spoon off any grease. Allow to boil until reduced by half. Slake the arrowroot with a little water and add to the sauce. Bring to the boil, reduce the heat and cook for 1–2 minutes. Taste and season.

Arrange the vegetables around the meat. Pour the sauce over the meat and sprinkle a little parsley on the potatoes.

Blanquette de Veau
Creamy veal stew (serves 4–6)

This recipe can also be adapted to use other white meats such as chicken, rabbit or sweetbreads. Serve with plain boiled rice (Riz Blanc).

	Imperial	American
1 kg stewing veal	2 lb	2 lb
2–3 onions, *or* 12 button onions		
2–3 carrots		
a bouquet garni		
6 peppercorns		
salt and pepper		
100 g button mushrooms	4 oz	4 oz
75 g butter	3 oz	6 tbsp
juice of $\frac{1}{2}$ lemon		
40 g plain flour	$1\frac{1}{2}$ oz	$\frac{1}{3}$ cup
150 ml single cream	$\frac{1}{4}$ pt	$\frac{2}{3}$ cup
2 egg yolks		
finely chopped parsley		

Trim the meat and cut into cubes. Place in a large pan and cover with cold water. Bring slowly to the boil, then remove the scum from the surface. Add the onions (button ones are peeled and left whole, large ones are cut into sections). Cut the carrots into quarters and add them with the bouquet garni. Season with the whole peppercorns and about 1 teaspoon of salt. Cover with a lid and simmer gently for $1\frac{1}{4}$ hours or until the veal is tender.

Lift the meat and vegetables into a warm serving-dish, cover with a lid and keep warm while the sauce is prepared. Boil the stock well to reduce it and intensify the flavour until about half a litre (1 pt/ $2\frac{1}{2}$ cups) remains. Wash the mushrooms.

Melt 25 g (1 oz/2 tbsp) of butter in a pan. Add the lemon juice and mushrooms. Cover with a lid and cook gently for 5 minutes, then put on top of the veal.

Melt the rest of the butter in another pan, add the flour and cook for 2–3 minutes. Remove from the heat and add the veal stock. Bring to the boil, stirring well, and cook for 5–10 minutes.

Blend the cream and egg yolks together. Add some of the hot sauce, stir together and return the mixture to the pan. Reheat without boiling. Taste and season, then pour the sauce over the meat and vegetables. Sprinkle with finely chopped parsley.

Blanquette de Veau. *Top:* The meat, vegetables and herbs simmering gently. *Centre:* Mixing the liaison. *Bottom:* The finished dish.

Tourtière de ma Grandmère

Grandmother's pie (serves 4)

This pie is good either hot or cold, and is excellent for picnics or a cold buffet.

	Imperial	American
flaky pastry made with 225 g plain flour (*see page 208–209*)	8 oz	2 cups
For the filling:		
275 g lean minced pork	10 oz	10 oz
275 g minced veal	10 oz	10 oz
1 small clove garlic		
a sprig of thyme		
salt and pepper		
1–2 tbsp seasoned flour	1–2 tbsp	1–2 tbsp
50 g butter	2 oz	$\frac{1}{4}$ cup
2 shallots, finely chopped		
25 g white breadcrumbs	1 oz	$\frac{1}{2}$ cup
2–3 tbsp finely chopped parsley	2–3 tbsp	2–3 tbsp
1 egg for glazing		
2 tbsp white wine	2 tbsp	2 tbsp
2 tbsp white stock	2 tbsp	2 tbsp

Make the pastry. Put aside in a cool place to relax. Mix the minced meats with the garlic and finely chopped thyme. Season, and roll into balls about the size of a walnut. Dip in seasoned flour. Melt the butter in a frying-pan, add the meat balls and fry until light golden brown. Drain.

Pour off 1–2 tablespoons of the fat. Add the shallots and stir over the heat for 2–3 minutes, without allowing them to colour. Add the breadcrumbs and parsley. Stir for 1 minute.

Roll out one-half of the pastry on a lightly floured board and line into an 18 cm (7 in) flan ring. Arrange the meat balls in the flan, piling them up. Sprinkle the breadcrumb mixture over the top and season again. Roll out the remaining pastry. Moisten the edges of the flan ring and place the pastry on top. Trim the edges and pinch them firmly together so that it is well sealed. Make a 1 cm ($\frac{1}{2}$ in) hole in the centre of the pastry. Brush over with beaten egg and bake in a hot oven, Mark 7 (220°C/425°F), for 10 minutes, then reduce the temperature to Mark 5 (190°C/375°F) and continue cooking for approximately 30 minutes altogether.

Remove the flan ring. Pour the wine and stock into the tourtière through the hole in the top and continue cooking for a further 15 minutes. Serve hot or cold.

Right: Tourtière de ma Grandmère. In the background (*right*) you will see another pie with the meat balls piled up ready to be covered with the pastry. Notice (*left*) how the pastry is placed over the rolling pin to make it easy to lift.

Les Abats

Offal

La Langue (*Tongue*)

Ox tongue is an economical piece of meat and can weigh from 700 g to 1.75 kg ($1\frac{1}{2}$–4 lb). It can be used fresh as in Langue de Boeuf Romaine or salted, boiled and pressed. The latter is often sold sliced by butchers and delicatessens and is used in the recipe for Medaillons à la Milanaise.

Lambs' tongues are much smaller and are not salted. Soak them in cold water for an hour before cooking. Drain and simmer in salted water for $1\frac{1}{2}$–2 hours or until the skin can be removed easily. Trim off all fat and sinew, then braise or casserole until tender.

Le Foie (*Liver*)

Most recipes in France use calves' liver as this is regarded as the finest for flavour and texture. It is very suitable for grilling, frying and can be casseroled.

Lambs' liver is generally cheaper and more easily available and can be used quite satisfactorily in all recipes which call for calves' liver, although it does not have quite the same delicacy.

Pigs' liver has a much stronger flavour and, for this reason, is not quite so popular. Soaking in cold salt water for an hour or two will help to remove some of the strong flavour. Although it can be used in the same way as calves' or lambs' liver it is more usually used in pâtés and terrines.

Ox liver comes from a mature animal and is therefore a much tougher piece of meat. It can be slowly casseroled or braised.

It is very easy to make liver tough and it must be cooked carefully for good results. Either fry or grill quickly until just cooked or casserole it slowly. If it is to be grilled or fried, soak in a little milk for an hour or so as this helps to tenderise it and improve the flavour. When casseroling liver, seal in hot fat quickly and then simmer very gently; never let it boil.

Les Rognons (*Kidneys*)

Lambs' or calves' kidneys can be used for all entrées. Calves' kidneys are much bigger so allow only one per person or one between two depending on the size. Allow two lambs' kidneys per person. Pigs' kidneys have a stronger flavour. Allow half to one per person. Ox kidney is tough and very strong in flavour. It is suitable for soups and any dish which requires long slow cooking. Always soak all kidneys in cold salted water before cooking.

Les Ris (*Sweetbreads*)

Sweetbreads are the thymus and pancreas glands. The thymus are the knobbly ones which come from the neck, and the pancreas are smooth and come from the stomach.

Calves' sweetbreads are the most succulent and are usually sold in pairs. Lambs' sweetbreads are much smaller and have less flavour.

Ox sweetbreads are large and tougher but can be used if they are given long slow cooking. They come from young beef and can be good value for money. Sweetbreads from pigs and mature animals are never used.

All sweetbreads must be soaked in water for 2–3 hours to remove any blood. Then place them in a pan of cold water and bring to the boil, simmer for 2–3 minutes, then drain and refresh. Remove all the loose tissue and sinews.

Calves' and ox sweetbreads should then be pressed between two plates until quite firm before further cooking.

Foie de Veau à la Bourgeoise

Liver casserole (serves 3–4)

Wine will tenderise the liver as well as flavour the sauce in this tasty dish.

	Imperial	American
500 g lambs' *or* calves' liver	1 lb	1 lb
50 g bacon	2 oz	2 oz
250 g carrots	8 oz	8 oz
250 g button onions	8 oz	8 oz
25 g butter	1 oz	2 tbsp
2 tsp plain flour	2 tsp	2 tsp
150 ml red wine	$\frac{1}{4}$ pt	$\frac{2}{3}$ cup
300 ml stock	$\frac{1}{2}$ pt	$1\frac{1}{4}$ cups
2 tsp tomato purée	2 tsp	2 tsp
1 small clove garlic, crushed		
salt and pepper		
triangular fried croûtons		
chopped parsley		

Slice the liver thinly and cut the bacon into small dice. Peel the carrots and onions, and turn the carrots or cut into batons. Blanch the onions in boiling salted water for 5 minutes. Drain well.

Melt the butter in a pan. When it is hot, add the liver and cook quickly on both sides until brown, then remove from the pan. Cook the carrots and onions gently until golden brown. Stir in the flour and cook for 1–2 minutes. Replace the liver in the pan and add the wine, stock, tomato purée, garlic and seasoning. Cover with greaseproof paper and a lid and cook in a moderate oven, Mark 4 (180°C/350°F), for about 45 minutes or until the liver and vegetables are tender.

Prepare and fry the croûtons.

Place the liver on a hot serving-dish and arrange the vegetables down each side. Keep hot.

Boil the sauce for a minute or two until it thickens slightly. Taste and adjust the seasoning. Pour the sauce over the liver. Sprinkle with the parsley, arrange the fried croûtons around the dish and serve.

Foie de Veau au Raisins

Liver with raisins (serves 3–4)

Liver cooked in a rich fruity sauce.

	Imperial	American
500 g calves' *or* lambs' liver	1 lb	1 lb
25 g raisins	1 oz	$\frac{1}{4}$ cup
25 g sultanas	1 oz	$\frac{1}{4}$ cup
150 ml red wine	$\frac{1}{4}$ pt	$\frac{2}{3}$ cup
2 shallots, *or* 1 small onion		
50 g butter	2 oz	$\frac{1}{4}$ cup
2 tbsp wine vinegar	2 tbsp	2 tbsp
2 tsp brown sugar	2 tsp	2 tsp
2 tsp plain flour	2 tsp	2 tsp
300 ml stock	$\frac{1}{2}$ pt	$1\frac{1}{4}$ cups
1 tsp tomato purée	1 tsp	1 tsp
a bouquet garni		
salt and pepper		
50 g mushrooms	2 oz	2 oz

Place the raisins, sultanas and wine in a bowl and leave for about 2 hours.

Slice the liver and finely chop the shallots or onion. Melt the butter in a pan. When it is hot, add the liver and cook quickly to brown on both sides. Remove and keep hot. Fry the shallots or onion in the same pan until soft. Add the vinegar and sugar and stir until dissolved, then add the flour and mix well. Drain off the wine from the fruit and add this with the stock, tomato purée, bouquet garni and seasoning. Bring to simmering point and replace the liver. Cover with greaseproof paper and a tightly-fitting lid and cook over a gentle heat or in a moderate oven, Mark 4 (180°C/350°F), for 30 minutes.

Slice the mushrooms and add them to the pan with the sultanas and raisins. Cook for a further 10 minutes. Taste and adjust the seasoning.

Arrange the liver on a hot serving-dish. Remove the bouquet garni and pour the sauce over.

Langue de Boeuf Romaine

Roman-style tongue (serves 6–8)

	Imperial	American
1 ox tongue (unsalted)		
salt and pepper		
5–6 carrots		
4 onions		
a bouquet garni		
75 g dripping	3 oz	6 tbsp
40 g plain flour	1½ oz	⅓ cup
1 tbsp meat extract	1 tbsp	1 tbsp
2 tbsp tomato purée	2 tbsp	2 tbsp
1 tbsp sugar	1 tbsp	1 tbsp
2 tbsp water	2 tbsp	2 tbsp
150 ml wine vinegar	¼ pt	⅔ cup
25 g sultanas	1 oz	¼ cup

Soak the tongue in water and 2 tablespoons of salt for 1 hour. Place in a pan of boiling water for 10 minutes. Drain and refresh under cold running water. Place the tongue in a clean pan with 2 sliced carrots, 2 sliced onions and the bouquet garni. Season well. Cover with cold water, bring slowly to the boil, then simmer for 2–2½ hours. Lift out and drain. Take out the bones and the root and remove the skin. Strain the cooking liquor.

To make the sauce, finely dice 1 carrot and 1 onion. Melt half the dripping in a frying-pan. When it is hot, add the diced vegetables and brown them slowly. Add the flour and colour this too, stirring well over a low heat. Add 300 ml (1 pt/2½ cups) of the strained cooking liquor. Add the meat extract and tomato purée. Stir and season well. Simmer for 10–15 minutes.

Slice the remaining carrots and onion. Melt the rest of the dripping in a large pan. When it is hot, add the vegetables. Turn them in the fat, then add the tongue. Brown it gently on all sides (this should take about 10 minutes). Add the sauce and check the seasoning. Cover with greaseproof paper and a lid and cook in a moderate oven, Mark 4 (180°C/350°F), for a further 1–1½ hours. At the end of this time the meat should be quite tender when tested with a skewer. Remove from the pan, cover and keep hot.

Place the sugar in a large pan with approximately 2 tablespoons of water. Cook over a moderate heat until a good caramel is obtained. Add the vinegar and stir well. Allow it to reduce by three-quarters over a good heat. Strain the sauce in which the tongue has been cooked. Add the caramel, then stir in the sultanas. Taste and adjust the seasoning.

To serve, slice the tongue and arrange neatly in a hot serving-dish. Pour over the sauce, keeping some back to hand separately. Serve at once.

Tante Marie tip:
This dish freezes well but for freezing reduce the sauce by half; further reduction can take place when reheating.

Médaillons à la Milanaise

Sliced ox tongue with savoury stuffing (serves 4)

This is an ideal light luncheon or supper dish.

	Imperial	American
4 thin slices of ox tongue		
500 g ripe tomatoes	1 lb	1 lb
and 150 ml water,	¼ pt	⅔ cup
or 400 g can tomatoes	14 oz	14 oz
1 large onion		
1 clove garlic		
a bouquet garni		
1 tsp sugar	1 tsp	1 tsp
1 tsp tomato purée	1 tsp	1 tsp
salt and pepper		
1 small green *or* red pepper		
25 g butter	1 oz	2 tbsp
2–3 tbsp cooked long grain rice	2–3 tbsp	2–3 tbsp
1 tsp chopped capers	1 tsp	1 tsp
75 g cheese, grated	3 oz	1½ cups

If using fresh tomatoes, skin and pip them and cut into shreds. Slice the onion finely and crush the garlic with a little salt.

Place the tomatoes, water (if used), onion, garlic, bouquet garni, sugar, tomato purée and seasoning in a pan and simmer gently until the onions are soft and the mixture is thick. Remove the bouquet garni and check the seasoning.

Remove the seeds and pith from the pepper and cut into small dice. Place in a pan of cold salted water, bring to the boil and cook for 5–6 minutes. Drain well and refresh. Melt the butter in a pan and add the well-drained rice, pepper, capers and half the cheese. Season well and stir with a fork over a gentle heat until the cheese is melted. Spread a layer of this mixture on one half of each slice of tongue, fold in half and arrange the pieces, slightly overlapping, down the centre of a hot heatproof dish.

Pour the tomato mixture over the top and sprinkle with the rest of the cheese. Place in the top of a hot oven, Mark 7 (220°C/425°F), for 20–30 minutes to brown the top. Serve hot.

Tante Marie tip:
Try this dish using ham instead of tongue.

Rognons d'Agneau à la Grandmère

Grandmother's recipe for lamb kidneys
(serves 4)

An attractive dish of kidneys and mushrooms with a potato border.

	Imperial	American
8 lambs' kidneys		
50 g butter	2 oz	$\frac{1}{4}$ cup
1 onion, finely chopped		
3 rashers of lean bacon, diced		
salt and pepper		
100 g mushrooms	4 oz	4 oz
15 g plain flour	$\frac{1}{2}$ oz	2 tbsp
4 tbsp red wine	4 tbsp	4 tbsp
150 ml stock	$\frac{1}{4}$ pt	$\frac{2}{3}$ cup
$\frac{1}{4}$ cucumber		
1 tbsp sherry	1 tbsp	1 tbsp
250 g carrots	8 oz	8 oz
250 g turnips	8 oz	8 oz
1 tsp lemon juice	1 tsp	1 tsp
4 tbsp white wine	4 tbsp	4 tbsp
a little melted butter		
Pommes de Terre Duchesse made with 750 g potatoes	1$\frac{1}{2}$ lb	1$\frac{1}{2}$ lb
(*see page 179*)		
chopped parsley		

Skin the kidneys and soak them in cold salted water for 20 minutes. Cut them in half and remove the core.

Melt 25 g (1 oz/2 tbsp) of butter in a pan. When it is hot, add the kidneys and cook quickly to brown. Remove from the pan and add the onion and bacon. Season and cook until the onion is soft and transparent. Slice the mushrooms thinly and add to the onion. Sprinkle in the flour, mix well and cook for 2–3 minutes. Add the red wine and stock and bring to simmering point. Peel the cucumber, cut into 12 mm ($\frac{1}{2}$ in) dice and add to the mixture with the sherry. Replace the kidneys and cook gently for 20–30 minutes.

Meanwhile, peel the carrots and turnips and cut into julienne. Melt the remaining 25 g (1 oz/2 tbsp) of butter in a pan and add the vegetables, lemon juice, white wine and seasoning. Cover with greaseproof paper and a lid and cook very slowly until the vegetables are tender, shaking the pan from time to time.

Brush the edge of a serving-dish with the melted butter and pipe a border of Pommes de Terre Duchesse using a forcing bag with a large rosette pipe. Place the julienne of carrots and turnips in the centre. Pile the kidneys on top and pour over the sauce. Sprinkle with chopped parsley and serve.

Rognons d'Agneau à la Beaujolaise

Lambs' kidneys in Beaujolais (serves 4)

A simple dish of kidneys in red wine.

	Imperial	American
8 lambs' kidneys		
50 g butter	2 oz	$\frac{1}{4}$ cup
1 onion, finely chopped		
150 ml Beaujolais or other red wine	$\frac{1}{4}$ pt	$\frac{2}{3}$ cup
2 tbsp double cream	2 tbsp	2 tbsp
1 tbsp French mustard	1 tbsp	1 tbsp
salt and pepper		
chopped parsley		

Skin the kidneys and soak in cold salted water for 30 minutes. Cut them in half and remove the cores.

Melt the butter in a pan. When it is hot, add the onion and cook until soft and transparent. Add the kidneys and cook them quickly. When the kidneys are cooked, place them on a hot serving-dish.

Add the wine to the sauté pan, bring to the boil and reduce by half. Mix the cream and mustard together. Add to the wine and heat through without boiling. Season to taste, pour over the kidneys and sprinkle with chopped parsley.

Ris de Veau Braisé

Braised veal sweetbreads (serves 4)

The delicate flavour of this dish will provide a good contrast to many dishes for your dinner parties.

	Imperial	American
2 veal sweetbreads, or 500 g lambs' sweetbreads	1 lb	1 lb
1 onion		
2 carrots		
25 g butter	1 oz	2 tbsp
1–2 tbsp brandy (optional)	1–2 tbsp	1–2 tbsp
150 ml white stock	$\frac{1}{4}$ pt	$\frac{2}{3}$ cup
150 ml white wine	$\frac{1}{4}$ pt	$\frac{2}{3}$ cup
a bouquet garni		
salt and pepper		
$\frac{1}{2}$–1 tsp arrowroot	$\frac{1}{2}$–1 tsp	$\frac{1}{2}$–1 tsp

Soak the sweetbreads in water for 2–3 hours to remove any blood. Place in a pan of cold water, bring to the boil, then simmer for 2–3 minutes. Drain and refresh. Remove all the loose tissue and sinews.

Peel and finely chop the onion and carrots. Melt the butter in a pan, add the onion and carrots and cook gently without colouring for 7–10 minutes. Place the sweetbreads on top. Warm the brandy (if used), pour over and flambé. Add the stock, wine, bouquet garni and seasoning. Cover with greaseproof paper and a lid and simmer gently or cook in a moderate oven, Mark 4 (180°C/350°F), for 30–40 minutes or until the sweetbreads are tender.

Remove the sweetbreads from the pan, slice and place on a hot dish. Strain the braising liquor into a clean pan. Slake the arrowroot in a little water and add to the braising liquor. Return to the heat, bring to the boil and simmer for 1–2 minutes. Pour over the sweetbreads and serve.

Tante Marie tip:
For a richer sauce add 2 tablespoons of double cream to the sauce before pouring it over the sweetbreads.

Réchauffé

Reheated dishes

It is always useful to have a good repertoire of dishes using leftovers of meat. The following recipes are delicious ways in which you can do this.

Jambon de Picardie

Picardy ham (serves 4)

A quickly made entrée or supper dish.

	Imperial	American
4 large slices of ham		
2 shallots		
100 g mushrooms	4 oz	4 oz
40 g butter	1½ oz	3 tbsp
250 ml white wine	8 fl oz	1 cup
3 tbsp double cream	3 tbsp	3 tbsp
2 tbsp finely chopped fresh herbs	2 tbsp	2 tbsp
salt and pepper		

Finely chop the shallots and the mushrooms. Melt 25 g (1 oz/2 tbsp) of the butter in a pan. When it is hot, fry the shallots gently until soft but not coloured. Add the mushrooms and wine and cook for 5–7 minutes.

Melt the rest of the butter in another pan. Warm the slices of ham in this. Arrange them, overlapping, on a hot serving-dish.

Stir the cream and herbs into the sauce, taste and season and pour over the ham.

Tante Marie tip:
Slices of cooked or raw gammon are ideal for this dish. If using raw gammon, poach it gently in water for 8–10 minutes or until tender. Arrange the ham as above and pour the sauce over.

Pain de Boeuf

Meat loaf (serves 4)

An ideal way to use leftover roast or braised beef.

	Imperial	American
350 g minced cooked beef	12 oz	3¾ cups
25 g butter	1 oz	2 tbsp
1 onion, chopped		
25 g plain flour	1 oz	3 tbsp
300 ml milk	½ pt	1 cup
1 heaped tsp tomato purée	1 tsp	1 tsp
1 tbsp finely chopped parsley mixed with a little thyme *or* other fresh herbs	1 tbsp	1 tbsp
2 eggs		
salt and pepper		
a pinch of nutmeg		
300 ml Sauce Tomate	½ pt	1 cup
(*see page 33*)		

Melt the butter, add the onion and cook gently, without browning, until tender. Stir in the flour, cook for a couple of minutes, then remove from the heat and add the milk gradually. Bring to the boil, stirring all the time, then cook for 2–3 minutes. Stir in the tomato purée, beef, herbs, beaten eggs, seasoning and nutmeg. Put the mixture into a 15 cm (6 in) buttered cake tin. Stand in a roasting-pan containing boiling water and cook in a moderately hot oven, Mark 5 (190°C/375°F), for 45 minutes or until set.

To ensure the loaf comes out of the tin without breaking, turn the tin onto a hot serving-dish, cover with a cloth and leave for a few minutes before unmoulding. Heat the Sauce Tomate and gently spoon it over the top of the loaf; the loaf is liable to crack if the sauce is poured on straight from the pan.

Rissoles

Deep fried meat turnovers (serves 4)

To the French cook, rissoles are meat or fish mixtures wrapped in shortcrust pastry and deep-fat fried. This is another excellent way of using up leftover meat and the rissoles are tasty enough to serve as appetisers with drinks.

	Imperial	American
225 g plain flour	8 oz	2 cups
salt and pepper		
50 g butter	2 oz	$\frac{1}{4}$ cup
50 g lard	2 oz	$\frac{1}{4}$ cup
For the filling:		
1 onion		
1 clove garlic		
25 g dripping	1 oz	2 tbsp
15 g plain flour	$\frac{1}{2}$ oz	2 tbsp
100 g minced cooked beef, lamb, veal *or* chicken	4 oz	$1\frac{1}{4}$ cups
1 tsp tomato purée	1 tsp	1 tsp
1 tsp chopped herbs	1 tsp	1 tsp
6–8 tbsp stock	6–8 tbsp	6–8 tbsp
fat for deep frying		
For serving:		
300 ml Sauce Tomate (*see page 33*), *or* Sauce Piquante (*see page 29*)	$\frac{1}{2}$ pt	$1\frac{1}{4}$ cups

Sift the flour and a $\frac{1}{4}$ teaspoonful of salt into a bowl, then rub in the butter and lard with the fingertips until the mixture resembles fine breadcrumbs. Bind together with a little cold water.

Chop the onion finely and crush the garlic with a little salt. Heat the dripping in a pan, add the onion and garlic and fry gently until soft. Add the flour and cook for 1–2 minutes. Mix in the minced meat, tomato purée and chopped herbs with sufficient stock to moisten without making the mixture too soft. Add seasoning to taste. Spread on a plate and cool quickly.

Roll out the pastry thinly and cut into 6.5 cm ($2\frac{1}{2}$ in) circles. Brush around the edge of each with water and place a teaspoonful of the mixture in each. Fold over to form half-moon-shaped patties and seal the edges well.

Heat a deep pan of fat to 190°C (375°F) and fry the rissoles quickly in a frying-basket until golden brown. Drain on kitchen paper.

Serve hot with Sauce Tomate or Sauce Piquante.

Tante Marie tip:
These rissoles can also be dipped into beaten egg and sieved white breadcrumbs or crushed vermicelli before being fried.

Poultry and Game

In every part of France there are local recipes for cooking poultry and game. From Provence you have a thyme-flavoured Poulet Sauté à la Provençale. Each region has its own special recipe for duck. Game is cooked with the wild mushrooms of autumn or with innumerable other ingredients; even the humble cabbage is glorified by the succulence of partridges. There are many, many recipes, but you need only to understand the basic preparation and cooking of poultry to begin to tackle them. Once you know how to truss and joint, roast, poach and sauté, you can cook an infinite number of dishes: not only using chicken and duck, but also goose, turkey, pheasant, partridge, pigeon, hare and rabbit, to give appetising changes to your menus.

Young birds are best to use for roasting. With poultry, you can judge this by feeling the breastbone; on a young bird the cartilage is still flexible at the tip. As the bird ages, this develops into hard bone and a bird at this stage needs long, slow cooking to make it tender and tasty.

When you order poultry by weight, remember that fresh birds are weighed before being dressed and that this weight includes the head, innards and legs, so you must allow for loss of weight. On a frozen bird you are told the dressed weight including the giblets.

If you are cooking frozen poultry or game, make quite certain that it has time to defrost completely before cooking, otherwise it is liable to be undercooked and is then a potential source of food poisoning.

The flavour of individual recipes depends partly on the way in which the poultry or game is cooked, but even more on the use of herbs, vegetables, cream and wine to add flavour and texture to the dish.

Le Poulet

Chicken

Chickens are available throughout the year. When you buy a farm-fresh bird allow for about 22 per cent loss of weight in preparation. A useful size for family cooking is a bird weighing about 1.75 kg ($3\frac{1}{2}$ lb) when dressed. This will serve four portions. A larger bird of 2–3 kg (4–6 lb) will serve six, while a capon weighs about 3–4 kg (6–8 lb). Old birds are usually boiled. They have a stronger flavour and need long, slow cooking to tenderise them. For individual portions, recipes can be adapted to use young baby chicken or poussin weighing 350–500 g (12 oz–1 lb) each.

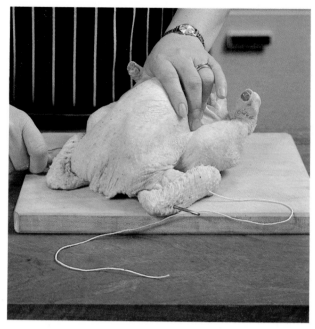

Trussing a Chicken

Chicken and other birds are trussed when they are cooked whole in order to keep them in good shape so that they look neat and cook evenly.

2. Put the needle through again, this time going through the other end of the wing.

1. Tuck the tips of the wing and the flap of skin under the bird. Take a trussing needle which is long enough to go from one side of the bird to the other. Thread this with reasonably fine cotton string. Take the needle through from one wing to the other, going through the flap and under the wing bones.

3. Pull the string firmly and tie the two ends together in a bow, so it is easy to remove when the bird is cooked.

4. Take a second piece of string and thread into the trussing needle. Lift up the legs and put the needle through the bird, at the angle of the leg.

6. Lift the 'parson's nose' and put the string under to hold it in position, then pull tight.

5. Take through again, going through the leg near the joint and under the bone.

7. Tie in another bow. The chicken should be a firm plump shape with the legs held neatly in position. Tie a short piece of string around the legs to hold them tight. After cooking pull one end of each string to remove.

Poulet à l'Estragon

Roast chicken with tarragon (serves 4–6)

Tarragon is a favourite flavouring in France for roast chicken which is often served in this way when the herb is in season from late spring to the first frost of autumn.

	Imperial	American
1 (1.5–2 kg) roasting chicken, drawn and trussed	3½–4 lb	3½–4 lb
75 g butter	3 oz	6 tbsp
1 handful of sprigs of tarragon		
1 clove garlic		
salt and pepper		
a little oil		
2 tbsp brandy	2 tbsp	2 tbsp
4 tbsp chicken stock	4 tbsp	4 tbsp
a little chopped tarragon		

Remove any pin feathers on the bird (see page 144). Place 25 g (1 oz/2 tbsp) of butter with the sprigs of tarragon, peeled garlic and seasoning inside the chicken. Truss, then place the bird in a roasting-pan with the rest of the butter. Season and brush over with the oil. Roast in a moderately hot oven, Mark 6 (200°C/400°F), basting occasionally. Allow 20 minutes per ½ kg (1 lb) plus 20 minutes over.

When the chicken is tender and golden brown, remove from the oven and tilt the bird so the buttery sauce inside it pours into the roasting-pan. Warm the brandy in a small pan and flame it over the chicken. Lift the chicken onto the serving-dish and remove the trussing string.

Blend the stock with the hot pan juices, boil again, taste and season. Stir in the chopped tarragon and pour over the chicken. Serve hot.

Poulet à la Grandmère

Grandmother's chicken (serves 4–6)

Stuffed garnished chicken: an ideal recipe to use for Sunday lunch.

	Imperial	American
1 (1.5–2 kg) roasting chicken, drawn and trussed	3½–4 lb	3½–4 lb
25 g butter	1 oz	2 tbsp
3 rashers of fat bacon to bard the chicken		
50 g lean bacon	2 oz	2 oz
10 button onions		
3 medium potatoes		
a little chicken stock, if necessary		
For the stuffing:		
1 small onion		
25 g butter	1 oz	2 tbsp
liver from the chicken, chopped		
100 g sausagemeat	4 oz	4 oz
2 tbsp finely chopped parsley	2 tbsp	2 tbsp
4 tbsp white breadcrumbs	4 tbsp	4 tbsp
salt and pepper		

First prepare the stuffing. Chop the onion finely and soften it in the butter without allowing it to brown. Add the chicken liver, sausagemeat, parsley, breadcrumbs and seasoning. Mix together well. Stuff the breast and body of the bird with this mixture, then truss the bird. Spread the breast with the butter and cover the breast with the rashers of bacon. Place the bird in a casserole (a heavy iron one is ideal).

Cut the lean bacon into dice and arrange round the sides of the bird with the peeled whole onions.

Cover with a lid, place in a moderately hot oven, Mark 5 (190°C/375°F), and cook for approximately 30 minutes. At the end of this time cut the potatoes into dice, add to the casserole and continue cooking for a further 30 minutes. Remove the lid, take off the bacon rashers and cook until the chicken is golden brown and tender (this should take a further 35–40 minutes).

To serve, remove the trussing strings and place the chicken on a hot serving-dish. Arrange the potatoes and onions at each end of the dish. Add some stock to the sauce if needed, and pour it over the chicken.

Poule au Pot Farci à la Lorraine
Stuffed poached chicken (serves 5–6)

A stuffed chicken which is poached and served with winter vegetables in a creamy sauce.

	Imperial	American
1 (1.5–2 kg) chicken, drawn and trussed	3½–4 lb	3½–4 lb
giblets from the chicken		
1 onion stuck with 2 cloves		
1 stick celery		
a bouquet garni		
8 peppercorns		
2 tsp salt	2 tsp	2 tsp

For the stuffing:

	Imperial	American
2 cloves garlic		
100 g breadcrumbs	4 oz	1¾ cups
4 tbsp milk	4 tbsp	4 tbsp
100 g veal	4 oz	4 oz
100 g lean bacon	4 oz	4 oz
2 tsp finely chopped parsley	2 tsp	2 tsp
100 g sausagemeat	4 oz	4 oz
a sprig of thyme, chopped		
a pinch of nutmeg		
1 egg		
salt and pepper		
500 g carrots	1 lb	1 lb
275 g turnips	10 oz	10 oz
4 leeks		

For the sauce:

	Imperial	American
40 g butter	1½ oz	3 tbsp
40 g plain flour	1½ oz	⅓ cup
juice of ½ lemon		
3 tbsp double cream	3 tbsp	3 tbsp
2 egg yolks		

First make the stock. Place 1 litre (2 pt/4½ cups) of water in a large pan, and add the onion, celery, bouquet garni, all the giblets except the liver, peppercorns and salt. Bring to the boil, skim and allow to simmer gently while you prepare the chicken.

To make the stuffing, crush the garlic. Place the breadcrumbs and milk in a bowl. Chop together or mince the veal, bacon, chicken liver, garlic and parsley. Squeeze the milk out of the breadcrumbs and mix them with the sausagemeat, thyme, nutmeg, egg and seasoning. Blend very thoroughly and stuff the body and breast of the chicken with this mixture. Truss the bird, then place in the pan of stock, adding more water if required to nearly cover the bird. Cover with a lid and simmer very gently for approximately 2 hours or until tender.

Meanwhile, prepare the carrots and turnips and cut into quarters. Add these and the cleaned leeks after 1 hour of cooking.

When the chicken and vegetables are tender, take 1 litre (2 pt/4½ cups) of the stock and place in another pan. Boil hard to reduce the quantity by half.

To prepare the sauce, melt the butter in a pan, add the flour and cook, stirring all the time, for 2–3 minutes. Remove from the heat and blend in the reduced stock and the lemon juice. Bring to the boil, stirring all the time, then cook for 4–5 minutes.

Drain the chicken and cut into portions, as described in the following recipe. Take the stuffing and cut into slices. Arrange on a dish with the vegetables.

Blend the cream with the egg yolks. Add some of the hot sauce, mix and return to the pan. Warm through without boiling. Taste and season. Strain some sauce over the meat and vegetables and serve the rest in a sauce-boat.

Tante Marie tip:
This recipe is ideal for a boiling fowl. A roasting chicken will cook in about 1 hour.

Poulet Gratiné aux Champignons

Cheese topped chicken with mushrooms
(serves 4–6)

A purée of mushrooms gives a distinctive flavour to this creamy chicken dish. Serve it with fluffy boiled rice.

	Imperial	American
1 (1.5 kg) chicken, drawn and trussed	3½ lb	3½ lb
giblets from the chicken		
2 carrots		
2 onions		
1 bayleaf		
6–8 peppercorns		
1 tsp salt	1 tsp	1 tsp
1 litre water	1¾ pt	4½ cups
100 g mushrooms	4 oz	4 oz
75 g butter	3 oz	6 tbsp
25 g plain flour	1 oz	3 tbsp
150 ml double cream	¼ pt	⅔ cup
2 egg yolks		
50 g Gruyère cheese, grated	2 oz	1 cup

Rinse the chicken giblets and place them all (except the liver) in a large pan with the carrots, onions, bayleaf, peppercorns, salt and water. Bring to the boil, then simmer for 1 hour.

Add the trussed chicken, cover with a lid and simmer gently until tender. A young bird will take about 1 hour, but an older boiling fowl needs about 2–2½ hours to get really tender.

Wash the mushrooms and chop very finely, either with a knife or in a liquidiser or food processor. Melt 25 g (1 oz/2 tbsp) butter in a pan, add the mushrooms and cook gently for 3–4 minutes.

When the chicken is cooked, lift it out of the pan and drain. Carve off the legs and drumsticks and divide into the two joints. Cut off the wishbone with a piece of breast meat and cut off the breast from each side of the bird. Cut each into two. Remove the skin, place the chicken on a serving-dish and keep warm. Strain the stock. To make the sauce, melt the rest of the butter in a pan and add the flour. Cook for a few minutes, then add 300 ml (½ pt/1¼ cups) of the strained chicken stock and the mushroom purée. Bring to the boil, stirring all the time, then simmer for 5 minutes. Mix the cream and egg yolks together. Pour the hot sauce onto them, stir and return to the pan. Taste and season, then repeat without boiling. Pour the sauce over the chicken and sprinkle with the cheese. Brown lightly under a very hot grill.

Suprêmes de Volaille Henri IV

Chicken breasts with Béarnaise Sauce
(serves 4)

An excellent dinner-party dish, which can be cooked very quickly if the chicken is cut and the sauce is made in advance.

	Imperial	American
2 (1.5 kg) chickens, or 4 chicken breasts	3–3½ lb	3–3½ lb
4 small artichokes or canned artichoke hearts		
juice of 1 lemon		
salt		
2 tomatoes		
50 g shelled peas	2 oz	2 oz
2 tbsp seasoned flour	2 tbsp	2 tbsp
65 g butter	2½ oz	5 tbsp
Sauce Béarnaise (see page 32)		

To prepare the suprêmes of chicken breast, scrape the flesh from the wishbone and remove it from the carcase. Take off the legs, then cut along each side of the breastbone using a filleting or boning knife, and bring the breast flesh away from the bone so that you have this in one piece, cutting through the wing joint. Remove the skin.

For fresh artichokes cut each one 4 cm (1½ in) from the base and pare down the leaves with a sharp knife. Scrape out the 'choke' to form a cup, then rub over the surface with the lemon juice. Cook in boiling salted water for approximately 20–25 minutes or until tender. If you are using canned artichokes, remove the choke, if necessary, and warm through.

Cut the tomatoes in half, scoop out the centres and sprinkle with a little salt. Turn upside down and allow to stand for 30 minutes. Cook the peas in boiling salted water until tender.

Coat the chicken breasts with the seasoned flour. Melt 50 g (2 oz/¼ cup) butter in a frying-pan, add the chicken breasts and cook until golden brown on each side and cooked through (8–10 minutes). Cook until just tender, but do not overcook or the chicken will toughen.

Put a knob of the remaining butter in each half tomato. Place on a baking-tray and heat through in a moderately hot oven, Mark 6 (200°C/400°F), for 5 minutes.

Arrange the suprêmes of chicken on a hot serving-dish. Make the Sauce Béarnaise and fill the artichoke hearts with this. Fill the tomatoes with the cooked peas. Arrange alternately around the chicken. Serve at once.

Salade de Poulet à la Niçoise
Chicken salad from Nice (serves 6)

This is a colourful well-flavoured dish to use for a buffet party.

	Imperial	American
1 cold cooked chicken		
250 g French beans	8 oz	8 oz
300 ml Mayonnaise (*see page 30*)	$\frac{1}{2}$ pt	$1\frac{1}{4}$ cups
1 *or* 2 red peppers, depending on size		
2 tbsp tomato purée	2 tbsp	2 tbsp
a few chopped tarragon leaves		
salt and pepper		
lemon juice to taste		
4 tomatoes		
a few black olives, stoned		
4 tbsp oil	4 tbsp	4 tbsp
1 tbsp vinegar	1 tbsp	1 tbsp
1 clove garlic		
a little French mustard		
chopped parsley		

Top and tail the French beans, then cook in boiling salted water for about 20 minutes or until tender. Drain, and refresh under the cold tap. Make the mayonnaise.

Cut the peppers in half and remove the seeds and core. Blanch in boiling salted water for 5 minutes. Drain and refresh with cold water. Drain again, chop very finely indeed and stir into the mayonnaise.

Add the tomato purée, tarragon, seasoning and lemon juice. Remove the chicken from the carcase and cut into pieces. Mix it with half the mayonnaise.

Cut the tomatoes in half, scoop out the centres and fill with the olives.

Whisk the oil and vinegar together. Season to taste with the salt, pepper, crushed garlic and mustard. Toss the beans in this dressing.

To serve, pile the chicken mixture in the centre of a platter. Coat with the rest of the mayonnaise. Arrange the tomatoes at each end, and the beans along the sides. Sprinkle the beans with chopped parsley.

Tante Marie tip:
If this is used for a fork buffet, cut the chicken into bite-sized pieces and cut the beans into shorter lengths.

Salade de Poulet à la Niçoise.

Vol-au-Vent

Puff pastry made with 250 g (9 oz/2 cups) strong flour (see page 210).

2. Take the circle, turn it over and place on a dampened baking-tray. Brush with beaten egg, taking care not to let it drop down the sides. Using a small knife, held as shown above, make a criss-cross pattern on the pastry.

1. Take a plate measuring about 19 cm (7½ in) in diameter and a 9 cm (3½ in) cutter. Roll out the chilled pastry on a lightly floured board until it is large enough for two circles the size of the plate, leaving 1 cm (½ in) of pastry at each side. Cut the circles, holding the knife at an angle so the edge of each circle is cut at a slant. Using the cutter, take a circle from one round only. Lift the surplus pastry and fold into layers so that it can be used again. Wrap and chill.

3. Lift the other circle of pastry onto the base and fit it on neatly. This piece is kept the same way up as this shaping helps to counteract the natural tendency of puff pastry to shrink inwards. The criss-crossed base will rise up to form the lid.

4. Knock up the edges to encourage them to rise well and evenly.

6. Brush the top with beaten egg and make a design on it, using the back of a small knife.

5. Flute the edges, pressing the pastry with the thumb of one hand, while bringing the back of the knife in at an angle. Chill for about 20 minutes.

Start baking in a very hot oven, Mark 7–8 (220–230°C/425–450°F), for 10 minutes then, without opening the door, reduce the temperature to Mark 5 (190°C/375°F) and continue cooking for a further 20-25 minutes. When the pastry is golden brown and set, remove from the oven, cut around the lid and lift this off. Scoop out any uncooked pastry inside the case with a spoon. Return to the oven to dry off and complete cooking. When ready, cool on a wire rack and either use immediately or place in an airtight container. If it has to be reheated, place in a hot oven for a short time.

Vol-au-Vent à la Reine

Chicken vol-au-vent (serves 4–5)

A large crisp puff pastry case with a filling of chicken and mushrooms in a Velouté sauce. This mixture can also be used to fill individual bouchée cases.

	Imperial	American
1 cooked vol-au-vent case (*see pages 140–141*)		
1 (1.5 kg) chicken, poached	$3\frac{1}{2}$ lb	$3\frac{1}{2}$ lb
25 g butter	1 oz	2 tbsp
50 g mushrooms	2 oz	2 oz
1 tsp lemon juice		
salt and pepper		
300 ml Sauce Velouté (*see page 27*)	$\frac{1}{2}$ pt	$1\frac{1}{4}$ cups

To finish:
finely chopped parsley

Either make the pastry case or, if it has been made beforehand, reheat it in a hot oven until crisp.

Shred the chicken, removing all skin and bone. Melt the butter in a pan and add the mushrooms, lemon juice and seasoning. Cover with greaseproof paper and a lid and cook gently for 5 minutes.

Make the Sauce Velouté. Stir in the chicken and mushrooms and heat gently. Taste and season. Fill the hot pastry case with this mixture and put the top on. Sprinkle a line of the parsley around the cap and serve hot.

Tante Marie tip:
Other cooked poultry such as turkey can also be used in the same way.

Right: Vol-au-Vent à la Reine.

Jointing a Raw Chicken

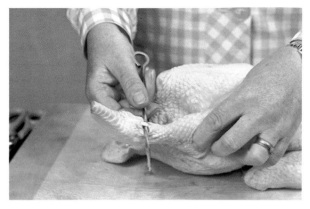

1. Pull out any remaining 'pin' feathers by placing a small knife under each one and pulling briskly. Remove the sinews from the drumsticks. To do this, slit the skin and put a skewer through under the sinew. Twist and pull to take it out of the leg.

4. With the angle of the joints facing upwards, cut between the joints, taking the knife down the natural crease to divide the thigh from the drumstick.

2. Pull the thigh and drumstick away from the breast. Cut through the skin with a sharp knife.

5. Trim off the end of the leg with the sinew. Put in the stockpot with other trimmings.

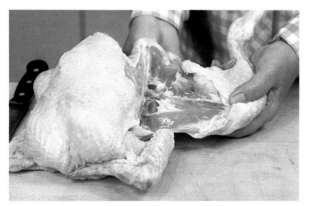

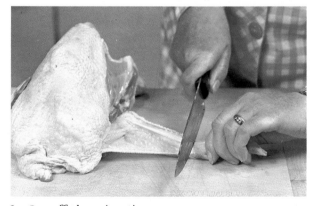

3. Press to open out at the joint. Cut through the flesh and between the ball-and-socket joint to separate the leg from the body.

6. Cut off the wing tips.

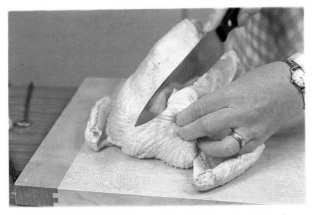

7. Take a large pinch of the breast flesh and cut down behind it, so that this is attached to the wing.

10. Lift this up and over the joint. This will then stay in position when it is cooked.

8. Slice through at the joint.

11. Separate the breast by cutting through the bones. The breast is then halved.

9. Hold so that the piece of flesh drops downwards.

12. The joints, ready to cook.
Back row, left to right: drumstick, thigh, breast, thigh, drumstick.

Front row, left to right: wing, breast, wing.

Coq au Vin
Cockerel in red wine (serves 4)

Originating in Burgundy, this classic casserole is made with cockerel or chicken cooked in red wine with herbs, onions and mushrooms to make a smooth and succulent dish. Serve it with a red wine.

	Imperial	American
1 (1.5 kg) cockerel *or* chicken	3½ lb	3½ lb
40 g butter	1½ oz	3 tbsp
1 tbsp oil	1 tbsp	1 tbsp
75 g lean rashers of bacon	3 oz	3 oz
350 g button onions	12 oz	12 oz
3 tbsp brandy	3 tbsp	3 tbsp
1 tbsp plain flour	1 tbsp	1 tbsp
600 ml red wine	1 pt	2 cups
a bouquet garni, containing a sprig of thyme, 1 bayleaf and a sprig of rosemary		
1 tbsp sugar	1 tbsp	1 tbsp
a pinch of nutmeg		
175 g button mushrooms	6 oz	6 oz
salt and pepper		

To finish:
heart-shaped fried croûtons (*see page 23*)

Joint the bird as shown on pages 144–45. Place the butter and oil in a heavy sauté pan and heat well. Add the bacon cut in strips and the onions. Turn them in the pan until golden brown. Remove, and keep on one side. Place the joints of the bird in the pan and brown them evenly. Warm the brandy, pour on and flame it. Take out the joints. Sprinkle in the flour and cook for 2–3 minutes, stirring well. Return the joints, onions and bacon to the pan. Add the wine, bouquet garni, sugar, nutmeg, mushrooms and seasoning. Cover with greaseproof paper and a lid and cook over a low heat or in a moderate oven, Mark 4 (180°C/350°F), for approximately 1 hour.

Check that the chicken is tender and lift the joints onto a hot serving-dish. Pile up the mushrooms at each end and arrange the onions along the sides of the dish. Remove the grease from the sauce. Reheat, taste and season the liquor and strain over the bird. Garnish with the croûtons.

Poulet Sauté à l'Italienne
Italian chicken (serves 4)

In common with many dishes from the Côte d'Azur this dish has a strong Italian influence. It can be served with a border of noodles.

	Imperial	American
1 (1.5 kg) roasting chicken	3½ lb	3½ lb
50 g butter	2 oz	¼ cup
1 tbsp oil	1 tbsp	1 tbsp
1 onion, finely chopped		
1 shallot, finely chopped		
15 g plain flour	½ oz	2 tbsp
150 ml white wine	¼ pt	⅔ cup
300 ml Sauce Tomate (*see page 33*)	½ pt	1¼ cups
150 ml chicken stock	¼ pt	⅔ cup
100 g mushrooms	4 oz	4 oz
100 g ham	4 oz	4 oz
salt and pepper		
1 tbsp finely chopped parsley and basil	1 tbsp	1 tbsp

Joint the chicken as shown on pages 144–45. Heat the butter and oil in a sauté pan, add the joints and sauté until well browned. Remove from the pan and add the onion and shallot. Cook until tender. Sprinkle in the flour, cook for a minute, then add the wine, Sauce Tomate and stock. Bring to the boil, return the chicken to the pan and cook for approximately 45 minutes or until nearly tender. About 10 minutes from the end of the cooking time, add the chopped mushrooms and ham and continue to simmer.

Lift the chicken onto a serving-dish. Boil the sauce to reduce it slightly. Taste and season. Pour it over the chicken and sprinkle with the herbs. Serve hot.

Poulet Sauté à la Provençale
Provençale chicken (serves 4)

This superbly flavoured casserole can be prepared in advance. Cover the bacon-wrapped joints and place in the refrigerator, and have all the other ingredients ready. An hour or so before you want to eat, start to sauté the joints, which can safely be left to simmer in the wine until they are cooked. Completing the dish takes only a few minutes.

	Imperial	American
1 (1.5–2 kg) roasting chicken	3½–4 lb	3½–4 lb
8 sprigs of thyme		
8 rashers back bacon		
4 tomatoes		
50 g butter	2 oz	¼ cup
1 tbsp oil	1 tbsp	1 tbsp
1 large onion		
2 tsp plain flour	2 tsp	2 tsp
300 ml wine	½ pt	1¼ cups
salt and pepper		
1 clove garlic		
6–8 slices of French bread, fried in oil		
finely chopped parsley		

Joint the chicken as shown on pages 144–45. Place a sprig of thyme on each joint, wrap round with a rasher of bacon and tie with a piece of thin string. Skin and pip the tomatoes and cut into shreds. Heat the butter and oil together in a sauté pan, add the joints and fry until they are a good rich brown. Remove the chicken, add the chopped onion and tomatoes and fry for several minutes. Pour off excess fat. Sprinkle in the flour. Mix well, then pour on the wine and add the seasoning and garlic crushed with a little salt. Bring to the boil. Replace the chicken, cover with a lid and simmer gently for 45 minutes–1 hour.

When the chicken is tender, remove the string from the joints and place them in a hot serving-dish. Reduce the liquor in which the chicken was cooked until it is the consistency of thin cream. Adjust the seasoning and pour over the chicken. Garnish with the French bread and dust thickly with the parsley.

Tante Marie tip:
If the sauce should boil away too much, add a spoonful or two of water to correct the consistency.

Poulet Sauté à la Provençale.

Fricassée de Poulet à l'Angevine
Chicken casserole from Angers (serves 4)

This fricassée is quickly prepared and has a delicate creamy flavour. Cider can replace the wine for a slightly different, but very good, flavour.

	Imperial	American
1 (1.5 kg) chicken	3½ lb	3½ lb
50 g butter	2 oz	¼ cup
8 button onions		
100 g button mushrooms	4 oz	4 oz
250 ml dry white wine	8 fl oz	1 cup
salt and pepper		
150 ml double cream	¼ pt	⅔ cup

Joint the chicken as shown on pages 144–45. Melt the butter in the pan, add the chicken and lightly brown. Remove the joints from the pan, add the onions and mushrooms and fry until golden brown. Add the wine and seasoning and replace the chicken in the pan. Cover with greaseproof paper and a lid and cook over a low heat until tender (about 45 minutes–1 hour). Place the chicken on a hot serving-dish, add the cream to the sauce and reboil. Remove any grease, adjust the seasoning and pour over the chicken.

Poulet Sauté Duroc

Chicken casserole Duroc (serves 4)

A garnish of tomatoes, mushrooms and potatoes adds colour and flavour to this sauté chicken.

	Imperial	American
1 (1.5–2 kg) roasting chicken	3¼–4 lb	3¼–4 lb
40 g butter	1½ oz	3 tbsp
1 tbsp oil	1 tbsp	1 tbsp
4 tbsp seasoned flour	4 tbsp	4 tbsp
1 small onion, finely chopped		
2 tsp plain flour	2 tsp	2 tsp
1 tsp tomato purée	1 tsp	1 tsp
150 ml dry white wine	¼ pt	⅔ cup
450 ml chicken stock	¾ pt	1¾ cups
1 clove garlic		
salt and pepper		
100 g mushrooms	4 oz	4 oz

For the garnish:

	Imperial	American
500 g small new potatoes	1 lb	1 lb
8 small tomatoes		
25 g butter	1 oz	2 tbsp
finely chopped parsley		

Joint the chicken as shown on pages 144–45. Melt the butter and oil together in a sauté pan. Dip the chicken joints in the seasoned flour. When the butter and oil are hot, add the chicken and brown it well all over. Remove the chicken, add the onion and cook for a few minutes until brown. Drain off excess fat, then stir in the flour and tomato purée. Add the wine, stock and garlic crushed with a little salt. Bring to simmering point, then replace the chicken. Season. Cover with greaseproof paper and a lid and simmer gently on the hob or cook in a moderately hot oven, Mark 4 (180°C/350°F), for 45 minutes. At the end of this time add the sliced mushrooms. Cook for a further 10 minutes.

Meanwhile, cook the potatoes in boiling salted water until tender. Skin the tomatoes and cook gently in the rest of the butter.

Pile the chicken onto a hot serving-dish. Pour over the sauce and garnish with the tomatoes and potatoes. Dust with the parsley.

Poulet Sauté à la Bordelaise

Bordeaux-style chicken (serves 4)

This chicken is lightly sautéd to a delicate golden brown, and cooked in stock with herbs and shallots or onions. Garnished with these and artichokes it makes a gourmet dish.

	Imperial	American
1 (1.5 kg) roasting chicken	3–3½ lb	3–3½ lb
75 g butter	3 oz	6 tbsp
1 tbsp oil	1 tbsp	1 tbsp
225 g shallots *or* pickling onions	8 oz	8 oz
150 ml chicken stock	¼ pt	⅔ cup
1 bayleaf		
salt and pepper		
a few parsley stalks		
4 fresh globe artichokes		
a little lemon juice		

Joint the chicken as shown on pages 144–45. Heat 50 g (2 oz/¼ cup) of butter with the oil in a heavy pan. When it is hot, place some joints in the pan and fry until golden brown on both sides. Remove from the pan and sauté the rest of the joints. Remove these too, add the onions and toss in the butter until golden brown. Lift out of the pan.

Return the chicken to the pan, with any juice that has dripped out. Add the stock and bayleaf. Season well, cover with a lid and cook for approximately 1 hour or until tender. After 30 minutes, add the onions.

Prepare the artichokes (see page 160). When cooked, remove the 'choke' (the whiskery centre) and the leaves. Cut the base into quarters. Melt the remaining butter, add the lemon juice and toss the artichokes in this.

When the chicken is tender, remove the joints and arrange on a serving-dish. Boil the sauce to reduce it, taste and season and remove any grease. Pour over the chicken and garnish with the artichokes.

Tante Marie tip:

If fresh artichokes are not available, or if you are short of time, use canned or frozen ones instead.

Le Pintade

Guinea fowl

Guinea fowl can be obtained at any time of the year. The flavour is midway between that of chicken and pheasant, and there is a good proportion of meat to bone. The size varies from a small bird of 550 g (1¼ lb) to larger birds of 1.5 kg (3 lb).

Pintade à la Vigneronne

Braised guinea fowl with grapes
(serves 4)

An excellent dish for an early autumn dinner party when grapes are at their best.

	Imperial	American
1 (1.5 kg) guinea fowl, *or*	3 lb	3 lb
2 small 750 g guinea fowl, drawn and trussed	1½ lb	1½ lb
50 g butter	2 oz	¼ cup
1 tbsp oil	1 tbsp	1 tbsp
1 small onion		
1 carrot		
1 leek		
2 sticks celery		
2 tbsp brandy	2 tbsp	2 tbsp
300 ml red wine	½ pt	1¼ cups
a bouquet garni		
300 ml white stock	½ pt	1¼ cups
salt and pepper		
100 g white grapes	4 oz	4 oz
100 g black grapes	4 oz	4 oz

For the garnish:
fried diced croûtons
finely chopped parsley

Truss the bird in the same way as a chicken (see pages 134–35). Heat the butter and oil in a pan, add the bird and brown on all sides. Chop the onion, carrot, leek and celery. Remove the bird from the pan, reduce the heat and add the chopped vegetables. Cook for 9–10 minutes or until lightly coloured. Pour off any excess fat and replace the guinea fowl in the pan. Warm the brandy slightly, and flame it as you pour it onto the bird. Add the wine, bouquet garni and stock, and season moderately. (Care must be taken to add sufficient seasoning to flavour the bird, but not too much as the sauce is reduced before serving.) Cover with a lid and cook in a moderate oven, Mark 4 (180°C/350°F), for 45 minutes–1 hour or until tender. Do not overcook or the flesh can become too dry.

Remove the pips from the grapes. Fry the croûtons of diced bread in oil until crisp and golden brown. Remove the guinea fowl from the pan and keep hot. Strain the cooking liquor into a clean pan. Take 4 tablespoons of this and cook the grapes in it for 2–3 minutes. Then return the liquor to the pan and allow the sauce to reduce over a good heat until thick and syrupy. When the sauce has reached the correct consistency, taste and adjust the seasoning. Strain and keep hot.

Remove the trussing strings and carve the guinea fowl. Place the pieces on a hot serving-dish and arrange the grapes down each side. Pour over the sauce and garnish each end of the dish with diced croûtons sprinkled with the parsley.

Le Canard

Duck

Duck used to be seasonal but, with modern farming methods, they are now available all year round. Live weights are about 2–3.6 kg (4½–8 lb) for fully grown birds, but they lose about one-third of their weight in preparation. There is a smaller ratio of flesh to bone than on a chicken, so you will find that a small duckling will serve two people and one with a dressed weight of 1.75 kg (4 lb) is just enough for four portions, or you might prefer to have a larger one of 2.25–2.75 kg (5–6 lb).

Canard à l'Orange

Duck in orange sauce (serves 4)

This roast duck is served in a rich brown sauce flavoured with orange, and garnished with orange segments. Everything can be prepared in advance ready to finish the actual cooking with a minimum of effort. You can have the duck ready to roast, the sauce made and oranges cut and stored in a plastic box in the refrigerator, so there is little last-minute cooking to do when you are entertaining.

	Imperial	American
1 (2–2.5 kg) duck, drawn and trussed	4–5 lb	4–5 lb
1 carrot		
1 onion		
75 g butter	3 oz	6 tbsp
4 oranges		
300 ml Sauce Demi-glace (*see page 29*)	½ pt	1¼ cups
1 bunch watercress		

Remove any pin feathers on the duck (see page 144) and singe off any hairs. For ease of carving the wishbone can be cut out before the bird is trussed. Prick the skin and rub with a little salt to make it crisp.

Cut the carrot and onion into large pieces. Place the duck in a roasting-tin with the carrot and onion, spread with butter and cover with foil. Roast in a hot oven, Mark 6 (200°C/400°F), for approximately 1½ hours. Remove the foil for the last 30 minutes of the cooking time.

Meanwhile, peel the zest from two of the oranges and cut into fine julienne strips. Blanch these in boiling water for 5 minutes or until tender.

Remove the skin from these two oranges and cut the fruit into segments. Decorate the third orange with a canelle knife and slice thinly.

When the duck is cooked, remove it from the pan, cut off the wing tips, and place on a serving-dish. Pour off the excess fat, then add the unstrained Sauce Demi-glace and the juice of the remaining orange, together with any juice left from the preparation of the other oranges. Stir well. Reheat, strain and add the strips of orange zest. Pour this sauce over the duck and arrange the orange segments down the back of the bird. Place cutlet frills on the ends of the drumsticks. Garnish with the watercress. Place the orange slices around the edge of the dish and serve.

Tante Marie tip:
If you prefer, you can carve this in the kitchen. Cut off the drumstick and thigh and divide in two. Carve off the breasts and cut each one in two. Arrange on the platter, pour over the sauce and garnish.

Canard au Muscadet
Duck in muscadet (serves 4)

A good brown stock is made beforehand to give the superb flavour to the sauce for this roast duck garnished with colourful vegetables.

	Imperial	American
1 (2 kg) duck, drawn and trussed	4 lb	4 lb
giblets from the duck		
25 g dripping	1 oz	2 tbsp
1 kg veal bones, chopped	2 lb	2 lb
2 carrots		
2 onions		
1 stick celery		
300 ml muscadet	$\frac{1}{2}$ pt	$1\frac{1}{4}$ cups
a bouquet garni, with tarragon, parsley and chervil		
salt and pepper		
1 tbsp tomato purée	1 tbsp	1 tbsp
75 g butter	3 oz	6 tbsp
2 tbsp brandy	2 tbsp	2 tbsp
2–3 tsp arrowroot	2–3 tsp	2–3 tsp
For the garnish:		
225 g button onions	8 oz	8 oz
500 g carrots	1 lb	1 lb
500 g celeriac	1 lb	1 lb
75 g butter	3 oz	6 tbsp
finely chopped parsley		

First prepare the stock, which must be cooked for 3–4 hours. Place the dripping in a large pan and heat. Add the veal bones and all the giblets except the liver and fry until brown. Add the chopped carrots, onions and celery, cover with a lid and cook gently, stirring occasionally. After 10 minutes drain off the fat, add 150 ml ($\frac{1}{4}$ pt/$\frac{2}{3}$ cup) muscadet, the bouquet garni and seasoning. Boil hard for a moment, then add 1.5 litres (3 pt/$7\frac{1}{2}$ cups) of water and the tomato purée. Simmer for 3–4 hours.

Prick the duck and rub with salt. Remove the wishbone, truss the bird and place in a roasting-pan. Spread with the butter and cover with foil. Roast in a moderately hot oven, Mark 6 (200°C/400°F), allowing 30 minutes per 500 g/1 lb. Remove the foil for the last 30 minutes of the cooking time.

Meanwhile, prepare and cook the vegetables for the garnish. Peel the onions and boil until tender. 'Turn' the carrots and celeriac and cook in boiling salted water until tender. When the duck is cooked, lift it out, remove the trussing string and keep warm.

Pour off the excess fat from the roasting-pan. Déglace with most of the muscadet and the brandy. Add 300 ml ($\frac{1}{2}$ pt/$1\frac{1}{4}$ cups) of stock. Boil together well, strain and skim off any fat. Blend the arrowroot with a little muscadet and mix well. Add the hot liquid, return to the pan and reboil. Taste and season. Pour into a sauce-boat.

Carve the duck. Take off the legs and cut each in two. Slice off each breast and cut in two. Arrange on a platter. Toss the vegetables in butter, then garnish each piece of duck with separate heaps of these. Sprinkle with the parsley.

L'Oie

Goose

Roast goose should be tender and succulent with a crisp brown skin. This can be achieved by slow roasting as suggested in the following recipe, which also minimises shrinkage of the meat. There will be a good bowlful of dripping from the goose and this can be used, as it is in southwest France, to give a superb flavour to your cooking.

Oie Rôti à la Paysanne

Country-style roast goose (serves 8)

	Imperial	American
1 (5 kg) goose, drawn and trussed	10 lb	10 lb
salt and pepper		
100 g butter	4 oz	$\frac{1}{2}$ cup
1 onion, chopped		
50 g fresh breadcrumbs	2 oz	1 cup
100 ml milk	3 fl oz	$\frac{1}{3}$ cup
liver from the goose		
2-3 chicken livers		
1 tbsp chopped parsley	1 tbsp	1 tbsp
4 sage leaves, chopped		
1 egg		
4 dessert apples, peeled, cored and diced		
For the stock:		
1 litre water	2 pt	$4\frac{1}{2}$ cups
giblets from the goose		
1 onion		
1 carrot		
1 stick celery		
1 leek		
6 peppercorns		
a bouquet garni		

Prick the goose well and rub with salt. Melt 25 g (1 oz/2 tbsp) of butter in a pan, add the onion and cook until tender. Soak the breadcrumbs in the boiling milk. Squeeze lightly and mix with the onion, chopped livers, parsley, sage, egg, apples and seasoning.

Remove any fat from the interior of the goose and place in the roasting-pan. Pull out any remaining pin feathers (see page 144) and singe off any hairs. Fill the breast and body with the stuffing. Put a rack in the roasting-pan and place the goose on top. Spread with the remaining butter and roast, un-

covered, in a moderately slow oven, Mark 3 (160°C/325°F), for 3 hours. If necessary, increase the heat for the last 20 minutes to brown the skin a little more.

As soon as the goose is in the oven, make the stock. Put all the ingredients in a pan, bring slowly to the boil, skim, then allow to simmer gently for 2–3 hours.

When the goose is cooked, the juice will run clear if the flesh is pierced. Lift onto a serving-dish and remove the string. Keep warm. Pour the fat off into a bowl, then put the roasting-pan on the hob and heat through. Add 300 ml ($\frac{1}{2}$ pt/$1\frac{1}{4}$ cups) of the stock you have made and boil fast for several minutes. Season to taste. Strain and serve separately.

La Dinde

Turkey

Turkeys vary in size from very small ones of 2.70 kg (6 lb) to large ones of 13.5 kg (30 lb) or even more. For a bird under 7.2 kg (16 lb), choose a hen as this is meatier than a cock bird of this size. Turkeys develop a better proportion of flesh as they get larger and a cock bird can be the best buy when a large turkey is required. Allow about 350–450 g (12–16 oz) dressed weight of bird per portion.

Roast a turkey in a moderately hot oven, Mark 6 (200°C/400°F), for the first hour then reduce the temperature to Mark 4 (180°C/350°F) for the remainder of the cooking time. Calculate the actual cooking time as follows (weight after stuffing):

Up to $4\frac{1}{2}$ kg (10 lb): 20 minutes per 500 g/1 lb
5–7.5 kg (11–15 lb): 15 minutes per 500 g/1 lb
8 kg (16 lb) and over: 10 minutes per 500 g/1 lb

The turkey is an all-important feature of dinner at Reveillon – the French New Year's Eve, when you might enjoy oysters beforehand and have a rich gâteau or ice after the turkey. This recipe for a turkey with a chestnut and apple stuffing is good for Christmas dinner, too.

Dinde Farcie aux Marrons

Turkey stuffed with chestnuts (serves 10)

	Imperial	American
1 (4.5 kg) turkey, drawn and trussed	10 lb	10 lb
500 g chestnuts	1 lb	1 lb
175 g fresh *or* salted belly of pork	6 oz	6 oz
2 dessert apples		
liver from the turkey		
2 shallots, *or* 1 small onion, chopped		
2–3 tbsp chopped parsley	2–3 tbsp	2–3 tbsp
1 egg, beaten		
salt and pepper		
100 g lard	4 oz	$\frac{1}{2}$ cup
100 g butter	4 oz	$\frac{1}{2}$ cup
6–8 rashers streaky bacon		
1 tbsp brandy	1 tbsp	1 tbsp

For the stock:

giblets from the turkey		
1 onion		
1 carrot		
1 stick celery		
a bouquet garni		

For the garnish:

250 g lean streaky bacon	8 oz	8 oz
500 g chipolata sausages	1 lb	1 lb
3 dessert apples		
25 g butter	1 oz	2 tbsp
1 bunch watercress		

Slit the chestnuts, place in boiling water and boil for 15–20 minutes. Drain, and remove the skins. Alternatively, roast them for 15 minutes in a moderately hot oven, Mark 5 (190°C/375°F), then skin. Stew them in water for about 30 minutes or until soft.

Cut the pork into small cubes and cook for about 10 minutes with a little water.

Peel and core the apples and cut into dice. Mix with the pork, chopped turkey liver and the roughly broken chestnuts. Add the shallots or onion, parsley, beaten egg and seasoning.

Stuff the turkey with this farce, truss the bird and place in a roasting-pan with the lard. Spread a good layer of butter all over the bird and cover with streaky bacon rashers and aluminium foil. Roast in a moderate oven, Mark 6 (200°C/400°F), for 1 hour, then reduce the temperature to Mark 4 (180°C/350°F), allowing 20 minutes per 500 g (1 lb) plus 20 minutes over. Baste at intervals and remove the foil and bacon for the last 1 hour. Reduce the temperature if necessary.

Meanwhile, make the stock and prepare the garnish. For the stock, wash the giblets well and place them in a pan with about 1 litre (2 pt/ $4\frac{1}{2}$ cups) of water. When they come to the boil, lift off the scum, add the vegetables and bouquet garni, cover with a lid and allow to simmer for 2 hours.

For the garnish, remove the bacon rinds and stretch the rashers, using the back of a knife, then cut in two. Roll up and place on skewers, so that they are ready to grill. Divide each chipolata sausage into two small ones: press the back of a knife across the centre of the sausage, then twist the sausage and cut. Grill the bacon rolls and sausages. Peel, core and slice the apples and fry in the butter.

To serve, lift the turkey onto a warm serving-dish and remove the trussing string or skewers. Keep hot. Pour off the excess fat from the roasting-tin and add the brandy and 300 ml ($\frac{1}{2}$ pt/$1\frac{1}{4}$ cups) of the turkey stock. Boil to reduce slightly, season to taste and remove any remaining grease with kitchen paper.

Garnish with the bacon rolls, sausages, fried apple slices and the washed watercress.

Tante Marie tip:
Instead of fresh chestnuts you can use dried ones. In this case you need only 225 g (8 oz). These should be soaked in cold water for 8–10 hours, then cooked in water until tender.

Dinde Farcie aux Marrons.

Salade de Dinde à l'Anversoise

Turkey and chicory salad (serves 4–6)

This salad is an attractive way of serving cold turkey. The taste of citrus fruits and chicory gives a refreshing flavour.

	Imperial	American
500 g cooked turkey	1 lb	1 lb
25 g whole almonds	1 oz	$\frac{1}{4}$ cup
25 g butter	1 oz	2 tbsp
salt and pepper		
4 heads chicory		
3 dessert apples		
150 ml double cream	$\frac{1}{4}$ pt	$\frac{2}{3}$ cup
150 ml single cream	$\frac{1}{4}$ pt	$\frac{2}{3}$ cup
1 lemon		
a little castor sugar		
2 oranges		
1 grapefruit		
a little paprika pepper		

Remove the skin from the turkey and shred the flesh. Blanch the almonds by pouring boiling water onto them and slipping off the skins. Melt the butter in a frying-pan, add the almonds and fry until golden brown. Drain on kitchen paper and sprinkle with salt.

Slice 2 heads of chicory into thin rings. Peel and quarter the apples, remove the cores then dice.

Whisk the creams lightly together, then beat in the strained lemon juice, seasoning and the sugar. Mix this with the turkey, apples, sliced chicory and almonds. Cut the peel from the oranges and grape-fruit and cut out the segments of fruit. Sprinkle lightly with a very little sugar.

Arrange the leaves of the remaining heads of chicory decoratively at each end of the serving-dish and pile the turkey mixture into the centre. Arrange the orange and grapefruit segments around the sides and sprinkle the turkey with the paprika.

Le Lièvre

Hare

In autumn and winter you can serve hare as your main dish. They are most plentiful in Britain in January and February.

They are paunched but not skinned, and hung head downwards for about a week, the time depending on the weather. The teeth are a good indication of age: they are white in a young animal but get yellow and discoloured with age.

Young hares can be used in any recipe, but old ones need to be marinaded and can then be made into casseroles, pâtés and terrines.

Civet de Lièvre

Jugged hare (serves 4–6)

This is a well-flavoured casserole, with a garnish of onions, mushroom and bacon.

	Imperial	American
1 hare, jointed		
blood from the hare		
150 ml red wine	$\frac{1}{4}$ pt	$\frac{2}{3}$ cup
a bouquet garni		
2 carrots, sliced		
2 onions, sliced		
50 g butter	2 oz	4 tbsp
1 tbsp plain flour	1 tbsp	1 tbsp
150 ml stock	$\frac{1}{4}$ pt	$\frac{2}{3}$ cup
1 clove garlic		
1 tsp arrowroot (*optional*)	1 tsp	1 tsp
For the garnish:		
350 g glacé onions (*see page 173*)	12 oz	12 oz
50 g butter	2 oz	4 tbsp
100 g lean bacon, cut into lardons	4 oz	4 oz
100 g mushrooms, sliced	4 oz	4 oz

Marinade the hare for a day in the wine with the bouquet garni, carrot and onion, turning occasionally. Drain before cooking.

The following day, heat the butter in a thick pan. When it is hot, add the hare and brown well on all sides. Add the carrots and onions and brown these too. Sprinkle in the flour, stir well, and allow it to brown without burning. Pour over the wine from the marinade and sufficient stock to cover. Add the bouquet garni and garlic crushed with a little salt, and plenty of seasoning. Cover with greaseproof paper and a lid and cook gently for approximately 2½ hours, either over a low heat on the hob or in a moderately slow oven, Mark 3 (160°C/325°F).

Towards the end of the cooking time, prepare the glacé onions, bacon and mushrooms. Melt the butter in a pan, add the strips of bacon and fry until brown. Remove from the pan, add the mushrooms and cook gently, then season to taste. Keep hot.

When the hare is cooked, lift it onto a hot serving-dish. Remove the excess grease from the sauce. Strain the liquor into a clean pan. Reduce it over a good heat or, if preferred, thicken it with a little arrowroot slaked with cold water. Simmer to cook the arrowroot. Add 2 or 3 tablespoons of this gravy to the blood from the hare. Mix well. Pour it back into the pan and heat it through, taking care not to let it overheat or the blood will curdle the sauce. Taste and season.

Pour this gravy over the hare. Arrange the mushrooms and bacon at each side of the dish. Pile up the glacé onions at each end and serve hot.

Le Lapin
Rabbit

Rabbits for cooking may be domestic or wild. They are paunched and skinned without hanging. Tenderness depends upon age and an old rabbit requires longer cooking. A young rabbit has sharp smooth claws and its ears are soft and easily torn. The meat is 'white' and can be cooked in the same way as veal and chicken. It needs a good sauce if it is to be moist and well flavoured.

Lapin aux Champignons
Rabbit with mushrooms (serves 4)

Dry cider is used to flavour this tasty way of serving rabbit.

	Imperial	American
1 rabbit, jointed		
100 g streaky bacon or belly pork	4 oz	4 oz
25 g butter	1 oz	2 tbsp
1 tbsp oil	1 tbsp	1 tbsp
4 tbsp seasoned flour	4 tbsp	4 tbsp
600 ml dry cider	1 pt	2½ cups
1 clove garlic		
a bouquet garni		
salt and pepper		
150 g mushrooms	6 oz	6 oz
liver from the rabbit		
1 heaped tsp French mustard	1 tsp	1 tsp
1 egg yolk		

Cut the bacon or pork into lardons. Melt the butter and oil in a pan, add the lardons and fry until brown. Remove from the pan. Coat the joints of rabbit in the seasoned flour, add to the pan and sauté until golden brown. Pour in the cider, replace the bacon and add the crushed garlic, bouquet garni and seasoning. Simmer gently.

Slice the mushrooms and add these to the pan, so they cook in the sauce. Simmer the rabbit gently for 1 hour or until tender.

Lift the joints onto a serving-dish and boil the sauce to reduce a little. Chop the liver and mix with the mustard and egg yolk. Thicken the sauce with this just before serving, taking care not to overheat. Pour the sauce over the rabbit and serve.

Lapin au Caramel

Caramelised rabbit (serves 4)

This unusual recipe gives an extremely good flavour to the rabbit, and has a particularly delicious sauce.

	Imperial	American
1 rabbit, jointed		
75 g castor sugar	3 oz	$\frac{1}{3}$ cup
75 g butter *or* good dripping	3 oz	6 tbsp
1 litre stock	2 pt	$4\frac{1}{2}$ cups
salt and pepper		
100 g bacon, chopped	4 oz	$\frac{3}{4}$ cup
100 g onion, sliced	4 oz	$\frac{3}{4}$ cup
2 tbsp plain flour	2 tbsp	2 tbsp
2 tbsp tomato purée	2 tbsp	2 tbsp
1 clove garlic		
a bouquet garni		
a strip of orange peel		
3 tbsp Madeira wine	3 tbsp	3 tbsp
2 tbsp single cream	2 tbsp	2 tbsp
10 stoned olives, black and green		

For the garnish:
fried croûtons

Coat each rabbit joint in the castor sugar. Melt 50 g (2 oz/$\frac{1}{4}$ cup) of butter in a sauté pan. When it is hot, add the rabbit and fry until the sugar is slightly caramelised. Remove the rabbit and pour in a little stock. Season and swill the pan round. Return the rabbit to the pan and put aside for a moment.

Heat the rest of the butter in a large pan. Add the bacon and onion and fry until brown. Stir in the flour and brown this slowly and carefully. Pour on the rest of the stock and bring to boiling point. Add the tomato purée, garlic crushed with a little salt, bouquet garni and orange peel. Season. Add the rabbit, together with the liquor from the other pan. Cover with greaseproof paper and a lid and cook gently for approximately $1\frac{1}{2}$ hours.

To serve, pile up the rabbit in a hot serving-dish. Remove the bouquet garni and orange peel from the pan. Stir in the Madeira and cream. Taste and season if necessary. Pour this sauce over the rabbit. Toss the olives in a little hot oil and pile them up at each end of the dish. Garnish with the fried croûtons. Serve very hot.

Le Faisan

Pheasant

Autumn is the time for pheasant. In Britain, shooting is from 1 October to 31 January and the birds are at their best and most plentiful in November and December.

Pheasant needs to be hung by the neck in a cool airy place immediately after shooting. The length of time depends on the weather and the flavour required, as this becomes more gamey as time goes on. The time can vary between 3 and 14 days, though a week is average. The bird is ready when a tail feather can be pulled out easily.

The cock is the larger bird, but the hen has the reputation of being the tastier. A brace of birds will serve about 5–6 people.

Faisan en Cocotte

Casserole of pheasant (serves 2–4, depending on size of pheasant)

A tasty casserole, which requires little last-minute attention.

	Imperial	American
1 pheasant, drawn and trussed		
40 g butter	$1\frac{1}{2}$ oz	3 tbsp
1 tbsp oil	1 tbsp	1 tbsp
150 ml stock	$\frac{1}{4}$ pt	$\frac{2}{3}$ cup
salt and pepper		
a bouquet garni		

For the garnish:
12 button onions		
75 g butter	3 oz	6 tbsp
1 tsp sugar	1 tsp	1 tsp
12 button mushrooms		
juice of $\frac{1}{2}$ lemon		

For the sauce:
| 4 tbsp Madeira wine | 4 tbsp | 4 tbsp |

To finish:
finely chopped parsley

Melt the butter and oil in a deep sauté pan. When it is hot, add the pheasant and brown on all sides. Pour on the stock, season well and place the bouquet garni at the side. Cover with a lid and cook in a moderately hot oven, Mark 5 (190°C/375°F), for 1 hour.

Meanwhile, prepare the garnish. Peel the onions and place them in a pan of cold salted water. Bring to the boil, then cook for 2–3 minutes. Remove and drain. Melt half the butter in a pan, add the onions, sugar and seasoning and shake over a moderate heat until the onions are golden brown and glazed all over. Melt the rest of the butter in a small pan, add the lemon juice, seasoning and mushrooms. Cover with greaseproof paper and a lid and shake over a gentle heat until just tender.

Remove the pheasant from the pan and keep hot. Increase the heat and reduce the liquor in which the bird was cooked until only 3 tablespoons remain. Pour in the Madeira, swill round well and adjust the seasoning. Arrange the pheasant on a hot dish with the mushrooms at one end and the onions at the other. Pour over the gravy, and sprinkle with the parsley.

Faisan en Cocotte.

Faisan à la Crème

Pheasant with port and cream (serves 2–4, depending on size of pheasant)

	Imperial	American
1 pheasant, drawn		
giblets from the pheasant		
1 carrot		
2 onions		
3 tbsp oil	3 tbsp	3 tbsp
25 g plain flour	1 oz	3 tbsp
150 ml dry white wine	$\frac{1}{4}$ pt	$\frac{2}{3}$ cup
300 ml stock	$\frac{1}{2}$ pt	$1\frac{1}{4}$ cups
a bouquet garni		
a piece of pork fat		
50 g butter	2 oz	$\frac{1}{4}$ cup
4–5 tbsp port	4–5 tbsp	4–5 tbsp
150 ml double cream	$\frac{1}{4}$ pt	$\frac{2}{3}$ cup
salt and pepper		

Cut the giblets and any trimmings, such as wing tips, into small pieces. Prepare the carrot and onion and cut into dice. Heat half the oil in a pan, add the giblets and brown. Add the vegetables, brown, then sprinkle in the flour. Mix in and brown lightly. Add the wine, stock and bouquet garni and simmer gently for 30 minutes.

Cut the wishbone out of the pheasant, then truss the bird, checking that all little feathers have been removed. Cover with the pork fat and tie this on securely. Heat the butter and remaining oil in a heavy pan, add the pheasant and sauté until well browned. Cover with a lid and place in the oven, if necessary transferring it to a heatproof dish. Cook in a moderately hot oven, Mark 6 (200°C/400°F), for 35 minutes or until just tender. Baste occasionally.

When the pheasant is cooked, strain the sauce. Remove the pork fat, and pour off the excess fat from the pan. Add the port and allow to reduce slightly, then pour in the sauce and cream. Cover with a lid and cook the pheasant gently in this for 15 minutes. Taste and season.

Lift the bird out of the casserole. Carve off the legs and divide into two, then carve the breast into slices. Arrange on a serving-dish and coat with some of the sauce. Hand the rest of the sauce in a sauce-boat.

La Perdrix

Partridge

The season for partridge in Britain is from 1 September to 31 January. They are usually most plentiful in the early autumn. The average length of time for hanging is about a week, but may be a day or two more or less, depending on the weather. Young partridges can be roasted, but older ones should be cooked in a casserole. Allow one bird per person. Like other game birds, partridges are always barded with fat to keep them moist.

Perdreaux aux Choux

Partridges with cabbage (serves 4)

This is a good recipe for old birds, as they will become very tender. By the time this casserole is served it is difficult to decide whether the partridge or the vegetables have the better flavour.

	Imperial	American
4 partridges, drawn and trussed		
thinly sliced pork fat or fat bacon		
25 g dripping	1 oz	2 tbsp
500 g cabbage	1 lb	1 lb
2 large carrots		
1 onion		
100 g lean bacon, e.g. gammon	4 oz	4 oz
a bouquet garni		
salt and pepper		
300 ml white stock	$\frac{1}{2}$ pt	$1\frac{1}{4}$ cups
250 g Continental boiling sausage	8 oz	8 oz

Singe the partridges to burn off any remaining feathers. Cut off the feet at the first joint. Tie on the piece of fat, using fine string. Heat the dripping in a pan, add the birds and brown on each side.

Slice the cabbage finely and blanch in boiling water for 1 minute. Drain well, then place in a casserole. Dice the carrots, onion, bacon and add, with the bouquet garni, to the cabbage. Season with salt and black pepper. Add the browned partridges, embedding them in the vegetables. Add the stock,

cover with a lid and cook in a moderately slow oven, Mark 3 (160°C/325°F), for $2\frac{1}{2}$–3 hours or until tender. Thirty minutes before the end of the cooking time, add the boiling sausage cut into chunks.

When the birds are cooked, remove the string and pork fat. Taste and season. Serve in the casserole in which they were cooked.

Perdreaux à la Catalane

Catalonian partridges (serves 4)

Do not be frightened by the amount of garlic used in the sauce. Prepared in this way it becomes very mild indeed.

	Imperial	American
4 partridges		
pork fat or fat bacon		
2 tbsp dripping	2 tbsp	2 tbsp
50 g ham	2 oz	2 oz
2 tbsp plain flour	2 tbsp	2 tbsp
100 ml white wine	3 fl oz	$\frac{1}{3}$ cup
225 ml stock	$7\frac{1}{2}$ fl oz	1 cup
1 tbsp tomato purée	1 tbsp	1 tbsp
a bouquet garni, with parsley, thyme, bayleaf and a piece of orange peel		
12 cloves garlic		

For the forcemeat:

	Imperial	American
2–3 chicken livers, chopped		
25 g breadcrumbs	1 oz	$\frac{1}{2}$ cup
50 g lean ham, chopped	2 oz	2 oz
2 tsp chopped parsley	2 tsp	2 tsp
1 clove garlic, crushed		
$\frac{1}{2}$ egg		
salt and pepper		

Mix all the ingredients for the forcemeat together and fill the partridges with this mixture. Truss the birds and tie on the piece of fat. Melt the dripping in a pan, add the partridges and sauté until golden. Add the diced ham, cook for 1 minute, then stir in the flour and cook again. Add the wine, stock, tomato purée and bouquet garni, cover with a lid and allow to simmer for 10 minutes.

Meanwhile, peel the garlic and blanch in boiling water for 5 minutes. Drain, then add to the sauce. Continue cooking together in a moderately hot oven,

Mark 3 (160°C/325°F), until tender. This may take only 45 minutes for tender young birds, or 2½ hours for old ones, but the latter will, however, become very tender and palatable when cooked in this way.

When tender, remove the bouquet garni. Take the barding fat and trussing string off the birds. Arrange them on a platter, taste and season the sauce and pour it over.

Le Pigeon
Pigeon

There is no close season for pigeon so they may be obtained at any time, though most are shot in the autumn or spring. Hang for 1–3 days. Allow one bird per person.

Pigeonneaux aux Legumes en Cocotte
Pigeon casserole (serves 4)

	Imperial	American
4 pigeons, drawn and trussed		
salt and pepper		
8 sage leaves		
75 g butter	3 oz	6 tbsp
1 gammon rasher		
350 g button onions	12 oz	12 oz
3 carrots		
2 turnips		
150 ml white wine	¼ pt	⅔ cup
300 ml stock	½ pt	1¼ cups
a bouquet garni		
225 g shelled peas	8 oz	8 oz
1 lettuce heart or 6 leaves, shredded		

Pull off any little feathers remaining on the pigeon. Season, then place 2 sage leaves in each bird. Melt the butter in a heavy pan, add the pigeons and brown on all sides. Lift them out, add the gammon cut into strips and the peeled onions. Cook until lightly browned, then add the carrots and turnips cut into small pieces. Add the white wine, stock, bouquet garni and seasoning.

Replace the pigeons in the pan. Cover with a lid and cook in a moderate oven, Mark 4 (180°C/350°F), for 1¼ hours, add the peas and lettuce and continue cooking for a further 10 minutes or until tender.

Taste and season. Remove the trussing strings and serve en cocotte (in the casserole).

Pigeonneaux aux Legumes en Cocotte.

Vegetables

France is a large country and has a climate ranging from temperate in the north to the very hot around the Mediterranean. Those of you who have spent time there will know how the produce varies as you travel from north to south. Wherever you go, fields of vegetables abound in conditions well suited to their growth.

In the Loire, the asparagus fields stretch for mile upon mile, and the delicate ferns bending in the breeze are a sight to remember. In Provence there are large red tomatoes of all shapes and deep purple aubergines growing in profusion.

Browsing around the local market is another experience not to be missed. Large green artichokes, yellow onions, glistening tomatoes, aubergines, courgettes, peppers and strings of white garlic: all in pristine array. Small peas, crisp French beans, large white cauliflowers or plump lettuce: whatever the season, there is an abundance of vegetables harvested at their best.

The French housewife is usually a discerning shopper who takes her pick of the produce offered. She likes small young vegetables and buys them fresh in their proper season. She knows that, not only are they cheapest then, but are also at their best. She cooks them with care, often braising them as in Céleri Braisé, or turning a simple cabbage into something special by the addition of a cream sauce to make Chou Vert à la Crème. Even plain boiled vegetables taste different if tossed in butter with herbs added, as are Fèves à la Maître d'Hotel and Petits Pois au Fenouil. Sometimes the French housewife will choose a salad instead, and will frequently serve her vegetable or salad as a separate dish after the main course, thus winning for it the appreciation it deserves.

Les Artichauts
Globe artichokes

Globe artichokes are most readily available in Britain from June to September. Look for heads which are well formed and plump with tight leaves which are greyish-green and have a bloom. Avoid any with brown-tipped or streaked leaves or a dry open centre.

Globe artichokes can be served whole with the centre filled with a stuffing or sauce. The diner pulls off the leaves, dips the fleshy part in the centre filling and eats it, then discards the inedible part of the leaf. The base or 'fond' is eaten using a knife and fork. Finger bowls are needed for this dish! Serve the artichoke on a plate large enough to take all the debris, or provide a side plate for it.

When artichokes are very plentiful, cook the bases only, trimmed down to the edible part, and serve with a savoury filling.

Preparation of an artichoke. You will see that the stalk has been broken off and the fibres pulled out of the base. After cooking, an attractive decoration can be made by removing the top of the centre leaves (*right*) as a cap. The artichoke in the background (*right*) has been decorated in this way. On the left you will notice the whiskery 'choke', behind which are a few of the leaves taken from the centre.

To cook artichokes, remove the fibres that penetrate the 'fond' by snapping off the stalk instead of cutting it. Cut the artichoke down evenly, removing about one third of its top. Cut the tip off each leaf with kitchen scissors. Cook in boiling salted water with either a lemon skin or 1 tablespoon of malt vinegar in the water. The acid helps to prevent discoloration. Cook until tender. The time varies from 20–40 minutes, depending on the size and quality of the artichoke. To test, remove one of the bottom leaves and check that the base is tender enough to eat.

Lift out and refresh swiftly under cold running water. Pull out the centre leaves and take the 'choke' out of the middle of the artichoke. A spoon handle is an easy tool to use. Rinse with water to remove any remaining whiskers and drain thoroughly. If the artichokes have to be kept hot, place them in a colander or steamer over a pan of hot water. When they are to be eaten cold, they can be chilled quickly in iced water, then drained.

Les Asperges

Asparagus

Home-grown asparagus is in season in Britain in May and June and imported asparagus is available to extend the season. It is sold in bundles or by weight and is graded according to the thickness of the stems and the size of the heads. Buy plump fleshy stems with tight heads. Thin stalks are called sprue and should be tender, not woody. They are useful for making soups and sauces.

To prepare asparagus for cooking, scrape the stems and trim the base of each. Wash carefully and tie bunches of similar-sized stalks together. They are best cooked in an asparagus pan: a tall slim pan, designed so the stalks are cooked in the water but the fragile heads are steamed. However, if you do not have an asparagus pan, simmer gently in a large pan instead. Cook for 15–25 minutes depending on the thickness and age of the stems. When tender, remove from the pan carefully so the heads are not damaged. Drain well.

Asperges à la Flamande

Flemish-style asparagus (serves 4–6)

	Imperial	American
1 kg asparagus	2 lb	2 lb
4 eggs		
4 tbsp chopped parsley	4 tbsp	4 tbsp
50 g melted butter	2 oz	$\frac{1}{4}$ cup
salt and pepper		

Cook the asparagus in gently boiling salted water until tender. Drain well and arrange on a hot serving-dish. Hard-boil the eggs and rub them through a sieve while still hot. Mix with the parsley, butter and seasoning and pour over the asparagus. Serve at once.

Tante Marie tip:
This dish can also be made with young leeks.

Asparagus stalks are scraped downwards using a small knife, then rinsed and tied in bundles. On the left is a tall asparagus pan.

Les Aubergines

Aubergines (egg plants)

Aubergines grow well in all the Mediterranean countries, particularly the south of France, and can be grown under glass in Britain. They are available all the year round but are cheapest in the early autumn. Look for aubergines with smooth shiny skins. Avoid any which are wrinkled or have brown marks on the skin.

After they have been cut or sliced, it is wise to sprinkle them with a little salt (dégorger) and allow to drain for about 30 minutes so that some of the moisture and the slightly bitter flavour is drawn out of them. Wash them and dry well on kitchen paper before cooking.

Cutting an aubergine.

Aubergines Farcies

Stuffed aubergines (serves 4–8)

	Imperial	American
4 aubergines		
salt and pepper		
50 g mushrooms	2 oz	2 oz
4 ripe tomatoes		
oil for frying		
1 tbsp finely chopped herbs	1 tbsp	1 tbsp
1 clove garlic		
2 tbsp seasoned flour	2 tbsp	2 tbsp
white breadcrumbs		
extra chopped parsley		

Cut the aubergines in half lengthways and, using a sharp pointed knife, make an incision all round the flesh, taking care not to cut the skins (see above).

Make diagonal cuts across the surface. Rub salt into the cuts, turn upside down and allow to drain.

Finely chop the mushrooms, skin and pip the tomatoes and chop roughly. Heat 1 tablespoon of oil in a small pan, add the mushrooms and cook gently until soft. Add the tomatoes, herbs and crushed garlic and mix well. Pat the aubergines dry on kitchen paper, then sprinkle the flour on the cut side. Heat sufficient oil to cover the base of a frying-pan, add the aubergines, cut side down, and fry until golden brown and tender. Remove from the pan, carefully scrape out the pulp, then chop and mix this with the mushrooms and tomatoes. Fill the aubergine shells with this mixture, cover with a thin layer of the breadcrumbs, sprinkle over with a little of the oil in which the aubergines were cooked. Brown under a hot grill. Dust with the parsley before serving.

Gratin d'Aubergines
Cheese covered aubergines (serves 4)

Aubergines topped with eggs and cheese make an ideal vegetable entrée or supper dish.

	Imperial	American
500 g aubergines	1 lb	1 lb
salt and pepper		
350 g tomatoes	12 oz	12 oz
250 g red peppers	8 oz	8 oz
3 shallots, *or* 1 onion		
2 cloves garlic		
oil for frying		
a bouquet garni		
1 tsp paprika pepper	1 tsp	1 tsp
2 tbsp finely chopped parsley	2 tbsp	2 tbsp
3 eggs		
50 g cheese, grated	2 oz	1 cup

Cut the aubergines into 6 mm ($\frac{1}{4}$ in) slices and sprinkle with salt. Place on a wire rack and allow to drain.

Skin and pip the tomatoes and cut them into quarters. Cut the peppers in half and remove the core and seeds. Blanch them for 5 minutes in boiling salted water. Drain, then cut into strips. Chop the shallots or onion finely and crush the garlic.

Heat 2 tablespoons oil in a pan, add the tomatoes and turn in the hot oil until soft. Add to the pan the shallots, garlic, bouquet garni, salt, pepper and paprika. Stir well, then add the peppers. Cover with a tight-fitting lid and simmer gently for 10–15 minutes. Remove the bouquet garni and add the parsley.

Dry the slices of aubergine on kitchen paper. Heat some oil in a pan, add the aubergine slices and fry quickly on both sides, if necessary adding a little more oil, until lightly browned. Lift them out, drain on kitchen paper and place in a heatproof dish.

Whisk the eggs lightly, remove the tomato mixture from the heat and add the beaten eggs. Taste and season. Pour over the aubergines. Sprinkle with the cheese and place in the top of a hot oven, Mark 7 (220°C/425°F), for 15–20 minutes.

Tante Marie tip:
To prevent the aubergines absorbing too much oil during cooking, beat another egg well. Dip the aubergine slices in this before placing them in the fat. This tip may not be traditionally French but it works well.

La Betterave
Beetroot

There are two main types of beetroot available in Britain: small globe beet which are available during the summer months, and the long beetroot which you can buy throughout most of the year. They are usually sold cooked. If you want raw ones, you may have to order them in advance.

Both cooked and uncooked beetroot will lose their colour unless a small amount of acid – usually vinegar or lemon – is added at the start of cooking.

Small round yellow beetroot are an unusual variety obtainable from some seed suppliers. They make a colourful and interesting addition to salads.

Betteraves à la Crème
Beetroots in cream (serves 4)

	Imperial	American
500 g cooked beetroot	1 lb	1 lb
50 g butter	2 oz	$\frac{1}{4}$ cup
salt and pepper		
2 tsp wine vinegar	2 tsp	2 tsp
150 ml double cream	$\frac{1}{4}$ pt	$\frac{2}{3}$ cup

To finish:
finely chopped fresh herbs

Skin the beetroots and cut them evenly into small dice. Melt the butter in a saucepan. When it is hot, add the beetroots. Stir carefully, season well, then add the vinegar and cream. Reduce the heat and simmer gently for 2–3 minutes to ensure that the mixture is quite hot. Pile it into a hot vegetable dish and sprinkle the herbs on top.

Tante Marie tip:
This dish is a pleasant accompaniment to grilled or fried pork chops.

Les Carottes

Carrots

Carrots, which are easily available all the year round, are often sold in bunches when they are young in the spring and summer. They are very tender and only need washing and scraping. Main-crop carrots can be scraped when they are new but need peeling later. Buy clean bright coloured carrots. Avoid any which are broken and have woody cores, or young ones which are green around the stem.

Carottes à la Polonaise

Polish-style carrots (serves 4–6)

	Imperial	American
500 g carrots	1 lb	1 lb
50 g butter	2 oz	4 tbsp
salt and pepper		
150 ml water	$\frac{1}{4}$ pt	$\frac{2}{3}$ cup
225 g fresh peas, *or*	8 oz	8 oz
100 g frozen peas	4 oz	4 oz
4 tbsp double cream	4 tbsp	4 tbsp
paprika		

Peel the carrots and cut them into thin julienne strips. Melt the butter in a pan and add the carrots, seasoning and water. Cover with a lid and cook over a very gentle heat for about 15 minutes. If the water reduces too quickly, add a little more.

Meanwhile, shell the peas and cook in boiling salted water. When the carrots are almost tender, add the cooked peas and continue cooking until all the water has evaporated and the vegetables are coated in butter. Just before serving, add the cream, check the seasoning and heat through. Pile into a hot serving-dish and sprinkle with a little paprika.

Carottes aux Fines Herbes

Carrots with herbs (serves 3–4)

	Imperial	American
500 g carrots	1 lb	1 lb
1 tsp sugar	1 tsp	1 tsp
salt and pepper		
25 g butter	1 oz	2 tbsp

To finish:
**a mixture of fresh herbs,
e.g. parsley, chives,
tarragon, and a little
fennel or dill**

Choose young sweet carrots for this recipe. Wash them well and scrape or rub lightly. Place them in a saucepan with the sugar, seasoning and butter and cover with cold water. Cook quickly over a good heat until all the water has evaporated and the carrots are lightly coated in butter. Sprinkle over the finely chopped herbs. Pile them up in a hot dish.

Carottes à la Vichy

Vichy carrots (serves 3–4)

This dish was originally cooked in Vichy water.

	Imperial	American
500 g carrots	1 lb	1 lb
25 g butter	1 oz	2 tbsp
$\frac{1}{2}$ tsp sugar	$\frac{1}{2}$ tsp	$\frac{1}{2}$ tsp
salt and pepper		
finely chopped parsley		

Wash and scrape or peel the carrots. If they are large, cut them into even-sized pieces. Place them in a saucepan with the butter, sugar and seasoning and sufficient water to barely cover them. Cook quickly until all the water has evaporated and the carrots are tender and lightly coated in butter. Pile them into a hot dish and sprinkle with the parsley just before serving.

Le Céleri
Celery

Home-grown celery is available in Britain from September to March. It is considered to be at its best in October as the early frosts give it a good flavour and crisp sticks. Some of it is washed and packed, but some comes with the black soil of the Fens clinging to it. This is done deliberately as the celery keeps better with the soil around it. It has an excellent flavour.

Imported celery is available from January to July. It is packed unripe and turns green when it is ready for eating. Good quality heads should be compact, plump at the base with plenty of inside sticks with pale green leaves. The sticks should be straight, crisp and smooth.

Céleri Braisé
Braised celery (serves 4)

	Imperial	American
1 head celery		
1 onion		
1 carrot		
40 g butter *or* good dripping	1½ oz	3 tbsp
2 rashers of bacon		
salt and pepper		
a bouquet garni		
white stock		

Wash the celery carefully. Remove the green part of the leaf and cut away the root. Cut the outer sticks of celery into pieces about 10 cm (4 in) long and the heart into four. Dice the onion and carrot for the braise. Blanch the celery for 2–3 minutes in boiling salted water. Remove and drain. Soften the onion and carrot in the butter, then add the bacon. Place the celery on top of the braise and season well. Add the bouquet garni and sufficient stock to barely cover the celery. Cover with a piece of buttered greaseproof paper and a tight-fitting lid. Cook in a moderate oven, Mark 4 (180°C/350°F), for 1 hour or until tender.

Lift out the celery and place in a hot serving-dish. Strain off the liquor from the braise and thicken with beurre manié (see page 16) until the sauce has a pouring consistency. Pour over the celery and serve.

Le Céleri-Rave
Celeriac

Celeriac tastes like celery and looks like a rough brown turnip or swede. Size is variable. Press the root well; it should feel firm all the way through. Avoid any which are soft or spongy. Peel thickly and immediately put into acidulated water to prevent discoloration.

Céleri-Rave à la Paysanne
Country-style celeriac (serves 4–6)

	Imperial	American
1 small celeriac		
3–4 small onions		
3–4 small carrots		
1 small head celery		
25 g butter	1 oz	2 tbsp
about 300 ml white stock	½ pt	1¼ cups
salt and pepper		

To finish:
finely chopped parsley

Peel the celeriac, cut into cubes and place in acidulated water. Peel the onions and carrots and cut into quarters. Wash the celery and cut into short lengths. Melt the butter in a thick pan, add the onions and carrots and stir over a moderate heat until lightly coloured. Add the celeriac and celery and mix until coated with butter.

Pour on sufficient stock to cover the vegetables, season well and cover with greaseproof paper and a lid. Bring to the boil, then simmer gently for about 50 minutes or until all the vegetables are tender.

Serve with the liquor in a hot dish. Sprinkle the parsley on top.

Tante Marie tip:
Although this dish is much nicer made with celeriac, it can be made entirely with branch celery.

Les Champignons
Mushrooms

Mushrooms are always available. Button mushrooms are slightly more expensive. Buy small white or cream-coloured ones for fish dishes or any cream-coloured sauces. Avoid any which are broken, scabby or discoloured.

Open or flat mushrooms have more flavour but, unfortunately, can darken a sauce. Buy dry clean ones, avoiding any which are sweating. Use soon after purchase as they easily deteriorate with storage. Good-quality mushrooms should not need skinning; there is plenty of flavour in the skins. Wipe each one clean with a damp cloth, or give them a quick wash just before using.

Beignets des Champignons
Mushroom fritters (serves 4–6)

	Imperial	American
250 g small button mushrooms	8 oz	8 oz
150 ml white wine	$\frac{1}{4}$ pt	$\frac{2}{3}$ cup
salt and pepper		
2–3 tbsp seasoned flour	2–3 tbsp	2–3 tbsp
fat for deep frying		
For the fritter batter:		
50 g plain flour	2 oz	$\frac{1}{2}$ cup
a pinch of salt		
5 tbsp tepid water	5 tbsp	5 tbsp
2 tsp olive oil	2 tsp	2 tsp
1 egg white		

Wipe the mushrooms, trim the stalks and place in a bowl with the wine. Sprinkle with a little salt and black pepper and allow to marinade for several hours or overnight.

To make the fritter batter, sift the flour and salt into a bowl. Make a well in the centre and pour the water and oil into it. Stir in the flour gradually from the sides of the bowl and beat well until the mixture is smooth. Put aside in a cool place for 30 minutes. Just before using, whisk the egg white until stiff and fold into the batter.

Heat a deep pan of fat to 190°C (380°F). Drain the mushrooms and toss them in the seasoned flour. Dip each one into the batter to coat, then drop carefully into the hot fat. Do not use a basket when frying fritters because the batter will stick to the mesh. It is therefore essential that the pan is not overfilled and that small quantities only are cooked at one time. Cook for 2–3 minutes or until golden brown. Drain well on kitchen paper. Serve immediately.

Tante Marie tip:
These fritters are also delicious served as a savoury with drinks or as a hot hors d'oeuvre.

Le Chou Vert
Green cabbage

Various types of home-grown cabbage are available all the year round. Choose those with tight firm light-green or white hearts. The outside leaves should be fresh, crisp and dark and the stalks dry and clean. Avoid cabbages with big holes in the outer leaves or with slimy stalks.

Chou Vert à la Crème
Cabbage in a cream sauce (serves 4–6)

	Imperial	American
1 large firm cabbage		
Sauce Béchamel made		
with 125 ml milk	$\frac{1}{4}$ pt	$\frac{2}{3}$ cup
and 125 ml single cream	$\frac{1}{4}$ pt	$\frac{2}{3}$ cup
(*see page 27*)		
salt and pepper		

Cut the cabbage into four and remove the hard stalks. Wash well, plunge into a pan of boiling salted water and cook rapidly for 15 minutes or until just tender. Drain the cabbage thoroughly and chop moderately finely.

Make the Sauce Béchamel and stir in the chopped cabbage. Return to the heat. Mix well, taste and adjust the seasoning. Place in a hot serving-dish and serve immediately.

Tante Marie tip:
For economy use 300 ml ($\frac{1}{2}$ pt/$1\frac{1}{4}$ cups) creamy milk instead of half milk and half cream.

Chou Vert au Riz à la Tomate

Green cabbage with rice and tomato (serves 4)

	Imperial	American
1 large firm cabbage		
50 g long grain rice	2 oz	$\frac{1}{3}$ cup
300 ml white stock	$\frac{1}{2}$ pt	$1\frac{1}{4}$ cups
salt and pepper		
50 g butter	2 oz	$\frac{1}{4}$ cup
150 ml Sauce Tomate	$\frac{1}{4}$ pt	$\frac{2}{3}$ cup
(see page 33)		
50 g Gruyère cheese, grated	2 oz	1 cup

Remove the tough outside leaves and wash the cabbage. Cut into four and remove the hard stalk. Shred the cabbage and blanch in boiling salted water for 5–7 minutes. Drain, refresh and press to remove the excess moisture.

Meanwhile, cook the rice gently in the boiling stock. Season lightly as the rice will absorb most of the stock.

Melt the butter in a pan, add the cabbage, cover with a lid and finish cooking the cabbage. Shake the pan from time to time.

Drain the rice when it is cooked and add to the cabbage with the tomato sauce. Taste and adjust the seasoning.

Place in a buttered heatproof dish, cover with the cheese and brown under a hot grill.

Le Chou Rouge

Red cabbage

These are available in Britain from August to January. Look for tight heads. The outside leaves of young cabbages have a bloom on them.

Chou Rouge à la Flamande

Flemish red cabbage (serves 4)

This is particularly good with pork or goose.

	Imperial	American
1 small red cabbage (about 500 g)	1 lb	1 lb
2 tbsp wine vinegar	2 tbsp	2 tbsp
salt and pepper		
2 tbsp brown sugar	2 tbsp	2 tbsp
2 large cooking apples, peeled, cored and sliced		

Remove any soiled outer leaves from the cabbage. Cut into quarters and slice finely. Place in a pan with 4 tablespoons of water and sprinkle with the vinegar. Toss all together, season, cover with a lid and cook very gently indeed. Simmer for 1 hour, then add the sugar and apples. Stir together and continue to simmer for a further 30 minutes–1 hour or until tender.

Le chou rouge.

Le Choufleur
Cauliflower

Home-grown varieties of cauliflower are available in Britain for most of the year and imported ones are to be found from November to April. They are most expensive in the late spring and early summer. Good-quality cauliflowers have firm round creamy-white heads. The outside leaves should be fresh and crisp. Do not buy any with limp leaves or with yellow, blotched or bruised heads.

Soufflé de Choufleur
Cauliflower soufflé (serves 4–6)

	Imperial	American
1 medium cauliflower		
75 g butter	3 oz	6 tbsp
sieved white breadcrumbs		
50 g plain flour	2 oz	$\frac{1}{2}$ cup
300 ml milk	$\frac{1}{2}$ pt	$1\frac{1}{4}$ cups
2 eggs		
2 egg whites		
salt and pepper		

Remove the tough outside leaves and scoop out the stalk of the cauliflower with a knife or ball cutter. Plunge into boiling salted water and cook for approximately 15–20 minutes or until just tender. Drain thoroughly and refresh. Drain well again.

Coat the inside of an 18 cm ($7\frac{1}{4}$ in) soufflé dish with about 25 g (1 oz/2 tbsp) of butter and dust with the breadcrumbs.

Melt the remaining butter in a pan, remove from the heat, stir in the flour, return to the heat and cook for 2–3 minutes. Remove from the heat, add the milk gradually, then bring to the boil, stirring all the time. Liquidise the cauliflower with the Sauce Béchamel, or pass the cauliflower through a vegetable mill or fine sieve and mix with the Sauce Béchamel. Pour into a large bowl. Separate the eggs, add the 2 egg yolks to the sauce and season well. Whisk the 4 whites very stiffly and fold them lightly into the cauliflower mixture. Pour into the prepared soufflé dish. Bake in a moderately hot oven, Mark 6 (200°C/400°F), for 40 minutes or until golden brown. Serve at once.

Les Choux de Bruxelles
Brussels sprouts

Sprouts are available in Britain from October to April. Buy tight even-sized ones.

Choux de Bruxelles à la Limousine
Brussels sprouts with chestnuts (serves 6)

This recipe comes from Limousin in the area just west of the Massif Central. It is a delicious way of serving Brussels sprouts.

	Imperial	American
500 g chestnuts	1 lb	1 lb
500 ml white stock	$\frac{3}{4}$ pt	2 cups
750 g small Brussels sprouts	$1\frac{1}{2}$ lb	$1\frac{1}{2}$ lb
salt		
50 g butter	2 oz	$\frac{1}{4}$ cup

Make a slit in the skin of each chestnut and blanch in boiling water for 3–5 minutes. Remove the shell and inner skin. Allow plenty of time for this, as it can take about 30 minutes. (The chestnuts can be prepared in advance.) Cook the chestnuts gently in the boiling stock for 20–30 minutes.

Meanwhile, prepare the sprouts and cook in boiling salted water until just tender. Drain the chestnuts and sprouts when they are cooked. Heat the butter in a pan, add the sprouts and chestnuts and toss together in this. Pile into a hot dish and serve.

Tante Marie tip:
For speed use 300 g (12 oz) whole canned chestnuts instead of fresh ones. They need no further cooking; just heat them through in the butter.

Le Concombre
Cucumber

These are readily available but tend to be more expensive in the winter. Normally they are used only as a salad ingredient in Britain, but are delicious cooked. Good quality cucumbers are straight, firm and an even dark green; they are hot-house grown. Ridge (outdoor cucumbers), or misshapen hot-house ones taste as good but if they are very bulbous they usually have a lot of seed. Do not buy soft ones or any which are turning yellow as they tend to be bitter.

Concombres à la Crème
Cucumbers with cream (serves 4)

	Imperial	American
40 g butter	$1\frac{1}{2}$ oz	3 tbsp
1 small onion		
salt and pepper		
2 small cucumbers		
40 g plain flour	$1\frac{1}{2}$ oz	$\frac{1}{3}$ cup
300 ml milk	$\frac{1}{2}$ pt	$1\frac{1}{4}$ cups
1 egg yolk		
150 ml single cream	$\frac{1}{4}$ pt	$\frac{2}{3}$ cup
finely chopped parsley and chervil		

Melt the butter in a small saucepan and add the very finely chopped onion. Season and cover with grease-proof paper and a lid. Cook over a very gentle heat for approximately 5 minutes or until soft but not coloured. Shake the pan from time to time. Peel the cucumbers and cut into 5 mm ($\frac{1}{4}$ in) slices, add to the pan and cook for a further 5 minutes. Remove from the heat, sprinkle in the flour and mix well. Add the milk, stir and simmer for 10 minutes over a low heat. Beat the egg yolk with the cream and stir into the pan. Taste and season. Reheat, stirring all the time until it thickens without boiling. Pour into a hot serving-dish. Dust with the parsley and chervil.

Les Courgettes
Courgettes (Zucchini)

Home-grown courgettes are available in Britain from June to September and imported ones are to be found in the shops for most of the year. They are very easy to grow and usually prolific in their yield.

They have green or green-and-yellow skins, but seeds for golden ones are available and these can make an interesting colour contrast in some dishes.

Courgettes should be 10–15 cm (4–6 in) long with smooth silky skins, and the insides should be creamy-white. Young ones need not be peeled. Larger ones have less flavour and the skin may have to be removed. Do not buy any which have brown-marked or wrinkled skins.

Beignets des Courgettes
Courgette fritters (serves 4)

	Imperial	American
500 g courgettes	1 lb	1 lb
3 tbsp plain flour	3 tbsp	3 tbsp
1 tbsp dried white breadcrumbs	1 tbsp	1 tbsp
salt and pepper		
1 egg, beaten		
50 g butter	2 oz	$\frac{1}{4}$ cup
1 tbsp oil	1 tbsp	1 tbsp

Trim the ends of the courgettes, then cut into quarters lengthways. Blanch in boiling salted water for 2–3 minutes, then drain.

Mix the flour and breadcrumbs with 1 teaspoon of salt and a sprinkling of black pepper. Dip the courgette sections in the beaten egg, then in the seasoned flour mixture, to coat evenly.

Heat the butter and oil in a frying-pan, add the fritters and fry until golden brown and tender. Drain and serve hot.

Left: Concombres à la Crème.
Right: Beignets des Courgettes.

L'Endive

Chicory

This is sometimes called Belgian chicory. Confusion can arise as this vegetable is called endive on the Continent, while the coarse, crinkly, blanched lettuce-like vegetable that we know as endive is called chicory there. Belgian chicory has crisp white heads which have a subtle bitter-sweet flavour, and are excellent in salads or as a cooked vegetable. It is available in Britain from September to May. Buy heads which are tightly formed, avoiding any which are loose and have yellow leaves.

When preparing chicory do not leave it soaking in water as this tends to make it too bitter.

Endives au Lard

Chicory with bacon (serves 4–8)

8 small heads chicory
8 rashers lean bacon
juice of 1 lemon
salt and pepper
a little sugar
melted butter for serving
  (*optional*)

Wash the chicory very well. Remove a thin slice from the root and any damaged or brown leaves. Place in a pan of boiling water and cook for 5–7 minutes. Drain and refresh. Wrap each root round with thin slices of bacon and tie securely with thread. Place in a buttered heatproof dish.

Mix the lemon juice with sufficient water to cover the chicory. Season well, adding the sugar, and pour over the chicory. Cover with buttered paper and cook in a moderately hot oven, Mark 6 (200°C/400°F), for 30 minutes. Remove from the oven, drain, take off the threads and place on a clean serving-dish. Serve, if liked, with melted butter.

Les Epinards

Spinach

There are four types of spinach generally available in Britain. The round-leaved summer variety and the prickly winter spinach both have tender dark leaves. New Zealand spinach has smaller tougher leaves and the spinach beet (or perpetual spinach) has large coarse leaves. The latter is not often found in shops but is a great favourite for growing in the garden or allotment.

Spinach bruises easily and wilts quickly. Buy crisp undamaged leaves. Wash it very carefully as grit clings to the leaves.

To cook, remove the tough stalks, wash the spinach in several changes of water and plunge into boiling salted water. Cook for 7–10 minutes or until tender. Drain in a colander and refresh under the cold tap. Press out the surplus water, using a small plate or saucer. It is then ready to use as required.

Try using small tender leaves of spinach coarsely shredded as a salad.

Epinards à la Bourgeoise

Spinach ring (serves 6–8)

	Imperial	American
1 kg spinach	**2 lb**	**2 lb**
300 ml Sauce Béchamel	$\frac{1}{2}$ **pt**	**1$\frac{1}{4}$ cups**
(*see page 27*)		
salt and pepper		
a pinch of nutmeg		
2 eggs		
40 g butter	**1$\frac{1}{2}$ oz**	**3 tbsp**
4 tbsp single cream	**4 tbsp**	**4 tbsp**

Prepare, cook and drain the spinach as above. Make the Sauce Béchamel, seasoning well with salt and pepper and adding the nutmeg. Beat the eggs and mix them into the sauce with the spinach. Add the butter to the mixture while it is still hot and mix well. Place in a buttered 18 cm (7 in) ring mould and cook in a moderate oven, Mark 4 (180°C/350°F), for 40–50 minutes. Unmould onto a round hot serving-dish. Heat the cream and season well. Just before serving, pour the hot cream over the spinach ring.

Tante Marie tip:
If fresh spinach is not available, substitute 500 g (1 lb) frozen spinach.

Epinards au Gratin

Spinach with a cheese topping
(serves 4–5)

	Imperial	American
1 kg fresh spinach	2 lb	2 lb
25 g butter	1 oz	2 tbsp
100 g cheese, grated	4 oz	2 cups
salt and pepper		

Prepare and cook the spinach as above.

Melt the butter in a pan, add the spinach and place over a good heat to drive off the excess liquid. Remove from the heat, stir in half the cheese, season well and place in a well-buttered heatproof dish. Sprinkle over the rest of the cheese and brown under a grill or in the top of a very hot oven, Mark 8 (230°C/450°F).

Les Fèves

Broad beans

In Britain broad beans are at their best from May to July, but are available up to August. Early season ones may be imported. Buy beans with light green pods which are well filled. Large mottled pods have tough beans in them. Very young, immature beans can be cooked and eaten whole, in the pods.

Fèves au Lard

Broad beans with bacon (serves 4–5)

	Imperial	American
1 kg young broad beans	2 lb	2 lb
10–12 spring onions		
40 g butter	1½ oz	3 tbsp
75 g lean bacon	3 oz	3 oz
2 tsp plain flour	2 tsp	2 tsp
450 ml white stock	¾ pt	2 cups
salt and pepper		

To finish:
finely chopped parsley

Cut the onions in half. Melt the butter in a heavy pan. Cut the bacon into strips and soften the onions and bacon together in the butter. Do not let the onions brown. Stir in the flour and mix well. Add the beans and pour on the stock. Season well and simmer gently until cooked. (The length of time will depend on the size of the beans, but they will probably take 10–15 minutes.) Place them in a hot serving-dish and pour over the liquor in which they were cooked. Dust with the parsley.

Tante Marie tip:
If there is a lot of liquor left in the pan after the beans have cooked, increase the heat and reduce the liquor until it is the consistency of a thin sauce, then pour over the beans. If the beans are very old, the skins may be removed before serving.

Fèves à la Maître d'Hôtel

Broad beans with lemon and parsley
(serves 4–5)

	Imperial	American
1 kg broad beans	2 lb	2 lb
salt and pepper		
50 g butter	2 oz	¼ cup
juice of ½ lemon		
finely chopped parsley		

Cook the beans in boiling salted water until tender. Drain well. Return to the pan and toss over a gentle heat until the surplus moisture has evaporated. Season well, then add the butter and lemon juice. Toss until the beans are evenly coated. Place in a warm vegetable-dish, coat thickly with the parsley and serve at once.

Les Haricots Verts

French beans

These are small thin beans. The colour varies from pale to mid-green according to the variety. They are imported to Britain all the year round but the main season is from June to August. Out of season they can be expensive. Choose beans with flat straight pods which break crisply and evenly. Young beans should be stringless. Dry and bulging pods will usually be tough.

Haricots Verts à la Bretonne

French beans Breton style (serves 4)

	Imperial	American
500 g French beans	1 lb	1 lb
1 small onion		
50 g butter	2 oz	$\frac{1}{4}$ cup
25 g plain flour	1 oz	3 tbsp
450 ml well flavoured white stock	$\frac{3}{4}$ pt	2 cups
salt and pepper		

Prepare the beans and blanch for 5–7 minutes in boiling salted water. Remove from the pan and drain thoroughly. Refresh under cold water.

Chop the onion very finely. Heat the butter in a pan, add the onion and cook over a gentle heat until soft and transparent. Remove from the heat and stir in the flour. Return to the heat and stir gently for 2–3 minutes. Pour in the stock, season, bring to the boil, then add the beans. Cook gently for 15–20 minutes. Place in a hot dish and serve.

Les Oignons

Onions

Home-grown onions are available in Britain from September to February and many different types are imported the whole year round. Spanish onions are large but have the most delicate flavour. Home-grown varieties usually have a stronger flavour. Small button onions, often sold as pickling onions, are ideal for garnishing and are available from September to November. The colour of the skin varies with the type. Buy onions with bright dry skins, avoiding any which are wet, shrivelled or soft around the neck. Onions are easy to grow and store well provided they are kept dry and away from frost.

To prevent tears when peeling onions, remove the skins carefully, leaving the stalk and the root on the onion without cutting into the flesh. It is the juice from the flesh which causes the irritation. When they are all peeled, slice and chop them quickly, discarding the stalk and root.

Oignons Glacé

Glazed onions (serves 4)

	Imperial	American
500 g button onions	1 lb	1 lb
salt		
50 g butter	2 oz	$\frac{1}{4}$ cup
chopped parsley		

Peel the onions carefully, leaving the stem as long as possible so they stay whole during cooking. Cook in boiling salted water for 7–10 minutes according to size. Refresh and drain well. Heat the butter in a pan, add the onions and finish cooking them in this, turning occasionally, until golden brown and cooked right through. Drain and serve as a garnish, or separately on a hot dish sprinkled with the parsley.

Paillettes des Oignons

Fried onion rings (serves 4)

	Imperial	American
350 g large onions	12 oz	12 oz
150 ml milk	$\frac{1}{4}$ pt	$\frac{2}{3}$ cup
4–5 tbsp plain flour	4–5 tbsp	4–5 tbsp
salt and pepper		
fat for deep frying		

Peel the onions and slice them into thin rings. Separate the layers and stir them in the milk. Add the flour and seasoning. Mix together lightly with a fork until the onion rings are coated with the batter.

Heat the fat to 190°C (380°F) and add the onion rings, taking care to separate them so they do not stick together. Cook until dark golden brown. Drain well before serving. If necessary, sprinkle with a little salt.

Tante Marie tip:
Spanish onions are ideal for this recipe.

Les Panais

Parsnips

Parsnips are in season in Britain from September to March, but are best from October onwards as their flavour is improved by a touch of frost. They should be white or cream-coloured and look crisp and clean. Brown patches on the top or woody roots denote poor quality.

Panais Frits

Fried parsnips (serves 4)

	Imperial	American
500 g parsnips	1 lb	1 lb
1 tbsp wine vinegar	1 tbsp	1 tbsp
1 tbsp sugar	1 tbsp	1 tbsp
fritter batter made with		
50 g plain flour	2 oz	$\frac{1}{2}$ cup
(*see page 167*)		
3–4 tbsp seasoned flour	3–4 tbsp	3–4 tbsp
fat for deep frying		
finely chopped parsley		

Peel the parsnips and cut them into even-sized pieces. Place them in a pan of boiling salted water with the vinegar and sugar. Cook until just tender, drain well and refresh. Dry the parsnips on kitchen paper.

Make the fritter batter and heat a deep pan of fat to 190°C (380°F). Pass the parsnips through the seasoned flour, coat with the batter and fry until golden brown. Do not use a frying-basket as the batter will stick to the mesh. Serve in a hot dish dusted with the parsley.

Les Petits Pois

Peas

In France peas are generally gathered younger and are smaller than English peas and rightly deserve to be called petit pois (little peas). Mangetout (sugar peas) are cooked and served whole. These are available at the start of the season which in Britain is from May to September. Buy peas with bright crisp pods, not large dry pods which are bulging with peas. The best test is to taste them raw; they should be sweet and juicy.

Petits Pois au Fenouil

Peas flavoured with fennel (serves 4)

	Imperial	American
1 kg peas	2 lb	2 lb
1 bunch fennel, tied with		
string		
To finish:		
25 g butter	1 oz	2 tbsp
1 tbsp chopped fennel	1 tbsp	1 tbsp

Shell the peas. Cook in a saucepan of boiling salted water, with the bunch of fennel, until tender. Drain well, refresh under the cold tap and remove the fennel. Melt the butter in a saucepan, add the peas and heat through.

Pile up the peas in a hot serving-dish and sprinkle with the chopped fennel.

Petits Pois à la Française

French-style peas (serves 4)

	Imperial	American
1 kg peas	2 lb	2 lb
50 g butter	2 oz	$\frac{1}{4}$ cup
1 tbsp plain flour	1 tbsp	1 tbsp
salt		
$\frac{1}{4}$ tsp sugar	$\frac{1}{4}$ tsp	$\frac{1}{4}$ tsp
12 spring onions		
3–4 lettuce leaves		
2–3 sprigs each parsley		
and chervil		

Shell the peas and place them in a pan with the butter and flour. Stir together over a very gentle heat. Add the salt, sugar, onions and shredded lettuce leaves. Add sufficient cold water to just cover the peas. Add the parsley and chervil. Simmer for 20–30 minutes according to the size of the peas. Serve with a little of the liquor in which they were cooked.

Tante Marie tip:
If frozen peas are used instead of fresh ones, use only 350 g (12 oz/3 cups). Adjust the cooking time to allow both onions and peas to become just tender.

Les Poireaux

Leeks

In Britain leeks are mainly home-grown, and are in season from August to April. Buy those which are trimmed and look crisp and clean. They should have fresh green leaves and be white for half their length. Buy leeks of similar size for even cooking. Avoid any which are limp and have yellow leaves.

To prepare for cooking, trim the leaf end to a point as there is more edible flesh on the inner than on the outer leaves. Cut through the leek halfway down its length and wash, cut end downwards, under cold running water. Make certain that all the grit is washed out of the layers and then tie together in small bundles if the leeks are to be boiled. The coarse green leaves can be chopped and used for flavouring soups, braised meats and vegetables, etc.

Poireaux au Jus

Leeks cooked in stock (serves 4)

	Imperial	American
500 g small leeks	1 lb	1 lb
600 ml white stock	1 pt	2½ cups
75 g butter	3 oz	6 tbsp
salt and pepper		
25 g plain flour	1 oz	3 tbsp
finely chopped parsley		

Prepare the leeks as above, place in a pan of boiling salted water and blanch for 5 minutes. Drain well and refresh. Replace in the empty pan with the stock and 25 g (1 oz/2 tbsp) butter and the seasoning. Cover with a lid and cook for 20–30 minutes, depending on the size of the leeks. When tender, lift them out of the stock, drain well and arrange in a hot dish.

Melt the rest of the butter in a clean pan, add the flour and cook for 2–3 minutes. Strain on the liquor in which the leeks were cooked, then bring to the boil, stirring all the time. Boil for 5 minutes. Taste, add seasoning if necessary and pour over the leeks. Sprinkle with the parsley just before serving.

Les Pommes de Terre

Potatoes

Home-grown new potatoes are available in Britain from May to August and imported ones from November to September. If they are fresh, you should be able to rub the skins away from the flesh with the fingers and they should have a delicious slightly earthy flavour. Buy small even-sized ones in small quantities. They shrivel and lose their delicate flavour if stored for long and turn green if exposed to the light.

To prepare for cooking, scrub well and boil without peeling. The skins can be removed after cooking but try serving them with their skins left on and tossed in butter.

Main-crop potatoes are available from September to May. Buy clean firm potatoes which are free from damage or blemish. They may be bought in large quantities but must be stored in a dry, cool, dark place. Warmth will cause them to sprout, and light will turn them green. Frost will also damage them.

Potatoes can be cooked in many ways: boiled, baked, steamed, casseroled or fried. As well as being served as a vegetable accompanying a dish, they are often used as a garnish. For example Pommes de Terre Duchesse for Filets de Sole à la Suchet; Pommes de Terre Paille for Steak Vert Pré; Pommes de Terre Château for Boeuf Braisé; Pommes de Terre Noisette for Tournedos à la Choron; Pommes de Terre Pont Neuf for Entrecôte Henri IV.

For four average servings, use 750 g (1½ lb) of old potatoes or 500 g (1 lb) of new potatoes. Unless otherwise stated, about half this amount is sufficient for garnishing.

Pommes de Terre Persillées

Parsley potatoes (serves 4)

	Imperial	American
750 g new potatoes	1½ lb	1½ lb
600 ml chicken stock	1 pt	2½ cups
salt and pepper		
a little butter		
3–4 tbsp finely chopped parsley	3–4 tbsp	3–4 tbsp

Scrape the potatoes and cut in half lengthways. Place them in a well-buttered heatproof dish. Pour over sufficient hot and well-flavoured stock to just cover them. Season well, dot with small knobs of butter and sprinkle with a little of the parsley. Cover with a piece of buttered greaseproof paper and cook in a moderately hot oven, Mark 6–7 (200–225°C/400–425°F), for 40 minutes. Remove the paper and, just before serving, cover the top with a thick layer of the remaining parsley. Serve in the dish in which they have been cooked.

Pommes de Terre à la Dijonnaise

Mustard potatoes (serves 4)

	Imperial	American
500 g new potatoes, washed and skinned	1 lb	1 lb
50 g butter	2 oz	¼ cup
salt and pepper		
1–2 tbsp finely chopped fresh herbs	1–2 tbsp	1–2 tbsp
4 tbsp double cream	4 tbsp	4 tbsp
1 tsp Dijon mustard	1 tsp	1 tsp

Cut the potatoes into very thin rounds. Heat the butter in a heavy pan, add the potatoes and sauté over a good heat. Turn them carefully from time to time with a metal spatula or fish-slice. When lightly brown, add approximately 300 ml (8 fl oz/1 cup) of hot water. Season well. Cover with a piece of grease-proof paper and a lid and continue cooking over a low heat for a further 20 minutes. Just before serving, heat the herbs, cream and mustard. Mix gently. Pile the potatoes up in a hot dish and pour over the cream mixture. Serve at once.

The two following recipes can be made with either new or old potatoes. Choose small new ones or cut old ones into pieces and 'turn' them to a similar size.

Pommes de Terre Berrichonne

Casseroled potatoes (serves 4)

	Imperial	American
750 g potatoes	1½ lb	1½ lb
25 g butter	1 oz	2 tbsp
100 g streaky bacon	4 oz	4 oz
1 onion, finely chopped		
white stock		
a bouquet garni		
salt and pepper		
finely chopped parsley		

Peel or scrape the potatoes and 'turn' if necessary (see page 25). Heat the butter in a pan, add the bacon and onion and fry gently, then add the potatoes and cook until lightly brown. Pour in sufficient stock to cover the potatoes, add the bouquet garni and season well. Cover with a lid and cook until the potatoes are tender. Serve in a hot dish sprinkled with the parsley.

Pommes de Terre Vapeur

Steamed potatoes (serves 4)

These are particularly good to serve with fish.

750 g (1½ lb) potatoes
salt

Peel or scrape the potatoes and 'turn' if necessary (see page 25). Place in a steamer over boiling water. Sprinkle over a little salt, cover with a lid and steam until tender. They will take half as long again to cook as boiled potatoes: approximately 30–35 minutes. When they are cooked, remove the steamer, place a dry folded cloth or some kitchen paper over the potatoes and cover partially with a lid. Allow to stand in a warm place for a few moments before serving.

Pommes de Terre Mousseline

Creamed potatoes (serves 4)

	Imperial	American
750 g old potatoes	1½ lb	1½ lb
salt and pepper		
boiling milk		
25 g butter	1 oz	2 tbsp
a pinch of nutmeg (*optional*)		

Wash and peel the potatoes and cut into even-sized pieces. Cover with cold water and add a good teaspoon of salt. Bring to the boil and cook until tender. Drain at once. Return to the pan, place over a gentle heat and toss the potatoes until they are quite dry.

Heat some milk to boiling point. Meanwhile, pass the potatoes quickly through a sieve or vegetable mill into a hot bowl. Make a well in the centre, add the butter, then pour in the boiling milk gradually. The exact quantity of milk needed will depend on the type of potatoes used. Beat very well indeed with a wooden spoon or spatula. The more vigorous the beating, the lighter and fluffier the result will be. Season to taste, adding a tiny pinch of grated nutmeg if desired. Pile the potatoes in a hot serving-dish.

Pommes de Terre Savoyard

Potato dish from the Haute Savoie (serves 4)

	Imperial	American
500 g old potatoes	1 lb	1 lb
1 large onion		
40 g butter	1½ oz	3 tbsp
salt and pepper		
white stock		
50 g Gruyère cheese	2 oz	1 cup

Peel the potatoes and onion. Cut the potatoes into 12 mm (½ in) dice and slice the onion thinly. Melt the butter in a thick pan, add the potatoes and onion and season well. Cover with thickly buttered grease-proof paper and a lid and cook over a gentle heat until the onion and potatoes are quite tender. Shake the pan from time to time to prevent the vegetables from sticking. When the vegetables are cooked, place in a well-buttered heatproof dish and pour in sufficient stock to partially cover. Add extra seasoning if needed. Cut the Gruyère cheese into wafer-thin

slices. Spread it all over the surface of the dish. Cook in the top of a moderately hot oven, Mark 6 (200°C/400°F), for 20–30 minutes. Serve very hot.

Pommes de Terre Fondant

Soft roast potatoes (serves 4)

	Imperial	American
750 g potatoes	1½ lb	1½ lb
salt		
600 ml white stock *or* milk and water	1 pt	2½ cups
50 g melted butter	2 oz	¼ cup
finely chopped parsley		

Peel the potatoes and 'turn' them (see page 25). Blanch in boiling salted water for 5 minutes, then drain. Place in a heatproof dish and add sufficient stock or milk and water to come halfway up the potatoes. Brush with the butter and cook in a moderately hot oven, Mark 6 (200°C/400°F), for approximately 45 minutes or until the liquid is absorbed, the potatoes are soft and the tops golden brown. Brush with more butter once or twice during cooking.

The potatoes can be served either in the dish in which they were cooked, or piled into a clean hot one. Sprinkle with the parsley and serve.

Pommes de Terre Duchesse

Duchess potatoes (serves 4)

	Imperial	American
500 g old potatoes	1 lb	1 lb
25 g butter	1 oz	2 tbsp
2 egg yolks, *or*		
1 whole egg		
salt and pepper		
a pinch of nutmeg		
beaten egg to glaze		
chopped parsley, *or*		
paprika pepper		

Peel the potatoes and cut into even-sized pieces. Place in a pan of cold salted water, bring to the boil and cook until tender. Drain. Return to the pan and toss over a gentle heat to dry off. Pass them through a sieve or vegetable mill into a hot bowl. Add the butter, egg yolks and seasoning. Beat the mixture very well. If the mixture still appears to be too soft for piping, return it to the pan and place over a gentle heat, beating well until some of the moisture has evaporated.

Place the mixture in a forcing bag with a large rosette pipe. Pipe out into cone shapes on a lightly greased baking-tray and cook in the top of a moderately hot oven, Mark 6 (200°C/400°F), for 10 minutes. Remove from the oven, brush over lightly with beaten egg and return to the oven until golden brown. Serve sprinkled with the parsley or paprika.

Tante Marie tip:
These potatoes can be frozen very satisfactorily. Pipe them onto baking-trays, or kitchen trays covered in sheet plastic. Freeze uncovered until firm, then transfer to plastic boxes. To cook, brush with beaten egg while still frozen, then either allow to defrost before cooking, or cook from the frozen state, allowing a little extra time.

Left: Pommes de Terre Duchesse and a dish of Carottes à la Vichy surrounded by a selection of vegetables. Clockwise from left: Courgettes, mushrooms, red cabbage, aubergine, cabbage, Webb lettuce, celery, Cos lettuce, beetroot, celeriac, tomatoes, onions, peppers, kohlrabi and beans.

Pommes de Terre Château

Castle potatoes (serves 4)

	Imperial	American
1 kg potatoes	2 lb	2 lb
salt		
50 g unsalted butter	2 oz	$\frac{1}{4}$ cup
a little chopped parsley		

Peel the potatoes and pare them down to the size of a large olive. Place in a pan of cold salted water, bring to the boil and cook for 2–3 minutes. Strain into a colander and drain well.

Method 1

Place the potatoes in a roasting-pan of hot fat and cook in a moderately hot oven, Mark 6 (200°C/400°F), for approximately 45 minutes. Baste occasionally. When the potatoes are cooked, drain off the fat and add a little butter. Place in a pan, cover with a lid and toss them over a low heat.

Method 2

Heat 50 g (2 oz/$\frac{1}{4}$ cup) of unsalted butter in a pan, add the well-drained potatoes and cover with a lid. Cook, shaking frequently, until the potatoes are golden brown and tender. Remove from the pan and drain.

To serve, sprinkle with salt and the parsley.

Pommes de Terre Noisettes

Fried potato balls (serves 4)

	Imperial	American
1 kg potatoes	2 lb	2 lb
salt and pepper		
50 g unsalted butter	2 oz	$\frac{1}{4}$ cup

Select large potatoes if possible. Wash and peel them and then, using a vegetable ball cutter, scoop out small balls. Place in a pan of cold salted water and bring them to the boil. Drain well, then dry on kitchen paper. Heat the butter in a shallow pan. When it begins to turn golden brown, add the potatoes and seasoning. Cover with a lid and cook, shaking the pan from time to time. They will probably take 5–7 minutes to finish cooking. Drain on kitchen paper. Serve at once.

Pommes de Terre Paille

Straw potatoes

potatoes
fat for deep frying
salt

Peel the potatoes and cut thin slices on a mandoline. Cut the slices into very fine julienne about 4 cm (1½ in) long. Soak in cold water before cooking to remove the starch, then drain and dry carefully on kitchen paper.

Heat a pan of deep fat to 195°C (390°F). Place the potatoes in a frying-basket and lower into the fat. Cook until golden brown. Remove from the pan and drain on kitchen paper. Sprinkle with salt just before serving.

Pommes de Terre Pont Neuf

Chipped potatoes

potatoes
fat for deep frying
salt

Peel the potatoes and cut into 1 cm (⅜ in) slices, then cut into batons of the same thickness and 6 cm (2¼ in) long. Wash well and dry on kitchen paper. Heat the fat to 160°C (320°F). Place the potatoes in a frying-basket and lower into the fat. Cook until the potatoes are soft but not coloured (this is called fat-blanching). Remove from the fat and increase the heat to 195°C (390°F) and cook the potatoes again until crisp and golden brown. Remove from the pan, drain on kitchen paper and sprinkle with salt just before serving.

Croquettes de Pommes de Terre

Potato croquettes (serves 4)

	Imperial	American
500 g old potatoes	1 lb	1 lb
2 egg yolks		
15 g butter	½ oz	1 tbsp
salt and pepper		
2 tsp finely chopped parsley	2 tsp	2 tsp
a pinch of nutmeg		
3–4 tbsp seasoned flour	3–4 tbsp	3–4 tbsp
1 egg		
1 tbsp oil	1 tbsp	1 tbsp
50–75 g white breadcrumbs	2–3 oz	1–1½ cups
a little plain flour		
fat for deep frying		

Peel the potatoes and cut into even-sized pieces. Cover with cold salted water. Bring to the boil and cook until tender but not broken. Drain well and pass through a sieve or vegetable mill. Return to the pan, place over a very gentle heat to dry off, then beat in the egg yolks, butter, seasoning, parsley and nutmeg.

Lightly flour a pastry board. Place the potatoes on this and, with floured hands, make into a roll and cut into 12 even-sized portions. Form each portion into a ball or sausage shape. Beat the egg and oil together. Dip each portion of potato into this mixture and then roll it in the breadcrumbs. Repeat this process, pressing the breadcrumbs firmly into the coated potato. Fry the potatoes quickly in hot deep fat at 195°C (390°F) until golden brown. Drain well on kitchen paper and serve hot.

Les Tomates

Tomatoes

Tomatoes are imported into Britain all the year round. Home-grown tomatoes are available from March to November although peak production is from May to September. Prime quality tomatoes are usually graded to give 6 or 8 to the 500 g (1 lb).

They are easy to grow in the greenhouse, garden or tub and seeds can be obtained for a variety of sizes and types: from tiny Tom Thumb, which have a lovely sharp flavour, to big fleshy irregularly shaped Continental ones. Long plum tomatoes can be grown as well as bright yellow ones, and all provide a contrast of flavour and colour for cooking and garnishing.

Tomates à la Duchesse

Duchess tomatoes (serves 3–6)

Tomatoes filled with Duchess potatoes which can also be used as an attractive garnish.

	Imperial	American
6 large tomatoes		
salt		
Pommes de Terre Duchesse mixture made with 500 kg potatoes (*see page 179*)	1 lb	1 lb
50 g cheese, grated	2 oz	1 cup

Cut the tomatoes in half. Carefully remove the pulp and seeds with a teaspoon or ball cutter. Lightly sprinkle the insides with salt, place upside down and allow to drain for 20–25 minutes.

Prepare the Duchess potatoes and place in a forcing bag with a large rosette pipe. Pipe the mixture into the tomato halves. Sprinkle with the cheese and cook in a hot oven, Mark 8 (230°C/450°F), for 8–10 minutes or until golden brown.

Tomates à la Provençale

Provençale tomatoes (serves 4)

Baked tomatoes with a garlic-flavoured topping.

	Imperial	American
3 cloves garlic		
2 tbsp chopped parsley	2 tbsp	2 tbsp
3 tbsp white breadcrumbs	3 tbsp	3 tbsp
500 g tomatoes	1 lb	1 lb
salt and pepper		
a little sugar		
3–4 tbsp oil	3–4 tbsp	3–4 tbsp

Chop the garlic very finely, then mix with the parsley and breadcrumbs. Cut the tomatoes in half and arrange in a well-buttered heatproof dish. Season, adding the sugar. Pile the garlic, breadcrumbs and parsley mixture on the top. Pour over the oil and cook in a moderately hot oven, Mark 6 (200°C/400°F), for 15–20 minutes. Serve very hot.

Les Topinambours

Jerusalem artichokes

In spite of their name, these artichokes have nothing to do with Jerusalem. The name is believed to come from girasole, the Italian name for sunflower, to which they are related. Although also distantly related to globe artichokes, they are completely dissimilar in appearance. Jerusalem artichokes are twisted knobbly tubers with a thin cream or purplish skin. Good quality ones are clean, firm and a good size.

To prepare Jerusalem artichokes for cooking, scrub well and remove any awkward knobs. They can be peeled or can be cooked first and the skins removed afterwards. After preparing they must be kept and cooked in acidulated water as they discolour easily.

Tomates à la Provençale.

Topinambours au Gratin

Jerusalem artichokes in cheese sauce
(serves 4)

	Imperial	American
500 g Jerusalem artichokes	1 lb	1 lb
300 ml Sauce Béchamel (*see page 27*)	$\frac{1}{2}$ pt	$1\frac{1}{4}$ cups
2 egg yolks		
25 g butter	1 oz	2 tbsp
75 g cheese, grated	3 oz	$1\frac{1}{2}$ cups
salt and pepper		

Cook the artichokes in boiling salted water until tender. Cut into rounds and place in a buttered heatproof dish.

Make the Sauce Béchamel. Mix the egg yolks lightly, add the sauce and beat well. Add the butter gradually then three-quarters of the cheese. Taste and season. Pour over the artichokes, sprinkle the rest of the cheese over the top and brown in a hot oven, Mark 7 (220°C/425°F), or under a hot grill until golden brown.

Les Légumes Sec
Dried vegetables

Les Haricots Blanc
Haricot beans

These are small white beans which must be soaked overnight. Cover with sufficient water so they are still covered after they have swollen. To cook, drain the beans and place in a pan of boiling water. Cook for 2–3 hours. Do not add salt until 30 minutes before the end of cooking, as earlier addition of salt hardens the beans.

Haricots à la Crème

Haricot beans with cream (serves 4)

	Imperial	American
225 g dried haricot beans	8 oz	1 cup
1 onion		
1 clove		
1 clove garlic		
1 carrot		
1 stick celery		
a sprig of thyme		
salt and pepper		
25 g butter	1 oz	2 tbsp
1 tbsp double cream	1 tbsp	1 tbsp

Soak the beans overnight. The following day place in a saucepan with plenty of water. Add the onion stuck with the clove, crushed garlic, whole carrot, stick of celery and thyme. Boil gently for 2–3 hours or until tender, adding more hot water if needed. Season well with salt and pepper about 30 minutes before the end of the cooking time.

When the beans are cooked, remove the herbs, carrot, celery and onion. Drain the beans well in a colander, return to the pan and add the butter and cream. Season and serve hot.

Top: Topinambours au Gratin.
Bottom: Endives au Lard (*see page 171*).

Les Lentilles

Lentils

Lentils in France are a grey-green colour and are much harder than the orange ones usually seen in Britain. The orange ones can be cooked without soaking, but the French type should be soaked overnight before cooking.

Lentilles à la Lorraine

Lorraine-style lentils (serves 4)

	Imperial	American
225 g lentils	8 oz	1 cup
salt and pepper		
3–4 rashers lean bacon		
2 large onions		
50 g butter *or* good beef dripping	2 oz	$\frac{1}{4}$ cup
Beurre Manié (*see page 23*)		
1 small clove garlic		
a pinch of sugar		

Wash the lentils well and cook in plenty of boiling water for 20–30 minutes or until nearly tender, then add sufficient salt to season and continue cooking until soft. Drain, but reserve the liquor in which they were cooked.

Cut the bacon into strips and finely chop the onions. Melt the butter or dripping in a thick pan and add the bacon. When it is just beginning to turn golden, add the onions and soften them together over a low heat, keeping well stirred. Do not let them brown. When they are quite soft, add the lentils and as much of their liquor as is necessary to make a thin sauce. Cook for 5 minutes, stirring occasionally. Thicken with sufficient Beurre Manié to give a thick purée, then add the clove of garlic crushed with a little salt. Season, adding the sugar, and serve very hot.

Les Salades

Salads

Salads can be presented in many different ways, each country having its own specialities. In France, a salad plays a very important part in the menu. Often the hors d'oeuvre is a simple tomato, cucumber or potato salad, but it can be a more elaborate salade composée, such as Courgettes à la Caillou,

Salade Printanière or Salade Panachée. These salads, which make full use of ingredients in season and are pleasing to the eye as well as to the palate, also make a colourful addition to a buffet table.

Crisp green salads provide a refreshing vegetable course. Different types of lettuce like crisp Webbs Wonder or a long-leafed Cos add variety, as do curly endive, batavia or escarole which have a slightly bitter flavour and are often used in France. Even tender young dandelion leaves are served. They are all tossed in a well-flavoured Sauce Vinaigrette just before they are eaten.

Salade Verte

Green salad (serves 4)

1 lettuce
salt
garlic (*optional*)
fresh herbs (*optional*)
Sauce Vinaigrette (*see page 33*) **made with:**
   8 tbsp oil
   1 tbsp red *or* white wine vinegar
   salt
   a pinch of sugar
   a little made mustard
   pepper

Separate the lettuce leaves and wash in water containing either salt or 1 tablespoon of malt vinegar. Rinse well, then shake dry in a salad basket or tea towel.

Cut the garlic in half, if used, and rub a large salad bowl with this.

Make the Sauce Vinaigrette. Mix the oil and vinegar together by whisking, blending in a liquidiser, or shaking together in a bottle. Add seasonings to taste. Pour into the salad bowl and place the lettuce on top. Sprinkle with fresh herbs if used. Toss at the table.

Tante Marie tip:
Remember to choose a large salad bowl, so that the lettuce can be tossed without spilling the Sauce Vinaigrette.

Courgettes à la Caillou
Courgette salad (serves 6)

	Imperial	American
500 g courgettes	1 lb	1 lb
4–6 tomatoes		
salt and pepper		
150 ml Sauce Vinaigrette	$\frac{1}{4}$ pt	$\frac{2}{3}$ cup
(see page 33)		
1–2 green peppers		
1 large lettuce		
2 hard-boiled eggs		
finely chopped basil		

Cut the courgettes into 4 cm (1½ in) lengths and then into strips about the thickness of a little finger (do not peel). Place in a pan of boiling water and cook for 4–5 minutes. Refresh until cold then drain well and place on a clean cloth or kitchen paper to dry. Cut the tomatoes in half and scoop out the centres with a ball cutter or a teaspoon. Dust the insides lightly with salt, turn upside down on a wire rack and allow to drain.

Meanwhile, make the Sauce Vinaigrette. Season well and mix with the courgettes. Cut the peppers in half, remove the core and cut into very fine julienne about 4 cm (1½ in) long.

Roll the lettuce leaves tightly, like a cigar, then cut into fine strips crossways (this is called a chiffonade).

Cut the drained tomatoes into strips. Keep back some of the courgettes for decoration and mix the rest with the tomatoes. Leave to marinade, turning them from time to time, then place in a serving-dish, heaping them up into a dome shape. Place small piles of the lettuce and peppers alternately around the edge of the dish and neatly arrange the quartered hard-boiled eggs and the remainder of the courgettes on the top. Sprinkle with the basil and serve cold.

Salade Printanière
Spring salad (serves 6)

A colourful salad using young spring vegetables.

	Imperial	American
Sauce Vinaigrette (see page 33) made with:		
1 small onion		
1 clove garlic		
salt and pepper		
8 tbsp oil	8 tbsp	8 tbsp
3 tbsp wine vinegar	3 tbsp	3 tbsp
1 lettuce		
1 bunch radishes		
100 g mushrooms	4 oz	4 oz
225 g new carrots	8 oz	8 oz
juice of 1 lemon		
225 g cooked young French beans	8 oz	8 oz

Peel the onion and grate 1–2 teaspoons of it. Crush the garlic with a little salt. Place the onion and garlic in a bowl with the oil, vinegar and seasoning and whisk together.

Wash the lettuce and radishes and drain well. Wipe the mushrooms with a damp cloth and scrape the carrots. Cut the radishes into rounds. Thinly slice the mushrooms and toss in the lemon juice. Grate the carrots and cut the beans into lozenges.

Arrange the lettuce leaves in a salad bowl, scatter with the radishes, followed by the mushrooms, carrot and finally the French beans. Pour over the Sauce Vinaigrette and serve cold.

Courgettes à la Caillou.

Salade Panachée
Mixed salad (serves 6)

A colourful salad, which is particularly useful in the winter when most salad ingredients are expensive or difficult to buy.

	Imperial	American
225 g haricot beans, soaked overnight	8 oz	1 cup
salt and pepper		
3–6 spring onions		
3–4 hard-boiled eggs		
1 red pepper		
50 g black olives	2 oz	$\frac{1}{3}$ cup
50 g green olives	2 oz	$\frac{1}{3}$ cup
Sauce Vinaigrette (*see page 33*) **made with:**		
3 tbsp oil	3 tbsp	3 tbsp
1 tbsp wine vinegar	1 tbsp	1 tbsp
1 tbsp finely chopped fresh herbs	1 tbsp	1 tbsp
salt and pepper		

The day before making the salad, wash the beans and place them in a large bowl. Cover with water and allow to stand in a cool place overnight.

The following day, cook the beans in plenty of boiling water for approximately $1\frac{1}{2}$ hours. Add the salt and continue cooking for a further 30 minutes or until tender. Drain, refresh and drain again.

Make the Sauce Vinaigrette and mix with the beans and sliced spring onions. Season well. Slice the eggs. Remove the core and seeds from the pepper and cut into strips. Stone the olives.

Pile the beans into the centre of a large dish and decorate with a lattice of red pepper strips. In between these, place the black olives. Arrange the slices of egg around the dish and decorate with green olives. Serve cold.

Salade Belle Hortense
Celery and walnut salad (serves 6)

Sauce Rémoulade gives a distinctive flavour to this salad.

	Imperial	American
300 ml Sauce Rémoulade (*see page 31*)	$\frac{1}{2}$ pt	$1\frac{1}{4}$ cups
1 head celery		
25 g chopped walnuts	1 oz	$\frac{1}{4}$ cup
225 g small round beetroot	8 oz	8 oz
a few walnut halves		

Make the Sauce Rémoulade. Slice the celery and mix it with the chopped walnuts and sauce, then pile into a salad bowl. Overlap the slices of beetroot around the edge of the bowl so the celery salad shows in the centre. Decorate with the walnut halves.

The Cheeseboard

An attractive and well-chosen cheeseboard will give pleasure to your family and guests on any occasion. If you have wine with your meal try serving cheese in the French style: after the main course and vegetables but before the pudding. In this way you can appreciate the wine that you serve with the cheese, whether you continue to drink the same wine you had with the previous course or serve a specially chosen red wine to honour the cheese.

The variety of cheeses served does not need to be great; a small selection of cheeses of different types can be most enjoyable. Choose contrasting types and ensure they are in peak condition. Brie and Camembert are always great favourites. Both are soft cheeses which need to be selected with care. Buy them a few days before they are required. If you want a whole Brie for a special occasion, order it beforehand so your supplier can have one in good condition for you. This is, however, a large cheese weighing about 2.25 kg (5 lb) so you will need only a section for most occasions. A Camembert, however, is a small cheese of about 250 g (9 oz). When choosing these cheeses the feel and the smell are the two points to assess. A few days before they are ripe the centre will yield slightly to the touch and when the cheeses are ripe they will feel soft and springy. A smell of ammonia is a sure indication that a cheese is past its prime and will not be good to eat. If you have a slightly under-ripe cheese which you want to ripen quickly, keep it in a warm kitchen. Use a cool place to slow down development when necessary. A cut Camembert often has a tendency to run, so stand the box on its side with the cut section uppermost. Pont l'Eveque, Carré de l'Est and Livarot are other similar cheeses.

To contrast with these soft cheeses, a blue-vein cheese has a tangy taste. Creamy-textured Roquefort made from ewe's milk and matured in the famous Roquefort caves is surely the choicest one. Bleu de Bresse has a sharper flavour and firmer consistency. Goat cheeses are less readily obtainable outside France, but they are delicious. The fearsome smell often belies the delicate flavour, although a few are strong. Some are prettily decorated. The Banon is wrapped in chestnut leaves and tied with straw, and others are cured in grey ash, like the nearly pyramidal Valençay. Ste Maure, from the Loire Valley, is traditionally shaped like a small log.

More readily available are some of the processed cheeses like Gruyère, with its strong nutty taste, or the milder St Paulin or Port Salut. Tomme aux Raisins has a thifty coating of black grape-pips left over from the Vendange, which give a delicate flavour to the creamy-smooth cheese. Cream cheeses too can be obtained, such as Petit Suisse, or the herb and garlic-flavoured cream cheeses. Altogether the choice is considerable.

Store cheeses in a cool airy place, or on the lowest shelf of the refrigerator. The flavour is best if the cheese is served at room temperature, so take them out of refrigeration 2 hours or so before serving. With the cheese you can serve crisp biscuits, bread or rolls, and, if you like, some fresh unsalted butter.

Sweets and Ices

Although fresh fruit is often served as a dessert in France, there are also many puddings to choose from, to suit all tastes and occasions. Some are very simple; a Crème Caramel is always popular, as are Petit Pots au Chocolat: a rich, light chocolate mousse served in individual dishes.

Frequently the French housewife will buy the pudding for Sunday lunch from the mouth-watering selection of gâteaux displayed in the window of the local pâtisserie. This chore is often given to her husband. For me, Sunday is identified not only by the sound of church bells, but by the sight of husbands walking home with their children, carrying beautifully tied cake boxes and bunches of flowers.

Some puddings are regional; there is the Tarte des Demoiselles Tatin in the Loire, and Amandine in Boulogne. Fruit flans vary in content according to local fruits. Normandy is famous for apple flans. In Alsace they are made with Crème Pâtissière covering the apples and, wherever you go in France, you will find them in one form or another.

Profiteroles au Chocolat are another favourite. Croquembouche – the traditional French wedding cake – is a pyramid of these cream-filled choux buns, coated in caramel and topped with a froth of spun sugar. It is sometimes made with meringues.

At home or in a restaurant, a hot soufflé never fails to please. A taste of this feathery light pudding will soon show you why this is so. To fully appreciate a soufflé, a sauce should be served to complement the texture: Crème Anglaise with a Soufflé au Chocolat or a sharp Sauce d'Abricots with a vanilla one. Add a little liqueur to either sauce or soufflé for that extra special touch.

Ice creams are, of course, always a good stand-by. Try making your own; they are delectable.

Whatever type of pudding is needed, the choice is infinite for the enterprising cook.

Meringues

Meringues in any form are always a great favourite as a sweet. Perfect ones are easy to make if a few simple rules are followed.

1. Make certain that all utensils to be used are completely free from grease and are quite dry, as fat and moisture prevent the egg whites from stiffening.

2. Separate the eggs carefully so that no yolk is in the white – yolks contain fat.

3. Make certain that the sugar is completely dry.

4. Whisk the eggs evenly. Make sure that none of the mixture stays around the sides of the bowl. (Uneven whisking results in a rough mixture which does not hold its bulk.)

5. Fold in the sugar very gently. After beating in 1 tablespoon, sift in half the sugar and, using a metal spatula, cut through the mixture 3–4 times only. Add the rest of the sugar and blend the mixture completely.

6. Use immediately.

Meringue Suisse

Swiss meringue (makes 10–12)

	Imperial	American
4 egg whites		
250 g castor sugar	9 oz	1 cup and 2 tbsp
1 tsp vanilla sugar	1 tsp	1 tsp
a little icing sugar		

Grease 2 or 3 baking-trays with melted lard and dust evenly with flour. Alternatively, line the baking-trays with silicone parchment. Have a forcing bag ready for use, with a plain or rosette pipe of your choice.

Whisk the egg whites until they stand in stiff peaks. Add 1 tablespoon of sugar and continue to whisk for 3–4 minutes or until the mixture is stiff again. Lightly fold in the rest of the sieved sugar in 2 batches. Do not overfold. Place in a forcing bag with the pipe.

Pipe out onto the prepared baking-tray. Dust the meringues with the icing sugar. Turn the tray upside down and give a brisk tap to remove any excess sugar. Bake in a very slow oven, Mark $\frac{1}{4}$ (110°C/225°F), for 2–3 hours according to size.

Tante Marie tip:
To store meringues, keep them in an airtight tin in a dry atmosphere.

Chamonix (*right*) and Petits Vacherins.

Petits Vacherins

Small meringue nests (makes 10–12)

	Imperial	American
Meringue Suisse made with 4 egg whites (*see opposite*)		
1 (425 g) can pineapple, or 1 small fresh pineapple	15 oz	15 oz
1–2 tbsp kirsch	1–2 tbsp	1–2 tbsp
300 ml double cream	$\frac{1}{2}$ pt	$1\frac{1}{4}$ cups

Grease and flour 2 or 3 baking-trays. Prepare the meringue mixture as in the previous recipe.

Place the meringue in a forcing bag with a small rosette pipe. Pipe into 5 cm (2 in) rounds and build up the sides. Dust with icing sugar. Bake in a very slow oven, Mark $\frac{1}{4}$ (110°C/225°F), for 2–3 hours. When cooked, remove from the oven, place on a wire rack and allow to cool.

Cut the pineapple into small dice and macerate in the kirsch. Whisk the cream until thick. Whisk in the kirsch, then fold in the pineapple. Fill the centres of the vacherins just before serving.

Tante Marie tip:
As an alternative to pineapple use other fruit such as fresh strawberries or raspberries, tinned or fresh apricots or peaches.

If using strawberries or raspberries do not add them to the cream. Pipe the cream into the vacherins and decorate with the whole fruit.

Chamonix
Chestnut meringues (makes 10–12)

This is another way in which to use the meringue mixture. It is a variation of Mont Blanc aux Marrons: the deliciously rich sweet of chestnut purée and cream created by Escoffier. This version takes its name from Chamonix, the town which lies in the shadow of Mont Blanc in the Haute Savoie.

	Imperial	American
Meringue Suisse made with 2 egg whites (*see opposite*)		
1 (225 g) can sweetened chestnut purée	8 oz	8 oz
150 ml double cream	$\frac{1}{4}$ pt	$\frac{2}{3}$ cup
a little grated chocolate		

Grease and flour 2 or 3 baking-trays. Prepare the meringue mixture – see Meringue Suisse (page 188).

Place the meringue in a forcing bag with a 12 mm ($\frac{1}{2}$ in) plain pipe. Pipe into 5 cm (2 in) discs. Dust with icing sugar. Bake in a very slow oven, Mark $\frac{1}{4}$ (110°C/225°F), for 2–3 hours. When cooked, remove from the oven, place on a wire rack and allow to cool.

When cool, place the chestnut purée in a forcing bag with a 3 mm ($\frac{1}{8}$ in) plain pipe and pipe a nest on the edge of the meringue. Whisk the cream until thick and spoon or pipe it into the centre. Sprinkle with the chocolate.

Crème Renversée au Caramel
Caramel custard (serves 4–5)

Caramel custard is always popular. Here is a basic recipe with two colourful variations. To obtain the greatest amount of caramel sauce, make the custard the day before it is turned out.

		Imperial	American
For the caramel:			
100 g sugar		4 oz	$\frac{1}{2}$ cup
4 tbsp water		4 tbsp	4 tbsp
For the crème renversée:			
450 ml milk		$\frac{3}{4}$ pt	2 cups
1 vanilla pod			
2 eggs			
4 egg yolks			
75 g castor sugar		3 oz	$\frac{1}{3}$ cup

Fold a dry tea towel diagonally into four. Wrap this around a ring mould or 19 cm ($7\frac{1}{2}$ in) moule à manqué.

To make the caramel, place the sugar and water in a pan. Cook gently, stirring occasionally, until the sugar has dissolved. Bring to the boil but do not stir while the syrup is boiling. Continue to boil until the sugar reaches a deep golden brown. Pour into the tin, holding it securely in the cloth, and twist the tin so the caramel partly coats the sides.

Place the milk and vanilla pod in a pan and warm gently. Mix the eggs, egg yolks and sugar together. Do not beat as this causes bubbles which form a thick skin on the custard. Remove the vanilla pod from the pan, pour the milk onto the egg mixture and stir gently to mix. Strain into the caramelised mould.

Stand the mould in a bain-marie or roasting-pan containing boiling water and bake in a moderate oven, Mark 3 (160°C/325°F), for 50–60 minutes. At the end of this time, insert the tip of a small knife into the custard. If the knife comes out clean, the custard is cooked. Remove from the oven and allow to stand until completely cold before unmoulding onto a serving-dish.

Tante Marie tip:
To clean the caramel from the mould place in a pan of hot water, cover with a lid and allow to soak until clean.

Crème Caramel au Grand Marnier

Caramel custard with Grand Marnier (serves 4–6)

	Imperial	American
caramel custard (*see page 189*)		

To finish:
2 oranges

	Imperial	American
150 ml double cream	$\frac{1}{4}$ pt	$\frac{2}{3}$ cup
2 tsp icing sugar	2 tsp	2 tsp
2 tbsp Grand Marnier	2 tbsp	2 tbsp

Make the caramel custard (see page 189). Cook in a ring mould.

Turn the mould out onto a serving-plate. Segment the oranges and arrange around the edge. Whip the cream with the sieved icing sugar and Grand Marnier and pipe or spoon into the centre of the caramel custard.

Crème Opera

Opera cream (serves 4–6)

	Imperial	American
caramel custard (*see page 189*)		

To finish:

	Imperial	American
225 g large strawberries	8 oz	8 oz
2 tbsp kirsch	2 tbsp	2 tbsp
150 ml double cream	$\frac{1}{4}$ pt	$\frac{2}{3}$ cup
3–4 meringue shells		

Make the caramel custard (see page 189). Cook in a ring mould.

Macerate the strawberries in the kirsch for 1–2 hours, then drain. Whisk the cream and kirsch until stiff. Break the meringues into small pieces and fold into half the cream. Pile into the centre of the mould. Place the rest of the cream in a forcing bag with a small rosette pipe. Pipe stars all over the cream in the centre. Arrange the strawberries around the centre and edge of the mould.

Crème Caramel au Grand Marnier. The whipped cream is piped into the centre.

Using Gelatine

Gelatine is available in two forms: as a powder or in thin transparent sheets known as leaf gelatine. At Tante Marie we generally use leaf gelatine as it is not discernible in lightly flavoured foods and is easier to dissolve. Powdered gelatine, however, is more easily obtainable. Either form can be used in any of the recipes requiring gelatine.

15 g ($\frac{1}{2}$ oz) gelatine is normally required to set 600 ml (1 pt/$2\frac{1}{2}$ cups) liquid
3 teaspoons powdered gelatine = 15 g ($\frac{1}{2}$ oz)

Extra gelatine may need to be used to obtain a good set if the food is being served in very hot weather or conditions.

Leaf gelatine

The leaves come in various thicknesses. There are normally 8–10 leaves to 25 g (1 oz) but always weigh a quantity of leaves from each packet to determine how many leaves are needed so you don't have to weigh them each time.

Always place the gelatine in a jug or bowl of cold water for 15–20 minutes to soften it before use, making sure that it is completely covered. It can then be squeezed out and dropped into hot liquids and will dissolve immediately.

If needed for cold mixtures, soften it in cold water, then dissolve in 1–2 tablespoons of boiling water or fruit juice. Strain into the mixture and fold in.

If leaf gelatine is stored in a cold dry place it will keep well.

Powdered gelatine

Powdered gelatine is usually sold in 57 g (2 oz) packets containing 5 envelopes. Each envelope or 3 teaspoons will set 600 ml (1 pt/$2\frac{1}{2}$ cups) of liquid.

Place the gelatine in a bowl with 2–3 tablespoons of water, fruit juice or other liquid. Allow to soak for 15–20 minutes. Place over a pan of hot water and allow to dissolve slowly. Add a little more water if necessary to obtain a solution. Strain before using.

Mousse aux Abricots

Apricot mousse (serves 6)

In France this mousse is usually made with the fresh apricots for which the Auvergne is famous. If good-flavoured ones are not obtainable, try using dried apricots. Wash them well and soak them overnight in cold water – then use as fresh.

	Imperial	American
500 g fresh apricots,	1 lb	1 lb
or 225 g dried apricots	8 oz	1 cup
7 g gelatine	$\frac{1}{4}$ oz	$\frac{1}{2}$ pkt
3 eggs		
50 g castor sugar	2 oz	$\frac{1}{4}$ cup
juice of 1 lemon		
150 ml double cream	$\frac{1}{4}$ pt	$\frac{2}{3}$ cup

To finish:
4 extra tbsp double cream, whipped
a few hazelnuts, chopped

Place the apricots in a saucepan with a little water and poach gently for about 10–15 minutes or until tender. Strain and sieve, or liquidise, then allow to cool.

Soften the gelatine in cold water (see above).

Place 2 whole eggs and 1 yolk in a bowl with the sugar. Whisk them over hot water until thick and creamy. Remove from the heat and continue to whisk until cool. Dissolve the gelatine in the hot lemon juice and mix in thoroughly. Fold in the apricot purée.

Put the bowl aside in a cool place and stir the mousse occasionally. Whip the cream lightly. When the mousse begins to thicken, whisk the remaining egg white until stiff and fold into the mousse together with the cream. Pour into a serving-bowl or individual bowls. When set, place the whipped cream in a forcing bag with a small rosette pipe and decorate with cream stars and the hazelnuts.

Crème Asphodèle

Lemon mousse (serves 6)

This light mousse with the sharp tang of lemons will prove a great favourite for family meals as well as special parties.

	Imperial	American
3 lemons		
120 g castor sugar	$4\frac{1}{2}$ oz	$\frac{2}{3}$ cup
3 eggs, separated		
7 g gelatine	$\frac{1}{4}$ oz	$\frac{1}{2}$ pkt
2 tbsp water	2 tbsp	2 tbsp

For the decoration:

mimosa balls and angelica, *or* 4–5 extra tbsp double cream, whipped	4–5 tbsp	4–5 tbsp

Soften the gelatine (see page 191).

Beat the sugar and egg yolks together until light and fluffy. Add the grated rind of 2 lemons. Squeeze all the lemons and strain the juice. Dissolve the gelatine in the water, mix with the lemon juice and quickly strain into the egg mixture. Mix well.

Put aside in a cold place or over ice and water until the mousse begins to set. Stir occasionally so it sets evenly. When the mixture is set sufficiently to hold a light trail, whisk the egg whites stiffly and fold them in lightly so they are completely incorporated in the mousse. Pour into a serving-dish and allow to set. Decorate with the mimosa balls and angelica leaves, or piped cream.

Tante Marie tip:

This mousse freezes well. Freeze in the serving-dish undecorated and cover when frozen. Decorate just before serving.

Crème Asphodèle with a plate of Cigarettes Russe (*see page 224*).

Mousse au Café

Coffee mousse (serves 5–6)

	Imperial	American
50 g chocolate	2 oz	$\frac{1}{3}$ cup
7 g gelatine	$\frac{1}{4}$ oz	$\frac{1}{2}$ pkt
2 eggs		
65 g sugar	$2\frac{1}{2}$ oz	$\frac{1}{3}$ cup
300 ml milk	$\frac{1}{2}$ pt	$1\frac{1}{4}$ cups
2 tsp instant coffee	2 tsp	2 tsp
dissolved in 1–2 tbsp	1–2 tbsp	1–2 tbsp
boiling water		
25 g walnuts	1 oz	$\frac{1}{4}$ cup
150 ml double cream	$\frac{1}{4}$ pt	$\frac{2}{3}$ cup

To finish:
4–5 extra tbsp double cream, whipped

To make medaillons, soften the chocolate on a plate over a pan of hot water. Draw $2\frac{1}{2}$ cm (1 in) circles, using a coin as a guide, on a piece of greaseproof paper. Spread the chocolate evenly on the circles and put aside in a cool place to harden completely.

Soften the gelatine in cold water (see page 191). Separate the eggs. Cream the egg yolks and sugar thoroughly. Warm the milk and add the coffee. Pour onto the yolk and sugar mixture. Mix well and replace over a low heat, stirring all the time until the custard coats the back of a spoon. Remove from the heat, stir in the softened gelatine immediately and strain into a bowl. Chop the walnuts and add to the custard.

Put aside in a cool place until the mousse begins to set round the edge. Stir occasionally so it sets evenly. Whisk the cream lightly, then whisk the egg whites stiffly. Fold in the cream and then the whites very carefully. Do not overfold. Pour into a serving-dish or mould and allow to set. Decorate with cream stars and the chocolate medaillons.

Tante Marie tip:
This type of mousse freezes well but it is best not to decorate it before freezing. Freeze unwrapped. When frozen, cover, and seal well. Remove the covering before it is defrosted.

Petits Pots de Chocolat au Rhum

Little chocolate pots with rum (serves 3–4)

A rich chocolate mousse.

	Imperial	American
120 g dessert chocolate	$4\frac{1}{2}$ oz	1 cup
2 eggs		
2 tbsp rum	2 tbsp	2 tbsp
a nut of butter		

Break the chocolate into small pieces and place in a bowl over a pan of hot water until the chocolate just melts.

Separate the eggs and lightly beat the egg yolks and rum together. Whisk the whites very stiffly. Beat the butter into the chocolate, which must still be liquid at this stage. Mix in the egg yolks and rum and fold in the egg whites carefully. If the liquid is added to the chocolate before the egg whites are ready, the chocolate thickens too quickly for the whites to be folded in evenly. Place in small pots and chill before serving.

Tante Marie tip:
If the rum is omitted from the recipe, substitute orange juice or sherry to produce the correct consistency.

Mousse au Café.

Bavarois

Bavarian creams

These cream mousses are, in spite of their name, typically French. These two recipes give variations in the way this sweet may be served.

Charlotte Montreuil

Peach charlotte (serves 6)

A delicate peach-flavoured bavarois fills this charlotte. Use canned peaches if fresh ones are not available.

	Imperial	American
For poaching:		
100 g sugar	4 oz	$\frac{1}{2}$ cup
300 ml water	$\frac{1}{2}$ pt	$1\frac{1}{4}$ cups
4 large peaches		
sponge finger biscuits, Biscuits à la Cuiller (*see page 225*)		
For the bavarois:		
15 g gelatine	$\frac{1}{2}$ oz	1 pkt
3 egg yolks		
25 g sugar	1 oz	2 tbsp
1 heaped tsp vanilla sugar	1 tsp	1 tsp
300 ml milk	$\frac{1}{2}$ pt	$1\frac{1}{4}$ cups
2 tbsp Maraschino	2 tbsp	2 tbsp
300 ml double cream	$\frac{1}{2}$ pt	$1\frac{1}{4}$ cups

Dissolve the sugar and water in a large pan over a gentle heat. Cut the peaches in half, remove the stones, and place in the syrup. Poach until tender. Remove the peaches from the pan, peel off the skins, place on a wire rack and allow to cool. Sieve sufficient peaches to give 150 ml ($\frac{1}{4}$ pt/$\frac{2}{3}$ cup) of purée. Slice the rest thinly.

Cut a circle of greaseproof paper to fit the base of a 15 cm (6 in) charlotte mould. Trim the biscuits and line the sides of the mould.

Soak the gelatine in cold water (see page 191).

Cream the egg yolks and sugars thoroughly. Heat the milk and pour onto the yolks. Stir well. Return to a clean pan and cook over a low heat, stirring all the time, until the mixture thickens and coats the back of a spoon. Do not allow it to boil. Add the softened gelatine to the custard and stir well until

dissolved. Strain into a clean bowl and stir in the peach purée.

When the custard begins to set, whisk well with a sauce whisk and add the Maraschino. Lightly whip 225 ml ($7\frac{1}{2}$ fl oz/1 cup) of the cream and fold into the setting custard.

Place the charlotte mould in a bowl containing crushed ice. Pour half the mixture into the mould and allow it to set. Arrange a layer of the sliced peaches (about 50 g/2 oz) on the top and pour on the rest of the bavarois mixture. Place in the refrigerator to set.

When the bavarois is firm, trim the biscuits. Turn out of the mould, remove the circle of paper from the top and decorate with a spiral of peach slices. Whip the rest of the cream and pipe around the edge.

Tante Marie tip:
If serving this dish in hot weather, or on a buffet table in a hot room, use 20 g ($\frac{3}{4}$ oz/$1\frac{1}{2}$ pkts) of gelatine.

Charlotte Montreuil.

Crème Bavarois à la Vanille

Vanilla cream mousse (serves 4–6)

The delicate flavour of this sweet is perfect after rich or spicy courses. Try this delicious cream mousse ring filled with strawberries.

	Imperial	American
15 g gelatine	$\frac{1}{2}$ oz	1 pkt
300 ml milk	$\frac{1}{2}$ pt	$1\frac{1}{4}$ cups
1 vanilla pod		
3 egg yolks		
65 g sugar	$2\frac{1}{2}$ oz	$\frac{1}{3}$ cup
300 ml double cream	$\frac{1}{2}$ pt	$1\frac{1}{4}$ cups

To finish:

	Imperial	American
4 extra tbsp double cream, whipped	4 tbsp	4 tbsp
a few halved walnuts		

Soften the gelatine in cold water (see page 191). Place the milk in a pan with the vanilla pod. Bring to the boil, remove from the heat and allow to stand for 10–15 minutes.

Mix the egg yolks with the sugar. Remove the vanilla pod from the pan and pour the milk onto the egg mixture. Return to the pan and cook over a gentle heat, stirring all the time, until the custard coats the back of a spoon.

Add the gelatine, stir well and strain into a clean bowl. Cool the custard, then place in the refrigerator or stand in a bowl of ice and water. Stir the mixture occasionally.

Whip the cream until it stands in very soft peaks. When the custard begins to set, fold in the cream. For good results the cream should be of the same consistency as the setting custard. Pour the mixture into a ring mould about 20 cm (8 in) in diameter and place in the refrigerator until set.

Before turning out onto a serving-dish, dip the mould in hot water for about 3 seconds. Turn out and decorate with cream stars and the walnuts.

Tante Marie tip:
Wet the serving-dish lightly so that the mousse can be moved a little if it is not in the centre of the serving-dish.

Crêpes Flambées au Grand Marnier

Pancakes flamed with Grand Marnier (serves 4)

France has a great tradition of pancake making. In this recipe the unusual addition of beer to the batter makes the pancakes very light and gives them a special flavour.

	Imperial	American
Note that, if you are using metric measurements, 125 g flour are needed to give the correct consistency.		
125 g plain flour	4 oz	1 cup
a pinch of salt		
1 tbsp icing sugar	1 tbsp	1 tbsp
3 egg yolks		
150 ml milk	$\frac{1}{4}$ pt	$\frac{2}{3}$ cup
150 ml light ale *or* lager	$\frac{1}{4}$ pt	$\frac{2}{3}$ cup
25 g butter	1 oz	2 tbsp
1 tbsp Grand Marnier	1 tbsp	1 tbsp
oil for cooking		

To finish:

	Imperial	American
1 tbsp sugar	1 tbsp	1 tbsp
2 tbsp water	2 tbsp	2 tbsp
2 oranges		
50 g butter	2 oz	$\frac{1}{4}$ cup
4 tbsp Grand Marnier	4 tbsp	4 tbsp

Sift the flour, salt and icing sugar into a bowl, add the egg yolks and milk and beat together until smooth. Add the beer, cool melted butter and Grand Marnier.

Heat a crêpe or omelette pan. When it is hot, pour over sufficient oil to cover the base. When this is hot, tip it out of the pan. Pour in sufficient batter to cover the base of the pan very thinly. Tilt the pan as you pour this in, so it is as thin as possible. When browned, turn or toss. Keep the crêpes on a plate placed over a pan of hot water. Cook all the batter in this way.

To serve, fold each crêpe into quarters or roll up and arrange in a heatproof dish.

Heat the sugar and water in a pan. Add the zest and juice of the oranges and the butter. Heat well and pour over the pancakes. Pour over the warm Grand Marnier and flame. Serve immediately.

Profiteroles au Chocolat

Cream filled choux balls with chocolate sauce (serves 4–6)

These are a great favourite at all times.

	Imperial	American
choux paste made with		
50 g plain flour	2 oz	$\frac{1}{2}$ cup
(*see page 207*)		
300 ml double cream	$\frac{1}{2}$ pt	$1\frac{1}{4}$ cups
1–2 tbsp milk	1–2 tbsp	1–2 tbsp
For the Sauce Chocolat:		
100 g plain chocolate	$\frac{1}{4}$ lb	$\frac{3}{4}$ cup
2 tbsp castor sugar	2 tbsp	2 tbsp
150 ml hot water	$\frac{1}{4}$ pt	$\frac{2}{3}$ cup
a pinch of salt		
50 g butter	2 oz	$\frac{1}{4}$ cup

Make the choux pastry and place in a forcing bag with a 12 mm ($\frac{1}{2}$ in) pipe. Grease a baking-tray and pipe the mixture into 12–16 small balls. Brush them over with beaten egg and cook in a hot oven, Mark 7 (220°C/425°F), for 10–15 minutes, then reduce the temperature to Mark 5 (190°C/375°F) and cook for a further 15–20 minutes until crisp and golden brown. Remove from the oven and make a small opening in the bottom of each choux ball to allow the steam to escape. Place on a wire rack and allow to cool.

To make the Sauce Chocolat, break the chocolate and place in a pan with the sugar, water and salt. Melt over a low heat, stirring all the time. Simmer gently for 20–30 minutes until the sauce is of a syrupy consistency. Just before serving, beat in the butter gradually.

Place the cream and milk in a bowl and stand in a bowl of ice. Whisk until it thickens. Using a forcing bag and very small pipe, pipe the cream into the profiteroles. Pile them up in a pyramid, then pour over the hot Sauce Chocolat just before serving.

Profiteroles au Chocolat.

Crème Pâtissière
Confectioners' custard

This is a smooth custard which is used in fruit flans and gâteaux, or as an alternative to cream in éclairs and Profiteroles au Chocolat.

	Imperial	American
300 ml milk	$\frac{1}{2}$ pt	1$\frac{1}{4}$ cups
1 vanilla pod		
1 egg		
1 egg yolk		
50 g sugar	2 oz	$\frac{1}{4}$ cup
25 g plain flour	1 oz	3 tbsp

Place the milk in a pan with the vanilla pod. Bring to the boil, remove from the heat and allow to stand for 10 minutes. Meanwhile, place the egg and egg yolk in a bowl and add the sugar and flour. Stir together well. Remove the vanilla pod from the milk, then wash and dry it. Add the milk gradually to the egg mixture, stirring well. Pour into a clean pan and place over a low heat. Bring to the boil, stirring all the time. At this stage it often appears lumpy, but it becomes smooth when boiled. Simmer for 3–4 minutes, stirring well. Pour into a bowl and cover with damp greaseproof paper to prevent the formation of a skin. When cold, use as required.

Compôte de Poires au Vin Rouge
Pears in red wine (serves 4)

	Imperial	American
300 ml red wine	$\frac{1}{2}$ pt	1$\frac{1}{4}$ cups
100 g sugar	4 oz	$\frac{1}{2}$ cup
2 cm (1 in) cinnamon stick		
4 pears		
a few browned flaked almonds		

Place the wine, sugar and cinnamon in a pan and cook over a gentle heat until the sugar dissolves.

Peel the pears and leave the stalk intact, or cut into halves and remove the core with a teaspoon or vegetable ball cutter. Place in the hot syrup, cover with a lid and simmer gently until the pears are translucent. Turn them once halfway through the cooking time so the whole of each pear is coloured by the syrup. Cook them very slowly.

When the pears are ready, remove from the syrup and place on a dish. Boil the syrup to reduce by half and pour over the pears. Sprinkle with the almonds and serve cold.

Tante Marie tip:
If using very hard pears, place them in a casserole, add the wine and sugar syrup and cook gently at Mark 3 (160°C/325°F) until tender.

Apple tarts are featured by almost every French pâtisserie. This is a splendid way of using windfall apples.

Tarte aux Pommes Grillé
Latticed apple tart (serves 4–6)

	Imperial	American
750 g apples	1$\frac{1}{2}$ lb	1$\frac{1}{2}$ lb
75 g sugar	3 oz	$\frac{1}{3}$ cup
Pâte Brisée made with		
250 g plain flour	9 oz	2$\frac{1}{4}$ cups
(*see page 207*)		
apricot glaze		
(*see page 23*)		

Wash the apples well, cut in quarters, remove the core and any discoloured or bad parts, but do not peel. Place in a thick saucepan with sufficient water to cover the base of the pan. Cover with a lid and cook over a low heat until tender. Pass through a sieve or vegetable mill. Return to a clean saucepan, add the sugar and cook until the apples become a thick purée. Spread on a plate and allow to cool.

Make the pastry, wrap and place in the refrigerator to cool for about 20 minutes.

Line an 18 cm (7 in) flan ring with about two-thirds of the pastry and cover with the cold apple purée. Dampen the edge with water. Roll out the remaining pastry and cut into 5 mm ($\frac{1}{4}$ in) strips. Arrange these in a lattice on the top of the tart.

Bake in a moderately hot oven, Mark 5 (190°C/375°F), for 25 minutes. Remove the flan ring and brush the top and sides of the tart with the hot apricot glaze. Return to the oven to brown for 5 minutes. Remove from the oven, place on a wire rack and allow to cool. Brush all over with the hot apricot glaze again. Serve hot or cold.

Gâteau Jalousie aux Pommes
Apple and almond puff (serves 6–8)

Jalousies are window shutters and the pastry is cut to resemble the shutters so typical of French houses.

	Imperial	American
puff pastry made with		
250 g strong flour	9 oz	$2\frac{1}{4}$ cups
(*see pages 210–211*)		
500 g apples	1 lb	1 lb
100 g sugar	4 oz	$\frac{1}{2}$ cup
For the almond paste:		
50 g ground almonds	2 oz	$\frac{1}{2}$ cup
50 g castor sugar	2 oz	$\frac{1}{4}$ cup
a little lemon juice		
1 egg white		
For the glaze:		
a little beaten egg		
icing sugar		

Make the pastry as shown on page 210. Cut the apples into quarters and remove the core and any damaged parts. Place in a pan with a little water and simmer until tender. Pass through a sieve or vegetable mill. Return to the pan, add the sugar and cook for a few minutes until slightly thick. Spread on a plate and allow to cool.

Make a soft almond paste with the almonds, sugar, lemon juice and egg white. Roll out the pastry to an oblong 35 × 30 cm, and 5 mm thick (14 × 12 in, and $\frac{1}{4}$ in thick). Trim the edges neatly. Cut the pastry in half lengthways. Place one of these pieces on a wetted baking-tray. Brush the border all round with the beaten egg. Spread the almond paste over the centre of the pastry and cover with the cold apple purée.

Lightly flour the second piece of pastry. Fold in half lengthways. Taking care to leave a 2.5 cm (1 in) border, use a sharp knife to cut the folded edge, the cuts being made at 1 cm ($\frac{1}{2}$ in) intervals. Unfold the pastry gently. You now have a rectangular piece of pastry which will have a plain border with the centre slashed at regular intervals. Lift this piece of pastry very carefully and place it over the piece on the baking-tray. Press all round to seal the edges.

Using the back of a knife, knock up and scallop the edges of the pastry. Brush lightly with the beaten egg. Place in the refrigerator to chill for 20 minutes. Bake in a very hot oven, Mark 8 (230°C/450°F), for 10 minutes, then reduce the temperature to Mark 6 (200°C/400°F) for a further 20–30 minutes. Remove from the oven and dust over lightly with the icing sugar. Return to a very hot oven and bake for a further 5 minutes to glaze the sugar. Remove from the oven, place on a wire rack and allow to cool.

Tante Marie tip:
It is wise to select your serving-dish for this tart before you start to shape it, as it often needs to be 'made to measure'.

Tarte des Demoiselles Tatin
Upside-down apple tart (serves 4–6)

The Misses Tatin lived in Lamotte Beuvron near Orléans and were reputed to have invented this dish by accidentally turning a pie out the wrong way. They decided it was much better this way – try it and see what you think.

	Imperial	American
flaky pastry made with		
100 g strong flour	4 oz	1 cup
(*see pages 208–209*)		
100 g butter	4 oz	$\frac{1}{2}$ cup
100 g sugar	4 oz	$\frac{1}{2}$ cup
1 kg cooking apples	2 lb	2 lb

Gâteau Jalousie aux Pommes.

Make the pastry as shown on pages 208–209, then put aside to relax.

Take a 19 cm (7½ in) diameter moule à manqué or shallow cake tin and spread half the butter in a thick even layer on the bottom. Cover this with half the sugar. Peel and core the apples and cut into wafer-thin slices. Arrange them in neat layers on top of the butter and sugar. Press them down very firmly. Cover with the rest of the sugar and the butter. Roll out the pastry on a lightly floured board and make a lid to cover the apples. Press down firmly.

Bake in a preheated oven, Mark 6 (200°C/400°F), for 20 minutes, then cover with greaseproof paper and cook for a further 1 hour. Test to see if it is cooked by lifting the crust slightly with a knife. The apples should be transparent and the sugar beginning to brown. Turn out onto a hot serving-dish, which is large enough to hold the pudding and its buttery sauce.

Tante Marie tip:
This is delicious served with Crème Chantilly.

Crème Hindoue

Pineapple cream (serves 4–6)

An attractive, easily made sweet. The mould can be made the day before it is needed, but the cream and apricot sauce should not be added more than 2–3 hours before it is served.

	Imperial	American
1 small pineapple, *or* 1 (425 g) can of pineapple slices	15 oz	15 oz
20 g butter	¾ oz	2 tbsp
100 g castor sugar	4 oz	½ cup
3 egg whites		
1 tsp vanilla sugar	1 tsp	1 tsp
65 g ground almonds	2½ oz	⅔ cup
300 ml double cream	½ pt	1¼ cups
a few finely chopped pistachio nuts		

For the Sauce d'Abricots:

	Imperial	American
400 g can apricots	14½ oz	14½ oz
1–2 tbsp rum *or* kirsch (*optional*)	1–2 tbsp	1–2 tbsp

If using fresh pineapple, remove the skin and slice the flesh very thinly. Cut out the core. If using canned pineapple, cut the slices in half transversely. Cut the slices in half to give semi-circles.

Spread a good layer of butter over the inside of a savarin or ring mould (about 19 cm/7½ in diameter) and coat with a little of the castor sugar. Arrange the pineapple slices, overlapping, in the mould.

Whisk the egg whites stiffly, then fold in the remaining castor sugar, vanilla sugar and ground almonds. Do not overfold. Pour the mixture into the prepared mould.

Place in a bain-marie or roasting-pan containing boiling water and cook in a moderate oven, Mark 5 (190°C/375°F), for 30–40 minutes. When it is springy to the touch, remove from the oven and allow to cool. When completely cold, unmould it onto a serving-dish.

Whip the cream until it stands in soft peaks and pipe or spoon into the centre of the mould.

To make the Sauce d'Abricots, drain the apricots and liquidise or sieve them with sufficient juice to give a thick sauce. Add the kirsch or rum if used and pour around the outside of the pudding.

Sprinkle the cream with the pistachio nuts and serve cold.

Tante Marie tip:
If pistachio nuts are difficult to obtain, finely chop a few flaked almonds with a very small amount of green colouring to give a light green tint. Do not use until just before serving as the colour can 'bleed'. Store excess in an airtight container.

Crème Chantilly

Whipped cream

	Imperial	American
150 ml double cream	¼ pt	⅔ cup
2 tbsp milk	2 tbsp	2 tbsp
1 tsp vanilla sugar	1 tsp	1 tsp

Take the cream from the refrigerator and whip with the milk over ice until it thickens. Do not overbeat. Fold in the vanilla sugar.

Amandine

Almond tart (serves 5–6)

An attractively decorated tart which is a speciality of the pâtisseries in Boulogne.

	Imperial	American
Pâte Sucrée made with		
125 g plain flour	5 oz	1¼ cups
(*see page 207*)		
50 g butter	2 oz	¼ cup
50 g castor sugar	2 oz	¼ cup
1 egg, separated		
50 g ground almonds	2 oz	½ cup
15 g plain flour	½ oz	1½ tbsp
grated rind of 1 lemon		
apricot glaze		
(*see page 23*)		
redcurrant jelly		

For the royal icing:

	Imperial	American
3 tbsp icing sugar, sifted	2 tbsp	2 tbsp
1 tsp egg white	1 tsp	1 tsp

Make the pastry, wrap and place in the refrigerator to relax. When chilled and firm, roll out the pastry on a lightly floured board and line into an 18 cm (7 in) flan ring. Flute the edges.

To make the filling, cream the butter and sugar until light, then add the egg yolk and beat again. Whisk the egg white stiffly, and fold into the butter mixture alternately with the almonds, flour and lemon rind. Fill the flan case with this mixture. Cook in a moderately hot oven, Mark 6 (200°C/400°F),

Amandine.

for 20–25 minutes. If the top becomes too brown, reduce the temperature to Mark 4 (180°C/350°F). When the flan is cooked, remove from the oven, place on a wire rack and allow to cool.

Place the apricot glaze in a pan, bring to the boil and brush thickly over the top of the tart and lightly over the sides. Allow to cool. Make the royal icing and place in a paper piping bag with a fine writing pipe, or cut a small piece from the tip of the bag to give a fine hole. Pipe parallel lines about 2.5 cm (1 in) apart on the top of the tart, then pipe in the opposite direction to make a lattice pattern. Allow to set. Boil the redcurrant jelly and whisk until smooth. Place this in another small paper piping bag, cut a small hole from the tip and pipe the jelly into alternate diamonds.

Small tartlets, called Amandines, can also be made in the same way, decorating them in straight lines instead of in a diamond pattern.

Tarte aux Abricots et Cerises

Apricot and cherry tart (serves 5–6)

A typical French fruit flan filled with confectioners' creamy custard. For a special occasion add 1–2 tablespoons of liqueur or rum to the custard.

	Imperial	American
Pâte Sucrée made with		
125 g plain flour	5 oz	1¼ cups
(*see page 207*)		
Crème Pâtissière made		
with 300 ml milk	½ pt	1¼ cups
(*see page 197*)		
450 g can apricots	1 lb	1 lb
225 g can cherries	8 oz	8 oz
2–3 tbsp sieved apricot jam	2–3 tbsp	2–3 tbsp
a little lemon juice		
(*optional*)		
2–3 tbsp redcurrant jelly	2–3 tbsp	2–3 tbsp

Make the pastry, wrap and place in the refrigerator to chill for about 20 minutes. Meanwhile, make the Crème Pâtissière and allow to cool. Drain the fruits and stone the cherries.

Roll out the pastry on a lightly floured board and line into an 18 cm (7 in) flan ring (see page 212). Line with greaseproof paper and fill with baking-beans.

Bake 'blind' in a moderately hot oven, Mark 5 (190°C/375°F), for 20 minutes. Remove the paper and beans, then return to the oven to dry out. When the pastry looks cooked, remove from the oven, remove the flan ring, place on a wire rack and allow to cool.

Boil the apricot jam and add the lemon juice or water to make it a smooth spreading consistency.

Boil the redcurrant jelly in a small pan and whisk until smooth. Brush the inside of the flan lightly with this to seal it, then spread in the cool Crème Pâtissière. Arrange the apricots and cherries in an attractive pattern. Brush the cherries with redcurrant glaze, and the apricots and the sides of the flan with apricot glaze. Lift carefully onto a large flat serving-dish, using fish slices or metal spatulas to support it while it is moved. Eat when freshly made.

Tante Marie tip:
If you want to get this partly ready, the pastry case can be made a day or two in advance and stored in an airtight container until required.

Tarte aux Abricots et Cerises.

Suprême au Moka
Coffee suprême (serves 4–6)

A creamy coffee sweet which is excellent for deep freezing.

	Imperial	American
120 g unsalted butter	4½ oz	½ cup
120 g castor sugar	4½ oz	½ cup
150 ml strong coffee	¼ pt	⅔ cup
2 egg yolks		
1 packet sponge finger biscuits		
2–3 tbsp Tia Maria (*optional*)	2–3 tbsp	2–3 tbsp

To decorate:
browned almonds
a few unblanched almonds, halved
mimosa balls, *or*
crystallised violets

Place the butter in a bowl and allow to stand in a warm place so that it will soften. Do not allow it to melt or run. Dissolve half the sugar in the hot coffee, pour into a shallow dish and allow to cool. Add the rest of the sugar to the butter and beat well until smooth and creamy. Add the egg yolks gradually, together with 4 teaspoons of the sweetened coffee. Dip half the biscuits into the coffee. Immerse them for long enough to absorb the coffee but do not allow them to break. Arrange down the centre of an oblong dish and sprinkle with half the Tia Maria if used. Spread a thin layer of the butter cream over the biscuits and arrange another row of soaked biscuits on top. Sprinkle with the rest of the Tia Maria and coat the top and the sides with the rest of the butter cream. Smooth the top with a palette knife and coat the sides with the browned almonds. Decorate the top with the halved almonds and mimosa balls or crystallised violets.

Tante Marie tip:
Strong fresh coffee gives the best flavour, but instant coffee can be substituted if desired.

Soufflé au Chocolat
Chocolate soufflé (serves 4–6)

An easy-to-make hot soufflé to delight your guests.

	Imperial	American
a little butter		
a little castor sugar		
100 g plain chocolate	4 oz	1 cup
4 eggs		
65 g sugar	$2\frac{1}{2}$ oz	$\frac{1}{3}$ cup
1 tsp vanilla sugar	1 tsp	1 tsp
40 g plain flour	$1\frac{1}{2}$ oz	$\frac{1}{3}$ cup
300 ml milk	$\frac{1}{2}$ pt	$1\frac{1}{4}$ cups
300 ml Crème Anglaise	$\frac{1}{2}$ pt	$1\frac{1}{4}$ cups
(see opposite)		

Butter a 15 cm (6 in) soufflé dish and dust out with castor sugar. Melt the chocolate in a bowl over a pan of hot water. Separate the eggs. Mix the yolks, chocolate, sugar, vanilla sugar and flour together. Heat the milk, pour onto the mixture and stir well. Return the mixture to the pan and stir over a low heat until it thickens. Pour into a large bowl. Whisk the egg whites until very stiff and fold them in lightly. Place the mixture in the prepared dish and smooth the top.

Cook in a moderately hot oven, Mark 5 (190°C/375°F), for 20–25 minutes, then increase the temperature to Mark 7 (220°C/425°F) for a few minutes to brown the top. Serve at once with Crème Anglaise.

Tante Marie tip:
This soufflé will 'hold' perfectly for about 30 minutes before it is cooked, so it can be made a little in advance, and put in the oven in time to serve at the end of the meal.

Crème Anglaise
Egg custard

	Imperial	American
2 egg yolks		
25 g sugar	1 oz	2 tbsp
1–2 tsp vanilla sugar	1–2 tsp	1–2 tsp
300 ml milk	$\frac{1}{2}$ pt	$1\frac{1}{4}$ cups

Place the egg yolks, sugar and vanilla sugar in a bowl and mix together. Heat the milk and pour onto the mixture. Stir well. Return to the pan and cook over a low heat, stirring all the time, until the mixture coats the back of a spoon. It must not be allowed to boil or the eggs will curdle. Strain at once and serve warm.

Tante Marie tip:
For a richer thicker sauce use an additional 1 or 2 yolks. If the eggs should overcook, liquidise the custard at high speed.

Fromage Blanc aux Bananes
Cream cheese and bananas (serves 3–4)

	Imperial	American
175 g cream cheese	6 oz	1 cup
2 tbsp double cream	2 tbsp	2 tbsp
2 tsp vanilla sugar	2 tsp	2 tsp
2 egg whites		
2 tbsp castor sugar	2 tbsp	2 tbsp
2 bananas		

Sieve the cream cheese into a large bowl. Gently stir in the cream and vanilla sugar. Whisk the egg whites very stiffly and fold them in lightly with the castor sugar. Peel the bananas, cut into slices and carefully fold into the cream cheese mixture. Place in a large serving bowl or individual dishes. Keep well chilled until required.

Ices and Ice Creams

Ices and ice creams were introduced into France in the seventeenth century. Water ices were known to both the Chinese and the Arabs since earliest times but it is recognised that the Chinese introduced the knowledge of ice cream making to the western world.

A Sicilian named Francisco Procopio opened a café in 1660 and gave the Parisiennes their first taste of iced sweets, which were an immediate success. By the middle of the eighteenth century the most elaborate iced sweets had been created by the great chefs of the day and no fashionable meal was complete unless it ended with an iced confection.

Nowadays, although more and more commercially made ice cream is served in France, it is still possible to find, even in some of the smallest hotels, home-made fruit sorbets and ice creams made with eggs, sugar, cream and the natural flavours of fresh fruit, praline, or liqueurs.

No book on French cookery would be complete without a section on ices and ice creams. All ices can be made quite simply in the freezing compartment of the refrigerator, although the use of an electric churner (sorbetière) or an ice bucket ensures a smoother result with some recipes.

How to freeze ices

All mixtures must be cooled to refrigerator temperature first.

Method 1: In a refrigerator
Turn the freezing section to its lowest setting. Pour the ice cream or sorbet into the container. Allow it to partly set, then remove and whisk well. Repeat this 2 or 3 times, stir in a whisked egg white, then freeze.

Method 2: Using an electric churner
Chill the container. Pour in the mixture, cover with the lid and place in the refrigerator freezing section or deep freeze. Plug in, switch on and allow to churn for about 30–45 minutes or until the mixture thickens. Remove the lid and paddler, etc. Place the mixture in a plastic box or foil container and freeze until required.

Method 3: Using an ice bucket
Ice buckets are available as an attachment to some mixers, or can be bought separately. Modern ones are turned by electricity but old-fashioned hand ones can still be discovered in antique and junk shops and work very well.

Assemble the ice bucket. Pack with alternate layers of ice and salt, using 3 parts of ice to 1 part of salt. Pour the chilled mixture into the freezing container, put in the dasher, cover and churn until the mixture thickens. Turn into a suitable container, e.g. a plastic box, and store in the freezer.

The following two ice creams are frozen in the ice compartment of the refrigerator or in a freezer and need no special equipment.

Parfait aux Noisettes

Hazelnut ice cream (serves 4)

	Imperial	American
75 g hazelnuts	3 oz	$\frac{2}{3}$ cup
50 g sugar	2 oz	$\frac{1}{4}$ cup
3 egg yolks		
150 ml double cream	$\frac{1}{4}$ pt	$\frac{2}{3}$ cup
To finish:		
50 g sugar	2 oz	$\frac{1}{4}$ cup
4 tbsp double cream	4 tbsp	4 tbsp

Roast the hazelnuts in a hot oven or under the grill. When evenly browned put them in a tea towel and rub off the skins. Keep aside 8 hazelnuts for the decoration. Grate the rest of the nuts in a nutmill or liquidiser.

Place the sugar in a small pan with a little water. Stir until dissolved, then boil without stirring until the sugar reaches 103°C (215°F). Test with a sugar thermometer, or *dip your fingers first into a bowl of cold water* then into the syrup. When it is ready, a slight thread will form when the fingers are gently drawn apart. (It is important to dip your fingers into cold water *each* time the syrup is tested.)

Pour the syrup onto the egg yolks and whisk well until light and fluffy. Whip the cream until thick and smooth. Fold the cream and grated hazelnuts into the yolks. Pour into a 'bombe' mould, or a plastic or foil container. Seal well and place in the freezing compartment of the refrigerator or in a deep freeze. Allow to set.

Dissolve the second quantity of sugar in a little water and boil to a caramel. Dip the nuts for decoration in this and allow to set on an oiled baking-tray.

To serve, undo the screw on the bombe mould if used and turn out the parfait onto a chilled dish. If there is any difficulty the mould can be dipped in cold water. Decorate with cream stars and the caramelised nuts.

Soufflé Glacé aux Fraises

Strawberry ice cream soufflé (serves 6)

	Imperial	American
150 g sugar	5 oz	$\frac{2}{3}$ cup
juice of $\frac{1}{2}$ lemon		
2 egg whites		
500 g strawberries	1 lb	1 lb
300 ml double cream	$\frac{1}{2}$ pt	$1\frac{1}{4}$ cups
1–2 tbsp kirsch	1–2 tbsp	1–2 tbsp
carmine colouring		
(optional)		

To finish:

4 tbsp double cream, whipped	4 tbsp	4 tbsp

Take a 13 cm (5 in) diameter soufflé dish and cut a double strip of greaseproof paper 11 cm (4$\frac{1}{2}$ in) deep and long enough to go round the dish. Tie this in position. Place in the refrigerator to chill.

Place the sugar in a saucepan with the strained lemon juice and approximately 2 tablespoons of water. Stir until dissolved, then boil to the soft-ball stage or 110°C (225°F). To test without a thermometer, drop a little of the syrup from a spoon into a bowl of water to see if it forms a soft ball. While the sugar is boiling, whisk the egg whites until very stiff. Pour the sugar syrup onto the egg whites. Whisk all the time and continue to whisk until cool.

Sieve the strawberries, keeping aside a few whole ones for decoration. Lightly whisk the cream. Fold the cream, strawberry purée and kirsch into the meringue mixture. Add a little carmine colouring if necessary. Pour the mixture into the prepared soufflé dish and freeze.

To serve, whisk the extra cream until stiff and place in a piping bag with a small rosette pipe. Peel the paper band carefully from the dish, then decorate the top of the soufflé with the cream and strawberries.

Tante Marie tip:
This ice cream soufflé is much nicer to eat if it is allowed to soften slightly before serving and not taken straight from the deep freeze. To serve it at its best, stand it in the refrigerator for 45 minutes – 1 hour.

Glace aux Framboises

Raspberry ice cream (serves 4–6)

This recipe can also be used to make ices from other soft fruits.

	Imperial	American
300 ml milk	$\frac{1}{2}$ pt	$1\frac{1}{4}$ cups
1 vanilla pod		
500 g raspberries	1 lb	1 lb
4 egg yolks		
75 g sugar	3 oz	$\frac{1}{3}$ cup
150 ml single cream	$\frac{1}{4}$ pt	$\frac{2}{3}$ cup

Place the milk in a pan with the vanilla pod. Bring to the boil, remove from the heat and allow to stand for 10–15 minutes. Pass the raspberries through a fine nylon sieve. For speed, they can be liquidised first.

Mix the egg yolks and sugar together. Remove the vanilla pod from the pan and pour the milk onto the yolks. Stir well and return to the pan. Cook slowly, stirring all the time until the custard coats the back of a spoon. Strain into a large bowl and put aside to cool. When it is cold, add the purée of sieved raspberries and the cream. Chill well, then freeze as described on page 203.

Place scoops of the ice cream in chilled coupe glasses and serve with thin wafer biscuits, such as Tuiles aux Amandes.

Glace Pralinée

Praline ice cream (serves 4–6)

	Imperial	American
4–5 egg yolks		
75 g castor sugar	3 oz	$\frac{1}{3}$ cup
450 ml milk	$\frac{3}{4}$ pt	2 cups
100 g crushed praline	4 oz	$\frac{2}{3}$ cup
(*see below*)		

Cream the egg yolks and sugar together. Heat the milk and pour over the mixture. Stir well and return to the pan. Cook very gently until the custard coats the back of a spoon. Strain into a large bowl and put aside to cool, then place in the refrigerator. When it is completely cold, add the crushed praline. Mix well and freeze as described on page 203.

Tante Marie tip:
A richer ice cream may be made by using single cream instead of milk.

Praline

Almond toffee

	Imperial	American
100 g unblanched almonds	4 oz	1 cup
100 g sugar	4 oz	$\frac{1}{2}$ cup
4 tbsp water	4 tbsp	4 tbsp

Rinse the almonds in cold water to remove the powdery substance clinging to the skins. Place the sugar and water in a small strong pan. Place over a low heat and stir with a wooden spoon until the sugar has dissolved. Increase the heat, add the almonds and continue to boil, brushing the sides of the pan with cold water if they become sugary. When the toffee reaches a rich brown colour, test it to see if it is ready. It should be 180°C (365°F). If you are not using a thermometer, drop a little from a spoon into a bowl of cold water. It should set quickly and be crisp to bite. If it is not quite crisp, allow to boil for a moment longer.

Pour the toffee onto an oiled slab or baking-tray and allow to cool, then crush it, using a pestle and mortar or a rolling-pin. Use as required. If it is to be kept, store in an absolutely airtight container and crush later.

Oranges Glacées Givrées

Orange water ice (serves 4)

	Imperial	American
8 oranges		
2 lemons		
75 g sugar	3 oz	$\frac{1}{3}$ cup
1 egg white		

Wipe the oranges and cut off the tops. Using a grapefruit knife or a teaspoon remove the pulp, taking care not to tear the shell. Serrate the cut edge of the oranges and the tops and place in the refrigerator to chill.

Pass the pulp through a sieve or vegetable mill, or liquidise in a blender or food processor and then sieve. Squeeze the lemons and mix with the orange juice. There should be 600 ml (1 pt/$2\frac{1}{2}$ cups) of juice; if it is less, add more orange juice or some water. Warm the liquid in a pan, add the sugar and allow to dissolve. Chill the liquid, then freeze until it thickens. Whisk the egg white and stir in. Freeze again until the liquid is very thick, then use it to fill as many oranges as possible (usually about 6). Cover with the top of each orange and freeze again until required.

Cakes and Pastries

French gâteaux look and taste splendid, but some of them are quite easy to make at home. If you want to produce them you will need a good recipe, some skills, imagination and the right ingredients.

As a light whisked sponge is the basis of many gâteaux, a picture guide is included to show you how to achieve this. Pastries can sometimes be tricky, so we have also provided picture guides showing you how to make flaky and puff pastry. Our well-tested recipes for other pastries are included as well.

Most people love to eat croissants, brioches and babas, so you will find recipes for these, together with an explanation of all the points that help to ensure success.

When making cakes and pastries, one factor which often gets overlooked is the choice of flour. White flours vary little in visible appearance, but do in fact vary considerably in quality.

Different wheats, grown in different parts of the world, have their individual qualities. The miller blends the wheats as the flour is made, to produce flours suitable for various purposes. There is a substance called gluten in flour which determines the way in which it behaves when used to make cakes, pastries and bread. 'Soft' flour has a low gluten content and this is the best one to use for cakes, biscuits and short pastries. 'Strong' flour, sold for bread-making, has a high gluten content which ensures that bread, flaky and puff pastries and choux paste all rise well.

It is not always easy to tell from the packet which type of flour is in it. If you want to find out, make a dough of a little of the flour mixed with water, then knead it in your hand. If it makes a stretchy dough, it is a 'strong' flour; if it makes a soft dough that will not develop this elasticitu, it is a 'soft' flour which is more suited to cake-making.

Flours vary in their absorbency, so quantities of liquids advised for pastries, etc, can only be approximate and some slight variation has to be expected. On average, allow 1 tablespoon of water to each 30 g (1 oz/4 tbsp) of flour used.

Pâte Brisée
Rich short crust pastry

This pastry is used for tartlets and flans, omitting the sugar for savoury dishes. The butter should be at room temperature.

	Imperial	American
250 g plain flour	9 oz	$2\frac{1}{4}$ cups
15 g castor sugar	$\frac{1}{2}$ oz	$1\frac{1}{2}$ tbsp
a pinch of salt		
125 g butter	$4\frac{1}{2}$ oz	$\frac{1}{2}$ cup
1 egg		

Sift the flour, sugar and salt onto a board. Make a well in the centre and add the butter and egg. Work up with the fingertips of one hand so that the butter and egg are first rubbed into the flour and then worked together to a ball of dough. Wrap in plastic, or put in a plastic box, and place in the refrigerator to chill for 20–30 minutes. Roll out and use as required.

Pâte à Choux
Choux paste

This is the pastry used to make éclairs, Profiteroles au Chocolat, fritters, etc.

	Imperial	American
50 g strong flour	2 oz	$\frac{1}{2}$ cup
25 g butter	1 oz	2 tbsp
150 ml water	$\frac{1}{4}$ pt	$\frac{2}{3}$ cup
1 egg yolk		
1 egg, beaten		

Sift the flour into a bowl. Place the butter and water in a medium-sized pan and warm until the butter has melted. Bring to the boil, then pour in all the flour at once and beat quickly, keeping it over the heat for a moment or two if necessary. Remove from the heat when it thickens to a smooth glossy paste which leaves the sides of the pan, then beat in the egg yolk. Gradually add the beaten egg, about 1 teaspoonful at a time, continuing to beat well. The mixture will become smooth, thick and shiny.

The paste is shaped with the help of a forcing bag and a plain 12 mm ($\frac{1}{2}$ in) pipe. The usual temperature for baking is Mark 7 (220°C/425°F) for 10 minutes, then reduce the temperature, without opening the oven door, to Mark 5 (190°C/375°F) for a further 25–30 minutes.

After two-thirds of the cooking time the oven door may be opened. Cook the choux paste until golden brown, crisp and fairly dry inside. If it is cooked in individual shapes, make a hole in the side or base after baking to allow steam to escape while cooling.

Pâte Sucrée
Sugar crust pastry

The traditional way to mix this pastry is on a board, but it can also be mixed in a bowl or with an electric mixer or food processor. Make sure that the butter is at room temperature.

	Imperial	American
Note that, if you are using metric measurements, 90 g butter are needed to give the correct consistency.		
150 g plain flour	5 oz	$1\frac{1}{4}$ cups
2 egg yolks		
50 g castor sugar	2 oz	$\frac{1}{4}$ cup
90 g butter	3 oz	6 tbsp

Sift the flour onto a board. Make a well in the centre and add the egg yolks, sugar and the butter cut into small pieces. Using one hand, rub the butter and egg yolks into the flour and sugar in the same way as rubbing in short crust pastry. When evenly mixed to a crumbly texture, blend together to a soft smooth ball of dough. Wrap in plastic, or put in a plastic box, and place in the refrigerator to chill for at least 20 minutes until firm. Roll out and use as required. The usual baking temperature is Mark 5 (190°C/375°F).

Pâte Demi-feuilletée

Flaky pastry

Flaky pastry is a light crisp layered pastry which rises well, though not to the extent of puff pastry. However, it is much quicker to make, and should not take more than 10–15 minutes to prepare. It is always best to chill it before baking.

	Imperial	American
100 g flour (strong flour is best)	4 oz	1 cup
a pinch of salt		
75 g fat, half lard and half butter	3 oz	6 tbsp
cold water to mix		

3. Add cold water. Flour varies in absorbency, but on average allow 1 tbsp water to each 30 g (1 oz/ 4 tbsp) of flour. Add 3 tbsp to begin with for this quantity.

1. Weigh the ingredients and sift the flour into a bowl with the salt.

4. Blend lightly together, using a palette knife or pastry blender.

2. Take half the butter and rub it into the flour either with the fingertips or using an electric mixer.

5. Complete mixing by hand, adding more liquid as necessary to make a soft but not sticky dough.

6. Roll out to an oblong on a lightly floured surface. Keep the sides straight and the ends square.

7. Mark the dough lightly into thirds.

8. Take one-half of the lard and place in rough pats on the top two-thirds of the pastry.

9. Fold the third nearest to you into the centre and then the section furthest from you onto this.

10. Give the pastry a half turn, seal the edges with the rolling-pin and press lightly across the centre before rolling into a strip again. Repeat the process, adding the rest of the butter. Fold again. Each time the pastry is turned it should be in the same direction.

Give a half turn and repeat the process again with the rest of the lard. Roll and fold once more, then wrap in plastic, or put in a plastic box, and place in the refrigerator to chill. Roll out and use as required.

Pâte Feuilletée

Puff pastry

Some dishes can be made only with this pastry. It is unique in the way it rises to make crisp light bouchée and vol-au-vent cases.

	Imperial	American
250 g strong flour	9 oz	2¼ cups
225 g chilled butter	8 oz	1 cup
a pinch of salt		
about 150 ml water	¼ pt	⅔ cup

4. Sprinkle on the rest of the water and work in the same way, taking care not to press the mixture forcibly together. It will go into a ball of dough when sufficient water has been added. Wrap in plastic or put in a plastic box, and place in the refrigerator.

1. Sift the flour and salt onto a pastry board and make a well in the centre.

2. Pour in about half of the water and work in some of the flour to a thick sauce-like paste, using two fingers only.

5. Take the chilled butter, place on the floured board, cover with a piece of greaseproof paper and tap with a rolling-pin to soften. Cut across in half, put the two pieces together and repeat until the butter is pliable though still cold.

3. Flick the rest of the flour over this and lightly mix together. Use the fingertips of both hands held palms upwards to 'flake' the mixture, working from the outside to the centre.

6. Roll the chilled dough into a circle about the size of a large dinner plate. Place the butter in the centre and bring the dough over from the sides.

7. Fold over the ends so the butter meets in the centre.

8. Give the pastry a half turn sideways, then ease it gently with the rolling-pin.

9. Roll out to a long rectangle, taking care not to actually roll over the ends.

10. Fold into thirds, taking the section nearest to you into the centre first.

11. Fold the top section over the centre. Seal the edges with the rolling-pin, give the pastry a half turn and roll and fold once more. Wrap and place in the refrigerator to chill for 20 minutes.

Repeat these two rolls and folds twice more, so the pastry is given six rolls altogether. Each time turn the pastry in the same direction. The pastry is then ready for use. It can be kept, well wrapped, in the refrigerator for up to two days, or it can be stored in a deep freeze.

Lining a Flan Tin

Flans can be made using different pastries such as Flaky Pastry, Pâte Sucrée or Pâte Brisée. The technique is similar whichever one is used. Use either a loose-based tin as illustrated, or a flan ring on a baking-tray.

3. Roll off with the rolling-pin to trim it quickly. Pastry trimmings can be re-rolled and used for other dishes.

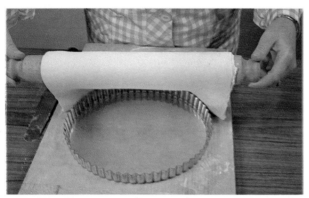

1. Roll the pastry until it is large enough to cover the base and sides of the tin. Put the rolling-pin on it and lift over the flan ring. Drop it gently into position.

4. Prick the top surface of the pastry lightly with a fork to help prevent the base from rising too much.

2. Lift the pastry so it fits into the base and sides without stretching (if it is stretched it will shrink). Use the back of the forefinger to fit it lightly into position.

5. Take a piece of greaseproof paper large enough to line the flan and crumple it in your hands to soften it. Place the paper in the pastry case and fill it with baking-beans, taking care to support the sides. The beans can be haricot beans, dried peas, macaroni or something similar. They can be kept in a storage jar in the larder and re-used an infinite number of times, as their purpose is simply to keep the pastry in shape.

Galette Bretonne

Breton shortcake

	Imperial	American
225 g plain flour	8 oz	2 cups
a pinch of salt		
100 g castor sugar	4 oz	$\frac{1}{2}$ cup
3 egg yolks		
150 g butter, softened	5 oz	$\frac{2}{3}$ cup
2 tsp orange-flower water	2 tsp	2 tsp
a little beaten egg to glaze		

Sift the flour into a bowl. Make a well in the centre, and place all the remaining ingredients in this.

With the fingertips make a paste, gradually incorporating the flour to form a smooth firm ball of dough. Work quickly so the butter does not become oily. Wrap the pastry in greaseproof paper, or put in a plastic box, and place in the refrigerator to chill for 1 hour.

Place the dough in the centre of an 18 cm (7 in) flan ring on a baking-tray and press out to the sides with the fingers. Smooth the surface, mark with a fork, and brush with the beaten egg. Bake in a moderate oven, Mark 4 (180°C/350°F), for 30–35 minutes, until golden brown and set. Remove from the oven, place on a wire rack and allow to cool.

Gâteau Cambacérès

Almond and brandy cake

A moist almond cake in a crisp pastry case.

	Imperial	American
Pâte Sucrée made with		
150 g plain flour	5 oz	$1\frac{1}{4}$ cups
(see page 207)		
50 g unsalted butter	2 oz	$\frac{1}{4}$ cup
3 eggs		
100 g castor sugar	4 oz	$\frac{1}{2}$ cup
50 g cornflour	2 oz	$\frac{1}{2}$ cup
100 g ground almonds	4 oz	1 cup
2 tbsp brandy	2 tbsp	2 tbsp

To finish:
apricot glaze
  (*see page 23*)
chopped almonds
lightly crushed lump sugar
chopped pistachio nuts *or*
  green coloured almonds
  (*see page 199*)

Make the pastry and place in the refrigerator to chill. Roll out and line a 19 cm (7$\frac{1}{2}$ in) moule à manqué or deep sandwich tin, smoothing the sides level.

To make the filling, melt the butter and put aside to cool. Whisk the eggs and sugar over hot water until light and fluffy. Remove from the heat and whisk until cool. Fold in the sifted cornflour, melted butter, ground almonds and brandy. Place in the pastry case and bake in a moderate oven, Mark 4 (180°C/350°F), for 40–50 minutes or until firm in the centre and coming away from the sides of the tin. Turn out onto a wire rack and allow to cool. When cold, brush the top and sides with the apricot glaze, then coat the top with a mixture of almonds, sugar and chopped pistachio nuts or green coloured almonds.

Biscuit Fin

Sponge cake

This fatless sponge is one of the lightest of cakes when it is well made. It is used as the basis of many gâteaux such as Gâteau à l'Ananas (see page 216).

	Imperial	American
3 eggs		
90 g castor sugar	3½ oz	⅓ cup *and* 2 tbsp
1 tsp vanilla sugar	1 tsp	1 tsp
75 g plain flour	3 oz	¾ cup

2. To test if the eggs are whisked sufficiently, press the whisk lightly on the surface, when a light imprint will show.

3. Remove from the heat and continue to whisk until the mixture feels cool. Test this by dipping your little finger in the mixture. A damp cloth placed under the bowl prevents it from slipping.

1. Prepare a 19 cm (7½ in) moule à manqué or other similar-sized cake tin by brushing it with melted lard. If desired, the base can also be lined with a circle of greaseproof paper.

Whisk the eggs and sugars over hot, but not boiling, water using a hand or electric whisk.

4. Sift in one-third of the flour at a time.

5. Fold in lightly and quickly, using a metal spatula. Repeat with each addition of flour. When all the flour has been added, make sure that it is smoothly mixed by lifting the mixture from the base of the bowl. Do not overfold.

6. Pour the sponge mixture into the prepared tin, and bake in a moderate oven, Mark 4 (180°C/350°F), for 25–30 minutes until the cake is golden brown and firm to the touch, and has slightly shrunk from the side of the tin.

A larger cake can be made using the same proportion of ingredients. One made with 4 eggs takes about 40 minutes to bake.

7. Turn out onto a wire rack.

8. Turn over again so the base of the cake is flat on the rack. It will then keep a perfect shape. When it is decorated this is the top, and the sides slope outwards. Cool before use.

Génoise Commune
Genoese sponge cake

A Génoise Commune is made in exactly the same way, except that 25 g (1 oz/2 tbsp) of butter is melted beforehand and the cool liquid butter is folded into the sponge alternately with the flour. The baking times are the same. This gives a moister sponge which will keep fresh longer.

Génoise Fine
Rich sponge cake

The Génoise Fine is also made using the same method, but 75 g (3 oz/6 tbsp) of butter is added. This needs a little more care to obtain a light sponge and is always a little more firm. Because of this it is excellent to cut up for petit fours.

Crème au Beurre Mousseline
Butter cream

A light smooth butter cream used on many gâteaux. It has the virtue of absorbing liquids easily so that fruit juices and liqueurs can be used for flavouring without risk of curdling.

	Imperial	American
65 g sugar	2½ oz	⅓ cup
4 tbsp water	4 tbsp	4 tbsp
2 egg yolks		
150 g unsalted butter	5 oz	⅔ cup

Place the sugar and water in a saucepan. Stir until the sugar has dissolved, then boil without stirring until the sugar reaches 102.6–104°C (215–220°F). Test with a sugar thermometer, or *dip your finger and thumb first into a bowl of cold water* then into the syrup. When it is ready, a slight thread will form when the fingers are gently drawn apart. Pour this syrup onto the egg yolks and beat well until cool. Beat in the butter gradually. The cream should be thick and buttery. If it has not quite thickened continue beating to complete the process. Add flavourings as required.

Gâteau à l'Ananas
Pineapple cake

A colourful cake which is as popular for a pudding as for afternoon tea.

Biscuit Fin made with 3 eggs
  (*see pages 214–215*)

For the filling:
2 tbsp pineapple jam

For the decoration:
sieved apricot jam to glaze
browned chopped almonds
pineapple rings (either
  canned *or* fresh)
glacé cherries
angelica

Grease a 19 cm (7½ in) moule à manqué or deep sandwich tin. Prepare, cook and cool the sponge cake as shown on pages 214–215. When it is cold, cut across into two layers.

Spread the cut surfaces with the pineapple jam and sandwich the cake together. Brush all over with the hot apricot glaze. Coat the sides with the chopped almonds. Decorate the top with pineapple slices (canned ones need to be sliced across to make thinner pieces), halved glacé cherries and leaves cut from angelica, making a decorative and bold design. Brush again heavily with the apricot glaze.

Tante Marie tip:
Do not store this cake in a biscuit tin. It must be covered and refrigerated to keep the fruit fresh. The filling can be varied by mixing a spoonful or two of Crème au Beurre Mousseline with a spoonful of pineapple jam.

Gâteau au Chocolat
Chocolate cake

The light sponge is combined with a smooth chocolate flavoured butter cream to make this gâteau. It is one which can be frozen very successfully.

	Imperial	American
Génoise Commune made with 3 eggs (*see page 215*)		
125 g plain chocolate	4½ oz	1 cup
Crème au Beurre Mousseline made with 2 egg yolks (*see opposite*)		

To finish:
chocolate vermicelli

Prepare and bake the cake as shown on pages 214–215, folding in the cool melted butter alternately with the flour. When baked, remove from the oven, turn onto a wire rack and allow to cool.

Meanwhile, cut the chocolate into small pieces, place in a bowl over a saucepan of warm water and allow to melt. Make the Crème au Beurre Mousseline. When this is ready, pour in the hot melted chocolate, mix well, then place in the refrigerator to cool for a short time. Cut the cake across in two layers and sandwich together with about a quarter of the butter cream. Spread some butter cream over the sides and coat in the chocolate vermicelli. Spread a very thin layer of butter cream over the top of the cake. Place the rest in a forcing bag with a small rosette pipe and pipe a line of rosettes across the centre of the cake.

Gâteau à l'Ananas (left) and Gâteau au Chocolat.

Pipe a straight line on either side of this, then a patterned one, and continue in this way until all of the cake top is decorated. Chill before serving.

Tante Marie tip.
Make sure the chocolate is hot when added to the butter cream. If it has cooled it will go into hard lumps as it is stirred in.

Gâteau Panaché

Four colour cake

This is a variation of the Gâteau au Chocolat (see page 216). Prepare the same cake and unflavoured Crème au Beurre Mousseline (see page 216).

	Imperial	American
finely chopped browned almonds		
pale green colouring		
a few drops of almond essence		
coffee flavouring		
50 g plain chocolate, melted	2 oz	$\frac{1}{3}$ cup
2 tsp vanilla sugar	2 tsp	2 tsp

When the cake has been baked and cooled, spread a little of the butter cream all round the sides and coat in the chopped almonds. Spread a thin layer of butter cream over the top of the cake. Divide the remaining butter cream in four. Colour one quarter pale green and add the almond essence, flavour another with coffee, the third with the hot melted chocolate and leave the remainder plain, but flavour strongly with the vanilla sugar. Mark the top of the cake into quarters and use a fine rosette pipe to pipe small stars of a different colour in each section.

Gâteau au Chocolat Suisse

Swiss chocolate cake

	Imperial	American
4 eggs		
100 g castor sugar	4 oz	$\frac{1}{2}$ cup
100 g plain chocolate	4 oz	$\frac{3}{4}$ cup
100 g unsalted butter	4 oz	$\frac{1}{2}$ cup
25 g plain flour	1 oz	3 tbsp
25 g fine white breadcrumbs	1 oz	$\frac{3}{4}$ cup
50 g ground almonds	2 oz	$\frac{2}{3}$ cup

Grease a moule à manqué or deep sandwich tin and line the base with greased greaseproof paper.

Separate the eggs and place the yolks in a bowl with the sugar. Melt the chocolate and butter by standing them on separate plates over pans of hot water. Cream the egg yolks and sugar until thick and creamy, then carefully beat in the softened butter, which must not be hot. Add the chocolate gradually. Whip the egg whites very stiffly and fold them into the mixture alternately with the flour, breadcrumbs and almonds. Pour into the prepared tin and bake in a moderate oven, Mark 4 (180°C/350°F), for 45 minutes. Unmould the cake carefully onto a wire rack and allow to cool.

Biscuit Roulé au Café

Coffee and walnut Swiss roll

	Imperial	American
4 eggs		
90 g castor sugar	3$\frac{1}{2}$ oz	$\frac{1}{3}$ cup and 2 tbsp
90 g plain flour	3$\frac{1}{2}$ oz	$\frac{3}{4}$ cup
extra castor sugar		
Crème au Beurre Mousseline made with 2 egg yolks (see page 216)		
very strong coffee		

To finish:
chopped walnuts
walnut halves

Grease a 23 × 30 × 1 cm (10 × 12 × $\frac{1}{2}$ in) Swiss roll tin and line with greaseproof paper.

Separate the eggs, and beat the yolks with the sugar until they are thick and will form a ribbon when the mixture is trailed across the bowl. Whisk the egg whites until stiff. Sift the flour as you fold it in, a third at a time, alternately with the egg whites. When just smoothly blended, pour into the prepared tin. Bake in a hot oven, Mark 7 (220°C/425°F), for 8–10 minutes until golden brown and set.

Turn out onto a sheet of greaseproof paper sprinkled with castor sugar. Cut the edge off the two long sides and one short one. Using a knife, mark just inside the remaining edge. Place another piece of greaseproof paper over the sponge and roll up firmly. Cover with a slightly damp tea towel for 5 minutes. Cool on a wire rack.

Make the Crème au Beurre Mousseline and flavour with the coffee, or an essence made from 2 teaspoons of instant coffee dissolved in 1 tablespoon of boiling water. Add sufficient to taste.

When the cake is cold, unroll it gently, remove the

greaseproof paper on top and spread with a layer of the coffee butter cream. Roll up again. Cut off the ends of the cake at a slight angle. Spread more butter cream halfway up the sides and coat with the chopped walnuts. Place the rest of the butter cream in a forcing bag with a rosette pipe, and pipe large swirls along the top of the cake. Decorate each swirl with a halved walnut.

Biscuit Roulé au Café.

Glace à l'eau

Glacé icing

	Imperial	American
225 g icing sugar	8 oz	2 cups
3-4 tbsp warm water	3-4 tbsp	3-4 tbsp
or fruit juice *or* coffee		

Sift the icing sugar into a bowl. Add, the water or other liquid, a spoonful at a time, and stir it in well. Add sufficient liquid to give a smooth coating consistency. Pour over the cake to be decorated and smooth quickly with a palette knife before it begins to set.

Glace au Fondant

Fondant icing

Fondant gives cakes a soft shiny coating and a really first-class smooth icing. It can be bought commercially or made by hand.

	Imperial	American
500 g granulated *or* lump sugar	1 lb	2 cups
4 tbsp water	4 tbsp	4 tbsp
75 g liquid glucose, *or* a pinch of cream of tartar	3 oz	3 tbsp

Place all the ingredients in a pan. Heat gently, stirring all the time, until the sugar has completely dissolved. Remove the spoon, increase the heat and boil rapidly. While it is boiling, brush down the sides of the pan to the level of the syrup with a pastry brush dipped in cold water, so that any syrup which splashes up the sides will be thoroughly dissolved. Cook to the soft-ball stage or 115°C (238°F). To test without a thermometer, drop a little of the syrup from a teaspoon into a basin of cold water. When the sugar has cooked enough, it will thicken so that a ball can be rolled off the spoon with the fingers. When pressed gently the ball is soft.

Pour the syrup onto a marble slab, enamel-topped table or very large old platter and allow it to cool to blood heat. A skin forms over the whole surface, and it must be sufficiently cool to lay a hand on top.

Using a metal sugar scraper or wooden spatula, stir the whole mixture very well so each part is thoroughly worked. Gradually the syrup will thicken and become opaque, and eventually it will become white and very stiff. With the palm of the hand, press the fondant down onto the slab, working it continuously so that it changes from a rough mixture to a smooth shiny one. Alternatively, take small pieces and knead with the fingers to make it smooth.

The fondant should be stored in a closed jar or plastic box or wrapped in a polythene bag. It will keep almost indefinitely if the container is airtight.

Tante Marie tip:
If, when the fondant has become thick and white, it is too hard to knead and break down, leave it covered with a damp cloth for 30 minutes. During this time the fondant will mature and become softer.

To ice with fondant

The thick white fondant icing is warmed and softened with sugar syrup then coloured and flavoured before it is used. Water can substitute for sugar syrup but a smaller amount of syrup will be required. Add the liquid glucose if the syrup is to be stored.

	Imperial	American
Stock syrup:		
350 g sugar	12 oz	1½ cups
50 g liquid glucose	2 oz	2 tbsp
300 ml water	½ pt	1¼ cups
food colouring		
flavouring, e.g. strong coffee essence, strained fruit juice, liqueurs, rum, etc		
sieved apricot glaze		

Dissolve the sugar, and glucose if used, in the water. Bring to the boil, then boil to 103°C (215°F). Cool and store until required.

Place the fondant in a pan with 2–3 tablespoons of the syrup, colouring if required and flavouring. (If this is liquid, add proportionately less syrup.) Place over a low heat and stir well. The pan must remain over the heat just long enough to become barely warm and the temperature should be such that you can keep your hand on the base of the saucepan in comfort. When it is warm, remove from the heat and continue to stir. Add more syrup as required to bring the fondant to a coating consistency. As a guide, 500 g (1 lb) fondant will absorb about 150 ml (¼ pt/⅔ cup). Brush the cake with a thin coating of the boiling apricot glaze.

Before coating, check the consistency of the icing: it should be such that it will form a light trail and coat the back of a wooden spoon. Bang it on a hard surface to bring air bubbles to the surface.

Place the cake on a wire rack over a bowl and pour the icing over the centre of the cake until it coats the top and sides. Use a clean palette knife to bring it over any part of the sides that is not covered. Allow to drip into the bowl. The icing will remain liquid for only a very short time, so work swiftly at this stage. Prick out any air bubbles. When it has stopped dripping, the icing in the bowl can, provided it is clean of crumbs, be placed in a closely covered container for re-use, together with any left in the pan.

Decorations which will set on the soft fondant are put on when the icing stops moving. Piped decoration except feather icing is done when it is set firm. It should be allowed to stand for several hours until set. The icing is then trimmed at the base and the cake lifted onto its serving-dish.

Fondant au Chocolat
Chocolate fondant

	Imperial	American
500 g fondant icing (*see opposite*)	1 lb	1 lb
100 g dark chocolate	4 oz	$\frac{3}{4}$ cup

Prepare the fondant. Cut the chocolate into pieces and melt in a bowl over a pan of hot water. When soft, stir into the fondant. Correct the consistency with more syrup if necessary.

Gâteau au Citron
Lemon cake

A pale yellow iced cake, flavoured with lemon.

	Imperial	American

Génoise Commune made
  with 3 eggs (*see page 215*)
finely grated rind of
  2 lemons		

For the filling:
Crème au Beurre Mousseline made with 1 egg yolk and flavoured with the juice of 1 lemon (*see page 216*)

For the decoration:

	Imperial	American
500 g fondant icing *or* glacé icing, made with	1 lb	1 lb
225 g icing sugar	8 oz	2 cups
juice of 2 lemons		
yellow food colouring		
mimosa balls		
angelica leaves		

Make the cake as shown on pages 214–215, adding the grated lemon rind with the flour. Bake, then allow to cool. Make the Crème au Beurre Mousseline and flavour with the lemon juice. Prepare the icing as shown on page 219 or 220, softening it with the strained lemon juice. Add a few drops of food colouring to give a pale yellow colour.

When the cake is cool, cut across in two or three layers, spread the cut surfaces with the crème au beurre, and sandwich together. Coat with the glacé or fondant icing. Decorate around the edge with groups of mimosa balls and angelica leaves.

Tante Marie tip:
A specially good filling can be made by stirring some lemon curd into the crème au beurre in place of the lemon juice.

Gâteau Mexicain

Mexican cake

A chocolate feather-iced cake.

	Imperial	American
75 g plain flour	3 oz	$\frac{3}{4}$ cup
25 g cocoa	1 oz	$\frac{1}{4}$ cup
50 g butter	2 oz	$\frac{1}{4}$ cup
4 eggs, separated		
125 g castor sugar	$4\frac{1}{2}$ oz	$\frac{2}{3}$ cup
1 tsp vanilla sugar	1 tsp	1 tsp
Crème au Beurre Mousseline made with 1 egg yolk (*see page 216*)		
50 g chocolate	2 oz	$\frac{1}{3}$ cup
a little sieved apricot jam		
a little white icing		
chocolate fondant *or* glacé icing (*see pages 221 and 219*)		

Grease a 19 cm ($7\frac{1}{2}$ in) moule à manqué or suitably sized cake tin. Sift the flour and cocoa together. Melt the butter. Beat the egg yolks, sugar and vanilla sugar until thick and creamy, when the mixture should form a ribbon when trailed across the bowl. Whisk the egg whites until stiff. Fold in the flour and cocoa alternately with the melted butter and egg whites, adding a third at a time.

Pour into the prepared cake tin and bake in a moderate oven, Mark 4 (180°C/350°F), for approximately 30 minutes or until firm. Remove from the oven, turn onto a wire rack and allow to cool.

Make the Crème au Beurre Mousseline, melt the chocolate in a bowl over a pan of hot water and stir it into the crème au beurre.

Cut the cake across in one or two layers, spread the cut surfaces with all of the butter cream and sandwich together. Brush with the boiling apricot glaze. Place the white icing in a greaseproof paper icing bag. Coat the cake with chocolate icing and immediately pipe fine parallel lines of white icing across the cake. With a skewer or the point of a knife, draw lines backwards and forwards to make a feather-icing pattern.

Gâteau Chambord

Chambord cake

An almond cake with a chestnut filling, named after the lovely château in the Loire Valley.

	Imperial	American
Génoise Commune made with 3 eggs (*see page 215*)		
50 g ground almonds	2 oz	$\frac{2}{3}$ cup
Crème au Beurre Mousseline made with 2 egg yolks (*see page 216*)		
1 (250 g) can sweetened chestnut purée	8 oz	8 oz
500 g fondant	1 lb	1 lb
or glacé icing, made with 225 g icing sugar	8 oz	2 cups
1 marron glacé		

Grease a 20 cm (8 in) square sandwich tin or moule à manqué. Prepare the cake as shown on pages 214–215, folding in the ground almonds with the flour. Pour the mixture into the tin and bake in the same way. When cooked, turn out onto a wire rack and allow to cool.

Mix two-thirds of the Crème au Beurre Mousseline with the chestnut purée. Cut the cake across in two layers, spread a cut surface with the chestnut mixture and sandwich together. Coat with the glacé or fondant icing (see pages 219 or 220) and allow to set. In each corner of the cake pipe a fleur de lys with a small star pipe, using the remaining crème au beurre, and place the marron glacé in the centre.

Tante Marie tip:
If you do not have a marron glacé, make an imitation chestnut. Take a nut-sized piece of almond paste, shape it, and dip three-quarters of it in melted chocolate. Allow to set before placing on the cake.

Orangines

Orange nut biscuits

	Imperial	American
50 g blanched almonds	2 oz	$\frac{2}{3}$ cup
50 g candied orange peel *or* mixed peel	2 oz	$\frac{2}{3}$ cup
50 g butter	2 oz	$\frac{1}{4}$ cup
50 g castor sugar	2 oz	$\frac{1}{4}$ cup
red food colouring		
40 g plain flour	$1\frac{1}{2}$ oz	$\frac{1}{3}$ cup

Finely chop the almonds and candied peel together. Cream the butter and sugar until light and fluffy, then add a few drops of food colouring to give a pale pink colour. Stir in the peel and almonds and flour. Drop small teaspoons of the mixture onto a greased baking sheet and flatten into rounds with a fork dipped in cold water. Press the mixture out thinly. Bake in a moderately hot oven, Mark 6 (200°C/400°F), for approximately 6 minutes. The biscuits should be tinged with brown around the edges. Leave on the baking-tray for a few minutes to harden slightly, then lift off onto a wire rack and allow to cool.

Gâteau Chambord and Tuiles aux Amandes (*see page 224*).

Tuiles aux Amandes
Almond wafers

These light wafer biscuits are shaped to look like French roof tiles – hence their name. They are particularly good to serve with ice cream.

	Imperial	American
50 g blanched almonds	2 oz	$\frac{2}{3}$ cup
50 g butter	2 oz	$\frac{1}{4}$ cup
2 egg whites		
65 g castor sugar	$2\frac{1}{2}$ oz	$\frac{1}{3}$ cup
50 g plain flour	2 oz	$\frac{1}{2}$ cup
$\frac{1}{2}$ tsp vanilla sugar	$\frac{1}{2}$ tsp	$\frac{1}{2}$ tsp
icing sugar		

Lightly grease 2 or 3 baking-trays. Chop the almonds very finely. Melt the butter until it runs, then allow to cool. Whisk the egg whites to a stiff froth, add the sugar and whisk again for 3–4 minutes until thick and white. Sift the flour and fold in, together with the melted butter, almonds and vanilla sugar. Drop teaspoons of the mixture onto the prepared baking-trays and spread into very thin rounds. Dust the wafers with a little sifted icing sugar. Cook in a moderately hot oven, Mark 6 (200°C/400°F), for approximately 5 minutes or until they are a pale gold colour, tinted golden brown around the edges.

Remove the wafers from the oven, loosen from the baking-trays with a thin-bladed knife and place over a very lightly greased rolling-pin, pressing gently with the hand to make them curve. Allow to cool until crisp. Carefully lift them off the rolling pin and store in an airtight container as soon as they are cold.

Cigarettes Russe
Russian cigarettes

This is another wafer biscuit which can be served with mousses and ices.

	Imperial	American

Note that, if you are using metric measurements, 60 g butter and plain flour and 100 g castor sugar are needed to give the correct result.

	Imperial	American
60 g butter	2 oz	$\frac{1}{4}$ cup
2 egg whites		
100 g castor sugar	$3\frac{1}{2}$ oz	$\frac{1}{3}$ cup and 1 tbsp
$\frac{1}{2}$ tsp vanilla sugar	$\frac{1}{2}$ tsp	$\frac{1}{2}$ tsp
60 g plain flour	2 oz	$\frac{1}{2}$ cup

Melt the butter in a saucepan, then allow to cool. Whisk the egg whites very stiffly in a clean dry bowl. Fold in the sifted sugars and flour, a third at a time, alternately with the cool but liquid butter.

Spread the mixture thinly into circles about 10 cm (4 in) in diameter on a greased and floured baking-tray. Bake in a moderately hot oven, Mark 5 (190°C/375°F), for about 5–7 minutes or until pale gold. Remove from the oven and leave on the baking-tray for a second or two to harden slightly. Using a palette knife, lift them carefully from the tray and roll each round a wooden skewer or spoon handle. If stored in a really airtight container, they will keep fresh for about a month.

It is advisable to make a trial run of one biscuit and bake it. If it is too hard to roll, add a little melted butter to the mixture; if it is too soft, add a pinch of flour to the mixture.

Tante Marie tip:
If you make these frequently it is worth asking a handyman to cut you some pieces of round wood dowelling to use for rolling the biscuits.

Langues de Chat
Cats' tongues

	Imperial	American

Note that, if you are using metric measurements, 75 g butter, sugar and flour are needed to give the correct result.

	Imperial	American
75 g butter	$2\frac{1}{2}$ oz	$\frac{1}{3}$ cup
75 g castor sugar	$2\frac{1}{2}$ oz	$\frac{1}{3}$ cup
2 egg whites		
75 g plain flour	$2\frac{1}{2}$ oz	$\frac{2}{3}$ cup

Place the butter in a bowl and work it with a wooden spoon until smooth and creamy. Add the sugar and work again until very soft and fluffy. Add the unbeaten egg whites very gradually and mix well with a whisk. Lightly beat in the sifted flour.

Grease and flour a baking-tray. Using a forcing bag and plain 1 cm ($\frac{3}{8}$ in) pipe, pipe the mixture into finger lengths on the prepared tin. Bake in a hot oven, Mark 7 (220°C/425°F), for 4–5 minutes or until tinged with brown around the edges. Remove from the oven, carefully place on a wire rack and allow to cool.

Biscuits à la Cuiller
Sponge finger biscuits

These are the biscuits used to make Charlottes. They can also be served with light puddings and ices.

Note that, if you are using metric measurements, 100 g plain flour are needed to give the correct result.

	Imperial	American
3 eggs, separated		
75 g castor sugar	3 oz	6 tbsp
100 g plain flour	3½ oz	1 scant cup
1 tsp vanilla sugar	1 tsp	1 tsp

Cut some strips of greaseproof paper approximately 15 cm (6 in) wide and the length of the baking-tray to be used.

Using a hand or electric whisk, cream the egg yolks with the sugar until thick and light in colour. They will form a ribbon when trailed across the bowl and this should remain visible for a count of three.

Whisk the egg whites stiffly and lightly fold into the mixture, alternately with the sifted flour and vanilla sugar. Place in a forcing bag with a plain 12 mm (½ in) pipe and pipe finger lengths of the mixture onto the greaseproof paper strips. Dust over with finely sifted icing sugar and tap off the surplus. Bake in a moderate oven, Mark 4 (180°C/350°F), for 10–13 minutes or until pale gold in colour and firm to the touch. Remove from the oven, turn the paper with the biscuits on it upside down on a wire rack and strip away the paper immediately. Do not allow to get cold as it will not come off then. Turn the biscuits over and allow to cool.

Eclairs au Chocolat
Chocolate éclairs

	Imperial	American
choux paste made with 50 g plain flour (*see page 207*)	2 oz	½ cup
For the filling:		
225 ml double cream, chilled	7½ fl oz	1 cup
a little milk		
1 tsp vanilla sugar (*optional*)	1 tsp	1 tsp
For the icing:		
50 g plain chocolate	2 oz	⅓ cup
1–2 tbsp hot water	1–2 tbsp	1–2 tbsp
¼ tsp butter *or* oil	¼ tsp	¼ tsp
100 g icing sugar	4 oz	1 cup

Make the choux paste. Place the mixture in a forcing bag with a 12 mm (½ in) plain pipe and pipe finger lengths of the mixture onto a greased baking-tray. Bake in a hot oven, Mark 7–8 (220–230°C/425–450°F), for 10 minutes, then reduce the temperature to Mark 5 (190°C/375°F) and continue cooking for a further 20–30 minutes or until golden brown and crisp. Remove from the oven and place on a wire rack. While still hot make a small hole in the side or base.

Whisk the cream until it is light and just standing in peaks. If it is very thick add a little milk. Stir in the vanilla sugar if used.

When the éclairs are cold, fill with the cream, using a forcing bag with a 3 mm (⅛ in) pipe.

To make the icing, chop the chocolate, place in a small pan with 1 tablespoon of water and the butter or oil and place the pan over a very gentle heat. When the chocolate has melted, beat it until smooth and allow to cool slightly. Stir in the sifted icing sugar. Thin the icing with a little more water if necessary. It should be of a consistency to coat the back of a spoon.

Dip the tops of the éclairs in the icing, place on a wire rack and allow to set. Before serving, place the éclairs in paper cases.

Exquis
Almond and chocolate tartlets

	Imperial	American
90 g ground almonds	3½ oz	1 cup
90 g castor sugar	3½ oz	⅓ cup and 2 tbsp
40 g plain flour	1½ oz	⅓ cup
1 egg white		

For the filling:

150 g plain chocolate	5½ oz	1¼ cups
40 g unsalted butter	1½ oz	3 tbsp
3 tbsp single cream	3 tbsp	3 tbsp

To finish:
chocolate fondant icing
(*see page 221*)
pistachio nuts

Mix together the almonds, sugar and flour. Add sufficient unbeaten egg white to make a stiff paste.

Grease some small tartlet tins with butter and dust evenly with flour. Roll out the paste very thinly, stamp out with a suitably sized fluted cutter and line into the tins. Bake in a slow oven, Mark 2 (150°C/300°F), for about 15 minutes or until cooked. Remove from the oven, carefully loosen from the tins with a thin-bladed knife and unmould. Place on a wire rack and allow to harden.

Meanwhile, make the filling. Break the chocolate into small pieces and place with the butter in a heatproof bowl over a pan of hot water. When the mixture has melted, remove from the heat and stir well, adding the cream. Beat the mixture very well for a minute or two. Before it has set, pour into the almond paste cases and smooth over the tops. Place in the refrigerator. When cold and completely hard, run a thin chocolate icing on the top of each case and decorate with half a pistachio nut.

Tante Marie tip:
It is very important to ensure that the chocolate filling is sufficiently set to take the warm icing over the top. If it has not hardened completely it will be melted by the warmth of the icing.

Madeleines
Shell sponge cakes

These light sponge cakes are cooked in shell-shaped tins to give them an attractive appearance.

	Imperial	American

Note that, if you are using metric measurements, 60 g flour, sugar and butter are needed to give the correct result.

60 g plain flour	2 oz	½ cup
60 g castor sugar	2 oz	¼ cup
60 g butter	2 oz	¼ cup
2 eggs		

Brush about 18 madeleine tins with melted lard. Mix a teaspoonful of flour with one of sugar and dust the tins with this.

Melt the butter and allow to cool. Break the eggs into a bowl, add the sugar and beat well over a pan of hot water until light and fluffy like a Génoise mixture (see pages 214–215). Remove from the heat and whisk till cold. Fold in the melted butter and sifted flour alternately. When just smooth, spoon into the tins, filling them about two-thirds full. Bake in a moderately hot oven, Mark 6 (200°C/400°F), for 8–10 minutes or until golden brown and set. Remove from the oven and take out of the tins with care. Place on a wire rack, shell pattern uppermost, and allow to cool.

Doigts de Dames
Lady's fingers

Crisp little meringues in three flavours.

	Imperial	American
4 egg whites		
250 g icing sugar	9 oz	2¼ cups
coffee essence		
1 tbsp cocoa	1 tbsp	1 tbsp

Sift the sugar and place in a bowl with the egg whites. Place over a pan of boiling water and whisk until very thick. Remove from the heat and whisk until cool.

Divide the mixture into three. Folding in the flavourings as lightly as possible, flavour one portion with coffee, the second with sifted cocoa and leave the third plain.

Pipe finger lengths of the mixtures onto greased, floured baking-trays. Bake in a slow oven, Mark 2 (150°C/300°F), for 5–6 minutes.

Noix au Caramel

Caramel walnuts (makes 18)

A crisp sweet to serve as a petit four with after-dinner coffee.

	Imperial	American
50 g ground almonds	2 oz	$\frac{1}{2}$ cup
50 g castor sugar	2 oz	$\frac{1}{4}$ cup
1 tsp lemon juice *or* rum	1 tsp	1 tsp
a little egg white		
36 (about 100 g) walnut halves	4 oz	$\frac{3}{4}$ cup

For the caramel:

350 g sugar	12 oz	$1\frac{1}{2}$ cups
4 tbsp water	4 tbsp	4 tbsp
1 tsp liquid glucose, or a pinch of cream of tartar	1 tsp	1 tsp

Mix the almonds and castor sugar with the lemon juice or rum and just enough egg white to blend together. Roll the mixture on a board and slice into 18 pieces. Roll into balls and sandwich the walnut halves with these.

Grease a baking-tray with oil and have a large bowl of hot water ready to use.

Place the sugar and water in a pan and add the liquid glucose or cream of tartar. Stir until dissolved, then boil to a golden toffee colour. Place the saucepan gently in the bowl of water and allow to stand in this while you dip the walnut and almond balls. Take these, one at a time, and dip into the caramel, using cooking tongs. Allow the excess caramel to drip off, then place on the prepared baking-tray. When set, place in paper cases and store in an airtight container until used.

Colettes

Soft chocolates (makes 16)

	Imperial	American
100 g plain chocolate	4 oz	$\frac{3}{4}$ cup

For the filling:

100 g plain chocolate	4 oz	$\frac{3}{4}$ cup
150 g unsalted butter	6 oz	$\frac{3}{4}$ cup
$1\frac{1}{2}$ tbsp double cream	$1\frac{1}{2}$ tbsp	$1\frac{1}{2}$ tbsp
1 tbsp rum	1 tbsp	1 tbsp
crystallised violets		

Chop the chocolate into small pieces and place in a bowl over a pan of hot water. Heat gently until the chocolate has melted. Do not allow to overheat. Using a teaspoon, line sweet paper cases with the chocolate. Allow to set, then recoat the sides. Chill, and when set remove from the paper cases.

Melt the chocolate for the filling in the same way, then beat in the butter, cream and rum. Allow to cool slightly. Using a forcing bag and rosette pipe, fill the chocolate cases with the mixture and decorate the top of each with a piece of crystallised violet. Refrigerate until set, then store in a cool, dry place.

Rochers à la Noix de Coco

Coconut rocks

The name belies the soft sticky centre of these cakes, although the golden top can look rocky.

	Imperial	American
125 g icing sugar	$4\frac{1}{2}$ oz	1 cup
2 egg whites		
100 g desiccated coconut	4 oz	1 cup

Place the sifted icing sugar in a bowl with the un-whisked whites. Place the bowl over a saucepan half filled with boiling water and whisk the mixture until white and creamy. Remove from the heat and beat until cold and thick enough to show the mark of the whisk. Fold in the coconut. Place the mixture in greaseproof paper bun cases and bake in a slow oven, Mark 2 (150°C/300°F), for 10–15 minutes, when the outside should be lightly coloured and crisp and the inside still soft and sticky.

Yeast Cookery

Yeast is used to make doughs rise for many kinds of bread and cakes. Croissants, brioches and babas are among the most delicious of the French breads and cakes made in this way.

In cooking any bread or cakes you will not get the best results unless you use the correct flour. A 'strong' flour has a high content of the substance gluten which makes the dough stretchy and allows it to rise well. Details are given on page 206.

Yeast can be either fresh or dried. Dried yeast is perfectly satisfactory to use, though perhaps a little slower, but only half the weight of fresh yeast is required. Mix the dried yeast with some of the measured liquid and allow it to stand for 10–15 minutes to soften, then use in the same way as fresh yeast.

Once the dough is prepared, it is placed in a slightly warm spot to rise: a warm area in the kitchen or a shelf in the airing cupboard are the usual places to use. If there is nowhere particularly suitable, stand your covered bowl of dough in a larger bowl of warm water – with the water no hotter than is really comfortable to your hand.

Baking is done in a very hot oven so the mixture rises when it first goes into the oven, then the yeast is killed and the dough bakes through. To test that rolls or bread are cooked, turn them upside down and tap with the fingernails. There will be a hollow sound when the bread is baked.

Croissants

Crescent rolls (makes 8–10)

Crisp, flaky rolls for breakfast time.

	Imperial	American
225 g strong flour	8 oz	2 cups
15 g sugar	$\frac{1}{2}$ oz	1 tbsp
1 tsp salt	1 tsp	1 tsp
15 g fresh yeast,	$\frac{1}{2}$ oz	1 tbsp
_or_ **7 g dried yeast**	$\frac{1}{4}$ oz	2 tsp
100–150 ml water to mix	about $\frac{1}{4}$ pt	$\frac{1}{2}$–$\frac{2}{3}$ cup
100 g butter	4 oz	$\frac{1}{2}$ cup
a little beaten egg		

Sift the flour, sugar and salt into a heap on a pastry board. Make a well in the centre and place the yeast in this. Add 2 tablespoons of tepid water and, with the tips of two fingers, mix it in until all the yeast has dissolved. Still keeping the well in the centre, add the rest of the water (it should be at blood heat). Continue working in the flour from the sides all the time to give a smooth and pliable dough. Cover and allow to rise in a warm place, such as the warming drawer of an electric cooker or a plate rack over a pan of simmering water, or in a warm airing cupboard, until it has risen to twice its bulk. This process should take about $1\frac{1}{2}$–2 hours.

Place in the refrigerator or a cold larder and chill until the dough is completely cold. It must still be covered at this stage.

Turn the dough onto a floured board and roll it to the size of a large dinner plate. Soften the butter by tapping it well with a rolling-pin to make it of the same consistency as the dough, in the same way as the butter is prepared for puff pastry (see pages 210–211).

Place the butter in the middle of the dough. Fold over the dough, first from the right, then from the left, into the centre, allowing it to overlap about 3 cm (1 in). Tap the dough with a rolling-pin all along the join to elongate the butter enclosed within. Fold over the top and bottom ends to join and overlap in the centre as before. Tap again with the rolling-pin.

Roll out the dough to an oblong shape. Fold in three exactly as for puff pastry (see page 211). Turn and repeat the rolling and folding. Wrap and put it aside in a cold place for 15 minutes. Repeat twice more, giving four rolls altogether. Put it aside for a further 15 minutes. Finally roll out the dough to a rectangle, about 30 × 46 cm (12 × 18 in) and about 3 mm ($\frac{1}{8}$ in) thick. Divide into two sections, cutting along the length of the dough. Cut into triangles. Use the uneven ends and the trimmings from the sides as a bolster to fatten each roll. Place a thin strip of trimming along the base of the triangle. Fold the dough once over this padding. Pull this fold sideways to elongate it. Using the flat of the hand, roll the dough towards the apex in one sweep. Form into a horseshoe shape. Lift carefully onto a dampened baking-tray. Allow the croissants to rise in a warm place (make sure it is not too hot or the butter will melt). When they have risen to twice their size, brush very lightly with the beaten egg. Bake in a very hot oven, Mark 8 (230°C/450°F), for about 15 minutes or until they are golden brown and sound hollow when tapped.

Tante Marie tip:
A favourite after-school treat for the French schoolchild is a croissant baked with a filling of chocolate which melts in the centre.

Brioches

Rich bread rolls (makes 8)

Serve for breakfast or with morning coffee.

	Imperial	American
225 g strong flour	8 oz	2 cups
$\frac{1}{2}$ tsp salt	$\frac{1}{2}$ tsp	$\frac{1}{2}$ tsp
15 g fresh yeast,	$\frac{1}{2}$ oz	1 tbsp
or 7 g dried yeast	$\frac{1}{4}$ oz	2 tsp
40 g castor sugar	$1\frac{1}{2}$ oz	3 tbsp
3 eggs		
100 g butter	4 oz	$\frac{1}{2}$ cup
a little beaten egg		

Sift the flour and salt in a mound on a marble slab or pastry board. Make a well in the centre and place the yeast in this. Add 2-3 tablespoons of warm water and, working it in with the fingertips, mix it in until all the yeast has dissolved. Add the sugar and eggs and mix well, gradually working in the flour from the sides. When thoroughly mixed, continue working the dough for 5 minutes to give it elasticity. Take the dough in one hand and throw it forcefully with a quick twist of the hand onto the slab. Repeat this several times. At first, the paste will adhere to the fingers, but gradually, as the dough becomes elastic, it will detach itself completely from the fingers. You will find that the dough is now smooth, shiny and free from lumps.

Work the butter to a soft paste. Take a piece about the size of a large walnut and work it into the dough until it is completely incorporated. Repeat, adding the same-sized pieces of butter and working in thoroughly between each addition. Place the dough in a bowl, cover and allow to rise very gently in a warm place. If the temperature is too hot the butter will melt and run out. When well risen, place in the refrigerator and allow to rise again very slowly for 2-3 hours, or overnight.

Turn the dough onto the lightly floured slab. You will find that the dough is now cold, firm and easy to manage. Divide it into even-sized pieces: this quantity should make about 8 average-sized brioches. Take one portion in the palm of one hand and roll it

with the four fingers of the other hand into a pear shape (the fingers are used flat). Take the pointed end, pinch it all round at a depth of approximately 2-3 cm (1 in) and give it a slight twist. Place it in a greased brioche tin. It is necessary to press it very lightly, so it fits the shape of the tin and the little cap stands up like the top of a cottage loaf. Repeat this process with each portion of the dough. Allow the portions to prove gently in a warm place. When they have risen to the top of the tin, brush *very* lightly with the beaten egg. Bake in a hot oven, Mark 6-7 (200-220°C/400-425°F), for 10 minutes or until golden brown. Remove from the oven, place on a wire rack and allow to cool.

Brioches (*top*) and Croissants.

Babas à l'Orange

Orange babas

Babas au rhum are the better-known version of this recipe, but this variation is equally delicious. The yeast sponge cakes are soaked in orange syrup and decorated with whipped cream and orange. Rum *or* orange-flavoured liqueur can be added to the syrup when you feel in festive mood.

	Imperial	American
15 g fresh yeast,	$\frac{1}{2}$ oz	1 tbsp
or 7 g dried yeast	$\frac{1}{4}$ oz	2 tsp
2 tbsp tepid water	2 tbsp	2 tbsp
2 eggs		
25 g butter	1 oz	2 tbsp
100 g strong flour	4 oz	1 cup
25 g sugar	1 oz	2 tbsp
$\frac{1}{4}$ tsp salt	$\frac{1}{4}$ tsp	$\frac{1}{4}$ tsp
2 oranges		

For the syrup:

	Imperial	American
300 ml water	$\frac{1}{2}$ pt	$1\frac{1}{4}$ cups
175 g sugar	6 oz	$\frac{3}{4}$ cup

To finish:

	Imperial	American
300 ml double cream	$\frac{1}{2}$ pt	$1\frac{1}{4}$ cups
apricot jam to glaze		

Place the yeast in a bowl with the tepid water and stir until it has dissolved. Break the eggs into the yeast and mix together. Melt the butter and allow to cool.

Sift the flour, sugar and salt into a warm bowl. Make a well in the centre and pour the yeast and egg mixture into this, with the grated rind of one orange. Beat the flour gradually into the liquid. When all the flour has been added, beat well for several minutes. Add the melted butter (which should be warm but not hot), and beat again until the dough is smooth and shiny. Cover and allow to rise in a warm place until it has doubled its bulk.

While the babas are proving, remove the peel very thinly from the second orange and cut into very fine julienne. Place in boiling water and cook until tender. Remove the pith and cut the orange into segments.

To make the syrup, place the water and sugar with the juice of the first orange in a pan over a gentle heat. Stir until the sugar has dissolved, then bring to the boil and simmer for 5 minutes.

Grease and flour 6 or 8 baba moulds. Knock back the dough and beat thoroughly again. Place it in a forcing bag with a plain 12 mm ($\frac{1}{2}$ in) pipe. Pipe it into the moulds.

Put these in a warm place until the dough has risen to the top of each mould. Place in a preheated oven, Mark 7 (210°C/425°F), for 6–8 minutes, then reduce the temperature to Mark 5 (190°C/375°F) and continue to cook for a further 8–10 minutes or until golden brown on the underside. If the tops brown too quickly, cover with greaseproof paper.

Reheat the syrup and pour into a large bowl. When the babas are cooked, remove them from the tins and soak them in the hot syrup immediately. Turn them constantly until all the syrup is absorbed. Place on a wire rack and glaze with the hot apricot jam.

Sprinkle the julienne of orange zest over the surface and pipe the cream into the centre of each baba when cold. Decorate with a piece of orange.

Tante Marie tip:
If required, the babas can be prepared in advance, soaked with the syrup, and deep frozen. Fill with cream and decorate when they are defrosted.

Wines and Menus

In French homes the main family meal is eaten in the middle of the day. There is a tendency to think that all French meals are rich and enormous. In fact it is the way in which the meals are presented. Whereas in other countries meat and vegetables are served at the same time, invariably the meal in France is divided so that more courses seem to be served. Although for special occasions such as weddings or first communions elaborate meals of many courses are usual, family meals tend to be quite simple.

The French housewife still prides herself on homemade soups. A meal would start with this or a simple hors d'oeuvre. This may be bought from the local charcuterie, or could consist of large juicy tomatoes sliced and sprinkled with Sauce Vinaigrette, chopped onion and parsley. Either fish or meat is served for the main course with a vegetable and cheese to follow. The meal could end with a sweet or fruit, but quite often cheese is sufficient. This is always served before the sweet so that red wine can be drunk with it. Potatoes are not so dominant in French meals, but plenty of crusty French bread is always served.

Those of you who have been to France will know that five or six course meals are usual, even in the simplest restaurants. Soup or hors d'oeuvre, possibly both, are served first, followed by fish and the main course. This could be steak, chicken, guinea fowl or a local speciality served as the plat du jour. The portions are not necessarily large by some standards but sufficient to balance with the rest of the meal. The vegetable or salad may be served at the end of this course so that it is eaten separately. Cheese and a sweet, or fresh fruit, complete the meal.

Compiling a balanced menu is important if the cook's efforts are to be fully appreciated. We all know the dishes we like to eat, but combining a selection of them is something which needs thought. Throughout the meal the courses should provide a contrast in texture, colour and flavour. You may enjoy a cheese soufflé or a cream caramel, but to serve them both at the same meal would be wrong; in colour, consistency and ingredients they are too similar.

Texture must be considered. A meal that can be eaten with little effort may be suitable for an invalid, but for the normal hale and hearty diner the textures must vary if the palate is to be kept alert and the meal enjoyed to the full. A salad to follow a rich sauce, or a crisp biscuit with a smooth mousse can give the definition you need. Try to vary courses so that colours are different; certainly provide a contrast between the main dish and the vegetables served with it. Imagination plays a large part in the enjoyment of eating. If it looks good, you expect it to taste good.

Flavour is, of course, most important. However well-presented a dish might be, the cook has wasted her time unless the flavour is good. Remember, too, not to repeat flavours and ingredients in a meal. Grapefruit to start and lemon mousse to finish are too similar. Potage Crécy is delicious, but do not follow it with Carottes à la Vichy.

It is also essential that the cook realises how long a dish takes to prepare, cook and serve. It is wise to plan the amount of preparation which can be done in advance. You will not be able to do full justice to your skills if overburdened with a complicated menu, unless time and space are available. Dishes which need a lot of last-minute finishing should be avoided by the cook–hostess, for she can enjoy a drink with her guests if she has planned a meal which can either be prepared in advance or kept hot.

The housewife is usually aware of the scope or limitations of her own kitchen. The professional Tante Marie cook, particularly if freelancing, may have to cook in unfamiliar surroundings. In this situation care must be taken to plan a meal which can be cooked without stress in a strange kitchen. Our experience has ranged from the extremely large kitchen with plenty of work surfaces, where you become exhausted by the distance between the cooker and the sink, to galley-type kitchens with no room to swing the proverbial cat. The amount of equipment available also varied. Some kitchens had everything; one had three small saucepans and no wooden spoon. Of course, you can take everything with you but there is a limit to the amount of equipment that can be carried. If the kitchen is under-equipped, it is far better to plan your menu so that as much work as possible can be done in advance and the prepared food taken with you for the final touches to be added.

Do remember that variety in the content and presentation of a meal, and the time and space available, are the vital points which must be considered for the success of a well-cooked meal.

Wines

No meal is complete without wine. Red, white and rosé wines, from cheap vins de table to expensive château bottled ones: the Frenchman is spoilt for choice. But, like everyone else, for everyday drinking he wants a modest wine to suit his purse. Quite often he keeps a good supply in his cellar, buying from a local producer or co-operative.

Wines should be treated with care if they are to be drunk at their best. Cheap wines are meant to be drunk immediately and not stored. Always store wine bottles on their sides so that the wine is in contact with the cork. This prevents the cork drying out and air reaching the wine. Store it at a constant cool temperature of around 10°C (50°F). Serve wines at the temperature at which the full flavour of the wine can be appreciated. Red wines are normally served at room temperature, and should be allowed to reach this temperature gradually. Bring them out of the cellar several hours before serving and stand them in a warm room until required. Do not spoil your wine by plunging the bottle into hot water, or putting it too near a direct source of heat such as a cooker or fire. Except for very old or very young wines, open them about an hour or so before they are drunk to enable the bouquet to develop. Good clarets should be decanted to aerate the wine and separate it from the sediment which is likely to be in the bottom of the bottle.

White and rosé wines should be served at cellar temperature. If this is not possible put them in a refrigerator for an hour or so before serving, or into an ice bucket filled with ice and water for 15–20 minutes. Always use ice and water as this chills more evenly. Ice alone chills unevenly and too severely for some delicate wines. If the wine is needed quickly place the bottle in the bucket neck down until it is opened – the first couple of glasses or so will chill quickly: while these are being drunk the rest of the wine can chill normally.

Champagne and sparkling wines are served slightly colder than other white wines. They need to be well chilled before opening or they will be difficult to open without the wine effervescing out of the bottle.

Tinted wine glasses obscure the colour of the wine; use clear ones so that it can be appreciated to the full. Glasses for red wines should have short stems so that the bowl can be held in the hand to keep the wine warm. Glasses for white wine should have long stems for the opposite reason – they prevent the hands touching the bowl. Champagne is better served in tulip-shaped glasses rather than the coupe glass so favoured by the Edwardians. Tulip glasses retain the bouquet and the bubbles. Glasses should be filled no more than two-thirds full so that the bouquet can develop and be appreciated.

Always rinse glasses well in clean water, as a film of detergent left on the glass destroys the bubbles. Glasses should be stored the right way up so that they remain fresh. If they are stored upside-down, stale air or the scent of wood or plastic from the surface on which they stand can spoil the taste of the wine.

Choosing a wine to serve with your meal needs a little understanding, since wines and food should complement each other. With a little experience even the most unsophisticated palate will recognise that certain wines taste better with certain foods. It is this and this alone which determines the choice of wine. The final decision must be one of personal preference.

Soups

In Britain, a dry fino sherry is drunk with a consommé but this is not the custom in France. No wine is served with thick soup.

Hors d'oeuvre

The choice of wine depends on what you are eating for this course. A light dry white wine makes a good introduction to a meal. Although some people may prefer not to drink a wine with dishes flavoured with vinegar, we like to serve a modest wine on these occasions as it brightens the start of a meal and makes the conversation flow. However, there is no doubt that wine does not go well with citrus fruit such as grapefruit.

With shellfish, have a chilled dry white wine such as a Muscadet or a Chablis. These wines go very well with fish pâtés too.

With meat pâtés and terrines, drink a moderate red wine such as a Côtes du Rhône or Beaujolais.

If you want to serve only one wine with a meal, plan your menu so that the same wine can be drunk with both the hors d'oeuvre and the main course.

Fish

Dry white wine is usually the best choice to serve with fish. A young Loire wine, such as a Sancerre, is a very pleasant wine, or a Graves from Bordeaux. For something special, choose a white Burgundy such as Pouilly Fuissé. Salmon, turbot or halibut are occasionally cooked in red wine. For such a dish, serve the same wine as is used in cooking.

White meats

Veal

With veal, drink a full-bodied dry white wine. A white Burgundy such as a Puligny Montrachet is splendid. Alternatively, choose a rosé. This is especially good with Veau Braisée Bouquetière.

Pork

Because this is such a rich meat, care must be taken in the choice of wine to serve with it. Traditionally, white wine is served, but many people enjoy a light red wine or rosé.

Red meats

Beef

There can be little doubt that a red wine is usually preferred with the full flavour of beef. With country casseroles like Estouffat Gascon, drink an inexpensive vin du pays such as Corbières. On the other hand, the lovely château-bottled wines of Bordeaux or Burgundy can be served to perfection with steaks or roasts.

Lamb

We like a Bordeaux wine or the red wines of the Rhône with lamb, as these offset the richness of the meat. Choose only a moderate quality wine for a pungent flavoured dish like Gigot d'Agneau au Romarin.

Poultry

Chicken and turkey

The way in which these birds are cooked usually dictates the choice of wine, but almost any medium dry white wine can be drunk. With a cream sauce, drink a fruity young Loire or Alsace wine; more highly seasoned dishes are excellent with a rosé or a medium quality red wine.

Simply cooked, a roast chicken or turkey will complement a really good red wine such as a château-bottled Bordeaux.

Duck and goose

These are both very rich, well-flavoured meats which need the fullness of a red wine. A Nuits St Georges or a Châteauneuf du Pape are most enjoyable with them.

Game

The well-known tradition is to drink claret with feathered game and burgundy with venison and hare. This is another occasion for serving your best wines.

Cheese

When cheese is served before the sweet, as it is in France, the red wine served with the previous course is often drunk with it. When a white wine accompanies the main course, choose a full-bodied red wine to drink with the cheese.

Puddings and desserts

This is the time to serve a sweet champagne or one of the lovely dessert wines of Bordeaux – a Barsac or Sauternes. Château d'Yquem is the most famous, but is, of course, very expensive. For a more reasonably priced wine, try a Côteaux du Layon from the Loire or a nutty Monbazillac from Bergerac in the Périgord.

Not all puddings can be eaten with wine. Chocolate spoils the flavour of the wine, and ices chill the palate too much. Fruit-based sweets, such as those with strawberries, raspberries, peaches and apricots are best.

Champagne, Alsace and rosé wines can be drunk throughout a meal.

Quantities

A bottle of wine holds approximately eight glasses. On most occasions, allow $\frac{1}{3}-\frac{1}{2}$ a bottle of wine per person. For six people, one bottle of white wine to go with the fish course and two bottles of red for the main course would normally be sufficient; but as some people may prefer more, it is a good idea to keep an extra bottle in reserve.

A half bottle of dessert wine will serve four.

Menus

We have given you a wide range of recipes. The following menus are suggestions of the way some of them might be put together.

A family lunch for all seasons
Potage Crécy
Longe d'Agneau Persillé
Pommes de Terre Berrichone
Salade de Saison
Fromage
Fruits

A summer lunch
Terrine Maison
Truites à l'Estragon
Beignets des Courgettes
Tarte aux Abricots et Cerises

A lunch for the cooler months
Hors d'oeuvre Variés
Blanquette de Veau
Riz Blanc
Profiteroles au Chocolat

A simple dinner party
Crudités
Côtes de Porc aux Pruneaux
Haricots Verts
Fromage
Crème Renversée au Caramel

Quick and easy
Avocats aux Crevettes
Steak Vert Pré
Salade Verte
Petit Pots de Chocolat au Rhum

Dinner for the cook/hostess
Moules à la Marinière
Poulet à la Grandmère
Céleri-Rave à la Paysanne
Amandine

Summer celebration
Asperges, Sauce Hollandaise
Pintade à la Vigneronne
Pommes de Terre Paille
Fromage
Soufflé Glacé aux Fraises
Orangines

A special dinner party
Consommé au Céleri
Filets de Sole aux Crevettes
Gigot d'Agneau au Romarin
Petits Pois à la Française
Fromage
Crème Asphodèle
Tuiles aux Amandes

Index

Abats 126–132
  Foie 126, 127
  Langue 126, 128
  Ris 126, 130
  Rognons 126, 129, 130
Abricots, Mousse aux 191
  Tarte aux, et Cerises 200
acidulated water 23
Agneau 102–110
  Carré, aux Courgettes 110
  Côtelettes, en Cuirasse 107
    Dubarry 107
  Côtes, Champvallon 106
  cuts 102–105
  Epaule, aux Navets 108
  Gigot, en Croûte 105
    au Romarin 105
  Longe, Persillé 106
  Navarin Printanier 110
  Noisettes, Chasseur 108
  Rognons, à la Beaujolaise 130
    à la Grandmère 129
  weights, average 102
Aïoli 31
almond and brandy cake 213
  and chocolate tartlets 226
  tart 200
  toffee 205
  wafers 224
almonds, to brown and skin 23
Amandine 200
appetisers, assorted 45
apple and almond puff 198
  tart, latticed 197
    upside-down 198
apricot and cherry tart 200
  glaze 23
  mousse 191
  sauce 199
Arlesienne scrambled eggs 55
Artichauts 45, 160–1
  preparation of 161
artichokes 45, 160–1
  Jerusalem 181
    in cheese sauce 182
    preparation of 161
asparagus 162
  Flemish-style 162
  with Hollandaise Sauce 46
  preparation of 162
Asperges 162
  à la Flamande 162
  preparation of 162

  Sauce Hollandaise 46
Assiette Anglaise 45
assorted appetisers 45
Aubergine(s) 163–4
  Caviar d' 49
  cheese covered 164
  Farcies 163
  Gratin d' 164
  hors d'oeuvre 45
  poor man's caviare 49
  preparation of 163
  stuffed 163
avocados 46
  with French dressing 46
  stuffed with prawns 46
Avocats 46
  aux Crevettes 46
  à la Vinaigrette 46

Babas à l'Orange 230
bacon and egg flan 63
Bagrance poached eggs 52
baked eggs 55
  with cream 55
  with kidney 55
  queen's 55
Basque tart 62
Bavarian creams 194–5
Bavarois 194–5
  Crème, à la Vanille 195
Béarnaise sauce 32
Béchamel sauce 27
beef 90–101
  boiled 97
  braised 98
  Chinon casserole 94
  Choron fillet steak 100
  cuts 90–3
  Flemish stew 94
  Gascon casserole 95
  Henri IV sirloin steak 100
  meat loaf 131
  peppered steak 100
  roast fillet steak 100
  rolls 96
  Roman-style tongue 128
  sliced ox tongue with savoury
    stuffing 128
  steak(s) 99–101
    Choron fillet 100
    Henri IV sirloin 100
    peppered 100
    roast fillet 100

Rossini 101
  with eggs 100
  with straw potatoes 100
  stock 34
  Vaucluse rolls 96
  weights, average 90
beetroot(s) 164
  in cream 164
  hors d'oeuvre 43, 45
Beignets des Champignons 167
  des Courgettes 170
Belgian chicory 171
best end of neck of lamb with
  courgettes 110
Betterave(s) 164
  à la Crème 164
  hors d'oeuvre 43, 45
Beurre au Fenouil 69
  Maître d'Hôtel 23
  Manié 23
Biscuit Fin 214–15
  Roulé au Café 218
biscuits 223–5, 226
  almond wafers 224
  cats' tongues 224
  Cigarettes Russe 224
  à la Cuiller 225
  Doigts de Dames 226
  lady's fingers 226
  Langues de Chat 224
  orange nut 223
  Orangines 223
  Russian cigarettes 224
  sponge finger 225
  Tuiles aux Amandes 224
Blanquette de Veau 123
blond roux 26
Boeuf 90–101
  Braisé 98
  Carbonnade de, à la Flamande
    94
  Châteaubriand 100
  cuts 90–3
  Entrecôte Henri IV 100
  Estouffat Gascon 95
  Langue de, Romaine 128
  Médaillons à la Milanaise 128
  Pain de 131
  Paupiettes de 96
  à la Vauclusienne 96
  Pot-au-Feu 40, 97
  Sauté de, au Chinon 94
  steaks 99–101

à Cheval 100
  au Poivre 100
  Vert Pré 100
  Tournedos à la Choron 100
    Rossini 101
  weights, average 90
boiled beef 40, 97
  soup 40, 97
  eggs 50
Bordeaux-style chicken 148
Boulogne omelette 57
braised beef 98
  celery 166
  guinea fowl with grapes 149
  veal 122
    sweetbreads 130
breadcrumbs 23
bread rolls, rich 229
Breton shortcake 213
Brioches 229
broad beans 172
  with bacon 172
  with lemon and parsley 172
brown roux 26
  sauce(s) 29
  stock 35
Brussels sprouts 169
  with chestnuts 169
butter cream 216
  sauces 32

cabbage, green 167–8
  in a cream sauce 167
  with rice and tomato 168
cabbage, red 168
  Flemish 168
  hors d'oeuvre 43
cake(s) 213–22
  almond and brandy 213
  Breton shortcake 213
  coffee and walnut Swiss roll
    218
  Chambord 222
  chocolate 216
  four colour 218
  lemon 221
  Mexican 222
  pineapple 216
  shell sponge 226
  sponge, fatless 214–15
    Genoese 215
    finger biscuits 225
    rich 215

cake(s) contd
  Swiss chocolate 218
Calmar 89
  à l'Armoricaine 89
  preparation of 89
Camembert mousse 60
  pancakes 56
Canard 150–1
  au Muscadet 151
  à l'Orange 150
  weights 150
caramel custard 189
    with Grand Marnier 190
  walnuts 227
caramelised rabbit 156
Carbonnade de Boeuf à la
  Flamande 94
Carré d'Agneau aux Courgettes
  110
  de Porc à l'Ananas 114
carrot(s) 165
  with herbs 165
  hors d'oeuvre 43
  Polish-style 165
  and rice soup 38
  Vichy 165
Carottes 165
  aux Fines Herbes 165
  à la Polonaise 165
  à la Vichy 165
casserole of pheasant 156
casseroled potatoes 176
castle potatoes 179
Catalonian partridges 158
cats' tongues 224
cauliflower 169
  soufflé 169
Caviar d'Aubergine 49
Céleri 166
  Braisé 166
  Consommé au 36
  Salade Belle Hortense 185
celeriac 166
  country-style 166
  hors d'oeuvre 43
Céleri-Rave 166
  hors d'oeuvre 43
  à la Paysanne 166
celery 166
  braised 166
  consommé 36
  and walnut salad 185
Chambord cake 222
Chamonix 189
Champignons 167
  Beignets des 167
  à la Grecque 48
  Potage aux 40
Champvallon lamb chops 106
Charlotte Montreuil 194
Châteaubriand 100
cheese dishes 58, 60–3
  covered aubergines 164
  sauce 27
  soufflé 58
  tart 61
  topped chicken with
    mushrooms 138
  types 186
cheeseboard, the 186

chestnut meringues 189
chicken 133–48
  Bordeaux-style 148
  breasts with Béarnaise sauce
    138
  casserole from Angers 147
  Duroc 148
  cheese topped, with
    mushrooms 138
  cockerel in red wine 146
  grandmother's 136
  Italian 146
  jointing, poached 138
    raw 144–5
  liver pâté, a quick 41
  Provençale 147
  roast, with tarragon 136
  salad from Nice 139
  stock 34
  stuffed, poached 137
  trussing 134–5
  vol-au-vent 140–2
  weights 133
chicory 171
  with bacon 171
chilled tomato soup 37
Chinon beef casserole 94
chipped potatoes 180
chocolate cake 216
  éclairs 225
  fondant 221
  pots with rum 193
  sauce 196
  soufflé 202
chocolates, soft 227
Choron fillet steak 100
  sauce 32
Choufleur 169
  Soufflé de 169
Chou Rouge 168
  à la Flamande 168
  hors d'oeuvre 43
Chou Vert 167–8
  à la Crème 167
  au Riz à la Tomate 168
Choux de Bruxelles 169
  à la Limousine 169
choux paste 207
Cigarettes Russe 224
Civet de Lièvre 154
cockerel in red wine 146
coconut rocks 227
cod, salt 70
  Niçoise fish flan 70
coffee mousse 193
  suprême 201
  and walnut Swiss roll 218
Colettes 227
Compôte de Poires au Vin Rouge
  197
Concombre(s) 170
  à la Crème 170
  Farci Parisienne 47
  hors d'oeuvre 43
confectioners' custard 197
Consommé au Céleri 36
cooper's eggs, the 49
Coq au Vin 146
Coquilles St Jacques 85
  Couronne de 86

  à la Nantaise 87
Côtelettes d'Agneau en Cuirasse
  107
  Dubarry 107
Côtes d'Agneau Champvallon
  106
  de Porc Charcutière 115
  aux Pruneaux 116
  à la Vallée d'Auge 116
country-style celeriac 166
  roast goose 152
Courgette(s) 170
  Beignets des 170
  à la Caillou 184
  fritters 170
  salad 184
Couronne de Coquilles St
  Jacques 85
Crab(e) Garni au Fenouil 81
  hot, with fennel 81
  Omaha 84
  preparation of 82–3
  salad 84
cream filled choux balls with
  chocolate sauce 196
  of mushroom soup 40
  sauce 27
  whipped 199
cream cheese and bananas 202
creamed potatoes 177
creamy chicken sauce 28
  scallop ring 86
  veal stew 123
Crème Anglaise 202
  Asphodèle 192
  Bavarois à la Vanille 195
  au Beurre Mousseline 216
  Caramel au Grand Marnier
    190
  Chantilly 199
  Evita 37
  Hindoue 199
  Jardinière 36
  Opera 190
  Pâtissière 197
  Renversée au Caramel 189
Crêpes 56
  au Camembert 56
  Ficelle de Picardie 56
  Flambées au Grand Marnier
    195
crescent rolls 228
crisp almond toffee 205
Croissants 228
Croquettes de Pommes de Terre
  180
Croustade de Pigeon 43
Croûtons 23
Crudités 43
cucumber(s) 170
  with cream 170
  hors d'oeuvre 43
  Parisian stuffed 47
culinary terms 16–18
custard, confectioners' 197
  egg 202

dawn eggs 51
  sauce 28
deep fried meat turnovers 132

demi-glace sauce 29
devilled herrings 64
Dinde 152–4
  Farcie aux Marrons 153
  Salade, à l'Anversoise 154
  weights 152
Doigts de Dames 226
Dover sole 70
  to skin and fillet 72–3
dried vegetables 182–3
  haricot beans 182
  lentils 183
Dubarry lamb cutlets 107
Duchess potatoes 179
  tomatoes 181
duck 150–1
  in muscadet 151
  in orange sauce 150
  weights 150

Eclairs au Chocolat 225
egg custard 202
  plant 163–4
eggs, baked 55
    with cream 55
    with kidneys 55
    queen's 55
  boiled 50
  cooper's, the 49
  dawn 51
  on the dish 52
    Isoline 52
    Mirabeau 52
    Portuguese 52
    Rothomago 52
  hard-boiled 51
    with mayonnaise 51
    with tomatoes 48
  poached 52
    Bagrance 52
  scrambled 55
    Arlesienne 55
  soft-boiled 50
    with herbs 50
    Montrouge 51
    with watercress 50
emulsion sauces 30–1
Encornet 89
Endive 171
  au Lard 171
English platter 45
Entrecôte Henri IV 100
Epaule d'Agneau aux Navets
  108
Epinards 171–2
  à la Bourgeoise 171
  au Gratin 172
equipment, kitchen 10–15
Escalopes de Veau à la Viennoise
  121
Estouffat Gascon 95
Estragon, Poulet à l' 136
  Truites à l' 80
Exquis 226

Faisan 156–7
  en Cocotte 156
  à la Crème 157
farmer's wife's omelette, the 57
fennel butter 69

fennel contd
grilled red mullet with 69
hot crab with 81
Provençale-style 48
Fenouil, Beurre au 69
Crabe au 81
Grillade au 69
à la Provençale 48
Fèves 172
au Lard 172
à la Maître d'Hôtel 172
Ficelle de Picardie 56
Filets de Merlan à la
Toulonnaise 77
Filets de Sole aux Crevettes 73
Cubat 71
à la Florentine 74
à la Suchet 74
fillets of sole with mushroom
purée 71
with prawns 73
poached with spinach 74
Suchet fillets 74
fish 64–81
preparation of Dover sole
72–3
preparation of round fish
66–7
soup 35
stock 35
flaky pastry 208–9
flan, bacon and egg 63
Niçoise fish 70
tin, lining a 212
flavourings 21
Flemish beef stew 94
red cabbage 168
-style asparagus 162
Foie 126, 127
de Veau à la Bourgeoise 127
au Raisins 127
Fond de cuisine 34
brun 35
fondant au Chocolat 221
icing 220
to ice with 220
Fondue au Jambon 60
four colour cake 218
Fraises, Soufflé Glacé aux 204
French beans 172–3
Breton style 173
hors d'oeuvre 45
dressing 33
onion soup 36
-style peas 174
Fricassée de Poulet à l'Angevine
147
fried mackerel with
mushrooms and tomatoes 70
onion rings 173
parsnips 174
potato balls 179
potatoes 180
sole 76
fritter(s) batter 167
courgette 170
mushroom 167
Fromage Blanc aux Bananes 202
Soufflé au 58
Fumet de Poisson 35

Galette Bretonne 213
de Morue à la Niçoise 70
game
hare 154
omelette 58
partridge 158
pheasant 156–7
pigeon 159
rabbit 155–6
stock 34
gardener's wife's soup, the 36
garlic flavoured roast pork 115
mayonnaise 31
Gascon beef casserole 95
Gâteau(x) 213–22
à l'Ananas 216
Biscuit Fin 214–15
Roulé au Café 218
Cambacères 213
Chambord 222
au Chocolat 216
Suisse 218
au Citron 221
Galette Bretonne 213
Génoise Commune 215
Fine 215
Jalousie aux Pommes 198
Mexicain 222
Panaché 218
gelatine 191
Genoese sponge cake 215
Génoise Commune 215
Fine 215
Gigot en Croûte 105
d'Agneau au Romarin 105
Glace à l'eau 219
au Fondant 220
Glace 203–5
aux Framboises 204
Oranges Glacées Givrées 205
Pralinée 205
Parfait aux Noisettes 204
Soufflé Glacé aux Fraises 204
glacé icing 219
glazed onions 173
globe artichokes 160–1
hors d'oeuvre 45
preparation of 161
goose 152
country-style roast 152
grandmother's chicken 136
pie 124
recipe for lamb kidneys 129
grannie's omelette 58
grapefruit, to segment 24
grapes, to remove pips 24
Gratin d'Aubergines 164
green cabbage 167–8
in cream sauce 167
with rice and tomato 168
green salad 183
sauce 31
vegetables 25
Grenoble trout 78
grey mullet 68
sole 71
Grillade au Fenouil 69
grilled red mullet with fennel
69
guinea fowl 149

braised with grapes 149
weight 149

haddock, smoked 70, 74
hake 80
ring 65
halibut 80
ham and cheese cream 60
pancakes 56
Picardy 131
hard-boiled eggs 51
with mayonnaise 51
with tomatoes 48
hare 154
jugged 154
Lorraine meat loaf 42
Harengs à la Diable 64
haricot beans 182
with cream 182
Haricots Blanc 182
à la Crème 182
Haricots Verts 172–3
à la Bretonne 173
hazelnut(s) ice cream 203
to skin and brown 24
Henri IV sirloin steak 100
herb sauce 28
herbs and spices 18–21
herrings, devilled 64
preparation of 66–7
Hollandaise sauce 32
Homard 85
à la Thermidor 85
home-made terrine 42
home-style sausages 117
Hors d'oeuvre 41–9
horseradish sauce 33
hot crab with fennel 81
Hunter's lamb 108

ice cream(s) 203–5
Glace aux Framboises 204
Glace Pralinée 205
hazelnut 203
Parfait aux Noisettes 203
raspberry 204
Soufflé Glacé aux Fraises 204
strawberry soufflé 204
ices 203–5
freezing of 203
Oranges Glacées Givrées 205
orange water ice 205
icings:
butter cream 216
chocolate fondant 221
Crème au Beurre Mousseline
216
Fondant au Chocolat 221
fondant 220
to ice with 220
Glace à l'eau 219
Glace au Fondant 220
water icing 219
Isoline eggs 52
Italian chicken 146

Jambon de Picardie 131
Ficelle de Picardie 56
Fondue au 60
Jerusalem artichokes 181–2

in cheese sauce 182
preparation of 181
John Dory 69
jugged hare 154

kidneys 126, 129, 130
lamb, in Beaujolais 130
lamb, grandmother's recipe
for 129
kitchen equipment 10–15
lore 23–5
kneaded butter 23

lady's fingers 226
lamb 102–10
bark 102
best end of neck, with
courgettes 110
Champvallon chops 106
cutlets, in armour 107
cuts 102–5
Dubarry cutlets 107
hunter's lamb 108
kidneys 129, 130
in Beaujolais 130
grandmother's recipe for
129
leg, in pastry 105
with rosemary 105
loin, stuffed 106
noisettes with mushroom
sauce 108
shoulder, with turnips 108
spring stew 110
stuffed loin 106
weights, average 102
Langue 126, 128
de Boeuf Romaine 128
Médaillons à la Milanaise 128
Langues de Chat 224
Lapin 155–6
au Caramel 156
aux Champignons 155
larding 24
latticed apple tart 197
leeks 175
cooked in stock 175
leg of lamb in pastry 105
with rosemary 105
Légumes Sec 182–3
Haricots Blanc 182
Lentilles 183
lemon cake 221
mousse 192
and parsley butter 23
sole 70
lemons for garnish 24
Lentilles à la Lorraine 183
lentils 183
Lorraine-style 183
liaisons 24
Lièvre 154
Civet de 154
liqueurs 22–3
little chocolate pots with rum
193
liver 126, 127
casserole 127
with raisins 127
lobster 85

lobster contd
    preparation of 85
    Thermidor 85
loin of lamb, stuffed 106
Longe d'Agneau Persillé 106
Lorraine meat loaf 42
    -style lentils 183

mackerel 69
    fried, with mushrooms and
        tomatoes 70
    preparation of 66–7
    stuffed 69
    in white wine 48
Madeira sauce 29
Madeleines 226
Maquereaux 69
    Farcis 69
    Mirelle 70
    au Vin Blanc 48
marinated mushrooms 48
mayonnaise 30
measures 9
meat 90–132
    loaf 42, 131
    reheated dishes 131–2
    turnovers, deep fried 132
    beef 90–101
    lamb 102–10
    offal 126–32
    pork 111–17
    veal 118–25
Médaillons à la Milanaise 128
Melon aux Fruits de Mer 47
    with seafood 47
menus 231–2, 234
Meringue(s) 187–9
    Chamonix 189
    chestnut 189
    Doigts de Dames 226
    lady's fingers 226
    nests 188
    Petits Vacherins 188
    Suisse 188
Merlan, preparation of 66–7
    Filets de, à la Toulonnaise 77
Mexican cake 222
Mirabeau eggs 52
mixed salad 185
    vegetables, hors d'oeuvre 43
Montrouge soft-boiled eggs 51
Morue 70
    Galette de, à la Niçoise 70
Moules 88
    à la Marinière 88
    preparation of 88
Mousse aux Abricots 191
    apricot 191
    au Café 193
    au Camembert 60
    coffee 193
    lemon 192
    vanilla cream 195
Mulet à la Provençale 68
mullet, grey, Provençale-style
    68
mullet, red, grilled with fennel
    69
Muscadet, Canard au 151
mushroom(s) 45, 167

cream soup 40
fritters 167
hors d'oeuvre 45
marinated 48
sauce 65
mussels, preparation of 88
    in wine 88
mustard potatoes 176
    sauce 64

Nantes scallops 87
Navarin Printanier 110
Niçoise fish flan 70
Noisettes d'Agneau Chasseur
    108
Noix au Caramel 227
Normandy pork chops 116

Oeufs
    Brouillés 55
        à l'Arlesienne 55
    en Cocotte 55
        à la Crème 55
        à la Reine 55
        aux Rognons 55
    à la Coque 50
    Durs 51
        à l'Aurore 51
        Sauce Mayonnaise 51
        aux Tomates 48
    Mollets 50
        à la Cressonière 50
        aux Fines Herbes 50
        Montrouge 51
    Pochés 52
        à la Bagrance 52
    sur le plat 52
        Isoline 52
        Mirabeau 52
        à la Portugaise 52
        Rothomago 52
    Tonnelier 49
offal 126–32
    kidneys 126, 129, 130
    liver 126, 127
    sweetbreads 126, 130
    tongue 126, 128
Oie 152
    Rôti à la Paysanne 152
Oignons 173
    Glacé 173
    Paillettes des 173
    Soupe à l' 36
olives, to stone 24
Omelette(s) 57–8
    Boulogne 57
    à la Boulonnaise 57
    aux Crevettes 58
    farmer's wife's, the 57
    à la Fermière 57
    game 58
    à la Grandmère 58
    grannie's 58
    à la Lyonnaise 57
    onion 57
    prawn 58
    à la Princesse 57
    St Hubert 58
onion(s) 173
    and anchovy bread 61

fried rings 173
glazed 173
omelette 57
sauce 27
soup, French 36
Opera cream 190
Orange(s) babas 230
    Glacées Givrées 205
    nut biscuits 223
    to segment 24
    water ice 205
Orangines 223

Paillettes des Oignons 173
Pain de Boeuf 131
Panais 174
    Frits 174
pancakes 56
    Camembert 56
    flamed in Grand Marnier 195
    ham and cheese 56
Parfait aux Noisettes 203
Parisian stuffed cucumber 47
parsley potatoes 176
parsnips 174
    fried 174
partridge(s) 158
    with cabbage 158
    Catalonian 158
pastry 206–12
    choux paste 207
    flaky 208–9
    puff 210–11
    rich short crust 207
    sugar crust 207
Pâté de Foies de Volaille 41
    Lorraine 42
Pâte 206–12
    Brisée 207
    à Choux 207
    Demi-feuilletée 208–9
    Feuilletée 210–11
    Sucrée 207
Paupiettes de Boeuf 96
    Vauclusienne 96
peach(es) charlotte 194
    to skin 25
pears in red wine 197
Pea(s) 174
    with fennel 174
    French-style 174
    soup 38
peppered steak 100
peppers, in hors d'oeuvre 45
Perdreaux à la Catalane 158
    aux Choux 158
Perdrix 158
perigord soup 40
Petit Fours 226, 227
    almond and chocolate tartlets
        226
    caramel walnuts 227
    Colettes 227
    Exquis 226
    Noix au Caramel 227
    soft chocolates 227
Petits Pois 174
    au Fenouil 174
    à la Française 174
    Potage Fontanges 38

Petits Pots de Chocolat au
    Rhum 193
Petits Vacherins 188
pheasant 156–7
    casserole 156
    with port and cream 157
Picardy ham 131
Pigeon 159
    casserole of 159
    Croustade de 43
    pie 43
    aux Legumes en Cocotte 159
pike 80
pineapple cake 216
    cream 199
Pintade 149
    à la Vigneronne 149
    weight 149
piquant pork chops 115
Pissaladière à la Mènagère 61
poached stuffed chicken 137
    eggs 52
        Bagrance 52
    salmon with butter sauce 80
    sole with spinach and cheese
        sauce 74
Poireaux 175
    au Jus 175
Polish-style carrots 165
Pommes de Terre 175–80
    Berrichonne 176
    Château 179
    Croquettes 180
    à la Dijonnaise 176
    Duchesse 179
    Fondant 177
    Mousseline 177
    Noisettes 179
    Paille 180
    Persillées 176
    Pont Neuf 180
    Savoyard 177
    Vapeur 176
poor man's caviare 49
Porc 111–17
    Carré de, à l'Ananas 114
    Côtes de, Charcutière 115
        aux Pruneaux 116
        à la Vallée d'Auge 116
    cuts 111–13
    Rôti de, à l'Ail 115
    Saucisses à la Ménagère 117
    Sauté, aux Aubergines 117
    weight, average 111
pork 111–17
    and aubergine casserole 117
    chops, Normandy 116
        piquant 115
        with prunes 116
    cuts 111–13
    garlic flavoured roast 115
    home-style sausages 117
    Normandy pork chops 116
    piquant chops 115
    roast, garlic flavoured 115
        with pineapple 114
    weight, average 111
Portuguese eggs 52
Potage aux Champignons 40
    Crécy 38

potage contd
Fontanges 38
Niçoise 37
Périgourdine 40
Vivier 35
potatoes 175–80
casseroled 176
castle 179
chipped 180
creamed 177
croquettes 180
dish from the Haute Savoie 177
Duchess 179
fried 179
hors d'oeuvre 43
mustard 176
parsley 176
soft roast 177
steamed 176
straw 180
Pot-au-Feu 40, 97
Poule au Pot Farci à la Lorraine 137
Poulet 133–48
Coq au Vin 146
à l'Estragon 136
Fricassée, à l'Angevine 147
à la Grandmère 136
Gratiné aux Champignons 138
jointing, poached 138
jointing, raw 144–5
Salade de, à la Niçoise 139
Sauté à la Bordelaise 148
Duroc 148
à l'Italienne 146
à la Provençale 147
Suprêmes de Volaille Henri IV 138
trussing 134–5
Vol-au-Vent à la Reine 140–2
weights 133
poultry 133–54
chicken 133–48
duck 150–1
goose 152
guinea fowl 149
turkey 152–4
praline 205
ice cream 205
prawn omelette 58
sauce 28
Princess omelette 57
Profiteroles au Chocolat 196
Provençale chicken 147
-style fennel 48
-style grey mullet 68
tomatoes 181
puff pastry 210–11

queen's baked eggs 55
Quiche Lorraine 63
quick chicken liver pâté 41

rabbit, caramelised 156
home-made terrine 42
with mushrooms 155
radishes 45
raspberry ice cream 204

Réchauffé 131–2
Jambon de Picardie 131
Pain de Boeuf 131
Rissoles 132
red cabbage 168
Flemish 168
hors d'oeuvre 43
red mullet, grilled, with fennel 69
reduction sauces 32
reheated dishes 131–2
deep fried meat turnovers 132
meat loaf 131
Picardy ham 131
rémoulade sauce 31
rice, saffron 89
rich bread rolls 229
short crust pastry 207
sponge cake 215
Ris 126, 130
de Veau Braisé 130
Rissoles 132
roast chicken with tarragon 136
fillet steak 100
pork, garlic flavoured 115
with pineapple 114
Rochers à la Noix de Coco 227
Rognons 126, 129, 130
d'Agneau à la Beaujolaise 130
à la Grandmère 129
rolls, crescent 228
rich bread 229
Roman-style tongue 128
Roquefort tartlets 63
Rothomago eggs 52
Rôti de Porc à l'Ail 115
Rouget 69
Grillade au Fenouil 69
round fish, preparation of 66–7
roux sauces 26–7
royal turbot soufflé 77
Russian cigarettes 224

saffron rice 89
salads 183–5
celery and walnut 185
courgette 184
green 183
mixed 185
spring 184
Salade(s) 183–5
Belle Hortense 185
Courgettes à la Caillou 184
de Dinde à l'Anversoise 154
Panachée 185
de Poulet à la Niçoise 139
Printanière 184
Verte 183
salmon poached with butter sauce 80
salmon trout 81
with herb mayonnaise 81
salt cod 70
Niçoise fish flan 70
Sauce d'Abricots 199
Aïoli 31
apricot 199
Aurore 28
Béarnaise 32
Béchamel 27

au Beurre 32
Blanc 32
brown 29
butter 32
cheese 27
chocolat(e) 196
Choron 32
cream 27
creamy chicken 28
à la Crème 27
aux Crevettes 28
dawn 28
Demi-glace 29
emulsion 30–1
au Fines Herbes 28
French dressing 33
garlic mayonnaise 31
green 31
herb 28
Hollandaise 32
horseradish 33
Madeira 29
Madère 29
Mayonnaise 30
Mornay 27
mushroom 65
mustard 64
onion 27
Piquante 29
prawn 28
Raifort 33
reduction 32
Rémoulade 31
roux 26–7
Soubise 27
spicy 29
Suprême 28
Tartare 31
tomato 33
Tomate 33
Velouté 27
Verte 31
Vinaigrette 33
au Vin Blanc 28
white 27
butter 33
wine 28
Saucisses à la Ménagère 117
Saumon Poché au Beurre Blanc 80
sausages, home-style 117
Sauté de Boeuf au Chinon 94
de Porc aux Aubergines 117
scallop(s) 85
creamy ring 86
Nantes 87
scrambled eggs 55
Arlesienne 55
sea bream 69
seafood 64–89
seasoned flour 25
sea trout 81
shellfish 81–9
shell sponge cakes 226
shoulder of lamb with turnips 108
sliced ox tongue with savoury stuffing 128
slip sole 70
small meringue nests 188

smoked haddock 70, 74
soft-boiled eggs 50
with herbs 50
Montrouge 51
with watercress 50
soft chocolates 227
roast potatoes 177
sole, Dover 70
preparation of 72–3
Farci 76
Filets de, aux Crevettes 73
Cubat 71
à la Florentine 74
à la Suchet 74
fried 76
fillets 71, 74–5
with prawns 73
with mushroom purée 71
fried 76
grey 71
lemon 70
limande 70
Meunière 76
poached with spinach and cheese sauce 74
to skin and fillet 72–3
slip 70
stuffed with prawns 76
Suchet fillets 74
Torbay 71
witch 71, 75
Soufflé(s)
cauliflower 169
cheese 58
au Chocolat 202
de choufleur 169
au Fromage 58
Glacé aux Fraises 204
royal turbot 77
strawberry ice cream 204
de Turbot Royale 77
Soup(e) boiled beef 40, 97
carrot and rice 38
celery consommé 36
chilled tomato 37
Consommé au Céleri 36
cream of mushroom 40
Crème Evita 37
Crème Jardinière 36
fish 35
French onion 36
gardener's wife's, the 36
à l'Oignon 36
pea 38
perigord 40
Pot-au-Feu 40, 97
Potage aux Champignons 40
Crécy 38
Fontanges 38
Niçoise 37
Périgourdine 40
Vivier 35
tomato and green pepper 37
spicy sauce 29
spinach 171–2
with cheese topping 172
ring 171
spirits 22, 23
sponge cake, fatless 214–15
Genoese 215

sponge cake contd
rich 215
finger biscuits 225
spring salad 184
stew 110
squid 89
Armorica 89
preparation of 89
steak(s) 99–101
Châteaubriand 99, 100
à Cheval 100
Contre-filet 99
with eggs 100
Entrecôte 99
Henri IV 100
Faux-filet 99
Filet Mignon 99
fillet 99
Choron 100
roast 100
minute 99
peppered 100
au Poivre 100
porterhouse 99
roast fillet 100
Rossini 101
rump 99
sirloin 99
Henri IV 100
with straw potatoes 100
T-bone 99
Tournedos 99
à la Choron 100
Rossini 101
Vert Pré 100
steamed potatoes 176
stock, brown 35
fish 35
white 34
strawberry ice cream soufflé 204
straw potatoes 180
stuffed aubergines 163
avocados with prawns 46
cucumber 47

loin of lamb 106
mackerel 69
ox tongue 128
poached chicken 137
trout 78
Suchet fillets of sole 74
sugar crust pastry 207
Suprême au Moka 201
Suprêmes de Volaille Henri IV
138
sweetbreads 126, 130
veal, braised 130
sweets 187–202
Swiss chocolate cake 218
meringue 188
roll, coffee and walnut 218

tart, almond 200
apple latticed 197
apricot and cherry 200
Basque 62
cheese 61
upside-down apple 198
Tartare sauce 31
Tarte aux Abricots et Cerises
200
Basquaise 62
des Demoiselles Tatin 198
aux Pommes Grillé 197
Tartelettes aux Roquefort 63
Terrine Maison 42
Thermidor, lobster 85
Tomates 181
à la Duchesse 181
à la Provençale 181
tomato(es) 181
Duchess 181
and green pepper soup 37
hors d'oeuvre 43
Provençale 181
sauce 33
to skin 25
soup, chilled 37
tongue 126, 128

Roman-style 128
stuffed sliced 128
Topinambours 181–2
au Gratin 182
preparation of 181
Torbay sole 71
Toulon style fillets of whiting
77
Tournedos à la Choron 100
Rossini 101
Tourte Poitevine 61
Tourtière de ma Grandmère 124
trout 78
Grenoble 78
preparation of 66–7
stuffed 78
in tarragon sauce 80
Truites à la Grenobloise 78
Caprice de Buffon 78
à l'Estragon 80
Truite Saumonée 81
Sauce Verte 81
trussing poultry and game
134–5
Tuiles aux Amandes 224
Turban de Colin 65
turbot, royal soufflé 77
turkey 152–4
and chicory salad 154
stuffed with chestnuts 153
weights 152
turned vegetables 25

upside-down apple tart 198

vanilla cream mousse 195
Vaucluse beef rolls 96
veal 118–25
braised 122
creamy stew 123
cuts 118–20
grandmother's pie 124
liver casserole 127
with raisins 127

Viennese escalopes 121
weight, average 118
Veau 118–25
Blanquette 123
Braisé Bouquetière 122
cuts 118–20
Escalopes à la Viennoise 121
Tourtière de ma Grandmère
124
weight, average 118
vegetable(s) 160–85
green 25
salad hors d'oeuvre 43
turned 25
velouté sauces 27–8
Vichy carrots 165
Viennese veal escalopes 121
vinaigrette sauce 32
vol-au-vent 140–1
chicken 142
à la Reine 142

water ice 205
icing 219
weights 9
whipped cream 199
white butter sauce 32
roux 26
sauce 27
stock 34
wine sauce 28
whiting, preparation of 66–7
Toulon style fillets 77
wines 21–2, 232–4
witch sole 71, 75

yeast cookery 228–30
Babas à l'Orange 230
Brioches 229
crescent rolls 228
Croissants 228
orange babas 230
rich bread rolls 229

Zucchini 170